Reading with Confidence

Joan Monahan

Polk Community College

Allyn and Bacon
Boston • London • Toronto • Sydney • Tokyo • Singapore

Vice President, Humanities: Joseph Opiela
Editorial Assistant: Kristen Desmond
Senior Marketing Manager: Lisa Kimball
Editorial–Production Service: Matrix Productions Inc.
Composition and Prepress Buyer: Linda Cox
Manufacturing Buyer: Suzanne Lareau
Cover Administrator: Jenny Hart
Electronic Composition: Omegatype Typography, Inc.

Between the time Website information is gathered and then published, it is not
unusual for some sites to have closed. Also, the transcription of URLs can result
in unintended typographical errors. The publisher would appreciate notification
where these occur so that they may be corrected in subsequent editions.

Library of Congress Cataloging-in-Publication Data

Monahan, Joan
    Reading with confidence / Joan Monahan.
        p.   cm.
    Includes index.
    ISBN 0-205-28329-2
    [1. Reading (Higher education)]   I. Title.

LB2395.3.M65   2000
428.4'071'1—dc21

                              99-047229

Printed in the United States of America

10 9 8 7 6 5 4 3 2 1   04 03 02 01 00 99

Contents

Preface

Today's complex world requires college students to process tremendous amounts of material from a variety of sources for a successful college experience. To meet these reading challenges successfully, they must learn to analyze, synthesize, and evaluate what they read.

The goal of *Reading with Confidence* is to help students develop the skills and strategies essential not only to reading with attention and comprehension, but also to thinking actively and effectively about their reading.

The text begins with basic skills on a literal level reinforced by exercises, readings, and activities. Students learn to organize ideas and information and make relationships between ideas. In later chapters, complex inferential skills are introduced until students are integrating all reading strategies learned in the complex activity of critically evaluating reading material—and thus reading with confidence.

Overview of Chapters

Chapter 1 gives students an overview of the techniques they will need to use in handling college reading. This instruction is given in the first chapter since many readers in developmental classes are also enrolled in college level courses; consequently, they have an immediate need to control the reading process effectively.

Chapter 2, 3, and 4 present literal-level reading strategies: decoding word meaning, identifying main ideas and distinguishing them from supporting details, and finding order in paragraphs and longer reading selections. Exercises in these early chapters are intended to improve students' ability to make connections and see relationships.

Reading and comprehending on a literal level is not sufficent for a student to have a successful college experience or, for that matter, a successful life experience. Students need to be able to organize ideas, analyze, and synthesize information in order to critically evaluate what they read.

To develop these more sophisticated thinking skills, Part II, beginning with Chapter 5, introduces strategies for making valid inferences and finding implied main ideas. Chapter 6 builds on students' ability to make inferences by distinguishing fact from opinion and recognizing bias in order to evaluate written arguments. Finally, Chapter 7 gives students strategies for interpreting an author's purpose and tone as well as methods for recognizing and understanding figurative language.

The chapters on study skills in Part III are meant to be used when an instructor believes the class will benefit from a specific skill; for example, the chapter on note taking might be offered after Chapter 3. This offers flexibility and change of pace for a class. Chapter 8 provides specific strategies for analytical study and methods of note taking. Chapter 9 explores work with following directions and reading visuals. Chapter 10 gives effective test-taking techniques and works well with classes after a first or second test. Chapter 11, finally, offers students an opportunity to apply all strategies learned in the text to evaluate critically several text offerings concerned with ethical issues.

Special Features

Organization

Chapter objectives are noted at the beginning of each chapter. An explanation of each skill to be developed is followed by examples and exercises. Each chapter works with paragraph and multiparagraph examples to give students sufficent practice with the skills introduced as they develop general knowledge with interesting and informative material. Each chapter contains two longer reading selections selected to engage student interest and give students an opportunity to apply skills learned in the chapter and previous chapters. Vocabulary is introduced in each chapter as it occurs in the sentences, paragraphs, and longer readings. Vocabulary is not defined so that students will become proficient in the use of the dictionary.

Three Steps to Active Reading

Students are encouraged throughout the text to practice pre-reading, anticipating, and associating strategies to help them in focusing, reading efficiently and carefully, and using appropriate skills for reviewing material.

Writing Suggestions

Writing activities are suggested in each chapter for instructors who wish to support the correlation between writing and reading activities. These writing activities can also be used to compile a portfolio of work or a journal for instructors who use this method of assessment.

Collaborative Activities

Each chapter contains suggestions for collaborative work since reading, often thought of as an essentially independent activity, is supported by and benefits from the interchange students make in attempting to fully comprehend, process,and retain information. Directions for collaborative work are explained in the text.

Critical Thinking Activities

Activities are included in each chapter to foster skills of critical thinking since reasoning, questioning, and evaluating are skills that students need practice in developing for successful college experiences.

Acknowledgments

Many colleagues and friends have been helpful in offering ideas and critiques. In particular, Jean Reynolds has offered continual support and encouragement. Linda Wolverton and Kathy Riley have shared books and ideas. The book would not have been possible without the assistance of many in the Learning Resources Division of Polk Community College. I am also grateful for the many helpful suggestions offered by the manuscript reviewers: Marilynn Anselmi, Halifax Community College; Mary Boyles, University of North Carolina at Pembroke; Eric Hibbison, J. Seargent Reynolds College; Michelle Jones, Valencia Community College; Leslie King, SUNY-Oswego; Catherine Ritter, Baltimore City Community College; and Nancy Smith, Florida Community College at Jacksonville. Finally, I also wish to thank my editor, Joe Opiela, and his assistant, Mary Beth Varney, for their patience and encouragement.

Strategies for Literal Comprehension

PART I

Chapter 1

Preparing for Meaningful Reading

> When you sell a man a book you don't sell him . . . paper
> and ink and glue—you sell him a whole new life.
>
> *Christopher Morley*

Books open doors to new worlds and new experiences. You have been reading for years. Have you read a good book recently? Oprah Winfrey says, "One of the greatest pleasures in my life is to be reading a really good book." Have you had that pleasure lately? Perhaps through reading books, magazines, newspapers, and material on the Internet you have explored new places, encountered interesting people, and been challenged by new ideas. Books like the Bible and written speeches like the Gettysburg Address and Martin Luther King's "I Have a Dream" have inspired changes. You are the person you are today, to some extent, as a result of the reading you have done in the past.

No doubt you have recently purchased textbooks for this term. These books can "sell you a whole new life" because, whatever the subject, you will be confronted with new ideas that can enlarge your views about life. You may be introduced to ideas that will help you take better care of your health. You may learn new techniques for speaking before a group. You may learn more about history, art, or psychology. What you can learn will depend on you, and on the courses you are taking.

On the other hand, all the possibilities for learning, and even the textbooks themselves, can sometimes appear overwhelming. There is so much to do, so many pages to cover, and so short a time to achieve success. As you consider your texts for this semester, consider the astronauts who must absorb the contents of piles of books before taking off into space. The purpose of this chapter is to help you develop strategies that will assist you in learning to save time as you learn to use your textbooks efficiently.

This chapter will consider:

- reasons for developing good reading strategies
- strategies you currently use
- strategies to prepare you for reading efficiently

Reasons for Developing Good Reading Strategies

Even though we live in the age of computers and television, reading with confidence is a habit that will serve you well throughout your life.

In College

In college you need to read and remember the material from textbooks in psychology, biology, and the humanities, just to mention a few courses. Success in college depends in a large part on your ability to read with understanding and to remember what you have read. The late Barbara Jordan, a lawyer and the only black congresswoman from Texas, learned in law school that she had to "read longer, . . . work harder, and study longer than others." But in the end she was "educated finally." You will read and absorb many textbooks and thousands of words before you are ready to accept a diploma at graduation.

On the Job

You may already know that on the job you will need to read articles and books about your job to keep up with changes and improve your position. For example, if you plan on a legal or law enforcement career, you will need to keep up with the laws that change frequently. A career in the health-care field also requires that you stay informed of new developments. In most careers you will need to read meeting notes and daily memos. Often you will need to grasp ideas quickly in order to make a required response. Good reading strategies are essential on the job.

As a Citizen

Keeping up with the daily news and being informed about local and world affairs will help you be an active member of your community. Is the town council or city commission planning a new development on land currently restricted for recreational use? Will this be a positive development for your area, for you, for your children? Every citizen needs to develop the ability to recognize propaganda and bias in order to analyze and evaluate events and make informed decisions.

As a Person

To become a more interesting person and find a relaxing, enjoyable activity, you read for pleasure. Recreational reading helps relieve the stress you will sometimes experience on the job. You will gain confidence in meeting new people and facing new adventures because you have developed new interests. College will not end your educational experiences. You will use reading to learn and grow intellectually as long as you live.

Your Present Reading Strategies

You already have certain reading habits and skills. What reading skills and strategies do you use at present? What skills would you like to improve? The following inventory will help you evaluate your present practices and strategies and suggest some ideas for areas to explore and improve in this course.

Inventory

Mark 4 for always, 2 for sometimes, and 0 for never.

_____ 1. I have a goal or purpose before beginning reading.

_____ 2. I can read several pages and have a clear idea of what I have just read.

_____ 3. When I read, I stop to anticipate what material will be discussed in the next few paragraphs.

_____ 4. I vary my speed for different reading assignments.

_____ 5. I read figures, graphs, and tables to help understand the text.

_____ 6. I survey headings and pictures before reading a chapter in a textbook.

_____ 7. As I read, I figure out the meaning of unfamiliar words from the context.

_____ 8. I remember and can recall accurately most of what I have read.

_____ 9. I underline important points and write comments in the margins of my textbooks.

_____ 10. I regularly review reading material and notes for each of my courses.

Add Your Points   Score _____

35–40   You are in an excellent starting position.
25–34   Circle the numbers of a few skills you want to begin using soon.
Below 24   This chapter will help you gain strategies to make textbook reading more beneficial for you.

Set at least one goal for yourself now. Select the strategy from the list that you most want to employ beginning now, and write it here.

_____

_____

_____

In addition to improving or developing strategies that will help you be a more successful reader, you can improve or develop other qualities to help you achieve reading and college success.

Be a Risk Taker

Act as though you believe in yourself and your abilities. An actor in a play must act the part he or she is playing. Your part is to believe in yourself as a college student. If you believe in yourself, you will not hesitate to ask questions in class. You will be an active participant in group activities. Asking questions and participating in group work involve taking risks. Risk taking will make you a stronger and more confident student.

Think about the following suggestions. Which would help you become more confident about your strengths? Which could you begin to practice in this reading course?

1. I can ask questions about something I do not understand. If I don't understand, probably someone else in the class also does not understand and will be grateful that I asked the question.
2. I can ask for an appointment to talk to the professor outside class. Talking to the instructor will increase my interest in and understanding of the material.
3. I can volunteer to answer questions in class. The world won't end if my answer is incorrect, and I will increase my understanding.
4. Even if I have difficulty responding in class, I can be an active participant in my group by volunteering suggestions and asking questions.

Write the suggestion you intend to practice.

_____

_____

Be Responsible

You are already committed to becoming a more active reader. Your reading of this textbook is evidence of that commitment. A first priority is to take responsibility for your homework and classwork. Only responsible people achieve success. Other demands on your time will often interfere with the demands of college study. Jobs, friends, school activities, and family duties often create conflicts for your time. You will need to practice skillful time management and make study a priority in order to become a successful student. Some suggestions follow to help you set the stage for using your reading time responsibly.

Read When You Are Most Alert

Most people have difficulty reading late at night because the muscles in their eyes are tired. Reading is a physical activity as well as a mental one. Know your best time for reading and study and plan to use the time when you are most alert.

Read in a Quiet Environment

Find a place free from sounds and movements. The library is an ideal place. If you read at home, disconnect the phone or let an answering machine take over. If children are your responsibility, get them settled in a quiet activity before you attempt your reading. If you have roommates, work out a schedule that allows you quiet time for study in the room.

Be Prepared to Handle Distractions

Attention, even in the most ideal circumstances, is a wandering creature. Have you ever been in a conversation with someone and suddenly realized that you have missed the last few remarks the person made? Or have you been startled by an instructor's question because you were thinking about all the things you had to do when class was over? The trick is to exercise more control over your concentration. This is not always easy, but the following three suggestions may help you gain more control over the distractions that interrupt your concentration.

1. Do an Attention Check.   Don't plan to read five pages without stopping. Read a page or even a paragraph, then stop to see if you are grasping the idea. Try to restate the general idea of what you have read in your own words. This habit of monitoring your reading and your understanding will help you banish distractions.

2. Treat a Wandering Attention with Gentleness.   If you find your mind wandering away from the subject frequently, give your attention a gentle tug. Don't get angry and upset with your wandering mind. If you are worried or angry when you start to study, mentally wrap the problem in colorful wrapping paper and put it aside to think about later or perhaps plan to ask someone for help. Draw your attention back quietly to your reading—don't strain to control your distractions. Fighting distractions only draws more attention to them. If these ideas don't capture your runaway attention, there's one more trick.

3. Give In to Your Distraction.   Whenever something demands your attention so strongly that you can't resist it, give in to the distraction. Is there a phone call you need to make or some task you need to do? Do it! Or stop and jot down a reminder of what you need to do. If the distraction is a worry, jot down the time when you will think about it later. Then you can return to your reading without the distraction.

Where and when do you plan to do most of your reading? Plan a regular time for study each day.

_____

_____

_____

How do you plan to handle distractions?

_____

_____

_____

Strategies to Get You Focused before Reading

Once you have selected a good place and time for reading where you can be relatively free from distractions, focus your attention on the reading task. The more you become involved in thinking, reacting, and asking questions about your reading, the more benefit you will derive from the reading.

Bill and Julio plan to watch a baseball game on television. Julio has been anticipating the game for weeks. He has played baseball and knows the rules and strategies of the game. He is familiar with the players on both teams and knows the strengths and weaknesses of both teams. Bill knows the names of the two teams and little more than that. Which viewer do you think will find greater enjoyment from the game and remember more about it later?

Before you take a picture with a camera, you focus the camera. Even if the camera is self-focusing, to get a good picture you need to view carefully from the viewfinder. Practicing techniques for focusing your attention on reading material *before* you read will prepare you for reading with attention and increase your understanding of difficult material. When you focus your attention before you read, you will become like Julio, the informed baseball viewer, prepared for the game of reading. Sometimes you will be required to read material that is difficult or appears uninteresting. Practicing the strategies that follow will stimulate your interest, making your reading time both productive and enjoyable.

First, think about your purpose for reading. *Second*, preview the reading assignment. *Third*, stop to anticipate or predict what you might learn, and *fourth*, associate this material with what you already know about the topic. These four strategies, explained on the following pages, will help you focus before you read.

First Strategy: Know Your Purpose for Reading

Knowing your purpose for reading will help you decide how to read the material. All reading should not be done at the same pace. Sometimes you will look over a reading assignment quickly to understand and become familiar with the general ideas covered. This method of reading is called making a survey, getting an overview, or *skimming*.

At other times you will want to read several pages rapidly because your purpose is to find specific information, like an answer to a question, a specific date, or a particular detail. This rapid reading method is called *scanning*.

College textbook reading often requires that you read slowly to understand difficult ideas. *Close*, or slow, careful reading is recommended for textbook comprehension. Special strategies for close reading are discussed throughout this text.

Some students neglect setting a purpose because they are in a rush to accomplish a reading task. They employ the same reading pace for all tasks. This method is inefficient. Consider these questions to see how different purposes suggest different approaches to the same reading material.

Are you reading to answer specific questions at the end?

If this is your purpose, you may want to use close reading to examine the questions carefully before you begin reading the assignment. Then you can decide to look over or scan the pages rapidly to find the answers.

Are you reading to learn about a process or procedure?

Often this kind of material will require close reading, especially if you are going to follow the procedure, for example, the directions for an experiment in chemistry that you are going to perform. Sometimes the steps will be clearly numbered or outlined. In this case, you might skim the explanation of the entire experiment, then read closely through a step, perform it, and go on to the next step. Rereading may even be necessary.

Are you reading to supplement your lecture notes?

Maybe you are looking for examples to clarify points made in a lecture class. In that case, skimming would be helpful. If the instructor has suggested that you need to read for more information on a particular topic, you may skim to locate the material and, when you find it, do close, careful reading.

Are you reading for information for a research paper?

Again, you may want to do two kinds of reading. If you are looking for specific information to support a point in your paper, skimming will serve the purpose. If you are looking for facts to support a point you wish to make, you might scan charts and graphs. If you have just selected a topic and need general background, however, you will probably want to read the source material closely.

Are you reading purely for entertainment or amusement?

Reading magazines and newspapers for your own enjoyment does not usually require close reading. You may, however, want to read an interesting article closely to use the information for conversation or personal reflection. Reading a novel for pleasure does not usually require close reading, either. However, if you haven't picked up the novel for a few days, you may want to skim a few pages you read previously. Reading a poem or short story for a literature class may be an enjoyable experience, but to understand the material you will want to do close reading. Rereading will probably be necessary. Having a clear purpose in mind before reading will help you determine how to read an assignment and may actually save you time.

Exercise 1-1   Establishing Purpose

Think about your purpose for reading in the following examples. Indicate whether you would read rapidly (scan); read selectively (skim); or read closely to accomplish the following tasks.

1. To look over material previously read to recall main ideas, I

   would _____.

2. To find a specific date to answer a question, I would

   _____.

3. To decide which articles in a newspaper I would like to read

   carefully, I would _____.

4. To read an assigned chapter in a biology text, I would first

    _____, and then _____.

5. To select articles that might give me supplementary material

    for an assignment, I would _____.

6. To check the index or table of contents of a book to find a specific topic, I would _____.

7. If I am using the Internet to find a specific topic, I would

    _____.

After completing this exercise, you may want to discuss with others in the class or a small group your reason for selecting a particular reading strategy.

Practice Scanning

You have probably already used the strategy of scanning in searching a phone book for the phone number of a friend. You ran your eyes quickly down the column of names looking for your friend's name. If you turned to the index at the back of a book looking for information on a particular topic, again you let your eyes move quickly. You did not read each word. Try this strategy on textbook material.

Exercise 1-2   Scanning Practice

Let your eyes move rapidly over this reading, picking up only words and phrases until you find the answer. To help guide your eyes in a rapid movement, place your finger in the center of the page and draw it quickly down the page.

Imagine you have just read an article on the history of calculating devices. A question at the end asks you, "Who made plans in the 19th century for a calculating machine?" Try scanning (running your finger down) the following paragraphs to

find the answer. (Hint: Look for the 19th century first. Numbers are easily located through scanning.)

The 17th century saw the beginnings of calculating machines. When Pascal was 19, he began to develop a machine to add long columns of figures. He built several versions, and since all proved to be unreliable, he considered this project a failure. But the machine introduced basic principles that are used in modern calculators. The next advance in mechanical calculators came from Germany in about 1672, when the great mathematician Gottfried Leibniz studied Pascal's calculators, improved them, and drew up plans for a mechanical calculator. In 1695, a machine was finally built, but this calculator also proved to be unreliable. In the 19th century, an eccentric Englishman, Charles Babbage, developed plans for a grandiose calculating machine. It was called a "difference engine," and had thousands of gears, ratchets, and counters. Four years later, in 1826, even though Babbage had still not built his difference engine, he began an even more elaborate project—the building of what he called an "analytic engine." This machine was capable of an accuracy to 20 decimal places. However it, too, could not be built because the technical knowledge to build it was not far enough advanced.

—Adapted from Karl J. Smith, *The Nature of Mathematics*

Did you find the answer—Babbage—in a second or two? Remember, scanning is a helpful strategy when your purpose is to find specific information quickly.

Practice Skimming

Just as scanning saves reading or rereading time, so does skimming. When you are shopping, you let your eyes pass quickly over the items on a counter to find what you are looking for. Try this surveying or skimming strategy with a textbook.

Exercise 1-3　Skimming Practice

An important skimming practice before you begin any college course is to become familiar with your textbook. Knowing the arrangement of the text and having an overview of all its parts will save you time. You will understand how material is presented and will know the special features of the text that will increase your understanding. Use skimming to become familiar with one of your textbooks. You can use this text if this course is the only one you are taking.

Name of text _____

Course _____

1. Study the textbook's table of contents. Can you see a relationship between the topics? What one topic looks most interesting?

   _____

   _____

2. Is there an introduction? It also may be called a "preface" and is found after the table of contents. (If there is one, it is a "must read" for an overview of the text.) Mention one idea you gained from the introduction.

   _____

   _____

3. Examine one chapter. How is it organized? Are there questions at the beginning or the end of the chapter? Are there pictures and/or graphs? Are there marginal notes or footnotes? Are there objectives at the beginning and a summary at the end of the chapter? Mention some of the helpful guides provided for the chapter.

   _____

   _____

4. Is there a glossary (a small dictionary) at the back of the text?

   _____

5. Is an answer key provided? (It may be at each chapter's end or at the back of the text.)

   _____

6. Is there an index to help you find information about special topics quickly? Look for the index in the back of the text.

_____

7. The author may have included extra, related material at the back of the book in an appendix. Does your text have any appendixes? If there are any, what do they cover?

_____

_____

8. What do you think is the most helpful or interesting feature of the text you are surveying? Why?

_____

_____

Second Strategy: Do a Preview

An important but often overlooked strategy is previewing: getting a general overview of a reading assignment just as you did in the textbook survey. Students often complain that they have read five pages of an assignment and have no idea what they read. They may not be *previewing,* skimming to become actively interested in new material to be read. Skimming to preview will focus the attention as well as prepare for the content.

When you attend a movie, you often see previews of coming attractions. The preview helps you anticipate a coming film by stimulating your interest. When you meet a new person, you look that person over and ask questions to learn more about him or her. This "preview" often tells you if you want to spend time getting to know the person better. That's the purpose of a skimming preview—to look over and become interested in the material. You will also activate your mind about the topic and begin to recall what you may already know about the subject.

When you surveyed a textbook in Exercise 1-3, you noticed the organization of a chapter. Often instructors make reading assignments by chapter. Getting an overview of a chapter or reading assignment is an important step. Things to note in skimming:

The title often a very brief summary of the content.

Introductory material a list of objectives for the reading, or an outline of major ideas to be covered.

Subheads the divisions that are road maps of the direction the reading matter is taking. (If there are no subheads, read the first sentence of each paragraph since the main idea of the paragraph is often stated in the first sentence.)

Visuals charts, tables, pictures, marginal notes. Visuals help capture your interest and add information. Marginal notes often explain important terms.

The end often contains a summary, discussion questions, questions to assess your understanding, or key words defined for memorization.

All college reading assignments have different kinds of aids to get you focused on the material. It is a good idea to skim all the elements suggested here. Then do some close reading of one or more elements to give you some background and start you thinking. A textbook on health has a chapter titled "Promoting Healthy Behavior Change." The chapter presents many features to use for *previewing*. There are objectives, subheads, visuals, terms defined in boxes, discussion questions, and a summary at the end. Skim the following objectives from this chapter.

Chapter Objectives

- Define health and wellness, and explain the interconnected roles of the physical, social, mental, emotional, environmental, and spiritual dimensions of health.
- Discuss the health status of Americans, the factors that contribute to health, and the importance of *Healthy People 2000* objectives in establishing national goals for promoting health and preventing premature death and disability.
- Evaluate the role of gender in health status, health research, and health training.
- Identify the leading causes of death and the lifestyle patterns associated with the reduction of risks.
- Examine how predisposing factors, beliefs, attitudes, and significant others affect your behavior changes.
- Survey behavior change techniques, and learn how to apply them to personal situations.
- Apply decision-making techniques to behavior changes.

—From Rebecca J. Donatelle and Lorraine G. Davis, *Health: The Basics*

The objectives were given as commands to define, evaluate, and so on. Now go back to the objectives and do a closer reading.

You can learn a great deal about the chapter from this closer reading. Think about restating the objectives as statements of fact. You will need to think carefully as you make these restatements. For example, the first objective stated as a fact might read:

1. "There is a difference between health and wellness. A connection exists between our physical, social, mental, emotional, environmental, and spiritual dimensions that influences our health." As you reread and rethink these objectives, you can probably answer these yes/no questions about the chapter content.

Exercise 1-4   Rethinking the Objectives

Answer the following yes and no questions as you rethink the objectives. Each question relates to one of the objectives.

_____ 1. Are health and wellness the same thing?

_____ 2. Does your physical health have any effect on your emotional well-being?

_____ 3. Are there national goals for improving our health?

_____ 4. Is there a difference in health status, health research, and health training for males and females?

_____ 5. Are there lifestyle changes that could reduce the leading causes of death?

_____ 6. Are your behavior changes influenced by your beliefs and attitudes?

_____ 7. Can important people in your life influence your behavior changes?

_____ 8. Are there techniques to help you make behavior changes?

_____ 9. Can you learn these techniques and apply them to personal situations?

_____ 10. Can you learn to apply decision-making techniques to help make behavior changes?

You can see how previewing these objectives gave you many ideas about the content and prepared your mind for reading the chapter. In class or with a small group, you can discuss what you or others may already know about the issues raised by these questions.

Third Strategy: Anticipate

This third strategy offers further assistance in helping you focus your attention for reading. Thinking ahead puts you in tune with the message the writer has for you and keeps you actively involved in the reading process. Like an engine on a railroad track, once you begin to anticipate or predict, you have a direction and are ready to roll. Asking yourself questions like the following will help you anticipate or predict what you are going to learn.

1. How will this selection continue or advance the other material in this text?
2. What do I expect to learn from this reading?
3. How might I use this information?

You have used the chapter objectives from "Promoting Healthy Behavior Change" to do a simple preview. Now use the subheads from one section of this chapter titled "Behavior Change Techniques" to practice anticipating and predicting. The division headings are:

Shaping: Developing New Behaviors in Small Steps
Visualizing: The Imagined Rehearsal
Modeling
Controlling the Situation
Reinforcement: "Different Strokes for Different Folks"
Changing Self-Talk

Exercise 1-5   Anticipating and Predicting

Reread these subheads and ask the questions that help you anticipate and predict. The questions are underlined for you.

1. How do you think these subheads relate to the chapter title, "Promoting Healthy Behavior Change"?

_____

_____

_____

2. <u>What are some of the things you might anticipate</u> learning from this section?

_____

_____

_____

3. <u>How do you think you could use this information</u> about techniques for making behavior changes?

_____

_____

_____

Asking yourself questions about the material you are about to read helps you *anticipate* some of the ideas you will read about and should stimulate your interest in the material.

Fourth Strategy: Associate

Next, consider what you might already know about the topic. Use your own background and experience to relate to the material you are about to read. Try to recall anything you might already know about the topic. If the topic is one you think will be difficult for you, or if you have little background or experience with it, you might find that another, simpler treatment of the topic will help create some background. A high school or even an elementary textbook might be helpful. An easy encyclopedia article might also help.

Making associations—drawing relationships between what you already know and the new material—will make your reading experience more meaningful and will help you retain the ideas more easily. You may already have ideas in your memory from past reading and past experiences. Calling on what you already know prepares your mind to receive new information. Once you have opened a file drawer in your mind, the new material will be filed with the old.

Questions to help you make associations could be:

1. What do I already know about this topic?
2. What relationship does this topic have to my past experiences?
3. What have I read previously that relates to this topic?

Exercise 1-6 Making Associations

The questions just listed are underlined here to help you draw relationships and make associations with your previous knowledge.

1. <u>What do I already know about this topic of behavior change?</u>
   Do you know anyone, including yourself, who has tried to change a bad habit like smoking or gossiping? What techniques have they used?

   _____

   _____

   _____

2. <u>What relationship does this topic of "behavior change" have to my past experiences?</u>
   What experiences have you had in trying to change a habitual action such as staying up late on school nights or leaving homework until the last possible minute?

   _____

   _____

   _____

3. <u>What do I know about visualizing and modeling?</u>
   How might these strategies relate to changing a habit?

   _____

   _____

   _____

4. How do these topics relate to any personal reading I may have done?
   Have you ever read any books or articles about changing habits? How does this division of the chapter relate to the chapter as a whole?

   _____

   _____

   _____

This kind of prethinking about a chapter or reading assignment takes a few minutes, but the time devoted to focusing is well spent. The questions and activities are meant to show you the kinds of strategies that can help you read with more attention. With practice, you will learn to compose your own mental questions.

The important things to remember are that before reading you need to have a clear *purpose* for your task. Next, you need to *preview* by skimming and thinking. Then stop to *anticipate* and *predict* the content of what you are about to read. And finally, *associate* experiences from your own background with what you read to make the reading more meaningful.

Chapter Review

Fill in the blanks with the correct words.

1. _____ will be important in all areas of your life.

2. Developing your ability to _____ will improve your effectiveness as a reader.

3. Establishing a _____ for reading determines the kind of reading speed to use.

4. A reader should _____ to find the answer to a specific question.

5. _____ is important to help you become familiar with a text or a reading selection before actually reading it.

6. When you preview, you will _____ various sections of the reading material.

7. Textbooks provide many features to help you skim. List three.

   _____

   _____

   _____

8. When you think about and make predictions before you read, you are _____.

9. Relating your background information and experiences to the reading material is called making _____.

10. Having a regular time and place for study will help you handle _____.

Reading Selection 1

Because you have previewed headings, anticipated, and made associations with the topics covered in this section from a health text on behavior change techniques, you should be prepared to read this section closely. (If some time has passed since you completed Exercises 1-5 and 1-6, you may wish to review your answers.)

Behavior Change Techniques

Rebecca J. Donatelle and Lorraine G. Davis

Once you have analyzed all the factors influencing your current behavior and all the factors that may influence the direction and potential success of the behavior change you are considering, you must decide which of several possible behavior change techniques will work best for you.   1

Shaping: Using a series of small steps to get to a particular   2
goal gradually.

Imagined rehearsal: Practicing through mental imagery, to
become better able to perform an event in actuality.

Modeling: Learning specific behaviors by watching others
perform them.

Situational inducement: Attempt to influence a behavior by
using situations and occasions that are structured to
exert control over that behavior.

Positive reinforcement: Presenting something positive following a behavior that is being reinforced.

Shaping: Developing New Behaviors in Small Steps

Regardless of how motivated and committed you are to   3
change, some behaviors are almost impossible to change immediately. To reach your goal, you may need to take a number
of individual steps, each designed to change one small piece of
the larger behavior. This process is known as **shaping.**

Whatever the desired behavior change, all shaping   4
involves

- starting slowly and trying not to cause undue stress during the early stages of the program
- keeping the steps small and achievable
- being flexible and ready to change if the original plan
  proves uncomfortable
- refusing to skip steps or to move to the next step until
  the previous step has been mastered. Behaviors don't develop overnight, so they won't change overnight.

Visualizing: The Imagined Rehearsal

Mental practice and rehearsal can help change unhealthy   5
behaviors into healthy ones. Athletes and others have used a
technique known as **imagined rehearsal** to reach their goals.
By visualizing their planned action ahead of time, they were
better prepared when they put themselves to the test.

Modeling

Modeling, or learning behaviors through careful obser-   6
vation of other people, is one of the most effective strategies
for changing behavior. If you carefully observe behaviors you
admire and isolate their components, you can model the
steps of your behavior change strategy on a proven success.

Controlling the Situation

Sometimes, putting yourself in the right setting or with   7
the right group of people will positively influence your behaviors directly or indirectly. Many situations and occasions
trigger similar behaviors by different people. For example, in
libraries, churches, and museums, most people talk softly.
Few people laugh at funerals. The term **situational inducement** refers to an attempt to influence a behavior by using situations and occasions that are structured to exert control
over that behavior.

Reinforcement: "Different Strokes for Different Folks"

A **positive reinforcement** seeks to increase the likeli-   8
hood that a behavior will occur by presenting something positive as a reward for that behavior. Each of us is motivated by
different reinforcers. While a special T-shirt may be a positive
reinforcer for young adults entering a race, it may not be for a
50-year-old runner who dislikes message-bearing T-shirts, or
someone with a drawer full of them.

Most positive reinforcers can be classified under five   9
headings: consumable, activity, manipulative, possessional,
and social reinforcers.

- *Consumable reinforcers* are delicious edibles such as
  candy, cookies, or gourmet meals.
- *Activity reinforcers* are opportunities to watch TV, to go
  on a vacation, to go swimming, or to do something else
  enjoyable.
- *Manipulative reinforcers* are such incentives as lower
  rent in exchange for mowing the lawn or the promise of
  a better grade for doing an extra-credit project.
- *Possessional reinforcers* are tangible rewards such as a
  new TV or a sports car.
- *Social reinforcers* are such things as loving looks, affec-
  tionate hugs, and praise.

When choosing reinforcers to help you maintain a   10
healthy behavior or change an unhealthy behavior, you need
to determine what would motivate you to act in a particular
way. Your rewards or reinforcers may initially come from
others (extrinsic rewards), but as you see positive changes
in yourself, you will begin to reward and reinforce yourself
(intrinsic rewards). Keep in mind that reinforcers should
immediately follow a behavior. But beware of overkill. If you
reward yourself with a movie on the VCR every time you go
jogging, this reinforcer will soon lose its power. It would be
better to give yourself this reward after, say, a full week of ad-
herence to your jogging program.

What Do You Think?

What type of consumable reinforcers (food or drink) would be a healthy reward for your new behavior? If you could choose one activity reinforcer to reward yourself after you've been successful for one day in your new behavior, what would it be? If you could obtain/buy something for yourself (possessional reinforcer) after you reach your goal, what would it be? If you maintain your behavior for one week, what type of social reinforcer would you like to receive from your friends? 11

Changing Self-Talk

Self-talk, or the way you think and talk to yourself, can also play a role in modifying your health-related behaviors. Here are some cognitive procedures for changing self-talk. 12

Rational-Emotive Therapy.

This form of cognitive therapy or self-directed behavior change is based on the premise that there is a close connection between what people say to themselves and how they feel. According to psychologist Albert Ellis, most everyday emotional problems and related behaviors stem from irrational statements that people make to themselves when events in their lives are different from what they would like them to be. 13

Meichenbaum's Self-Instructional Methods.

In Meichenbaum's behavioral therapies, clients are encouraged to give "self-instructions" ("Slow down, don't rush") and "positive affirmations" ("My speech is going fine—I'm almost done!") to themselves instead of thinking self-defeating thoughts ("I'm taking too fast—my speech is terrible") whenever a situation seems to be getting out of control. Meichenbaum is perhaps best known for a process known as stress inoculation, in which clients are subjected to extreme stressors in a laboratory environment. Before a stressful event (e.g., going to the doctor), clients practice individual coping skills (e.g., deep breathing exercises) and self-instructions (e.g., "I'll feel better once I know what's causing my pain"). Meichenbaum demonstrated that clients who practiced coping techniques and self-instruction were less likely to resort to negative behaviors in stressful situations. 14

Blocking/Thought Stopping.

By purposefully blocking or stopping negative thoughts, a person can concentrate on taking positive steps toward 15 necessary behavior change. For example, suppose you are pre-occupied with your ex-partner, who has recently deserted you for someone else. In blocking/thought stopping, you consciously stop thinking about the situation and force yourself to think about something more pleasant (e.g., dinner tomorrow with your best friend). By refusing to dwell on negative images and by forcing yourself to focus elsewhere, you can save wasted energy, time, and emotional resources and move on to positive change.

Check Your Understanding

True/False

Try to answer the following true or false questions without rereading the article. If you need to look back for an answer, practice scanning.

_____ 1. "Shaping" refers to taking small steps to achieve a behavior change gradually.

_____ 2. Visualizing allows you to rehearse a new action mentally.

_____ 3. Studying the behavior of others is of no help in changing your own behavior.

_____ 4. If you are trying to stop smoking, spending time in the library or another nonsmoking area is helpful.

_____ 5. A "reinforcer" is a kind of reward for practicing a new behavior.

_____ 6. Consumable reinforcers like candy and cookies work best for all people.

_____ 7. Reinforcers are impossible to overuse.

_____ 8. Self-talk is usually harmful.

_____ 9. How people talk to themselves is an indication of how they feel.

_____ 10. The article suggests that it is possible to talk yourself through stressful events.

Writing

Changing behaviors is not always easy. Most students have some behaviors they would like to change. How might this chapter in the health text help you in achieving a change by adapting new strategies for reading? Review the headings in this reading and relate them to a strategy you plan to begin to use, such as setting a purpose or previewing.

Shaping _____

_____

_____

Visualizing _____

_____

_____

Modeling _____

_____

_____

Controlling _____

_____

_____

Reinforcement _____

_____

_____

Self-Talk _____

_____

_____

Reading Selection 2

Purpose

Now apply the strategies of previewing, anticipating, and associating to an entire article. The article suggests some other strategies or "keys" that can help you become a more successful college student. Your purpose for reading is to discover more ideas to make you a more confident reader.

Preview

1. Skim the article, noticing in particular the six italicized strategies or keys.

2. Skim the end questions and the vocabulary.

3. (Anticipate) Which ideas sound like new ideas to explore?

_____

_____

_____

4. (Associate) Have you used any of these skills in learning before?

_____

_____

_____

5. What ideas in these keys are related to strategies discussed earlier in this chapter?

_____

_____

_____

Six Keys to Quicker Learning

Patricia Skalka

A friend of mine was at a dinner party where two men   1
she knew were discussing *The Right Stuff*, a book about the
Mercury space program. While Ted went on and on about the
technical details he had picked up from the book, Dan offered
only a few tentative comments. "Ted got so much more out
of the reading than I did," Dan later said to my friend. "Is he
much smarter than I am?"

My friend, an educator, was curious. She knew the two
men had similar educational backgrounds and intelligence
levels. She talked with each and discovered the answer: Ted
just knew how to learn better than Dan did. Ted had made his
brain more <u>absorbent</u> by using a few simple skills.

For years, experts had believed that an individual's ability to learn was a fixed <u>capacity</u>. During the last two decades,
however, leading <u>psychologists</u> and educators have come to
think otherwise. "We have increasing proof that human intelligence is <u>expandable</u>," says Jack Lochhead, director of the
Cognitive Development Project at the University of Massachusetts in Amherst. "We know that with proper skills people can actually improve their learning ability."

Moreover, these skills are basic enough so that almost
anyone can master them with practice. Here, gathered from
the ideas of experts across the country, are six proven ways to
boost your learning ability.

1. *Look at the big picture first.* When reading new, unfamiliar material, do not <u>plunge</u> directly into it. You can
increase your comprehension and <u>retention</u> if you scan
the material first. Skim subheads, photo captions, and
any available summaries. With reports or articles, read
the first sentence of each paragraph; with books, glance
at the table of contents and introduction.

   All this previewing will help anchor in your mind
what you then read.

2. *Slow down and talk to yourself.* While speed-reading
may be fine for easy material, slower reading can be
much more effective for absorbing complex, challenging
works. Arthur Whimbey and Jack Lochhead, co-authors
of the high-school and college handbook *Problem Solving and Comprehension,* have <u>isolated</u> three basic differences in how good and bad learners study:

   - Good learners <u>vocalize</u>, or voice, the material, either
silently or aloud. They slow down, listening to each
word as they read.
   - Good learners, when <u>stymied</u>, automatically reread
until they understand the material. Poor readers, by
contrast, just keep going if they don't get it the first
time.
   - Good learners become "actively involved" with new
information. They think about what they read, challenge it, make it their own.

   In 1979, Whimbey introduced a slow, vocalized reading method into a five-week, pre-freshman program at
Xavier University in New Orleans. Many of the 175 students using this technique jumped two grade levels in

comprehension, and their college-aptitude test scores rose by as much as 14 percent.

3. *Practice memory-enhancing techniques.* When I was   9
eight and couldn't spell *arithmetic,* a teacher taught me
a sentence that has remained locked in my mind for
decades: "A rat in Tom's house may eat Tom's ice
cream." The first letters of each word spell *arithmetic.*

All such memory-enhancing techniques, called mne-   10
monics, transform new information into more easily remembered formulations.

Other first-letter mnemonics include "Homes" (the   11
names of the Great Lakes—Huron, Ontario, Michigan,
Erie, and Superior); "George Eaton's old granny rode a
pig home yesterday" (for spelling *geography*); and "My
very educated mother just served us nine pickles" (the
planet system in order—Mercury, Venus, Earth, Mars,
Jupiter, Saturn, Uranus, Neptune, Pluto).

Mnemonics can also work with images. The trick is   12
to invent visual clues that will make unfamiliar material mean something to you.

In studying Spanish, for example, you might learn   13
that the word for "duck" is *pato. Pato* sounds like the
English word *pot.* To link the two, imagine a duck wad-
dling about with a large pot over its head. You will have
a clear image that reminds you pot = *pato* = duck.

Once dismissed by researchers as a mere gimmick,   14
mnemonics are now considered an effective means of
boosting memory—doubling or even tripling the
amount of new material that test subjects can retain. "A
good memory is the key to all cognitive processes," according to William G. Chase, professor of psychology at
Carnegie-Mellon University in Pittsburgh. "And it is
something we can all have with practice."

Cognitive research shows that we have two kinds of   15
memory: short-term and long-term. Short-term memory
(STM) lasts for about 30 to 60 seconds. We call directory
assistance for a phone number, dial the number, and
then forget it. Long-term memory (LTM), however, can
last a lifetime. The secret to developing a good memory,
say Francis S. Bellezza, author of *Improve Your Memory
Skills,* is learning how to transfer useful information
from STM to LTM and how to retrieve that information
when needed.

Mnemonics can be the key that puts data into LTM   16
and gets the information back out again. Remember, the
mind and memory are like muscles—the more you use
them, the stronger they get.

4. *Organize facts into categories.* In studies at Stanford 17
University, students were asked to memorize 112 words.
These included names of animals, items of clothing,
types of transportation, and occupations. For one group,
the words were divided into these four categories. For a
second group, the words were listed at <u>random</u>. Those
who studied the material in organized categories consis-
tently outperformed the others, recalling two to three
times more words.

"Trying to digest new information in one lump is dif- 18
ficult," says Thomas R. Trabasso, professor of education
and behavioral science at the University of Chicago. "By
analyzing new material and dividing it into meaningful
chunks, you make learning easier."

For example, to remember the names of all former 19
U.S. Presidents in proper order, cluster the leaders into
groups—those before the War of 1812, those from 1812
until the Civil War, those from the Civil War to World
War I, and those after World War I. By thus organizing
complex material into logical categories you create a
permanent storage technique.

5. *Focus your attention.* The next time you are faced with 20
new material you need to master, ask yourself, What do
I want to learn from reading this, and how will I benefit
from the knowledge gained? "By telling ourselves what
the learning will do for us, we reduce our <u>resistance</u> to
studying and become better learners," says Russell W.
Scalpone, a psychologist and manager at A. T. Kearney,
Inc., an international management-consulting firm.

Scalpone recommends four other techniques for im- 21
proving concentration and focus:

- Establish a time and a place for learning. Take the
phone off the hook; close the door. By regulating your
environment, you create the expectation that learning will occur.
- Guard against <u>distractions</u>. Don't be shy about hanging a "Do Not Disturb" sign on your door. You have a
right to your time.
- Try a variety of learning methods. Diagramming, note
taking, outlining, even talking into a tape recorder are
study techniques that can increase concentration.
Use whatever study skills you are most comfortable
with. Be creative.
- Monitor your progress. Being busy is not always the
same as being productive. Stop occasionally and ask
yourself, Am I contributing right now to my learn-

ing goal? If the answer is yes, keep working. If no, ask yourself why. If you're not making progress because of tension or <u>fatigue</u>, take a break—without feeling guilty. Regular breaks can improve the learning process.

6. *Discover your own learning style.* Educators Rita and Ken Dunn tell the story of three children who each received a bicycle for Christmas. The bikes, purchased unassembled, had to be put together by parents. Tim's father read the directions carefully before he set to work. Mary's father laid out the pieces on the floor and handed the directions to Mary's mother. "Read this to me," he said, as he surveyed the <u>components</u>. George's mother <u>instinctively</u> began fitting pieces together, glancing at the directions only when stymied. By day's end, all three bikes were assembled, each from a different approach.   22

"Although they didn't realize it," says Rita Dunn, professor of education at St. John's University in New York City, "the parents had worked according to their own learning styles."   23

"Our approaches to unfamiliar material are as unique and specialized as we are, and a key to learning is recognizing—and accommodating—the style that suits us best," says Ken Dunn, professor of education at Queens College in New York City.   24

Learning styles can vary dramatically. The Dunns have developed a Productivity Environment Preference Survey, which identifies 21 elements that affect the way we learn. These factors include noise level, lighting, amount of supervision required, even the time of day.   25

What's *your* style? Try some self-analysis. What, for example, is your approach to putting together an unassembled item? Do you concentrate better in the morning or in the evening? In a noisy environment or a quiet one? Make a list of all the pluses and minuses you can identify. Then use this list to create the learning environment best for you.   26

Whichever style works for you, the good news is that you *can* expand your learning capacity. And this can make your life fuller and more productive.   27

Check Your Understanding

Review

Write each of the keys here. Skim the text for the keys if you need to.

1. _____

2. _____

3. _____

4. _____

5. _____

6. _____

Fill in the Blanks

Write in the word or words from the article to complete the statement.

1. STM stands for _____.

2. LTM stands for _____.

3. The Spanish word for "duck" is _____.

4. _____ are important for finding information

   in your memory.

5. Human intelligence is _____.

Multiple Choice

Write the letter or letters of the best choices to complete each statement.

_____ 1. The article is mainly about
   a. how your learning skills can be improved.
   b. how some people have good memories and others do not.
   c. how everyone learns the same way.
   d. how organizing is an aid to learning.

_____ 2. According to the article, good readers
   a. vocalize, either silently or aloud.
   b. become actively involved.
   c. think about what they read.
   d. all of the above.

_____ 3. Research into cognitive or intellectual development
   a. is no longer of interest.
   b. continues.

        c. has changed ideas about learning ability.
        d. is a waste of time.

_____ 4. The writer suggests that you can enhance your learning by
        a. using mnemonics.
        b. talking to yourself.
        c. organizing facts to be learned.
        d. all of the above.

_____ 5. The article suggests that
        a. some people are smarter than others.
        b. reading slowly is harmful to learning.
        c. everybody has the potential to become a successful learner.
        d. speed-reading of college texts is a timesaver.

True/False

Write the word true *if the statement is correct or* false *if it is not correct.*

_____ 1. The example of three parents who assemble bicycles shows that mechanical skills are easy to learn.

_____ 2. A good memory is very important to improving your intelligence.

_____ 3. Mental pictures or images are an aid in helping you remember things.

_____ 4. Your physical surroundings are not important in influencing your ability to learn.

_____ 5. You can improve your memory by transferring information from short-term memory to long-term memory.

_____ 6. Many people don't use the techniques mentioned in the article because they don't believe they'll work.

_____ 7. Some experts believe that good learners vocalize or read material aloud.

_____ 8. Mnemonics were once thought to be a gimmick or a game.

_____ 9. You can learn more easily if you divide new material into meaningful chunks.

_____ 10. We all learn in exactly the same way.

Vocabulary

Match the words in Column A with the words or phrases in Column B by writing the letter from Column B in the space before Column A for both exercises. Consult a dictionary for help with unfamiliar words.

I.

Column A	Column B
_____ 1. tentative	a. say aloud
_____ 2. absorbent	b. able to increase
_____ 3. retention	c. intellectual
_____ 4. enhancing	d. interference
_____ 5. gimmick	e. ability
_____ 6. cognitive	f. ability to hold on to
_____ 7. distraction	g. uncertain
_____ 8. capacity	h. capable of taking in, soaking up
_____ 9. expandable	i. improving
_____ 10. vocalize	j. trick

II.

Column A	Column B
_____ 1. plunge	a. blocked
_____ 2. isolated	b. ways to improve memory
_____ 3. stymied	c. opposition to
_____ 4. mnemonics	d. part of a larger whole
_____ 5. retrieve	e. without order
_____ 6. random	f. dive
_____ 7. fatigue	g. kept apart
_____ 8. component	h. by nature
_____ 9. instinctively	i. bring back
_____ 10. resistance	j. weariness

Writing

Write a detailed description of a key to quicker learning that you intend to use immediately. Explain why you think this key will be helpful and mention at least one occasion when you will use it.

Group Discussion: Thinking beyond the Text

An important way to assure that you have understood your reading is to participate in group discussions or collaborative learning experiences. Research shows that students who study in groups do better than students who work alone. This text offers opportunities in each chapter for small group discussions to discuss readings, compare answers, clarify material, and extend your learning beyond the text by doing critical thinking about your activities and your reading.

Group work requires your active participation as a listener, a leader, a recorder, or a responder. Work with other members of your group to discuss the following questions. Your instructor may ask for a report from your group following the discussion.

1. The writer has used quotes from books and interviews with friends and experts to support her ideas. Do you find the ideas convincing? Is there anything she could have done to make her points more convincing?
2. Who do you think is the intended audience for this article?
3. Which key do you think would be most helpful to you? Explain your reasons.
4. Do you think that some of the suggestions are just the opinion of the writer? Why or why not?

Chapter 2

Getting Involved with Words

A rich vocabulary is one of the most invaluable possessions
of the leaders in every profession.

Wilfred Funk

You use words constantly. You probably already have a base of at
least 15,000 words for everyday use. After college, you may well
have a vocabulary in the range of 30,000 to 60,000 words. More
than 2,000,000 words in the English language are available for your
use. The more you read, the more words you will command. The
more words you can command, the more efficiently you will read,
the more ideas you will have, and the more effectively you can
communicate. This chapter is intended to show you how to acquire a rich vocabulary. A rich vocabulary is an important key to a
successful college experience.

The chapter will consider:

- clues to word meaning from context
- unlocking word meaning by analyzing structure
- using your dictionary effectively
- methods for remembering new words

The first thing to know about words is that they can be tricky;
one word often has more than one meaning. You are familiar with
the word *gag*. Look at several of the different ideas this word can
convey according to *The Random House College Dictionary*.

a. to stop up the mouth of a person
b. to restrain by force from freedom of speech
c. to cause to choke
d. a thing put in a person's mouth to stop speech
e. an order to suppress speech
f. a joke

Use these meanings to explain the meaning of the word *gag* in the following sentences by putting the letter of the appropriate meaning before the sentence.

_____ 1. Bert *gagged* on the dreaded brussels sprouts.

_____ 2. We planned an elaborate *gag* for April 1st.

_____ 3. When violence erupted, a *gag* was put on open discussion.

_____ 4. The robber stuffed the *gag* in his victim's mouth.

_____ 5. The robber's victim was *gagged.*

_____ 6. The dictator *gagged* his opponents.

You used the meaning of the sentence to determine the correct meaning of *gag* in each instance.

You are probably familiar with the words *cell, colon,* and *culture.* However, when you find these words in one of your science texts, be on the alert. *Cell* does not refer to a prison. *Colon* is not a punctuation mark. *Culture* is not a particular way of living. Likewise, the words *sign, base,* and *root* all take on new meanings in your math text. Familiar meanings may not be the correct ones. The sentence or paragraph, called the *context,* will suggest the meaning for the word.

Energy is another familiar word. When we are tired, we may say, "I have run out of energy." This is not the same energy discussed in the paragraph that follows.

> If you ever read about an *energy* shortage, you can be sure it is false. There is no energy shortage, nor can there ever be. The earth holds the potential of producing unlimited low-cost power, which can help raise the living standards of humans across the globe. The sun, for example, produces more *energy* than humanity could ever need. Boundless *energy* is also available from the tides and the winds. In some cases, we need better technology to harness these sources of *energy;* in others, we need only apply technology we already have.
>
> —James M. Henslin, *Sociology*

A biology text has a slightly different and more complex definition of energy. Read the following paragraph.

> *Energy* is the capacity to do work. Implicit in the definition of *energy* as the "capacity" to do work is an important idea: Although some object might have had *energy* applied to

it, the *energy* might not necessarily produce immediately measurable work; that is, *energy* can be stored, but not yet released. *Energy* that is stored in a system and that may be made available to do work is called *potential energy*. As the coiled spring unwinds, its potential energy can be used to do work. Potential energy does not perform any work. The *energy* that actually performs work is called *kinetic energy*. *Kinetic energy* is the energy of matter that is in motion. As a coiled spring unwinds, its potential energy is converted to kinetic energy.

—Adapted from Mahlon G. Kelly and
John C. McGrath, *Biology*

Do some *close* reading to write definitions, using your own words as much as possible for these words from the second paragraph.

energy _____

potential energy _____

kinetic energy _____

Identify the kind of energy discussed in the first paragraph.

_____

Fortunately, many textbooks give you different aids to determine the meaning of special words. Sometimes a word is in bold print to show its importance. For example, you might find the word *synergism* in boldface in a business text. Some chapters have important words noted at the beginning or end of the chapter. You might find *monogamy* in a sociology text defined at the beginning of the chapter. The word *thanatology* in a psychology text might be defined at the end of the chapter. Some books define special words by a note in the margin, and other books have their own small dictionary, called a *glossary*, at the end of the book.

When the textbook draws special attention to a word, you know the word is important for you to add to your vocabulary. The long definition of energy in the first paragraph is a clue that the word will appear in your further reading in that text.

When you wrote the meanings of the energy words, you were using context clues to get the meaning. *Context* is the word's environment—the sentence or paragraph in which the word is found. Getting the meaning of a word from context is a major help in developing your vocabulary and will often save you the time of stopping to look up the word in the dictionary.

Clues to Learning Word Meaning from Context

Context clues to the meaning of an unfamiliar word are often available to the alert reader. Look at this sentence.

Canker, a disease of plants, especially fruit trees, is caused by various fungi and bacteria.

Here the meaning of *canker* is clear because it is defined or explained by the context. The dictionary might give you as many as eight other meanings. Perhaps you are familiar with a sore in your mouth called a canker; clearly that is not the meaning in this sentence. You were able to gather the meaning from the definition set off with commas.

Punctuation Clues

When you meet an unfamiliar word, look for punctuation clues. Marks like commas, dashes, and parentheses following an unfamiliar word will often indicate a word or phrase of explanation, definition, or restatement that unlocks the meaning of that word. Study the following example.

Hemophilia (literally "love of blood") is a rare disease in which the blood of the afflicted individual clots slowly or not at all.

This sentence gives you two definitions: the actual meaning of the word from the Greek language in parentheses and then a statement of explanation.

Signal Words as Clues

Another kind of context clue is sometimes given by a signal word. Such signals might be:

that is   meaning   such as   or

When you see these words, you can be alert to a definition or an example to follow.

Condiments, such as mustard, spices, and salsa, are tasty additions to many foods.

Did you notice the signal words and the punctuation? The sentence tells you how condiments are used and gives you examples of condiments. Can you think of other condiments?

Still other kinds of signal words prepare you for understanding an unfamiliar word because of an opposite or contrasting idea presented. The signal words might be:

not	rather than	on the other hand
instead of	however	but

Look at this example:

> He usually is a *laggard*; however, today he was energetic and completed his work on time.

Could you tell from the signal word and from the contrasting idea of energy and getting done on time that *laggard* means one who is slow moving? Of course, there are other signal words. These examples are just to start you thinking.

Less Obvious Clues

Sometimes context clues are not as clear as the examples just given. You must deal with the general idea of the context or read between the lines. This strategy is called *making an inference.* You may need to read an entire paragraph to decide the meaning of a word. Here's an example.

> I wanted to *retrieve* the time capsule that my classmates and I had buried some years ago. I had buried a comic book that was now worth a considerable sum, so I proceeded to the burial place with a shovel.

If you did not know the meaning of *retrieve,* you could figure out that the person is going to dig up the time capsule and "reclaim" or "recover" the comic book.

You might want to work with a group to discuss the clues and the meaning of the words in the following exercise. What is most important is recognizing the meaning of the word from the context and using whatever clues you can to determine meaning.

Exercise 2-1   Recognizing Context Clues

Using the clues of punctuation marks, signal clues, *and* general context, *write the meaning of the underlined words and the clue or clues that helped you define the word from context on the lines below the sentences.*

1. By making products out of <u>biodegradable</u> materials (materials that decay and are absorbed into the environment) we could reduce pollution.

   Meaning _____

   Clue _____

2. The politician's <u>ulterior</u>—hidden and concealed—motives confused the voters into voting for him.

   Meaning _____

   Clue _____

3. Carlos was <u>taciturn</u> rather than talkative after receiving the academic award.

   Meaning _____

   Clue _____

4. Kissing a lady's hand is a habit almost as <u>obsolete</u> as wearing hoop skirts.

   Meaning _____

   Clue _____

5. My story about the night's adventures was not <u>credible</u>. My family really didn't believe it.

   Meaning _____

   Clue _____

6. When talking with my boss, I was careful not to <u>allude</u> or refer to my previous job.

   Meaning _____

   Clue _____

7. Her <u>effervescent</u>, high-spirited, approach to life was an inspiration to all.

   Meaning _____

   Clue _____

8. The dress Samantha chose to wear to the funeral was <u>bizarre</u>; it had wild, outlandish colors and a sexy cut.

   Meaning _____

   Clue _____

9. Jarrod's decision to increase his study time was a <u>judicious</u>, carefully considered one.

   Meaning _____

   Clue _____

10. One should not feel <u>antipathy</u> toward people with AIDS. One should try instead to give comfort and understanding.

    Meaning _____

    Clue _____

Exercise 2-2 Context Clues in Paragraphs

Read the three paragraphs that follow and use all the clues that each paragraph provides to help you think of a definition for each of the italicized words. Then look at the list of words following the paragraph and select the term that seems to best define each one.

1. Hemophilia is a heredity *trait* that causes blood to clot slowly or not at all. The trait is most often passed by females to male children. Queen Victoria was a carrier of this trait. Since Queen Victoria and Prince Albert were *prolific* parents and their numerous offspring were *notorious* for marrying into the royal families of Europe, Queen Victoria sowed the seeds that *ultimately* led to the *demise* of the European dynasties because the males died of hemophilia.

   —Adapted from Irwin W. Sherman and Vilia G. Sherman,
   Biology: A Human Approach

Circle the correct definition.

1. **trait**
   a. quality
   b. evidence
   c. requirement

2. **prolific**
   a. kind
   b. fruitful
   c. barren

3. **notorious**
   a. infamous
   b. known
   c. accepted

4. **ultimately**
   a. absolutely
   b. horribly
   c. eventually

5. **demise**
   a. death
   b. growth
   c. health

2. If you live in the United States and speak English, your emotional life is *categorized* differently than if you come from Japan or Indonesia. . . . Some English words have no real *equivalent* in other languages. . . . English *distinguishes* among "terror," "horror," "dread," "apprehension," and "timidity" as types of fear. However, in Gidjingali, an Australian aboriginal language, one word, "gurakadj," *suffices*.

   —Lester A. Lefton, *Psychology*

Circle the correct definition.

1. **categorized**
   a. noted
   b. grouped
   c. mentioned

2. **distinguishes**
   a. notes differences
   b. combines
   c. experiences

3. **equivalent**
   a. answer
   b. potential
   c. equal

4. **apprehension**   5. **suffices**

   a. courage   a. lacks

   b. opinion   b. satisfies

   c. alarm   c. supplies

3. *Carcinoma* is one of four types of cancer. It occurs most often in the *epithelial tissues* (tissues covering body surfaces and lining most body cavities). Carcinoma of the breast, lung, intestines, skin, and mouth are examples. . . . *Symptoms* vary. For example, lung cancer might be indicated by a *persistent* cough, chest pains, and *recurrent* bronchitis.

   —Adapted from Rebecca J. Donatelle and
   Lorraine G. Davis, *Health: The Basics* .

Write your own definition for these words. Use a dictionary if necessary.

carcinoma _____

_____

epithelial tissues _____

_____

symptoms _____

persistent _____

recurrent _____

Exercise 2-3 Using Context to Supply a Missing Word

Use context clues to find the word that best completes the meaning of the sentences in the following paragraphs. Sometimes the sentence before or after the blank will be helpful. Try to think of a word before you look at the choices following the paragraph. Choose one word from the list of four with the same letter as the blank.

1. One of the most unwelcome participants in a group meeting is

   the person who thinks "No." This person's primary mission

seems to be (a) _____ the ideas and proposals that others voice. Such a participant seldom presents a (b) _____ idea but is always quick to say of someone else's (c) _____, "That won't work," or "That's not right."

Most groups meet to solve problems and find answers, but problems can't be solved or answers found in a (d) _____ atmosphere. Participants must be willing to approach group activities with the attitude that the only way to achieve (e) _____ is to listen and contribute freely. No one immediately (f) _____ an idea or answer someone else has presented; instead, each tries to see the merit of the idea or answer and explore it. To (g) _____ ideas and answers before they are discussed is not only rude but also extremely (h). _____ to those who are (i) _____ trying to reach intelligent (j) _____.

a. separating	killing	noticing	applauding
b. disastrous	wet	positive	negative
c. operation	idea	work	preparation
d. negative	forceful	varied	colorful
e. preparation	success	prediction	solution
f. increases	paints	vetoes	sells
g. grow	smother	fulfill	like
h. fulfilling	gross	anticipating	disheartening
i. negatively	genuinely	stupidly	loquaciously
j. topics	notes	purposes	decisions

2. In recent years the Soviet Union has been (a) _____

and what were once its satellite nations have undergone

massive (b) _____. Meanwhile most developing

(c) _____ face difficult challenges to bring them-

selves into the (d) _____ world, with poverty, lim-

ited resources, overpopulation, and hunger almost always

threatening them. While most U.S. citizens face less

(e) _____ threats, a declining economy, poverty, po-

litical corruption, environmental pollution, crime, racism,

sexism, delinquency, and family problems are common

realities lacking simple (f) _____. Before these

(g) _____ can be solved, people must better

(h) _____ how society works, or fails to work. Never

has the need to provide introductory sociology been more

(i) _____.

a. launched	dissolved	mediated	cruised
b. surveys	theories	changes	chapters
c. nations	problems	masters	presses
d. third	modern	old	negative
e. sexist	ancient	captive	drastic
f. recipes	solutions	formats	diagnoses
g. problems	parts	features	classrooms
h. contribute	support	separate	understand
i. forceful	satisfactory	credible	urgent

*For this paragraph, the missing words are in the group following
the paragraph. You may want to cross off each word as you use it.*

3. An increasing number of employers are providing day care

centers at their places of _____. They have

learned that employees are more _____ when they do not have to worry about babysitting _____ for their children. In addition, when child care is on company _____, employees do not need to be _____ from work when the baby-sitter fails to show up. Many companies are learning that on-site day care is a valuable _____ benefit. Employees are less likely to _____ their places of employment when day care is available. This means _____ do not have to worry about _____ employee turnover. Undoubtedly, more and more companies will be providing day care facilities. They are a benefit to both employer and _____.

productive	arrangements	business	fringe	change
companies	premises	rapid	absent	employee

Context clues are the easiest, quickest way to unlock the meaning of a word, but these clues have limitations, and you can be misled about a word's meaning. In the sentence, "She was ultimately reliable because you could always depend on her," you cannot be sure if she was absolutely (totally) reliable or eventually (when she got around to it) reliable. Both *eventually* and *absolutely* can mean the same as ultimately, yet there's a shade of difference. You need to look carefully at sentences before and after the unfamiliar word to determine word meaning.

Unlocking Word Meaning by Structural Analysis

The structure of a building is the arrangement of its parts. Words are built or structured as well. Learning the structure of words—their *prefixes, roots* and *suffixes*—can help you determine word meanings as well as add more words to your current vocabulary.

Prefixes consist of one or more letters at the beginning of some words. *Pre-* is a prefix meaning *before.* So the word **pre**fix means to fix before.

A root is the part of a word which may have prefixes or suffixes attached to it. *Port* is a root meaning *carry* that you can find in **port**er (one who carries) and ex**port** (to carry out).

Suffixes, like prefixes, can be one or more letters, but they occur at the end of a word. The word *porter* has the suffix *er,* which indicates a person, as it also does in *worker* and *teacher.*

No doubt you know the meaning of the word *inspect,* to look at closely. If you also know that the root *spec* or *spect* means "to look," you can unlock the meaning of countless words.

inspector—one who looks over something
inspection—the act of looking over
perspective—your view of facts or ideas
respect—to look at again with esteem
retrospect—a look back at
suspect—to look under outward appearances
expect—to look forward to something
prospect—to look for or explore
spectator—one who looks on
spectrum—in physics, a colored band the eye sees

If any of these words is unfamiliar, you will find it helpful to learn a few of the many prefixes in our language. These prefixes will also help you to detect the meaning of other words you encounter in your reading.

Working with Prefixes

Sometimes prefixes reverse the meaning of a word. The prefixes *il-, dis-, un-,* and *in-* may give the word a negative meaning. For example, **il**logical is "not logical," **dis**like is "to not like," **un**listed is "not listed," and **in**flexible is "not flexible or movable."

Other prefixes show relationships of time and place. As noted, often *pre-* means "before," a time relationship. The prefix *trans-* indicates "across," a place relationship.

Exercise 2-4   Using Prefixes to Discover Meaning

Here is a list of ten common prefixes and their meanings. Study the prefix, its meaning, and the example, and then write in a word from your own vocabulary that uses that prefix. You may want to do this as a group activity.

Prefix	Meaning	Example	Your Word
intro-	within, into	*introduce*	_____
omni-	all	*omniscient*	_____
hyper-	over, beyond	*hypertension*	_____
super-	over, above	*supernatural*	_____
anti-	against	*antidote*	_____
poly-	many	*polygon*	_____
sub-	under	*submarine*	_____
ex-	out of/from	*excavate*	_____
micro-	small	*microscope*	_____
auto-	self	*autobiography*	_____

Using your knowledge of these prefixes, complete the following sentences with the words from the list below. The context clues may also help. Write a definition of each word on the line below the sentence.

introspective	hyperbole	polygon	transgressing
subordinate	omniscient	antibodies	autocracy
microscopic	superfluous		

1. He worked under a tough boss and did not enjoy being a

   _____ .

   _____

2. Our blood system produces _____ against poisons in our systems.

   _____

3. He was _____, inclined to look within himself to consider his own motivations.

   _____

4. Young children think their parents are _____ because they seem to know everything.

   _____

5. The many-sided figure was called a _____.

   _____

6. An _____ is government ruled by a single ruler.

   _____

7. He tends to use _____ or exaggeration, saying he waited an eternity for me to dress for dinner.

   _____

8. A paramecium is too small to be seen with the naked eye. It is _____.

   _____

9. If you go over the speed limit, you are _____ the speed limit.

   _____

10. Her apologies were excessive, or _____, beyond what would be expected.

   _____

Exercise 2-5   More Work with Prefixes

Work with some more familiar prefixes by reading the prefix, its meaning, and the example. Then supply your own word beginning with the same prefix.

Prefix	Meaning	Example	Your Word
meta-	after/beyond	metaphor	_____
bene-	good	benediction	_____
homo-	same	homonym	_____
mal-	bad	malicious	_____
re-/retro-	backward, again	retreat	_____
tele-	distant	telegraph	_____
pro-	forward	propose	_____
de-	down	deposit	_____
post-	after	postscript	_____
sym-/syn-	together	sympathy, synthesis	_____

Use the following list of words with these prefixes to complete the sentences, and then define the words on the line below the sentence.

symmetry   postgraduate   malcontent   regenerate
demolish   metabolism   homogenized   benevolent
progressive   telepathy

11. Are they going to tear down or _____ that

    building?

    _____

12. After Sam graduated, he continued to take _____ courses.

_____

13. The two sides of a person's face go together, producing a kind of _____.

_____

14. He seemed never to be satisfied with the government's actions. He seemed a _____.

_____

15. Some animals have the ability to _____ parts that have been lost.

_____

16. Bodily energy is produced by the process of _____.

_____

17. When different elements are blended to make them the same, the product is _____.

_____

18. Communicating between minds without words or actions is called _____.

_____

19. Her ideas seemed to be ahead of the times, or _____.

_____

20. The millionaire who did much good in the community was

    known for her _____ actions.

    _____

_____

Working with Roots

The prefixes just given have come into our language from Greek or Latin. In the same way, many roots or base words came into our language from other languages. Learning a few basic roots will help you make rapid additions to your vocabulary.

_____

Exercise 2-6   Working with Roots

Study these roots, their meaning, and the words built from them. Then use some of the words to complete the sentences that follow.

Root	Meaning	Examples
phon	sound	*telephone, phonetic, symphony, telephonic*
graph	write	*autograph, graphic, photograph, biography*
cede/cess	go, move	*recession, recede, process, secede*
mis/mit	send	*missionary, permit, submit, remit, transmission*
volv	turn, roll	*revolve, revolution, involve, voluntary, involuntary*
vert	turn	*invert, reverse, divert, avert, conversation*

Complete these sentences using one of the examples from the list of roots.

1. When you are concentrating on a recipe, a sudden noise can

   _____ your attention.

2. The floodwaters had begun to move back or _____.

3. It was easy to picture his room from his _____ description.

4. Because I like the sound of beautiful music, I enjoy the _____.

5. She was asked to send in her resume, so she was quick to _____ it.

6. Some muscle movements are _____.

Exercise 2-7   Working with More Roots

First study the roots, their meanings, and the examples. Then use some of the words to complete the sentences that follow.

More Roots	**Meaning**	**Examples**
cred	believe	*credit, credibility, incredible, credulity*
cog/cogni	know	*recognize, incognito, precognition*
press	squeeze	*pressure, repress, impress*
port	carry	*import, export, portable, report*
form	make	*reform, information, formation*
duc	lead	*conductor, aqueduct, induct, deduct*

Choose a word from the examples to complete these sentences.

1. The rocks created an interesting _____.

2. Since the star did not want to be recognized, she traveled _____.

3. He sometimes played around with the truth, so I found the latest story he told me to be _____.

4. Anger is an emotion that sometimes should be hidden, so people attempt to _____ it.

5. The lake water was too shallow for our canoe; fortunately the canoe was _____.

6. The water was fed from one lake to another by an _____.

Working with Suffixes

Suffixes, the endings of words, are one more way to analyze a word from its makeup or structure. Recognizing suffixes added to a new or familiar word will help you to enlarge your vocabulary. The endings of words often change the part of speech; for example, a verb can become a noun, an adjective, or an adverb. You know that you can make most singular nouns plural by adding *-s* or *-es*. Verbs are easily changed by adding *-s*, *-ed*, or *-ing*. But other endings can change a word from one part of speech to another. A few examples:

> The verb *covet*, meaning to desire something like a car or money excessively, becomes the adjective *covetous* or the noun *coveter*, as in the following sentences: *Joe **covets** my Porsche. He is **covetous**. He is a **coveter**.*

> *Cognition*, a noun, means the act of knowing, while *cognitive* is an adjective: *My science homework required considerable **cognition**, but I **recognized** the ideas when I reviewed them. College requires much **cognitive** activity.*

Study the following list of common suffixes, their meaning, and the part of speech they usually indicate.

Suffix	Meaning	Example
-able/-ible (*adj.*)	able to	*manageable/ responsible*
-ance/-ence (*n.*)	a quality or state; an action	*independence/ performance*

Suffix	Meaning	Example
-ion/-tion (n.)	a condition or result	*confusion/information*
-less (n.)	without	*selfless*
-ent/-ant (adj.)	marked by, having	*important/different*
-ic/-al (adj.)	relating to, characterized by	*phonetic/heroic/ seasonal*
-ate (v.)	to act or cause	*originate/eliminate*
-ous/-ious (adj.)	full of	*fabulous/courageous/ ambitious*
-er/-or/-ist (n.)	one who	*writer/actor/terrorist*
-ify/-ize (v.)	to make	*justify/finalize*

Exercise 2-8   Practice Using Suffixes

Select one of the following words to create a new word by adding the appropriate suffix. You may need a dictionary to be sure of the correct spelling. The first one is completed for you.

elect	prevent	ideal	music	relent
resist	motive	false	glory	excel

1. (*-able/-ible*)   If she had exercised care, the accident would have been _preventable_.

2. (*-ance/-ence*)   Since Sue did well in math, it was no surprise when she received the award for _____.

3. (*-ion/-tion*)   We plan to vote in the coming _____.

4. (*-less*)   He would never give up; he was _____ in achieving his goals.

5. (*-ant/-ent*)   The mustard stain withstood frequent washings. It was _____.

6. (*-ic*/*-al*)   Tony played the violin; his father played the piano, and his sister sang. They were a _____ family.

7. (*-ate*)   Having a goal is helpful to _____ oneself to do homework.

8. (*-ous*/*-ious*)   The vivid sunset was one of the most _____ of the summer.

9. (*-er*/*-or*/*-ist*)   An _____ is a person with high standards.

10. (*-ify*/*-ize*)   A criminal will sometimes lie and _____ records.

Becoming familiar with common prefixes, roots, and suffixes is helpful in analyzing new words to determine their meaning. These exercises are not exhaustive, but they are intended to make you alert to the aid that word parts can provide in word recognition and vocabulary building. As with context, however, these clues are not totally reliable. The common prefix *in-* often means "not," as in the word *inaccurate*, meaning "not accurate" or "not correct." However, the word *income*, as you know, does not mean "not coming." Using context and structural clues is helpful, but to be sure of meaning, you should check new words in a dictionary as necessary.

Exercise 2-9   Putting It All Together

The words in this exercise are composed of roots, prefixes, and suffixes. Break each word into its parts to determine the meaning of the word. You may wish to turn back to look at the lists of prefixes, roots, and suffixes introduced previously. Then use the words in a sentence of your own. The first one is done for you as an example.

1. *symphony:* _____ sounds made together _____

    (*phon* = sound, *sym* = together)

    I enjoyed the symphony played on public radio.

2. *precognition:* _____ (						)

    _____

    _____

3. *incredible:* _____ (						)

    _____

    _____

4. *information:* _____ (						)

    _____

    _____

5. *suppress:* _____ (						)

    _____

    _____

6. *microphone:* _____ (						)

    _____

    _____

7. *exportable:* _____ (						)

    _____

    _____

8. *phonograph:* _____ (						)

    _____

    _____

9. *malform:* _____ (   )

_____

_____

10. *inversion:* _____ (   )

_____

_____

_____

Using the Dictionary

Perhaps the person who has expressed most clearly the value of the dictionary is Malcolm X, the controversial Black Muslim leader, later assassinated while giving a speech in Harlem. He was a powerful speaker for the rights of African Americans, particularly the urban poor. After leaving school in the eighth grade, he drifted into crime and finally spent some years in prison. While in prison, Malcolm X became frustrated with his inability to read and asked for a dictionary. Read a few comments from his autobiography:

> Every book I picked up had few sentences which didn't contain anywhere from one to nearly all of the words that might as well have been in Chinese. When I skipped those words, of course, I really ended up with little idea of what the book said. . . . I saw that the best thing I could do was get hold of a dictionary—to study, to learn some words.
>
> —Malcolm X, *The Autobiography of Malcolm X*

After he got a dictionary, pencils, and writing tablets, he began copying every detail, even punctuation, from page after page. Later, he said:

> I also learned of people and places and events from history. Actually the dictionary is like a miniature encyclopedia. . . . I suppose it was inevitable that as my word base broadened, I could for the first time pick up a book and read and now begin to understand what the book was saying.
>
> —Malcolm X, *The Autobiography of Malcolm X*

What does your dictionary have to offer you? That will depend on the kind of dictionary you own. Ideally, you will carry in your book bag a paperback dictionary containing about 50,000 words. At home you will have a hardback or desk dictionary containing as many as 150,000 words. All libraries and many homes have complete or unabridged dictionaries with even more words and information.

You already know that you can find the meaning of words and their correct spelling in the dictionary, but a good desk dictionary will give you much more.

Pronunciation of Words

A good dictionary is also a help in learning word pronunciation. Word entries are divided into syllables followed by the phonetic spelling of the word. For example, the word *commensurate,* meaning "equal in measure, amount, or duration," is divided into syllables as *com men su rate.* The phonetic spelling is "kə men(t)s rət." (An upside-down *e,* or *schwa,* indicates an unaccented vowel.) A key to help you with the sounds in the syllables can usually be found in the front of the book and also at the bottom of every other page. There you will find sample sounds like the *a* in *ash.* Using the pronunciation key in your dictionary, try pronouncing these familiar phrases. Then write them out on the lines below.

1. smīl yər on kan´ dəd kam´ rə

   _____

2. wən(t)s ə pȯn ə tīm

   _____

3. sā chēz

   _____

Parts of Speech

Following the phonetic spelling in a typical dictionary entry is an abbreviation indicating the part of speech, or how the word will be used in a sentence. The phonetic spelling for the word *command* is followed by *v.* This abbreviation indicates that it functions as a verb, as in the sentence, "The general commanded the troops." In other definitions for this word, you will see that it can also be used as a noun, as in, "The command to evacuate was issued."

Usage

Some words will have a special usage label informing you that they are slang or informal. The expression *dig in* is informal when it is used to mean "start eating." If you tell someone you "dig it," meaning that you understand, you are using *dig* as slang.

Definitions

You have already noticed that a single word can have many definitions. If you are trying to learn the meaning of a word, the first definition in your dictionary is usually the most important. But if you are looking for a word used in a scientific or technological text, you will need to skim the definitions to find the most appropriate meaning, which will be preceded by an abbreviation of the subject. The simple word *low*, which you understand as the opposite of *high*, means "simple structure" (like a single-celled animal) when it is preceded by *biol*. Words may also have special meaning in sports. The first meaning of the noun *loft* is a room or upper level, like a choir loft, but in golf the word means the slant of the face of the club head.

Synonyms/Antonyms

Synonyms, words that have the same meaning as the word you are looking up, are often included at the end of the entry after the abbreviation *syn*. You may also find *ant*. for *antonyms*, words with an opposite meaning from the entry word. The specialized dictionary known as a thesaurus is a better source for finding both synonyms and antonyms, however.

Illustrations

Most dictionaries contain illustrations, maps, and graphs that can be helpful in developing your understanding of a word. Malcolm X commented that years after his dictionary study, he had never forgotten the picture of the aardvark, a kind of anteater, appearing on the first page of his book. Sometimes the dictionary will give you another kind of illustration—an example in the form of a sample phrase or sentence with the word used in context.

Word History or Etymology

Many English words have their origin in other languages. Abbreviations for the language are included in brackets. For example, [Gr] indicates that Greek is the original source of the word or part of the word. These abbreviations are usually explained in the front of the dictionary. Sometimes, especially in an unabridged dictionary, you can find stories behind the meanings of words. For example, the word *chauvinist,* meaning one who shows prejudiced devotion to a cause, comes from French. The word is derived from the last name of Nicholas Chauvin, a loud-mouthed, patriotic soldier in Napoleon's army.

Study the following half-page of a dictionary to see examples of the many kinds of information you can find in almost any dictionary.

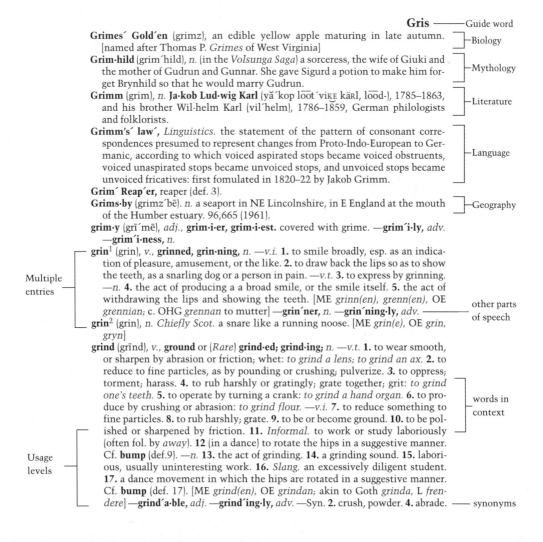

Gris ——Guide word

Grimes′ Gold′en (grimz), an edible yellow apple maturing in late autumn. [named after Thomas P. *Grimes* of West Virginia] ——Biology

Grim·hild (grim′hild), *n.* (in the *Volsunga Saga*) a sorceress, the wife of Giuki and the mother of Gudrun and Gunnar. She gave Sigurd a potion to make him forget Brynhild so that he would marry Gudrun. ——Mythology

Grimm (grim), *n.* **Ja·kob Lud·wig Karl** (yä′kop lōōt′viKE kärl, lōōd-), 1785–1863, and his brother Wil·helm Karl (vil′helm), 1786–1859, German philologists and folklorists. ——Literature

Grimm's′ law′, *Linguistics.* the statement of the pattern of consonant correspondences presumed to represent changes from Proto-Indo-European to Germanic, according to which voiced aspirated stops became voiced obstruents, voiced unaspirated stops became unvoiced stops, and unvoiced stops became unvoiced fricatives: first fomulated in 1820–22 by Jakob Grimm. ——Language

Grim′ Reap′er, reaper (def. 3).

Grims·by (grimz′bē). *n.* a seaport in NE Lincolnshire, in E England at the mouth of the Humber estuary. 96,665 (1961). ——Geography

grim·y (grī′mē), *adj.*, **grim·i·er, grim·i·est.** covered with grime. —**grim′i·ly,** *adv.* —**grim′i·ness,** *n.*

Multiple entries — **grin**[1] (grin), *v.*, **grinned, grin·ning,** *n.* —*v.i.* **1.** to smile broadly, esp. as an indication of pleasure, amusement, or the like. **2.** to draw back the lips so as to show the teeth, as a snarling dog or a person in pain. —*v.t.* **3.** to express by grinning. —*n.* **4.** the act of producing a a broad smile, or the smile itself. **5.** the act of withdrawing the lips and showing the teeth. [ME *grinn(en), grenn(en),* OE *grennian;* c. OHG *grennan* to mutter] —**grin′ner,** *n.* —**grin′ning·ly,** *adv.* —— other parts of speech

grin[2] (grin), *n. Chiefly Scot.* a snare like a running noose. [ME *grin(e),* OE *grin, gryn*]

grind (grīnd), *v.*, **ground** or (*Rare*) **grind·ed; grind·ing;** *n.* —*v.t.* **1.** to wear smooth, or sharpen by abrasion or friction; whet: *to grind a lens; to grind an ax.* **2.** to reduce to fine particles, as by pounding or crushing; pulverize. **3.** to oppress; torment; harass. **4.** to rub harshly or gratingly; grate together; grit: *to grind one's teeth.* **5.** to operate by turning a crank: *to grind a hand organ.* **6.** to produce by crushing or abrasion: *to grind flour.* —*v.i.* **7.** to reduce something to fine particles. **8.** to rub harshly; grate. **9.** to be or become ground. **10.** to be polished or sharpened by friction. **11.** *Informal.* to work or study laboriously (often fol. by *away*). **12** (in a dance) to rotate the hips in a suggestive manner. Cf. **bump** (def.9). —*n.* **13.** the act of grinding. **14.** a grinding sound. **15.** laborious, usually uninteresting work. **16.** *Slang.* an excessively diligent student. **17.** a dance movement in which the hips are rotated in a suggestive manner. Cf. **bump** (def. 17). [ME *grind(en),* OE *grindan;* akin to Goth *grinda,* L *frendere*] —**grind′a·ble,** *adj.* —**grind′ing·ly,** *adv.* —Syn. **2.** crush, powder. **4.** abrade. —— synonyms

words in context

Usage levels

Exercise 2-10 Dictionary Scavenger Hunt

Working with your group, find answers to the following questions. If you have different dictionaries, you will discover some of the many differences among dictionaries.

1. What is a synonym of *loquacious?*

   _____

2. What syllable will be pronounced most heavily in the word *fiasco?* Write the phonetic spelling of the word.

   _____

3. What do the words at the top of each dictionary page tell you?

   _____

4. Which forms of the word *smug* are used when you are comparing the attitudes of two or more people? (The forms are called *comparative* and *superlative.*)

   _____

5. From what language was the word *mystic* brought into English?

   _____

6. What part of speech is *pandemonium?*

   _____

7. How many different meanings are given for the word *frog?* (Be sure to note whether there is more than one entry.)

   _____

8. What is the slang meaning of *cool?*

   _____

9. What is another spelling for *sheik?*

   _____

10. What is the informal meaning of *kickoff?*

_____

11. How is a *fib* related to a *fable?*

_____

12. When would you capitalize the word *advent?*

_____

13. What is an antonym for *vivacious?*

_____

14. What meaning of *marry* is archaic or out of date?

_____

15. What is the British meaning of *stall?*

_____

16. Write the phonetic spelling of *dissipated.*

_____

17. Who was *Richard Phillips Feynman?*

_____

18. What historic event occured in *Hastings,* a seaport in England?

_____

19. What information appears at the beginning of your dictionary (before the definitions begin)?

_____

20. What information occurs after the last *z* word in your dictionary?

_____

No wonder Malcolm X found the dictionary a miniature encyclopedia!

Methods for Remembering New Words

Discovering the meaning of a word from its context, its structure, or the dictionary is just the beginning. Many of the new words that you come across you will want to store in your memory for future use. How you choose to work with words in order to remember them is a somewhat individual matter. Here are several methods to try, all involving paying repeated attention to the words.

Vocabulary Cards

Many students find this method effective and efficient. Cards can be carried with you and reviewed at odd moments, for example, when you are waiting in a doctor's office or for a friend who is always late.

Record each word on a 3" x 5" card. Place the word in the center of the card, and below the word add the phonetic pronunciation. Add other forms of the word in the bottom right corner of the card. If you know any other words formed from the same root, note those in the bottom left corner of the card. You may want to note the subject area where you found the word, such as philosophy or business. The illustration shows the front of a card for the word *apathy*.

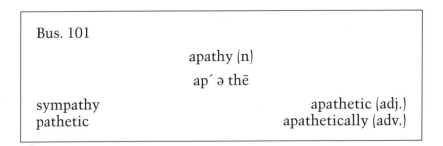

The back of the card can be used for a definition of the word and a sentence using the word in context, or you may decide on another arrangement. The point is to make the cards useful for review. As you review your cards, you can eliminate the cards for the words you know, reshuffle the cards, and continue the review. This sample shows the back of the card for the word *apathy*.

> lack of emotion, interest, or concern
>
> <u>Syn</u>. coolness, indifference   <u>Ant</u>. ardor
>
> When my friend suggested we see a movie, I showed apathy.

Computer or Personal Glossary Notebook

You may prefer to record the words you want to master in a notebook or on a computer. A looseleaf notebook has the advantage that you can remove the sheets for special study. You might want to use a half-page for thorough information. Your entry could look like this:

Word: _____ **Phonetic Spelling:** _____

Definition: _____

Synonyms   **Antonyms**   **Other Forms**

_____   _____   _____

_____   _____   _____

Source Sentence: _____

_____

An Original Sentence: _____

_____

If you are not using vocabulary cards, another way to review is to fold a sheet of notebook paper in four equal columns. Copy the words you want to review in the first column. Write a synonym for the word in the second column. Then fold the paper so you are looking only at the synonym. Write the word in the third column and fold back again so you see only the word, then write the synonym. Eliminate the words you know and start with a new list, perhaps adding new words.

Some students write sentences using vocabulary words that help them visualize the word. For example, taking the word *precognition* from Exercise 2-9, you might write a sentence like this: "The fortune-teller had a precognition that I would meet a tall handsome stranger." You can visualize the fortuneteller looking into a crystal ball and gaining knowledge of this future event.

If you prefer, you can record your words using your computer. The computer has the advantage that you can add words alphabetically, record them by subject area, then scramble the words and definitions to give yourself a review. Choose the method required by your instructor or the one that you find most helpful for developing your vocabulary.

Reviewing Vocabulary

Whatever method you develop for yourself, use it actively to build your vocabulary and increase your reading success. Decide what information you want to record about your new words to make them part of your growing vocabulary. You should use your new words in your speaking and writing as much as possible. Reviewing your words regularly, each day if possible or at least once a week, is very important.

Chapter Review

Fill in the blanks with the correct words.

1. Most college students need to _____ their vocabulary.

2. The three methods for unlocking the meaning of an unfamiliar word are: _____, _____, and the
   _____.

3. Many words are made of parts called _____,
   _____, and _____.

4. These parts can be examined individually to determine a word's _____.

5. Figuring out the meaning of a word from the sentence or paragraph in which it occurs is called learning from
   _____.

6. Although other clues are helpful, the most reliable source for meaning is the _____.

7. A word that has the same meaning as another is called a _____.

8. A word with an opposite meaning from another is called an _____.

9. Two ways to record words for study are _____ _____ and a personal _____ in a computer or notebook.

10. Use the _____ to find the pronunciation of a word, its part of speech, and something of its origin and history.

Reading Selection 1

Purpose

The following article is based on a study done for the National Institute of Mental Health. The article explores some popular notions about family life and the effect working mothers have on the family. Even if you are not married, you probably have some experience with family life that will provide you with background for the presentation of myths (popular beliefs) and facts from the study. Read to see how your ideas are reflected (or challenged) in the article. You also will want to prepare yourself for answering true-or-false questions and understanding the vocabulary used in the selection.

Preview

Skim the article, giving particular attention to the myths, which have a bullet point in front of them. Check the underlined vocabulary and skim the questions at the end of the reading.

Anticipate/Associate

Two television shows from the 1950s were used by many viewers as standards for what American family life should be. *Ozzie and Harriet* and *Father Knows Best* are examples of the idealized television models of family life at that time. Since that time, many factors have brought about changes in family life.

Are you a working mother, or did your mother work outside the home while you were growing up? Many people believe that this change alone has affected family life. What is your experience?

_____

_____

_____

Just What Family Values Are Normal?

Caryl Rivers and Rosalind C. Barnett

"Family values" is turning into a hot political topic, with both Republicans and Democrats <u>wrestling</u> over who has the best policies and programs—and the best sound bites. But the truth about the American family is much different from the political TV spots and news reports.   1

Almost daily, headlines <u>trumpet</u> the somber facts about the family. It's in "decline," with working parents <u>frazzled</u> wrecks and their kids prime candidates for psychiatrists' couches.   2

But the truth is quite different, as evidenced by a major study of American couples who are employed full time. The study was funded by a million-dollar grant from the National Institute of Mental Health (NIMH).   3

Contrary to myth, these couples are <u>coping</u> well with their often-stressful lives, with a low <u>incidence</u> of anxiety and depression, and few physical symptoms of the sort that accompany stress-related illness. They report warm relations with their children, and that their children are thriving.   4

What the Research Shows

The NIMH research explodes a number of myths about the new American Family: 5

- **Myth:** Moving away from the *Ozzie and Harriet* family—breadwinner father and homemaker mom—spells disaster.   6

- **Fact:** Two-earner couples even in tough times were not facing anxiety over finances. While families with a single breadwinner could be <u>plunged</u> into economic <u>chaos</u> by the loss of a job, these <u>couples</u> have a safety <u>net</u> because of their dual incomes. Their lifestyle is a good fit with today's economic reality. 7

- **Myth:** Parents who work full time are too busy to care for their kids. 8

- **Fact:** One study found that working parents spend as much time with their children as parents where one partner is not employed—but they do it on weekends and in evenings. 9

- **Myth:** Today's fathers can't compare with the wonderful dads of the *Father Knows Best* days. 10

- **Fact:** Fathers in dual-earner couples spend much more time with their kids than '50s fathers did. By the time their kids reach school age, men spend as much time parenting as do their wives. The reality of the '50s was not that "father knew best," but that he often wasn't around very much. Studies of '50s fathers showed they envied their wives' closeness with the kids. 11

- **Myth:** Working women and their children are wrecks. 12

- **Fact:** For women, paid employment has resulted in <u>heightened</u> self-esteem and improved physical and mental <u>health</u>. Scores of studies show that employed women are healthier than homemakers, and the scare stories about working women didn't come true. They are not dropping dead of heart attacks, nor are they dying earlier because of overwork. Paid work provides a buffer against depression and anxiety. As for their children, study after study shows no differences between children of working mothers and those of homemakers on any measures of child development. 13

- **Myth:** Women do it all on the "second shift" while <u>balky</u> men resist doing work around the home. 14

- **Fact:** In two-earner couples, men and women are both doing considerable work around the home—55 percent for women, 45 percent for men. The days of the couch-potato dad are over. 15

- **Myth:** It's always best for mom to be home full time. 16

- **Fact:** We add stress to today's parents' lives by insisting that the only "real" family is the '50s model. If we encourage women to drop out of the labor force or settle for crummy part-time jobs, their risk of anxiety and depression increases. If men take second jobs or work 17 much longer hours their stress will increase. Today's fathers see time with children as important to their lives, and men in our study showed heightened stress if their wives got to spend considerably more time with the children.

The 1950s Are Over

- **Myth:** Yesterday's parents were better parents.   18
- **Fact:** These couples have a good chance to be better parents than those of the *Ozzie and Harriet* era. The women do not suffer the high anxiety and depression that women endured in those years, and the men seem more closely bonded to their kids.   19

- **Myth:** The old "Family Values" will bring back "Happy Days."   20
- **Fact:** The 1950s are not coming back. Men's wages are flat or declining; good jobs are vanishing overseas, middle managers are being laid off. Those who believe the *Ozzie and Harriet* lifestyle is the only right one will be subject to stress, guilt and <u>marital</u> tensions.   21

Disturbing trends in the economy could harm working families, however. Downsizing—with fewer people asked to do more work, more <u>contingent</u> jobs with no benefits and no vacation time and the failure of a national health-care plan cut into the time working parents can spend with children or cause them more worry.   22

The answer to these problems is not to pretend that one wage can support a family or to track women into low-paying, part-time jobs which offer high stress, no benefits and little sense of control or challenge. Research shows that bad jobs have a negative impact on the quality of parenting. Sixty-six percent of all families today are working families. Only when we accept working parents as "normal" parents can we create corporate and community policies that help and support these families.   23

Check Your Understanding

Review

Look back at the underlined words in the article. How many of these words can you understand from the context? Which words are so unfamiliar that you need to plan a method for vocabulary study, such as cards?

Fill in the Blanks

Complete the statements by writing the answers in the blanks.

1. The letters NIMH stand for _____.

2. The facts in this article are based on _____.

3. Ideas we assume to be true without evidence are called

   _____.

4. According to the study, myths are not supported by

   _____.

5. The myths and facts in this article concern _____

   values.

True/False

Label the following statements as true or false according to the information provided in the article.

_____ 1. Working parents don't have time to spend with their children.

_____ 2. Having two incomes makes a family more financially stable.

_____ 3. Working women face more health problems than homemakers do.

_____ 4. Family values have changed since the 1950s.

_____ 5. Research shows that men share household duties.

_____ 6. Men today are generally couch-potatoes.

_____ 7. Working parents can be successful parents.

_____ 8. Today 66 percent of families are working families.

_____ 9. Business needs new policies to help working families.

_____ 10. Today one wage earner in a family is usually sufficient.

Vocabulary

The following exercise asks you to unlock the meaning of unfamiliar words using a variety of strategies. First, three under-

lined words in the article are familiar, but they are used creatively to make us visualize an action. For example, when the
article states that politicians are wrestling over the best policies, *they are not actually engaging in the sport; rather, they are*
struggling *with the problem. Explain the actual meaning of the*
two following phrases on the lines below.

1. *headlines* **trumpet** _____

   _____

2. *breadwinner* **plunged** *into economic chaos* _____

   _____

3. If you know that the Middle English word for marriage is

   mariage, explain the phrase *marital* **tensions.** _____

   _____

4. If you know that *frazzle* means to "wear to threads," ex-

   plain the informal meaning in the phrase *working par-*

   ents **frazzled** *wrecks.* _____

   _____

5. You know that height indicates how tall an object is.

   With the suffixes added, explain the meaning of the

   phrase *resulted in* **heightened** *self-esteem.* _____

   _____

For the following words in phrases, circle the letter of the dic-
tionary definition that best fis the way the word is used in con-
text. If necessary, go back to the passage for more context clues.

6. *somber* family facts   7. couples *cope* well with stress

   a. gloomily dark   a. struggle, with some success

   b. dull-colored   b. cover with a long mantle

   c. depressing   c. join two pieces of wood to fit

8. low *incidence* of stress

   a. influence of something unwanted

   b. rate of occurrence

   c. arrival of a ray of light

9. economic *chaos* caused by job loss

   a. inherent unpredictability of a natural system

   b. state of complete confusion

   c. a confused mass or mixture

10. *balky* men resist doing work

    a. stopping at an obstacle

    b. refusing to act

    c. failing to complete a motion

11. more *contingent* jobs

    a. dependent for existence on uncertain conditions

    b. happening by chance

    c. likely but not certain to happen

Writing

Select one of the myths mentioned in the article and describe in a short paragraph how your background and experience is similar or dissimilar to the myth.

Group Discussion

With your small group, discuss business or community practices that exist or should exist to help working families. Consider such things as after-school care, paternity leave (time off for fathers of new babies), working flex time (working hours made flexible to fit family schedules instead of the regular 9-to-5 hours). Be creative; do some brainstorming.

Reading Selection 2

Purpose

Another difficulty some relationships face is that in our highly mobile society friends and spouses may have to deal with a "commuter" relationship. If a friend or spouse takes a job in another city or attends a college in another city, the relationship will have to undergo changes. The next article discusses some of the adjustments that must be made. Your purpose for reading is to learn more about a modern obstacle to relationships and how some couples overcome the difficulties.

Preview

1. Skim the subheads, considering the ideas they suggest.
2. Check the questions and the vocabulary at the end.

Anticipate/Associate

1. From the preview, what do you think are some of the problems involved in long-distance relationships?

_____

_____

2. Have you or anyone you know had to deal with maintaining a relationship between two people working or going to school in two different cities? What were some of the resulting problems?

_____

_____

Commuter Marriage: Does It Work?

Elaine C. Ray

One Sunday afternoon in spring, my husband and I stood   1
near the church we'd just attended, having a tug-of-war with
my suitcase. "I don't feel like carrying this," he said. "Well,
fine, I'll carry it myself," I snapped back. Then, head held
high. I tried to walk gracefully down Harlem's Lenox Avenue
in high heels with a suitcase weighing me down on one side.

In reality, the issue wasn't the suitcase at all. The real   2
burden was juggling a long-distance marriage. I had recently
taken a job at a New England newspaper, and he had decided
to stay in New York, at least for the time being. As it turned
out my husband finally opted (as he puts it) to share his black-
eyed peas with me in Boston, and our stint as a commuting

couple ended after only three months. But for many professionals, following one's spouse from hither to yon isn't the most attractive or practical option, and separate-but-equally-committed status seems to work out just fine.

Long-distance marriage is nothing new. Over the years   3
the families of servicemen, railroad workers, salesmen, truckers, athletes and performing artists have endured long separations. What makes today's commuting couples different is that both husband and wife are making choices based on their needs and aspirations both as individuals and as a couple. Instead of abandoning their own professional goals to follow their husband's career track, many women are now initiating these moves to realize their own dreams. And since moving up often requires moving around, many couples who want both career advancement and marriage are opting to live apart.

For Love and Money

Fanny and Peter Pettijohn, both in their early 40s, are a   4
classic example of the modem commuter couple. Fanny, manager of the Florida region for the Bahamas Tourist Office, says that she is assigned a new territory every couple of years and has little choice about where an assignment will take her. Peter, a marketing manager for USAir/Piedmont Airlines, is in a similar situation. So, when they promised to love each other for "as long we both shall live," they knew it wouldn't necessarily be under one roof. But Fanny says the fact that she and Peter are both on the go is precisely what makes their one-year-old Miami-to-Toledo marriage tick; neither resents the necessary absences of the other. "If I had married a nine-to-five person," Fanny says, "there's no way our marriage could have worked."

Charles and Cheryl Ward, both 42 and married for 20   5
years, have been a commuter couple for the past 13 years. Their relationship runs like clockwork. Charles, a pay-per-view cable-television executive who lives in Los Angeles, phones Cheryl and their 8-year-old son, Che, in San Francisco every morning before they go off to work and school. Then he and Cheryl, an administrative assistant to the president and general manager of a television station, check in with each other several times during the workday. Charles calls again every evening before Che goes to bed. Then on Friday evening, he flies to San Francisco. "I've never lived more than an hour and a half from my family by plane," says Charles, who has found that his best career opportunities since 1976 have been in cities outside San Francisco.

"It's not ideal," he adds. "I'm not at home with my fam-   6
ily every night." But under the circumstances, he says, it
works out well. Charles explains that his first employer in
the cable-television industry sent him to work in San Diego,
then to Orange County, California, and then to Las Vegas—
all within a four-and-a-half year period. "If the whole family
had left San Francisco when I initially entered the cable-television business," says Charles, "we would have moved four
times in four years, and we weren't interested in doing that."

What commuter couples *are* interested in doing is ful-   7
filling the commitment to their marriages while pursuing career goals in separate cities. For some it's easier than for
others. Coordinating schedules, maintaining good communication, developing quality parenting and meeting financial
obligations are challenges that any married couple faces, but
for commuters the difficulties are <u>exacerbated</u> by the distance. "It's an extremely complicated way to live," says Dr.
Geraldine A. Manning, associate professor of sociology at
Boston's Suffolk University. Manning adds that trust, communication and strong commitment—key elements in all
marriages—are especially important in commuter relationships. "Family life is not easy in the best of circumstances."

Evelyn Gay and Omatunde Mahoney, who are in their   8
mid-30s and have been commuters for almost two years, say
that it's the solid commitment to their individual ambitions
as well as their goals as a couple that have kept their marriage
together. But they add that there's a need for constant adjustment to each other. Having dated for five years before they
married in 1987, they thought the 75 miles that stand between them would be no big obstacle. "We underestimated
the amount of separation involved," says Omatunde, who has
taken a leave of absence from his job at the Gambian Mission
to the United Nations to pursue a master's degree in international finance at Yale University's Graduate School of Management in New Haven, Connecticut, while Evelyn has
remained in New York City.

"I really never know when I'm going to see him," says   9
Evelyn, associate director for foreign <u>repatriation</u> for CBS
Records, Inc. When they can carve out time for each other,
it's not always an automatic transition. "You immerse yourself so much in what you're doing," Evelyn says, "that it's
somewhat difficult to bring someone back into your life
when he's around."

On the plus side, Evelyn admits that the absence has in-   10
deed made their hearts grow fonder. "It [the time spent apart]
makes us excited about seeing each other, and it gives us a
chance to appreciate what we miss by not being together,"
she says.

Coping with Conflicts

When asked how they deal with problems at a distance, 11 most couples say the separation helps them put disagreements in perspective. "It seems as if our communication has gotten better," says Greg Patterson, 31, a *Wall Street Journal* reporter who moved to Detroit last summer while Lucy, 31, his wife of five years, chose to finish her graduate studies in Massachusetts. "We don't argue as much," he says.

But Manning warns that "there is the potential for the 12 relationship to have a cheery <u>veneer</u> to it" while conflicts lurk beneath the surface. "What matters is how good the communication skills are and how strong the commitment is to begin with," she says.

Does separation give partners license to fool around? 13 Not necessarily. In conducting research for their book *Commuter Marriage,* authors Naomi Gerstel and Harriet Gross found that "physical <u>proximity</u> is not the determining factor controlling or causing extramarital encounters." They discovered that nearly one-third of commuters in their study had affairs while commuting, but that most of these individuals had been engaging in extramarital activity when they were living with their spouses. Only a small percentage, 8 percent, began an affair *after* the marriage became a long-distance one. Even more interesting, the study showed that 11 percent had had affairs while living with their partners and stopped doing so when the relationship became a long-distance one.

Greg Patterson describes his feelings about the sexual 14 separation this way: "Biologically, it's sometimes difficult, but when you're not with someone you realize how special they are to you, and you're just not interested [in anyone else]."

A Costly Affair

Spouses who live apart say that cost is a big considera- 15 tion in any couple's decision to pursue a commuter lifestyle. Two rents or two mortgages, long-distance phone calls and airfares are the economic realities of commuter marriage. Fanny and Peter Pettijohn, who earn what they describe as "very high salaries," have continued to maintain two households. The <u>perks</u> of their jobs in the travel industry help keep commuting expenses down.

The Wards make it clear that the distance is exactly 16 what has made them able to afford their comfortable lifestyle. Charles's itinerant career has paid off with a salary that now exceeds $100,000 a year, and Cheryl makes about $30,000. As she explains it, "The 12 years before we had Che, we were really adventuresome careerwise, allowing each other the flexibility to do whatever we wanted to do—regardless of how much money we earned."(During that time, Cheryl developed and ran a children's media center in Washington, D.C. She also managed a recording studio and operated her own art gallery in San Francisco.)

But for many couples, commuting is a strain on finances. When the Pattersons decided that he'd go and she'd stay, Lucy left their two-bedroom apartment for a one-bedroom place, and Greg found a small apartment in Detroit. Still, their combined rent adds up to $1,300 a month, $500 more than they paid when they lived together. Greg, who earns about $50,000, sends money to Lucy to supplement her part-time accountant's income. "If it were more financially <u>feasible</u>, it would be a lot easier to take," says Greg. "But with her tuition and two rents, it's difficult." Greg and Lucy are hoping that these temporary sacrifices will net them a big payoff.   17

Evelyn Gay and Omatunde Mahoney are also looking ahead. "This [living apart] is something that the two of us decided would be the best thing for *our* future," says Evelyn, who holds an M.B.A. and earns about $40,000. She maintains the couple's co-op in the Riverdale section of New York, while Omatunde shares his small New Haven apartment with a fellow student and relies on financial aid to cover most of his living and tuition expenses.   18

Who's Minding the Kids?

But while the <u>justifications</u> for living apart are clear to these consenting adults, what about the children? Commuting parents say establishing a stable home base (a primary and regular residence of one spouse) and spending "quality time" with children take on added importance in trying to achieve a sense of family. After Che was born and Cheryl returned to work, Charles took a <u>hiatus</u> from what was then a legal career in the recording industry and spent two years as a full-time parent. After that, though, the family resumed its long-distance status.   19

"He's grown up with it," says Charles about Che. Cheryl admits, however, that "sometimes Che will say that he wishes he could see his dad more often. Then I have to remind him that in many families children never get to see their fathers." She adds "He's come to understand that ours is really a special family."   20

When it comes to parental responsibility, Cheryl carries a greater share of the weight. "She takes up a lot of my slack," Charles acknowledges. "For her it's very much like being a single parent." Still, Cheryl says that parenting is a shared responsibility. She and her husband have similar child-rearing   21 philosophies, and when Charles gets home on Fridays, he makes time with Che a priority.

Though the Pettijohns have no children together, each   22
has two children from previous marriages. Peter's son and daughter live with their mother in Los Angeles. Fanny's 18-year-old son is finishing his senior year in high school while living with friends in Michigan, where Fanny lived before she was transferred to Miami last February. Her 15-year-old son lives with Fanny during the week and travels with her to be with Peter on those weekends when she goes to Toledo. Accustomed to traveling with her and traveling to visit their father and extended family in the Bahamas, Fanny says, her sons were not concerned about any additional traveling that her new marriage might bring. However, her youngest did express misgivings about his mother's remarriage. "He wanted to know why I had to get married," Fanny explains. Peter and Fanny have made it a point to include her younger son in their weekend activities, and when possible, all four of their children spend time with them. "At first it was very difficult," she says. "Now the camaraderie is great."

Manning stresses that it's too early to assess the full im-   23
pact of modern-day commuter marriage on children. But, she says, "if quality time is what matters, then being the child of a commuter marriage ought not to create problems."

Togetherness Is the Goal

Unfortunately, commuter couples often don't know   24
how they will cope until they've already committed themselves to the lifestyle. After he moved to Detroit, Greg Patterson was surprised to find that he was not as independent as he thought he was. "I realized that I don't have the emotional timber to be able to gain fulfillment in a situation where I'm split from my mate," he says, though he plans to hang in there until Lucy completes her studies and moves to Detroit this summer. "In hindsight, I don't know that I'd do it again." Greg points out that his adjustment is much more difficult than his wife's because she has an established network of friends and activities in Massachusetts while he's moved to a city where he doesn't know anyone.

"There are some," says Manning, "who carry around the   25
'togetherness model.' And those people may have a harder time handling the separation." She adds, "It doesn't help that society has presented a very stereotypical model of 'family'. And when the image doesn't mesh with the reality, that creates tremendous problems."

Evelyn Gay advises couples to make a timetable for end-   26
ing the commuter arrangement, even if it means, she explains,

"two years on and two years off. I wouldn't want separation to be a permanent situation."

While commuter marriage works over the long haul for   27 some families, such as the Pettijohns and the Wards, most couples agree with Evelyn that their arrangement is a short-term solution to achieving a long-term goal—a goal that includes living together at some point. But in the meantime these couples are broadening their view of marriage and expanding their options for individual fulfillment. "You're asking men to see their wives' lives and their own as equally important," says Manning. "Ideally, commuter marriage is a way for both men and women to pursue what's really meaningful to them."

Check Your Understanding

Review

List the problems you noted that arise in commuter marriages.

1. _____

2. _____

3. _____

4. _____

Fill in the Blanks

Complete the statements by writing the best word in the blank.

1. Jobs sometimes _____ married couples to live

   apart.

2. Commuter marriages are not considered _____.

3. Couples who live apart often _____ their

   time together.

4. Children should be a(n) _____ consideration

   when a couple considers a commuter marriage.

5. Sometimes commuter marriages are a short-term solution

to achieve a _____ goal.

True/False

Label the following statements as true or false according to the article.

_____ 1. The main idea of this article is that commuter marriages can work if the couple is willing to make adjustments.

_____ 2. Long-distance marriages are a completely new concept.

_____ 3. More women are now initiating commuter marriages.

_____ 4. Few couples are interested in the difficulties of commuter marriages.

_____ 5. Commuter marriages require commitment from both partners.

_____ 6. Traveling is an essential element of commuter marriages.

_____ 7. It is never difficult for couples to adjust after a separation.

_____ 8. Children always suffer from commuter marriages.

_____ 9. Couples sometimes agree to commuter marriages for financial reasons.

_____ 10. In the best circumstances, family life is relatively easy.

Vocabulary

Choose the best meaning for the italicized words as they are used in context and write the letter on the blank.

_____ 1. You need emotional *timber* for a commuter marriage.
   a. growing trees
   b. personal character
   c. a lumberjack's call

_____ 2. the *perks* of their jobs
   a. lively actions
   b. smart dressing
   c. extra benefits

_____ 3. relationships have a cheery *veneer*
  a. varnish
  b. thin layer of wood
  c. superficially pleasing appearance

_____ 4. *precisely* what makes it work
  a. definitely
  b. exactly
  c. rigidly particular

_____ 5. difficulties are *exacerbated* by distance
  a. aggravated
  b. increased
  c. irritated

_____ 6. He worked at *repatriation*.
  a. distribution of goods
  b. returning people to their homelands
  c. making witty replies

_____ 7. Commuter partners don't always have *proximity*.
  a. the right amount
  b. time for each other
  c. nearness

_____ 8. Living together is not always financially *feasible*.
  a. suitable
  b. possible
  c. probable

_____ 9. *justification* for living apart
  a. reasonable cause
  b. excuse
  c. judgment

_____ 10. took a *hiatus* from work
  a. writing supplies
  b. vacation
  c. break

Writing Exercise

Would you be willing to participate in a commuter marriage?
Defend your answer with three reasons from the article or three
personal reasons.

Group Discussion

With your group, share the pros and cons of a commuter mar-
riage from the article and also from your own thoughts and
feelings about this kind of a marriage.

Chapter 3

Recognizing Topics, Stated Main Ideas, and Supporting Details

> Words are but the signs of ideas.
>
> *Samuel Johnson*

One of the most important strategies you practice is that of finding Samuel Jackson's "signs of ideas" in the words of a passage. Identifying the *main idea* is of great help in unlocking the meaning of a paragraph or passage. Once you have grasped the main idea, the point of a written passage, you have taken the first step in understanding all of the writer's message. Finding the main idea is the strategy that will most help you in comprehending what you read.

The story is told of Jean Louis Agassiz, a naturalist and a professor, that he required a student to spend two full days examining a dead fish. The student observed many things about the fish. But Agassiz was not satisfied until the student was able to see the most simple, fundamental thing about the fish: that it was symmetrical, both sides corresponding in size and arrangement of parts. That was the main idea. If you can correctly determine the main idea of a passage, you will be making a giant step toward comprehending difficult reading assignments.

This chapter will help you:

- use strategies to unlock meaning
- find the topic of a paragraph
- distinguish among topics, main ideas, and supporting details
- locate the main idea in a paragraph
- underline and make marginal notes

Strategies to Unlock Meaning

How can you unravel the main idea from all the words in a passage? Have you ever listened to someone ramble on about a topic and wished to interrupt that person with the question, "What's the point you're trying to make?" You can ask speakers to explain their point, but you must often think carefully to find a writer's main idea. Writers you will be reading in your texts are usually careful to state their point. The sentences may be complex, vocabulary may be confusing, but the point or main idea is there.

Looking for Key Words

Locating key words in sentences is the first strategy to use in finding the subject or the topic of a reading. Finding the *subject* or *topic* is the first step in determining a stated main idea. As you put aside interesting details to see the big picture, you will be able to focus on the essential or key words in a passage that will lead first to the subject or topic and, in longer passages, to the main idea. Two questions will help you isolate the subject or topic:

1. *Who* or *what* is acting?
2. *Who* or *what* is being acted upon?

Exercise 3-1   Finding Key Words in Sentences

Find the key words in the following sentences by asking the two questions just given. Circle the key words and write them on the line below the sentence. The first one is done for you.

1. Many farmers in developing countries cannot afford to take advantage of the new, high-yield crop strains.

   Many farmers cannot afford new crop strains.
   _____

2. Choosing a computer and the software to use with it is a challenge because of the many options on the market.

   _____

3. Television can be a great educational resource with its programs that develop our knowledge and background about the environment, history, and social issues.

   _____

4. Humanitarians choose what is good for others and not just what they see as good for themselves.

   _____

5. Although many different daytime TV formats have been tried, daytime programming still consists primarily of soap operas and game shows.

   _____

6. Alexander Graham Bell, who invented the telephone, thought the instrument would be used primarily to educate the hearing impaired.

   _____

7. Often people try not to get involved when they see one person threatening another in public or a mother spanking a child in a supermarket.

   _____

8. My sister's wedding was an event to remember because of the family gathering, the food prepared, and the entertainment presented.

   _____

9. Holiday dinners, prepared so carefully and presented with love, can be marred by family and guests who rush to watch the kickoff of a football game.

   _____

10. The "group principle" was thought to be a new psychology, designed to replace the idea that individuals think, feel, and act independently.

    _____

Distinguishing between the General and the Specific

Have you heard the expression, "It's like looking for a needle in a haystack"? Try to visualize just how difficult that task would be. Sometimes trying to find the key words, the topic, and then the main idea in a paragraph or passage is a little like looking for that needle. A second helpful strategy for finding the topic and then the main idea is to develop your ability to distinguish between *general* and *specific* words, phrases, and sentences. Recognizing the difference between the general and the specific will help you see the topic and then the main idea in paragraphs or in a reading selection. If something is general, it is broad, including many things. *Fruit* is a general term. Something specific, on the other hand, is particular. *Berries* are a specific kind of fruit. Being even more specific, you could think of *strawberries* or *blueberries.*

Finding key words and recognizing the difference between the general and the specific will help you identify the topic of a paragraph and to distinguish the main idea from supporting details. It is important to recognize that related ideas can be more or less general and more or less specific. In determining the topic of a given paragraph, you need to identify a topic that is not too general or broad and not too specific or limited. If a given passage discusses disaster movies, the subject or topic "movies" is too general and the topic *"Titanic"* is too specific. If the passage discusses civil wars, the subject or topic "war" is too broad, and the topic "American Civil War" is too specific. The next exercise gives you practice in making these distinctions.

Exercise 3-2   Arranging Topics from the Most General to the Most Specific

Label the following topics as (1) most general, (2) less general, and (3) most specific. The first one is completed as an example.

1. __3__ Bill Cosby   2. _____ television
   __2__ comedian   _____ electronic equipment
   __1__ American   _____ RCA television

3. _____ diseases   4. _____ rock stars
   _____ childhood diseases   _____ Beatles
   _____ measles   _____ Ringo

5. _____ Lake Michigan   6. _____ automobile
   _____ body of water   _____ Ford
   _____ lake   _____ Taurus

7. _____ machine   8. _____ Great Lakes

   _____ automobile   _____ lakes

   _____ gas-powered engine   _____ Lake Michigan

9. _____ school   10. _____ swimming

   _____ college   _____ exercise

   _____ Notre Dame   _____ aerobic exercise

Did you notice that what is general and what is specific can change when different comparisons are made? An automobile is general when it is compared to a specific brand like a Ford, but it is less general and more specific compared to a machine. In item 5, *lake* is "less general," but it becomes "most general" in item 8. In other words, relationships between groups change as the topics change.

Take your ability to distinguish between general and specific a step further by applying it to sentences. A *general sentence* will give you a broad statement about a topic, while a *specific sentence* will include more specific words and sometimes more details. These words and details are important, but they should not distract you from the main point when you are looking for topics and main ideas.

Exercise 3-3   General and Specific Sentences

Read the following pairs of sentences and circle the key words in each sentence. Note the similarity of ideas in the pairs of sentences. In which sentence are more specific words used? Circle the letter of the more general sentence.

1. a. Studies suggest that heavier people are more likely to develop osteoarthritis.

   b. Research shows osteoarthritis of the knee is six times more common in overweight people.

2. a. Many children grow up as latchkey kids.

   b. Children who grow up as latchkey kids often learn to do things for themselves like surfing the Internet and preparing meals.

3. a. Trees are used to make paper for publishing the news.

   b. It takes more than 500,000 trees to supply just the Sunday newspapers to American homes each week.

4. a. Drinking six to eight glasses of water a day helps the body to maintain energy.

   b. A lack of fluid in the body can bring on fatigue.

5. a. Spring is a truly glorious season following the dreariness of winter.

   b. First the crocus, then the daffodils, and finally the tulips trumpet the news that spring is upon us.

6. a. Taking responsibility for your actions requires following up things you have started.

   b. It's not enough to call others to work on a project; you need to be present yourself and contribute ideas.

7. a. Every 25 seconds someone in America suffers a heart attack.

   b. Heart attacks are a serious health threat.

8. a. Tigers in their natural habitat are rapidly disappearing.

   b. Eight species of tigers have dwindled to only five.

9. a. For some people, the word *enthusiastic* simply means "spirited"; to others, the literal meaning "possessed by a god" is important.

   b. Some people enjoy the fine distinction between words of similar meaning and use words precisely.

10. a. In organization theory, the organizational pyramid is a result of functional growth.

    b. Each addition of workers in functional growth brings new supervisors and more higher-level management.

Finding the Subject or Topic

Apply your ability to distinguish between general and specific to identifying the subject or topic of a paragraph. Avoid topics that are too general or broad. Also avoid topics that are *too* specific, because they focus on a detail or two rather than the overall picture. A good topic is *comprehensive,* meaning that it covers all the ideas in the selection.

Exercise 3-4   Identifying Topics of Paragraphs

First circle the key words. Using the key words, determine the best topic from the list that follows each paragraph. Label the best description of the topic (T). Put (G) before the phrase that is too general or broad and (S) before the phrase that is too specific. The first paragraph is done for you as a model.

1. The Mayan civilization of Central and South America, which existed some three thousand years before Columbus's discovery of America, was highly developed. For example, Mayan astronomers accurately predicted eclipses of the sun and moon. Their calendar was even more accurate than ours. Mayan mathematicians and engineers built roads and pyramids similar to Egyptian pyramids, which their painters decorated using brilliant colors.

    __G__ a. Mayan history described

    __T__ b. Mayan civilization highly developed

    __S__ c. Mayan and Egyptian pyramids

2. Living with cancer is difficult, but for a child it is doubly difficult. Children with cancer need to focus away from their illness and develop self-esteem. One help for these children is the Children's Art Project at the Anderson Cancer Center in Houston. At the center, young cancer victims from all over the United States become involved in art projects that help them forget their illness and the anger, fear, and pain the illness causes. Through working with art activities, children learn to fight cancer and develop an amazing level of maturity for their age. Today 80 percent of children with cancer live to adulthood.

    _____ a. Cancer in children

    _____ b. Art helping children with cancer

    _____ c. Children's Art Project

3. We use many expressions about water in our speech. Did anyone ever tell you that you were "all wet"? Have you ever been "swamped" with homework? Did a friend ever give you an "icy stare"? Maybe someone told you not to be a "drip" and "to go with the flow." These expressions are one sign of how important water is in our lives. Our bodies are more than 60 percent water. The surface of the earth is about 70 percent water. Most of our 50 states are bounded by rivers, lakes, and oceans. We play in water and on it. Water is used to transport goods and people, to produce electricity, and to produce food.

_____ a. Water's importance to humans

_____ b. All life needs water

_____ c. Expressions that use the word *water*

4. Guion Bluford is an African-American astronaut. Bluford didn't dream of becoming an astronaut although as a boy he was interested in airplanes. Bluford built model airplanes and collected pictures of airplanes, but surprisingly, he was more interested in the way things flew than in the airplanes themselves. He liked to play table tennis and watch the flight of the ball. When he delivered newspapers, he tried to fold and throw each one differently. Bluford wanted to be an aerospace engineer. In high school, Bluford found reading difficult but had no trouble with math and science. In college he decided to become a pilot because that would make him a better aerospace engineer.

_____ a. Guion Bluford's life

_____ b. Bluford's interests as a youngster

_____ c. How Bluford became an astronaut

5. New uses are being planned for blimps, those huge airships that often fly over football games and are sometimes used to carry advertisements. Because blimps can hover in the air, unlike airplanes, and aren't as noisy and windy as helicopters, they can be used to do things helicopters and planes can't do. For example, they can be used to watch for the outbreak of fires in large forested areas or to watch shorelines for drug-smuggling activities. New plans for blimps include enlarging the gondola, the cabin attached to the bottom of the blimp. The new gondolas will have three decks and include restaurants, lounges, and bedrooms. Soon you will be able to purchase a ticket for a leisurely vacation in the sky.

_____ a. New uses for blimps

_____ b. Blimps as advertising billboards

_____ c. The history of blimps

6. Most people suffer some loss of vision as they grow older. Fortunately, many aids to eyesight have been perfected in the past century. Eyeglasses with plastic lenses and plastic rims have made glasses lighter and therefore easier to wear. Contact lenses, worn directly on the eyes, have become so comfortable and inexpensive that people wear them just to change their eye color. Bifocals and trifocals are now available without the visible lines that were difficult for some wearers to adjust to. Even sunglasses, those shields from the sun's glare, are new to this century.

_____ a. Improvements in eyeglasses

_____ b. Aids to eyesight

_____ c. Bifocals

7. Scientists are studying spider silk, the thread spiders use to build their webs, because spider silk has many special qualities. If a spider were to spin a line all around the equator (about 27,500 miles), the line would weigh only about 15 ounces. But even though the silk is very lightweight, it is also very strong, five times stronger than the same amount of steel. Spider silk is two times as elastic as nylon, and, finally, spider silk is waterproof. Scientists would like to make silk as light, tough, elastic, and waterproof as the spider's.

_____ a. Qualities of spider silk

_____ b. Spiders

_____ c. Scientists study spider silk

8. The city of Anchorage, Alaska, has an interesting geography. Anchorage covers an area about the size of Delaware and is surrounded by four mountain ranges that protect it from harsh winter weather. The city sits on a body of water called Cook Inlet, named for Captain James Cook, who sailed there in 1778 looking for the Northwest Passage. The inlet has two long arms that surround the city. One is called Knik, an Indian word meaning fire, and the other is called Turnagain. The inlet Turnagain was supposedly named because Captain

Cook repeatedly sent his ships toward land only to have them turn back again and again because of unusually low tides.

_____ a. Cook Inlet

_____ b. The geography of Anchorage

_____ c. Anchorage, Alaska

9. Time is one big mystery. People have been using many devices to measure time since prehistoric times. Probably early humans began by keeping track of full moons, which occur about once a month. Then huge standing stones may have been used. The unusual stone monuments at Stonehenge, England, are an example. About the time Stonehenge was being built, Egyptians were using shadow clocks, called *obelisks,* and sundials to measure time. Sand and water were also used. The sand or water trickled slowly through a tiny opening between one container and another. Some people still use a sand dial or sand clock to time the cooking of a soft-boiled egg. It wasn't until the fourteenth century that someone invented a mechanical clock.

_____ a. Time, a mystery

_____ b. Telling time with stones and sand

_____ c. Different time-telling devices

10. Plans are moving forward for a space station called Freedom. Europe, Canada, Japan, and the United States are all involved in the planning. As many as twenty shuttle flights will be necessary to assemble this space station, which will weigh more than 200 tons when completed. Up to eight people will be able to live in the space station with crews staying three to six months. The station is needed for a planned trip to Mars. Freedom would serve as a launching station, but even from Freedom the trip to Mars would take six months and then, of course, another six months to return to Freedom.

_____ a. A planned trip to Mars

_____ b. Space station plans

_____ c. The future of space travel

11. New Year's is celebrated in different ways and at different times by different people. Here are a few examples. The Chinese celebrate in mid-January or early February with

paper lanterns, big parades, and fireworks as they welcome the new year. Jewish people all over the world celebrate in September with ten days called the Days of Awe. In Africa, the new year begins with the rainy season in March or April. Since the dry season has ended and crops can soon be planted, Africans celebrate with singing and dancing. People of the Middle East who follow the Koran celebrate for thirteen days beginning on March 20. Little potted plants prepared several weeks before are cast into a river as a symbol of releasing bad luck.

_____ a. Different New Year's celebrations

_____ b. A Jewish New Year

_____ c. New Year's celebrations all over the world

Writing Subjects, Topics, or Titles for Paragraphs

The correct topics of the preceeding paragraphs give you a *general* idea of the content of the paragraph, not too broad and not too limited. Normally you will not find choices given about the topic of a paragraph, although longer passages will sometimes carry a title. A title is often a good clue about the subject or topic. But frequently it will be your responsibility as an active reader to determine the topic of paragraphs to assure your comprehension.

Exercise 3-5   Writing Topics

Identify the topics of the following paragraphs. You will need to note key words and make your topic specific enough without being too specific. The first one is done for you as an example.

1. Not long after the United States entered World War II, a Marine Corps officer named Philip Johnston, who had spent his childhood among the Navajos, came up with the idea of transmitting battlefield messages in the Navajo language so the enemy could not understand them. Several Indian languages had been used during World War I for battlefield communications, but the complexity of the Navajo language and the large pool of native speakers made it especially suitable. In May 1942, the first platoon of Navajo "code talkers"

completed training and proved so successful that other units were soon formed.

—Adapted from Garrick Bailey and Roberta Glenn Bailey,
A History of the Navajos: The Reservation Years

Topic: <u>Navajo language used as code language</u>

<u>in WWII.</u>

"Navajo language" would be too general a topic since the paragraph tells only one detail of the language. The topic "complexity of The Navajo language" focuses on a minor (though important) detail and would be too specific.

2. I [also] learned important lessons from my other personal heroes: Jackie Robinson, Thelonious Monk, Malcolm X, to name a few. Jackie's pride, courage, and fierce determination left an imprint on my soul. One way or another, with his bat or his glove, or his legs, or his mind, he kept trying to beat you. I wanted a touch of that in me. And the first time I heard Monk play so soulfully at the Village Vanguard, I was inspired by his wild, creative cool. I thought, "I wish I could do *anything* like he plays his music." Then Malcolm X came along, and his boldness, personal commitment, and intelligence impressed me. More than anyone else, he made me realize that life was broader than basketball, and that it was my responsibility to learn as much as possible about my world, especially my own people.

—Kareem Abdul-Jabbar and Alan Steinberg,
Black Profiles in Courage

Topic: _____

_____

3. Orchestra conductors often live well into their nineties. Arturo Toscanini lived to be 89, Paul Paray, 92, and Pablo Casals, 96. Do these musical masters have a secret that the rest of the world might like to know about how to live longer? It would seem so. A recent study showed that "arm jogging" was more beneficial for a long life than ordinary jogging or running. Conductors of course do this arm jogging daily to music. Couch potatoes take note: Wave your arms vigorously while changing the remote and work your way to good health.

Topic: _____

_____

4. It is important to distinguish between observations and theories. An observation is something that is witnessed and can be recorded. A theory is an *interpretation*—a possible explanation of *why* nature behaves in a particular way. Theories inevitably change as more information becomes available. For example, the motions of the sun and stars have remained virtually the same over the thousands of years during which humans have been observing them, but our explanations—our theories—have changed greatly since ancient times.

—Steven S. Zumdahl, *Introductory Chemistry*

Topic: _____

_____

5. The answer to preparing leaders for the new human relations role was training at all levels to develop skills in understanding logical and nonlogical behavior, understanding of the sentiments of the worker through listening and communications skills, and developing the ability to maintain an equilibrium between the economic needs of the formal organization and the social needs of the informal organization. The newly trained leadership could distinguish fact from sentiment and balance economic logic and the nonlogic of sentiment.

—Adapted from Daniel A. Wren,
The Evolution of Management Thought

Topic: _____

_____

6. Psychotherapists have exhaustively analyzed every form of dysfunctional family and social relationships. But the idea of "dysfunctional environmental relations" did not even exist as an idea. In the past decade, however, the idea that "nature heals" has begun to receive some recognition. When highly stressed people are asked to visualize a calming scene, they don't see a mall or a freeway. Instead they visualize

images of forests, seasides, starry skies. Nature and our relationship to our environment are important elements in our mental health.

—Adapted from Theodore Roszak,
"The Nature of Sanity," *Women's Health Digest*

Topic: _____

_____

Distinguishing among Topics, Main Ideas, and Details

Once you can distinguish the topic of a paragraph, you are better prepared to find the main idea in a selection. The main idea will give you a more *specific* idea about the content of the passage than the topic. The main idea is often expressed as a sentence in the paragraph. At the same time, the main-idea sentence states a point that will be explained and clarified by specific details in the whole passage. Remember that the terms *general* and *specific* can shift as relationships change.

In a given selection, the topic is general. The main-idea sentence is more specific than the topic but more general than other sentences, which explain, develop, and clarify the main-idea sentence. These most specific sentences are called *supporting details*. Supporting details may be examples, illustrations, and facts that give more information about the topic and main idea.

Exercise 3-6   Distinguishing Topics, Main Ideas, and Supporting Details

In the following groups of statements, label the topic (T), the main idea (MI), and supporting details (SD). The first one is completed for you.

1.

___T___ a. The speed of hurricanes

___SD___ b. First, there is the speed of the hurricane itself.

___MI___ c. Hurricanes have two kinds of speed.

___SD___ d. Next, clouds whirling inside a hurricane travel at a different speed.

2.

_____ a. The Electoral College is not a real college but a group of people elected in their state to vote for the president of the United States.

_____ b. Each state has as many electors as it has representatives in Congress.

_____ c. The Electoral College

_____ d. The electors from each state meet in their own state capital to cast their votes.

3.

_____ a. Emperor Nero (A.D. 37–68) ate frozen snow mixed with honey and fresh fruit.

_____ b. Some say that Marco Polo, a great explorer who lived from 1254 to 1324, brought recipes for ice mixtures back from India.

_____ c. Early origins of ice cream

_____ d. Modern ice cream has ancient beginnings.

4.

_____ a. Rain forests, an environmental treasure, are in danger of disappearing.

_____ b. Many countries are removing trees from the rain forests to make paper and other goods.

_____ c. Rain forests are also being cleared for homes and farmland.

_____ d. Rain forests in danger

5.

_____ a. Folks in Mexico add beetle larvae to spaghetti.

_____ b. Around the world, many cultures add bugs to their menu.

_____ c. Insects are an excellent source of protein.

_____ d. In Australia, the rear ends of ants provide a honey-like nectar.

_____ e. Bugs make tasty treats.

6.

_____ a. The red-haired orangutan is a part of the great ape family.

_____ b. An orang walks on the ground using both its long arms and its legs in a rolling movement.

_____ c. The orangutan enjoys the fruits and nuts of the trees in the tropical forests where it lives.

_____ d. Habits of orangutans

_____ e. Orangutans are not social animals except as young adults.

Finding the Stated Main Idea in a Paragraph

Many paragraphs will have their main idea stated in a sentence. Often the main idea is found at the beginning of the paragraph, but it is not always there. It may be at the end of the paragraph as a kind of summary of what appeared earlier. Sometimes it will be located in the middle of the paragraph. Being able to locate the main idea is an important skill for understanding your reading. Use the strategies you have already practiced to locate the main-idea sentence:

1. Look for and circle key words.
2. Decide what idea or topic sums up what the writer is expressing.
3. Compose in your mind a sentence that expands the topic into a sentence.
4. Determine what sentence in the paragraph most closely expresses the idea you have in your mind.

The following paragraph serves as an illustration.

(1) In most communities, newspapers cover more news at greater depth than competing media. (2) A metropolitan daily like the *Washington Post* typically may carry 300 items, many

more on Sundays—more than any Washington television or radio station and at greater length. (3) City magazines in Washington, for example, offer more depth on selected stories, but the magazines are published relatively infrequently and run relatively few articles. (4) Nationally, no broadcast organization comes close to the number of stories or the depth of the two major national newspapers, the *Wall Street Journal* and *USA Today.*

—John Vivian, *The Media of Mass Communication*

The topic may seem to be "newspapers," but that is too general since other types of media are also mentioned. "Newspapers and their competition" is a better choice because it limits the topic to the paragraph without making it too specific. With this topic in mind, consider what point the author is making about newspapers and their competition. Answering that question in your own words, you might think of something like, "Newspapers cover more stories in greater depth than either magazines, television, or radio." The sentence in the paragraph that expresses this main idea is the first sentence of the paragraph.

In locating the stated main idea in the following paragraphs, think first of the topic and then consider what the paragraph is stating about that topic.

Exercise 3-7   Locating the Stated Main Idea

In the paragraphs that follow, underline the main-idea sentence and write its letter on the blank before the paragraph. The main-idea sentence will not always be the first sentence. One paragraph may have two sentences both of which express the main idea.

_____ 1. (a) Our usual way of communicating is by talking. (b) Animals also use sounds to talk to each other. (c) A bird singing early on a bright, sunny morning may be sending a message to other birds. However, many animals and insects talk to each other by using senses other than hearing. (d) Some animals send messages by smell. (e) They mark their territory. (f) You have seen a dog put his mark on a tree. (g) Wolves, deer, and cats, from the house cat to the tiger and the cheetah, mark their territory with their scent. (h) Manatees, dolphins, tigers, and elephants are among the many animals that use touch to communicate. (i) Sight is another sense animals use to communicate. (j) A firefly's light is to attract a mate; a peacock spreads his beautiful feathers; a gooney bird does a dance.

_____ 2. (a) Sojourner Truth was an early fighter for the rights of women and African-Americans. (b) She was born a slave probably in 1797 and was named Isabella Baumfree. (c) Later, she changed her name to reflect her ideals. (d) *Sojourn* means to spend a short time in a place, and *Truth* is what she fought for. (e) She traveled the country preaching for women's rights and the freedom of slaves. (f) During the Civil War, Sojourner Truth cared for wounded soldiers and newly freed slaves. (g) President Lincoln appointed her to aid freed slaves.

_____ 3. (a) The town of Likely, California, got its name in a peculiar way. (b) There's a special system for approving names. (c) The first step is to submit the name to the state's Geographic Names Board because the state does not want duplicate names in the state. (d) If there are no other towns with that name, the name goes back to the town council for approval. (e) Once the council approves, the name goes to the U.S. Board on Geographic Names for approval. (f) The town that eventually was named Likely had submitted names three times for approval without getting it. (g) Finally, someone on the committee asked if there was a decent name that had not been claimed. (h) Someone else responded, "Not likely." (i) And that's how Likely became a town name.

_____ 4. (a) In the 1700s the founding fathers of the United States were talking about which bird should be named the national bird. (b) Some of them wanted the national bird to be the bald eagle. (c) Benjamin Franklin didn't like the idea, however. (d) He said that the bald eagle had a "bad moral character." (e) Instead, he proposed the turkey because the turkey was more respectable and a "true original native of North America." (f) Just imagine, if Franklin had not been outvoted, we wouldn't be eating turkey at Thanksgiving.

_____ 5. (a) He was only twenty-one, the son of a black U.S. Army officer and a Thai mother and named after a tough Vietnamese soldier. (b) He first learned to grip a golf club when he was three. (c) Bursting onto the professional golf scene in 1996, he quickly rewrote the record books for golf at the world-famous Augusta National Golf Tournament in 1997. (d) He was not only the youngest player and the first African American, but he won the Masters with the widest margin of victory. (e) People were spellbound by his long drives, his accurate putts, and the focus and concentration he displayed. (f) People were further charmed by his dazzling smile and his modesty. (g) He has been compared to Jackie Robinson, who broke the color barrier in baseball, and to Mozart and Chopin, who were early geniuses in music. (h) Because of his achievements and his manner, Tiger Woods has become a role model for young people the world over.

Simplifying Complex Main Idea Sentences

Sometimes the main idea sentence—or *topic sentence,* as it is sometimes called—can contain specific details. To understand the main-idea sentence, you must put aside the details for clearer comprehension. For example, the following sentence introduces a paragraph about the hazards of daily living.

Daily living can be hazardous to your health, as you will learn if you read labels and find that toilet bowl cleaner can produce hydrochloric acid, mildew remover can cause breathing problems, swallowing your mouth wash is potentially dangerous, and cooking oil spray can be fatal if deliberately inhaled.

The paragraph that follows this sentence develops further the specific dangers from each of these ordinary household products. To see the main idea clearly, however, you would want to simplify the sentence to something like: "Household products can be hazardous to your health." Read the following main-idea sentences and eliminate the specific details to write a short main idea sentence in your own words.

Exercise 3-8   Making Sense of Complex Main Idea Sentences

The following sentences provide practice in understanding and simplifying complex main-idea sentences. The sentences also suggest some words to define from context.

1. Steel, made from iron but with a low carbon content, is superior to iron because of its greater flexibility and strength.

   a. Which material has the lower carbon content? (If you are not sure, take out the phrase within the commas, which merely describes a quality of steel.)

   _____

   b. Which is more flexible? (Since the sentence is mainly about steel, the word *its* refers to steel.)

   _____

   c. Write the main idea of this sentence in fewer words, keeping only the core idea.

   _____

   _____

2. Steel *alloys* made with substances such as tungsten, manganese, and chrome offer qualities of strength and hardness not present in the original metal.

   a. Define an alloy from this context. _____

   _____

   b. What is the original metal? _____

   c. Write the main idea of this sentence in a few words.

   _____

   _____

3. The raw materials needed by every living organism to supply energy, to power the system, to make the parts operate, and to

keep functioning; and for matter needed to replace parts, to repair breakdowns, and to maintain structure are called *nutrients*.

    a. What are the needed raw materials called? _____

    b. What are the two things that these raw materials provide? (The semicolon provides the clue by dividing the two supporting ideas.)

    _____ and _____

    c. Write the main idea of the sentence in a few words.

    _____

    _____

4. Two general classes of *nutrients* exist. One class includes water, salts, and other materials that are obtained directly from the physical environment of the earth; the other class is foods that are found in the biological environment.

    a. From the context of sentences 3 and 4, what is a nutrient?

    _____

    b. From what two places are nutrients obtained?

    _____ and _____

    c. Rewrite the main idea of the two sentences as one.

    _____

    _____

(From this context, you probably can't be sure about the difference between a physical and a biological environment. In a biology class, if the difference was not previously explained in the text or does not follow, you would need to check the glossary or make a marginal note to ask the instructor.)

5. Marsupial carnivores, like the Tasmanian devil and the Tasmanian wolf, which are primarily *nocturnal*, can climb trees but are not considered truly *arboreal* since they sleep, usually

during the day, in caves and holes in the ground as well as in trees.

a. What is the meaning of *arboreal?* _____

b. What is the meaning of *nocturnal?* _____

c. Rewrite the main idea of the sentence in a few words.

_____

_____

6. DNA samples of saliva, obtained from the back of postage stamps, called into question the suspicion that the accused man had actually handled the murder weapon.

a. Did the DNA samples prove the accused was guilty? _____

b. Had the man handled the murder weapon? _____

c. Rewrite the main idea of the sentence in a few words.

_____

_____

Underlining and Making Marginal Notes

In many of the exercises in this chapter, you have been marking key words to help you identify the topic and the main idea sentence. When you are reading paragraphs and longer passages in texts, it is a good idea to mark the main idea in some way for easy recall and review. In his essay, "How to Mark a Book," editor and writer Mortimer Adler writes about the importance of using this strategy to become an active reader. Adler says:

If, when you've finished reading a book, the pages are filled with your notes, you know that you read actively. . . . To set down your reaction to important words and sentences you have read and the questions they have raised in your mind is to preserve those reactions and sharpen those questions.

Marking your text will improve your understanding of difficult material and also assist you in keeping your attention focused. You will more easily locate the main idea and be able to pull out important supporting details. Some students are hesitant to mark their texts because they intend to resell them. Good readers, however, often read with a pencil, pen, or marker in hand. Marking your text gets you more actively involved with the written material. You will not only be seeing the words, but your pen, pencil, or marker will be involved in simple note taking. Some helpful strategies for marking your texts follow.

First, what should you mark?

This is a personal decision. You might decide to underline or highlight main ideas so that these ideas stand out when you are making a quick review. You might circle or underline difficult vocabulary, so that you can check it in the glossary or a dictionary. Perhaps you want to argue with an idea presented or ask for clarification from your instructor. The possibilities for interacting with your text are many. Choose the interactions that will benefit you.

How should you mark your text?

Again, you will need to develop a system that works for you. You might choose to use colored markers. Some students use different colored markers for different purposes. One color might indicate a main idea; another color might be used to highlight a difficult vocabulary word or phrase.

1. If you wish to use a pencil only, a check (✓) in the margin might indicate a vocabulary word for attention.
2. A star (*) in the margin beside the lines of the main idea will mark that for attention.
3. Two vertical lines (||) or (!!) could indicate something you think is important.
4. If an example is particularly helpful, you might want to mark (ex) in the margin.
5. If the text gives four ideas, number them 1, 2, 3, 4 so that you can find them later.
6. A question mark (?) in the margin is a signal to ask for help later.

Develop your own system for marking your text. The more you interact with your reading, the more focused and attentive you will be. This is a hands-on experience that offers you the special rewards of better understanding and a boost in remembering material.

Here is a sample of one student's marginal notes on a short section taken from the first section of a text on American government.

Do not read the passage; just skim it, paying close attention to the marginal notes.

1st cause   The Civil War had <u>many</u> causes, including (1) the political
Def.   <u>conflict</u> between the North and South over nullification, a doctrine allowing states to declare federal laws null and void, and
secession, which involved the rights of states to leave the
2nd cause   Union; (2) the Northern states' increasing political strength in
3rd and   Congress, especially in the House of Representatives: (3) South-
4th causes ern agriculture versus Northern industry; and (4) the clash of
conservative Southern culture with more progressive Northern
ideas. Slavery, however, was clearly the key issue.

        During the war (1861–65), abolitionists kept their antislav-
ery pressure on. They were rewarded when President Abraham
Def.   Lincoln issued the Emancipation Proclamation, which provided
that all slaves in states still in active rebellion against the
United States would automatically be freed on January 1, 1863.

        Designed as a measure to gain favor for the war in the
??   North, the Emancipation Proclamation did not free all slaves—
it freed only those who lived in the Confederacy. Complete abo-
lition of slavery did not occur until congressional passage and
ultimate ratification of the Thirteenth Amendment in 1865.

—Karen O'Connor and Larry J. Sabato,
American Government

Using just the marginal notes, quickly answer the following questions.

Write the main idea: _____

Write the four causes of the war:

   1. _____

   2. _____

   3. _____

   4. _____

        From studying the marginal notes, you can see that marking
your text would make a review of the material easy. You might

choose to interact with this passage differently. The idea is to interact with marginal markings that make the text meaningful to you.

Chapter Review

Fill in the blanks with the correct words.

1. _____ _____ help you locate the topic of a selection.

2. In determining the _____ of a selection, you must distinguish between the too general and the too specific.

3. Determining the topic of a paragraph or selection is the first step in locating the _____ sentence.

4. Statements that are more specific than the main idea sentence are called _____ _____.

5. Correctly determining the _____ _____ _____ helps you comprehend more efficiently.

6. Marking your text helps you to read _____.

7. Main idea sentences are more _____ than supporting details.

Reading Selection 1

Purpose

Your purpose for reading the following selection is to learn some key techniques for a good start in math courses. You will also practice looking for main ideas and marking your text with helpful notes.

Preview

Paul Nolting, a mathematics professor, offers advice for math study in his book, *Winning at Math*. This first chapter talks about things to consider before enrolling in a math course.

1. Scan the subheadings carefully.
2. Check the questions and the vocabulary at the end.

Anticipate/Associate

1. Have you ever had difficulty with previous math courses? If you did, do you know why?

_____

_____

2. What ideas do the subheads suggest that might be clues to making math easier?

_____

_____

Different Skills to Be Used for Math Courses

Paul Nolting

Mathematics courses are considered to be totally differ-   1
ent from other college courses and require different study procedures. Passing most of your other college courses requires
only that you read and understand the subject material. However, to pass mathematics, an extra step is required: applying
the material by doing the problems.

EXAMPLE: Political science courses require reading the   2
textbook and understanding the material. But your instructor
isn't going to make you run for political office to apply
knowledge you obtained.

In mathematics you must understand the material,   3
comprehend the material and apply the material. Applying
mathematics is the hardest task.

Linear Learning Pattern

Another characteristic of mathematics is its linear learn-   4
ing pattern. *Linear learning pattern means that the material*

learned on one day is used the next day and the next day, and so forth.

If you fail to understand the classroom material the first   5
week, you may never catch up. Linear learning affects studying for tests in mathematics as well. If you study Chapter One and understand it, study Chapter Two and understand it and study Chapter Three and *do not understand it,* then when you have a test on Chapter Four, you're not going to understand it, either.

In a history class, if you study for Chapter One and   6
Chapter Two, and do not understand Chapter Three, and end up studying and having a test on Chapter Four, you could pass. Understanding Chapter Four in history is not totally based on comprehending Chapter Three.

To succeed in mathematics each previous chapter has   7
to be understood before continuing to the next chapter.

When students get behind in mathematics it is difficult to   8
catch up. Mathematics learning is a building process. All building blocks must be included to win at math. Mathematics learning builds up geometrically and compounds itself. Math is not a subject in which you can forget the material after a test. REMEMBER: To learn the new math material for the test on Chapter Five, first, you must go back and learn the material in Chapter Four. This means you will have to go back and learn Chapter Four while learning Chapter Five. The best of us can fall behind under these circumstances. However, if you do not understand the material in Chapter Four, you will not understand the material in Chapter Five either and will fail the test on Chapter Five.

Math as a Foreign Language

Another way to understand studying for mathematics is   9
to consider it a foreign language. Looking at mathematics as a foreign language can improve your study procedures. In the case of a foreign language, if you do not practice it, what happens? You forget it. If you do not practice mathematics, what happens? You are likely to forget it too. Students who excel in a foreign language study and practice it at least every other day. The same study habits apply to mathematics, because it is considered a foreign language.

Like a foreign language, mathematics has unfamiliar vo-   10
cabulary words or terms to be put in sentences called expressions or equations. Understanding and solving a mathematics equation is the same as speaking and understanding a foreign language. Mathematics sentences have words in them, such as equal (=), less (-), and unknown (a).

Learning how to speak mathematics as a language is the 11
key to success. Currently most universities consider computer and statistics (a form of mathematics) courses as foreign languages. Universities have now gone as far as to make mathematics a foreign language.

Mathematics is not a popular topic. You do not hear Dan 12
Rather on TV talking in mathematics formulas. He talks about major events in countries like Korea to which we can relate politically, geographically, and historically. Through TV—the greatest of learning tools—we can learn English, humanities, speech, social studies, and natural sciences but not mathematics. Mathematics concepts are not constantly reinforced like English or other subject areas in our everyday lives. Mathematics has to be learned independently. Therefore, it requires more study time.

High School Versus College Math

Mathematics as a college level course is almost two to 13
three times as difficult as high school mathematics. In college, the Fall and Spring math class time has been cut to three hours a week. High school math gives you five hours a week. Furthermore, college courses are taught twice as fast as high school courses; what is learned in one year in high school is learned in one semester (four months) in college. This enhances mathematics study problems for the college student; you are receiving less instructional time and proceeding twice as fast. The responsibility for learning mathematics has now shifted from the school to the student, and most of your learning will have to occur outside the college classroom.

Summer Versus Fall or Spring Semesters

Mathematics courses taught in summer semesters are 14
more difficult than Fall or Spring semester courses. Students in a six week summer session must learn math two and a half times as fast as regular semester students. Though you receive the same amount of instructional classroom time, there's less time to understand the material between class sessions. Summer semester classes are usually two hours a day and four days a week. If you don't understand the lecture on Monday, then you only have Monday night to learn the material before progressing to more difficult material on Tuesday. Since mathematics is a linear learning experience where every building block must be understood, you can fall behind quickly and never catch up. In fact, some students become *lost* during the first half of a math lecture and never understand the rest of the lecture. This is called *kamikaze* math, since most students don't survive the course. *If you*

have to take a summer mathematics course, take a ten or twelve week session so that you have more time to process the material between classes.

Course Grading System

The course grading system for mathematics is different 15 in college than in high school. While in high school, if you make a D or borderline D/F the teacher more than likely will give you a D and you may go on to the next course. However, in some college mathematics courses, students cannot make a D, or if a D is made, the course will not count toward graduation. Also, college instructors are more likely to give an N (no grade), W (withdraw from class), or F for barely knowing the material, because you will be unable to pass the next course.

Most colleges require students to pass two college level 16 algebra courses to graduate. In high school you may graduate by passing one to three arithmetic courses. In college you might have to take four mathematics courses and make Cs in all of them to graduate. *The first two high school mathematics courses will be preparation for the two college level algebra courses. Therefore you must* <u>dramatically</u> *increase the quality and quantity of your mathematics study skills to pass more mathematics courses with higher grades.*

Your First Math Test

Making a high grade on the first major math test is 17 *more important than making a high grade on the first major test in other college subjects.* The first major math test taken is the easiest and most often least prepared for. Students feel that the first major math text is mainly review and they can make a B or C without much study. These students are overlooking an excellent opportunity to make an A on the easiest major math test of the semester which counts the same as the more difficult remaining major math tests. These students, at the end of the semester, sometimes do not pass the math course or do not make an A because their first major test grade was not high enough to pull up a low test score on one of the remaining major tests.

Studying hard for the first major math test and obtaining 18 an A has several advantages.

- A high score on this math test *can* <u>compensate</u> *for a low score on a more difficult fourth or fifth math test*—and major tests count the same.
- Knowing you have learned the basic math skills required to pass the course. *This means you will not have to spend time relearning the misunderstood material*

covered on the first major test while learning new material for the next test.

- *Improving <u>motivation</u> for higher test scores.* Improved motivation can cause you to increase your math study time allowing you to master the material.
- *Improving confidence for higher test scores.* With more confidence you are more likely to work harder on the difficult math homework assignments which will increase your chances of doing well in the course.

College math instructors treat students differently than high school mathematics instructors. High school mathematics teachers warn you about your grades. Some college instructors may ask you, "How are you doing in the course?" Do not expect them to say, "You have been making Ds and Fs on your tests and you need to come to see me." That would be a rare response. *You must take responsibility and make an appointment to seek help from your instructor.* 19

Sometimes, due to the increase in the number of college math courses, there are more adjunct math faculty than full-time math faculty. This problem can restrict student and instructor interaction. Fulltime faculty have regular office hours and are required to help students a certain number of hours per week in their office or math lab. However, adjunct faculty are only required to teach their mathematics courses; they don't have to meet students after class even though some adjunct faculty will provide this service. Since mathematics students usually need more instructor assistance after class than other students, having an adjunct math faculty member could require you to find another source of course help. *Try to select a fulltime math faculty member as your instructor.* 20

Finding a Study Buddy

Getting a study buddy is suggested. You can't always depend on having the instructor available for help. A study buddy is someone in your class to call when you have difficulty working mathematics problems. *A study buddy can improve your study time.* 21

Before beginning to check your understanding, reread the selection and make marginal notes.

Check Your Understanding

Review

Using the subheads and your marginal notes, write a main-idea sentence for each of the subheads.

Linear Learning Pattern: _____

_____

Math as a Foreign Language: _____

_____

High School versus College Math: _____

_____

Summer versus Fall or Spring Semesters: _____

_____

Course Grading System: _____

_____

Your First Math Test: _____

_____

Finding a Study Buddy: _____

_____

Fill in the Blanks

Complete the statements by writing the best word in the blank.

1. Math has a _____ learning pattern.

2. To learn math, you need to _____ it;
   consequently, you will have many problems to solve for
   homework.

3. Your first math test is the _____.

4. Summer is not the _____ time to take a
   math course.

5. When you get behind in math, it is _____
   to catch up.

Multiple Choice

Select the letter of the answer that best completes the statement.

_____ 1. The main idea of the whole selection is
   a. Math is difficult.
   b. You have to have special intelligence for math.
   c. Learning math is different from learning other subjects for several reasons.
   d. Math teachers try to make the courses difficult.

_____ 2. Passing college math can prove difficult
   a. if you take the course in fall or winter.
   b. if you don't learn it in a linear pattern.
   c. if you don't make an A on the first test.
   d. because you can guess at the answers.

_____ 3. You can be successful on a chapter math test if you
   a. take your best estimated guess at the answers.
   b. understand the chapters preceding the test chapter.
   c. understand equations.
   d. do most of the assigned homework.

_____ 4. Math is like a foreign language because
   a. you must practice it frequently.
   b. it is a popular subject.
   c. math concepts are reinforced in daily living.
   d. everyone needs to understand more than one language.

_____ 5. Which of the following reasons is *not* an important reason for getting an A on the first math test?
   a. A high score on the first test will make up for a lower test score later.
   b. A good score on one test improves your motivation.
   c. A good score gives you confidence.
   d. Your instructor will be impressed.

True/False

Label the statements true or false.

_____ 1. Applying math is the hardest task.

_____ 2. If you don't understand Chapter 3 in math, go ahead to Chapter 4. It may get easier.

_____ 3. Learning how to speak math as a language is a key to success.

_____ 4. College math is usually easier than high school math.

_____ 5. The best time to take math is during the summer because you can complete it faster.

_____ 6. It is easy to get behind in math.

_____ 7. Even if you get a D in math, you can go to the next course because it will be different.

_____ 8. When you're having difficulty in math, it's a good idea to make an appointment to see your instructor.

_____ 9. Getting a good grade on the first math test can help motivate you for the next test.

_____ 10. The linear learning pattern of math is like building with blocks. Each one must be solidly in place before you add another one.

Vocabulary

Use the words from the list to complete the statements that follow.

kamikaze	equation	reinforce	circumstance
enhance	linear	motivation	procedure
dramatically	compensate		

1. If one thing follows another in a line, it has a(n)

   _____ pattern.

2. A(n) _____ is an expression that asserts the equality of two quantities.

3. Having good _____ leads to better grades.

4. If you follow a set _____ in a math problem,

   you should reach the correct conclusion.

5. If a person experiences difficulty with math, seeking appropriate help will _____ for the weakness.

6. Spaced review will _____ ideas to be learned.

7. Attempting a math course without sufficient time for homework and review is called _____, because you won't survive.

8. Learning each chapter of a math text completely will _____ increase your chances for success.

9. The _____ or the surroundings of your study area can

10. _____ your learning.

Writing

Write a paragraph about your previous experiences with math courses. How were you successful or not so successful?

Write a paragraph or letter to someone taking math for the first time in college. What advice would you give this person?

Group Discussion

1. How can the skills learned in math be helpful to you in daily living? (You might want to brainstorm this question.)
2. Why do colleges require math courses for graduation?

Reading Selection 2

Purpose

The writer of this selection, Richard Rodriguez, is a native-born American of Mexican ancestry. The selection describes his initial reluctance to learn English, the language of *los gringos* (the white people). Spanish was his private language, the language of his home, while English was a public language. Later he earned a Ph.D. and became a full-time writer. This selection is taken from his autobiography, *Hunger of Memory*. Read to discover how Rodriguez overcame his difficulties with learning English.

Preview

1. From reading the introduction above, why do you think Rodriguez may have been reluctant about learning English?

2. Study the questions at the end and review the vocabulary.

Anticipate/Associate

1. What classroom difficulties might someone have for whom English is a second language?

_____

_____

2. Does your family have customs, language, or even expressions that make your home or family different from others as speaking Spanish made the Rodriguez family different?

_____

_____

Public Language Versus Private Language

Richard Rodriguez

Supporters of bilingual education today imply that students like me miss a great deal by not being taught in their family's language. What they seem not to recognize is that, as a socially disadvantaged child, I considered Spanish to be a private language. What I needed to learn in school was that I had the right—and the obligation—to speak the public language of *los gringos*. The odd truth is that my first-grade classmates could have become bilingual, in the conventional sense of that word, more easily than I. Had they been taught (as upper-middle-class children are often taught early) a second language like Spanish or French, they could have regarded it simply as that: another public language. In my case such bilingualism could not have been so quickly achieved. What I did not believe was that I could speak a single public language. 1

Without question, it would have pleased me to hear my teacher address me in Spanish when I entered the classroom. I would have felt less afraid. I would have trusted them and responded with ease. But I would have delayed—for how long postponed?—having to learn the language of public society. I would have evaded—and for how long could I have afforded to delay?—learning the great lesson of school, that I had a public identity. 2

Fortunately, my teachers were <u>unsentimental</u> about their   3
responsibility. What they understood was that I needed to
speak a public language. So their voices would search me out,
asking me questions. Each time I'd hear them, I'd look up in
surprise to see a nun's face frowning at me. I'd mumble, not really meaning to answer. The nun would persist. "Richard,
stand up. Don't look at the floor. Speak up. Speak to the entire
class, not just to me!" But I couldn't believe that the English
language was mine to use. (In part, I did not want to believe it.)
I continued to mumble. I resisted the teacher's demands. (Did
I somehow suspect that once I learned public language my
pleasing family life would be changed?) Silent, waiting for the
bell to sound, I remained <u>dazed</u>, <u>diffident</u>, afraid.

Because I wrongly imagined that English was <u>intrinsi-</u>   4
<u>cally</u> a public language and Spanish an intrinsically private
one, I easily noted the difference between classroom language
and the language at home. At school, words were directed to
a general audience of listeners. ("Boys and girls.") Words were
meaningfully ordered. And the point was not self-expression
alone but to make oneself understood by many others. The
teacher quizzed: "Boys and girls, why do we use that word in
this sentence? Could we think of a better word to use there?
Would the sentence change its meaning if the words were differently arranged? And wasn't there a better way of saying
much the same thing?" (I couldn't say. I wouldn't try to say.)

Three months. Five. Half a year passed. Unsmiling, ever   5
watchful, my teachers noted my silence. They began to connect my behavior with the difficult progress my older sister
and brother were making. Until one Saturday morning, three
nuns arrived at the house to talk to my parents. Stiffly, they
sat on the blue living room sofa. From the doorway of another
room, spying the visitors, I noted the <u>incongruity</u>—the clash
of two worlds, the faces and voices of school intruding upon
the familiar setting of home. I overheard one voice gently
wondering, "Do your children speak only Spanish at home,
Mrs. Rodriguez?" While another voice added, "That Richard
especially seems so timid and shy."

That Rich-heard!   6

With great tact the visitors continued, "Is it possible for   7
you and your husband to encourage your children to practice
their English when they are home?" Of course, my parents
<u>complied</u>. What would they not do for their children's well-
being? And how could they have questioned the Church's authority, which those women represented? In an instant, they
agreed to give up the language (the sounds) that had revealed
and <u>accentuated</u> our family's closeness. The moment after the
visitors left, the change was observed. "*Ahora,* speak to us *en
inglés,*" my father and mother united to tell us.

At first, it seemed like a kind of game. After dinner each   8
night, the family gathered to practice "our" English (It was
still then *inglés*, a language foreign to us, so we felt drawn as
strangers to it.) Laughing, we would try to define words we
could not pronounce. We played with strange English sounds,
often over-<u>anglicizing</u> our pronunciations. And we filled the
smiling gaps of our sentences with familiar Spanish sounds.
But that was cheating, somebody shouted. Everyone laughed.
In school, meanwhile, like my brother and sister, I was required to attend a daily tutoring session. I needed a full year
of special attention. I also needed my teachers to keep my attention from straying in class by calling out, *Rich-heard*—
their English voices slowly prying loose my ties to my other
name, its three notes, *Ri-car-do*. Most of all I needed to hear
my mother and father speak to me in a moment of serious-
ness in broken—suddenly heartbreaking—English. The scene
was <u>inevitable</u>: One Saturday morning I entered the kitchen
where my parents were talking in Spanish. I did not realize
that they were talking in Spanish however until, at the moment they saw me, I heard their voices change to speak English. Those *gringo* sounds they uttered startled me. Pushed
me away. In that moment of <u>trivial</u> misunderstanding and
profound insight, I felt my throat twisted by unsounded grief.
I turned quickly and left the room. But I had no place to escape to with Spanish. (The spell was broken). My brother and
sister were speaking in English in another part of the house.

Again and again in the days following, increasingly angry,   9
I was obliged to hear my mother and father: "Speak to us *en
inglés*." (*Speak*.) Only then did I determine to learn classroom
English. Weeks after, it happened.: One day in school I raised
my hand to volunteer an answer. I spoke in a loud voice. I did
not think it remarkable when the entire class understood.
That day, I moved very far from the disadvantaged child I had
been only days earlier. The belief, the calming <u>assurance</u> that
I belonged in public, had at last taken hold.

Check Your Understanding

Review

*Reread the selection to underline and make marginal notes.
Define what Rodriguez means by these two terms.*

Public language: _____

_____

Private language: _____

_____

Fill in the Blanks

Complete the statements by writing the best word in the blank.

1. The "great lesson" of school for Rodriguez was that he had

   a _____ _____.

2. At first, English was for Rodriguez a _____

   language.

3. Rodriguez considered Spanish a _____

   language.

4. Speaking English at home was, at first, just a _____.

5. The Spanish name for Richard is _____.

Multiple Choice

Select the letter of the answer that best completes the statement.

_____ 1. The main idea of the selection is
   a. learning to speak English gave Rodriguez a public identity.
   b. Spanish is a beautiful language.
   c. Rodriguez was angry when his parents spoke English at home.
   d. children should be taught in the language they understand.

_____ 2. The change in the Rodriguez home after the nuns' visit was that
   a. Richard was punished for not learning English.
   b. the family became more religious.
   c. the family began to speak English in the home.
   d. b and c above.

_____ 3. Rodriguez's parents were
   a. uneducated.
   b. strict with their children.

      c. socially disadvantaged by their language.

      d. unable to provide for their children.

_____ 4. The nuns were

      a. sentimental about religion.

      b. very strict with punishments.

      c. unable to speak Spanish.

      d. determined that Rodriguez would learn to speak English.

_____ 5. From this passage, you might assume that later in life Rodriguez

      a. never spoke Spanish.

      b. appreciated the nuns' efforts.

      c. hated English.

      d. a and b above.

True/False

Label the following statements as true or false.

_____ 1. Rodriguez believes that all children in America have the "right—and the obligation" to speak English.

_____ 2. Learning to speak aloud in class was difficult for the writer.

_____ 3. Rodriguez's parents never learned to speak English.

_____ 4. Rodriguez had special tutoring in English for a year.

_____ 5. Learning to speak English was a proud achievement for Rodriguez.

_____ 6. The nuns ignored Rodriguez until he was ready to speak.

_____ 7. Not knowing English made the writer socially disadvantaged.

_____ 8. Rodriguez learned English in the first grade.

_____ 9. Learning a new language was easier for the writer than learning a new language would have been for his classmates.

_____ 10. Rodriguez's parents wanted their children to learn English.

Vocabulary

Use the words from the list to complete the sentences that follow. Cross out each word as you use it.

obligation	bilingual	conventional
evaded	unsentimental	dazed
diffident	intrinsically	incongruity
accentuated	complied	anglicizing
inevitable	trivial	assurance

1. Sharpening pencils is a(n) _____ task.

2. When the order was given, the sailor _____.

3. Essentially or _____, he knew the wisdom of the order.

4. After she fell, the painter was _____ for a moment.

5. We have a(n) _____ to obey traffic laws.

6. Mario _____ doing his homework as long as possible.

7. Some people, in an attempt to be unusual, resist the established or _____ way of doing things.

8. If you can speak two languages, you are _____.

9. I believed her _____ that she would help me.

10. The final test could not be avoided. It was _____.

11. To want success without expecting to make an effort is an example of a(n) _____.

12. The color of her hair _____ her beauty.

13. Richard was self-conscious or _____ about speaking out in class.

14. Pronouncing a Spanish name with an English accent is

_____ the name.

15. Failure to cry at a parent's funeral may appear to be

_____ .

Writing Exercise

Has learning a new skill ever proved difficult for you? Describe your difficulties in a paragraph. If you have not had this problem, write a summary paragraph describing the difficulties Rodriguez mentions.

Group Discussion

1. Why was Rodriguez angry when he heard only English spoken at home?
2. What was the importance or value of Spanish to this family?
3. Should children with a native language other than English be forced to learn English in school? Support your opinion with facts and examples from the article or from your own experience.

Chapter 4

Supporting Details and Other Guides to Paragraph Organization

> Organizing is what you do before you do something, so that when you do it, it's not all mixed up.
>
> *A. A. Milne*

Writers want you to understand what they have written. Consequently, paragraphs and whole essays often make use of supporting details arranged in an organized pattern. Becoming familiar with these clues to organization and using the clues to unlock and remember essential ideas in reading material is an important skill. As Milne suggests in the quotation above, most published writing is "not all mixed up" because writers organize their ideas.

This chapter will consider:

- the difference between major and minor supporting details
- how transitions, or signal words, form bridges linking ideas

When you can see order, information makes more sense and you can recall the facts more easily. Look at the patterns shown in Figure 4.1 for a few seconds. Now cover the patterns and draw them from memory.

Was the fourth grouping the most difficult to remember? If it was, that's because it doesn't seem to have an order. The first group consists of circles arranged in a circle. The second is triangles arranged in a triangle, and the third has the order of all triangles in a circle. The last group of circles and triangles, however, seems to have no order.

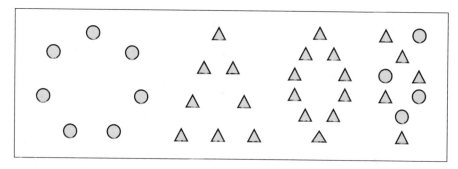

Figure 4.1

The Difference between Major and Minor Supporting Details

Details that support the main idea are part of a writer's organization. As you saw in Chapter 3, these supporting details give facts, reasons, and examples to develop the main idea of a paragraph. Some of the details give further support to the major detail. Look at the following paragraph as an example.

> Stereotyping is a kind of shorthand that can facilitate communication. Putting a cowboy in a black hat allows a movie director to sidestep complex character explanation and move quickly into a story line, because moviegoers hold a generalization about cowboys in black hats. They are the bad guys—a stereotype. Newspaper editors pack lots of information into headlines by drawing on stereotypes held by the readers. Consider the extra meaning implicit in headlines that refer to the "Castro regime," or a "Southern belle," or a "college jock." Stereotypes paint broad strokes that help create impact in media messages.
>
> —John Vivian, *The Media of Mass Communication*

The main idea is best expressed in the last sentence. Two major details introduced are stereotypes in movies and newspapers. Minor details are the example of "bad guys" in the movies and the Castro, belle, and jock examples from the newspapers. Because colorful details stick in our memory, it is important to distinguish major details from the minor. Ask yourself which details directly *support*, *prove*, or *explain* the main idea. Those are the *major supporting details*.

The *minor supporting details* support, explain, and give more information about the major details.

Exercise 4-1 Finding Major and Minor Supporting Details

Read each paragraph, then answer the questions about topic, main idea, and details that follow.

1. The amount of time a slave spent in slavery has varied widely around the world. In some cases, slavery was temporary. After serving a set number of years, a slave might be freed to return to his or her home country. Slaves of the Israelites were set free in the year of jubilee, which occurred every fifty years. Roman slaves ordinarily had the right to buy themselves out of slavery. They knew what their purchase price was, and some were able to meet this price by striking a bargain with their owner and selling their services to others. Such was the case with some of the educated Greek slaves. In most instances, however, slavery was lifelong. Some criminals, for example, became slaves when they were given life sentences as oarsmen on Roman war ships. There they served until death, which under this exhausting service often did not take long.

   —Adapted from James M. Henslin, *Sociology*

   a. The topic is

      1. Freedom for slaves

      2. Slavery

      3. Time spent in slavery

   b. Rewrite the main-idea sentence in your own words.

      _____

      _____

   c. Write the two major details that develop the main idea.

      1. _____

      2. _____

   d. Circle the number of the detail below that supports one of the major details you wrote above.

      1. Conditions of slavery varied around the world.

      2. Some criminals were slaves until death.

      3. Slavery was sometimes temporary.

2. The equity theory of motivation at work is so far focused on salary. A person's perception of pay may be based on two ideas: first, the person's pay relative to the pay of others; and second, the person's effort, education, skill level, training, and experience relative to the person's salary. In the first case, the comparison is made of the person's pay relative to what others are getting. In the second, the comparison is that of how hard the person worked, how long the person trained, and so on, relative to the pay received for the work. For example, a worker might be dissatisfied with his or her salary if the worker thought that another person doing the same job was paid more. A person who worked harder and had more experience than a co-worker yet received equal pay would also be dissatisfied.

—Adapted from Daniel A. Wren,
The Evolution of Management Thought

a. The topic is

1. Work satisfaction

2. The equity theory

3. A person's salary

b. Rewrite the main-idea sentence in your own words.

_____

_____

c. Write the two major details that explain the main idea.

1. _____

2. _____

d. Circle the number of the detail that further supports one of the major details in question c.

1. Workers can be dissatisfied in their job if someone doing the same job receives more pay.

2. Some workers have more experience than others.

3. Everyone in the same job should receive the same pay.

3. Some factors have been identified as important in determining who will remain in an occupation and who will change. Some factors—such as whether the person likes the occupation—lead to self-initiated occupation changes. For example,

people who really like their occupation may seek additional training or accept overtime assignments in hopes of acquiring new skills that will enable them to get better jobs. However, other factors, such as obsolete skills and economic trends, cause forced occupational changes. For example, continued improvement of robots caused some auto industry workers to lose their jobs, and economic recessions usually result in large-scale layoffs.

—Robert V. Kail and John C. Kavenaugh,
Human Development

a. The topic is

1. Job changes

2. Robots and job loss

3. Occupational insecurity

b. Rewrite the main-idea sentence in your own words.

_____

_____

c. Write the major details supporting the main idea.

1. _____

2. _____

d. Circle the number of the detail below that further supports one of the major details above.

1. Some workers seek additional training.

2. Some workers decide to change their jobs.

3. Several factors influence job changes.

4. Even before you take your first bite of pizza, your body has already begun a series of complex digestive responses. Your mouth prepares for the food by increasing production of saliva. Saliva contains mostly water, which aids in chewing and swallowing, but it also contains important enzymes that begin the process of food breakdown, including amylase, which begins to break down carbohydrates. From the mouth the food passes down the esophagus, a 9- to 10-inch tube that connects the mouth and stomach. A series of contractions and relaxations by the muscles lining the esophagus gently

moves food to the next digestive organ, the stomach. Here food mixes with enzymes and stomach acids. Hydrochloric acid begins to work in combination with pepsin, an enzyme, to break down proteins. In most people, the stomach secretes enough mucus to protect the stomach lining from these harsh digestive juices. In others, there are problems with the lining that can result in ulcers or other gastric problems.

—Rebecca J. Donatelle and Lorraine G. Davis,
Health: The Basics

a. The topic is

1. Digestive juices

2. Complex digestive responses

3. How saliva works

b. Rewrite the main-idea sentence in your own words.

_____

_____

c. Write the three major details that support the main idea.

1. _____

2. _____

3. _____

d. Circle the number of the detail below that further supports one of the major details you wrote above.

1. The mouth prepares for food.

2. Saliva contains mostly water.

3. Food moves from the esophagus to the stomach.

5. While recorded music has the power to move people to war and peace, to love and to sleep, it also reflects changing human values. In 1991, as U.S. troops were massing at the Persian Gulf to reclaim Kuwait, American record-makers issued music that reflected public enthusiasm for the war. Arista records put Whitney Houston's Super Bowl version of "The Star Spangled Banner" on a single, which sold 750,000 audio copies in only eight days. It was the fastest-selling single in Arista's history. Boston Dawn's remake of

the Shirelles' oldie "Soldier Boy," expressing a woman's love for her soldier overseas, included some rap lines from the soldier. It was very much a song of the times, and the record company, American Sound, had 25,000 back orders for the record almost as soon as it was released.

—John Vivian, *The Media of Mass Communication*

a. The topic is

　　1. Popular music today

　　2. Music as a reflection of human values

　　3. Different songs about war

b. Rewrite the main-idea sentence in your own words.

_____

_____

c. Only one major detail is given. Write it below.

_____

_____

d. Write the two minor details that support the major detail. (Note that these two minor details are developed with further details.)

　　1. _____

　　2. _____

Transitions, or Signal Words, Form Bridges Linking Ideas

As you can see, finding the relationships between major and minor ideas helps you to understand a paragraph or longer passage. Writers also provide other clues to their meaning with specific organizational patterns. Helpful in detecting order and therefore meaning are the specific words that make connections between ideas, sentences, and paragraphs. These connectors are called *transitions* or *signal words*. Noticing these words helps you see the relationships between ideas.

You will be looking at several of the most common kinds of order that writers use to present their ideas. When events or ideas are presented in *sequence*, the order in which they naturally occur, they are in *sequential order*. One kind of sequence is *time*, another is *place*, a third is *importance*, and a fourth is *process*, such as the sequential steps in how to make something. If you have cooked using a recipe, you are already familiar with process order. First you assemble the materials you are going to use, then you follow a sequence, a particular order for mixing the ingredients.

Sequential Transitions

When ideas are arranged in *time sequential order*, the pattern will look like the diagram here. Paragraphs about historical events are often in sequential order. To see this in graphic form, fill in your own dates and titles for major events in your life. The first and the last heading are provided. What events might you record? Think of events important to you from the past and the future—such as high school graduation, graduation from college, military service, marriage, and children—and place them in order.

Sequence of Events

Birth   Death

19____   19____   19____   19____   20____   20____   20____   20____

When events are arranged in sequential order in a paragraph, you will find clues to this order in the transitional or signal words used. These words signal the facts are arranged in the order of when, or how, they occur. A sample paragraph follows.

Buying a new car can be a rewarding experience for those who prepare for the event. <u>First</u>, they don't wait for an emergency. When their clunker will not go another mile, they could fall victim to a car salesperson. <u>Next</u>, experienced buyers don't fall in love with a racy sports car that will not really serve their needs. Falling in love can cost them more money than they intended to spend, and they can end up with a car that isn't suitable for them. <u>Further</u>, experienced buyers study publications like *Consumer Reports* for car prices and visit several dealerships. <u>Finally</u>, they know it is best to establish the purchase price of the new car before they discuss the trade-in price for their old car.

The underlined words connect or show an order for the process of car buying. The words in the list below are often clues to sequential order, whether of time, importance, place, or process:

immediately	next	last	soon
at this time	before	later	now
finally	then	since	until
following	after	when	during

Exercise 4-2   Locating Sequence Transitions in Sentences

To become familiar with sequential-order transitions, read the following sentences and circle the words that signal sequential order. Study the connections these words make between ideas.

1. Before taking the garbage outside, be sure to tie the bag carefully. Then you can clean the kitchen floor.

2. Until you remove the shell, a hard-boiled egg is difficult to eat.

3. First, the helicopter landed in the field. Next, the pilot jumped out. Finally, the stranded hikers were rescued.

4. At one time I thought my parents didn't know much. Some years later I was amazed to discover how much they had learned.

5. The last thing I did was prepare for bed after I finished studying.

6. During our study group we accomplished our objectives. Immediately following our work, we stopped for pizza.

7. Since I have completed reading the selection, I plan to take notes on the material soon.

8. I now knew I could focus on dieting after I had finished the last of the chocolate cake.

9. The first challenge was to find a part-time job. Next, I could consider buying a preowned car.

10. During computer class, Pedro enjoyed playing games. Some time later, he realized he had missed a few essential directions.

When you circled the signal words in the sentences, did you notice that some of the sentences mentioned the last event first? This was true in sentences 5 and 8. Thinking about the meaning of the transitional word is important to understanding order. For example, in the sentence

Test the water before you add chlorine.

you realize that the first step is to test the water. If the sentence is changed to

Before you add chlorine to the water, test the water's chemical content.

the order of the process is the same; first test, then add chlorine. The placement and meaning of the transition set up the relationship of ideas.

Exercise 4-3   Sequential Transitions in Paragraphs

Read the following paragraphs and circle the transition words that link the events of this anecdote together. Then complete the activities that follow.

Prelaw students and premed students boarded a train for the same destination. Each of the premed students had a ticket. Only one prelaw student had a ticket. The premed students thought the prelaw students were pretty stupid. Just then a prelaw student shouted, "The conductor is coming." Soon all the prelaw students were hidden in the bathroom. When the conductor arrived, he took everyone's ticket and then knocked on the bathroom door and said, "Ticket, please." The one ticket was passed under the door. The conductor took it and left.

Later the same two groups were returning from their trip. Now the premed students had only one ticket and planned to use the same trick. Surprisingly, this time the prelaw students had no ticket.

Soon the lookout called that the conductor was coming. Both groups of students rushed to crowd into the two opposite bathrooms. The premed students were puzzled. Before the conductor arrived, one prelaw student slipped out of their bathroom and knocked on the opposite door. "Ticket, please," he said.

The topic is

1. A train trip
2. Tricky prelaw students
3. Prelaw students hide in bathroom

If you wanted to recall this story to tell a friend, you could make an outline or list of events using the signal words to help you order events. Complete the following outline.

I. Prelaw students and premed students board train.

A. Premed students all have tickets.

B. _____

II. Prelaw student warns that conductor is coming.

A. _____

B. One ticket is passed under the door.

III. _____

A. Premed students have only one ticket.

B. _____

IV. Prelaw student announces conductor coming.

A. Both groups hide in two separate bathrooms.

B. _____

C. _____

Listing Transitions

Some transitional words prepare you for several thoughts presented along the same line. They introduce one or more ideas that the writer is using to support an idea already introduced. Often the topic sentence will use words or phrases like *there are three ways, two facts support this,* or *four reasons for this are.* These phrases are clues that a listing will follow. Here's an example. Note the underlined words.

> We are constantly communicating with others. On the job you will be using three kinds of communication: oral, written, and body language. <u>First</u>, you talk on the phone, at meetings, and face to face with your co-workers and customers. <u>In addition</u>, you will communicate by writing. Written communication will take the form of notes, reports, memos, e-mail, and faxes. <u>Also</u>, even when you are quietly working at your desk, your body language will convey a message. If you are slumped over your desk with a frown creasing your forehead, you convey one message. A smile and an alert posture convey another message.

The signal words *first, in addition,* and *also* introduce the major details that list the three kinds of communication that occur at work.

Some common listing links appear in the following list.

in addition	also	next	first
furthermore	another	finally	second
moreover	last	similarly	third

Exercise 4-4   Locating Listing Signals in Sentences

Circle the transitions used to connect ideas in the following sentences. Think about the connection being made.

1. Babe Ruth, a great baseball player, established two major league records. First, he hit 60 home runs in a season of 154 games. In addition, when he retired, he had hit 714 home runs. Moreover, Ruth was probably the best left-handed pitcher of his time.

2. Thirty-four years later, Roger Maris, playing for the Yankees, broke Ruth's record for home runs in a year. Furthermore, Hank Aaron, who came to the major leagues from the Negro American League, had a record of 755 home runs when he retired.

3. First, a female fox, called a vixen, looks for a safe den. She might use a badger's or a woodchuck's den as a nest for her cubs. Also, a hollow tree trunk or even thick undergrowth will do. Next, she gives birth to anywhere from three to nine cubs.

4. One reason for planning to study regularly is that you are developing a good habit. Another reason is that studying for finals is not difficult if you have reviewed daily.

5. Dan Jansen, the Olympic gold winner in speed racing in 1994, is a good model of perseverance paying off. He fell in the '88 Olympics and also in the '92 race.

6. The electric guitar, once considered a novelty, now shapes the sound and direction of modern musical style. Furthermore, it's played anyplace from concert halls to garages. Moreover, the National Museum of American History features an exhibition on the instrument called "The Rise of the Electric Guitar."

7. Take care of your teeth. First, you need your front teeth or incisors for cutting food into smaller pieces. Further, the canine teeth help you get meat off bones and strip an ear of corn. Finally, your molars help you grind food.

Exercise 4-5   Listing Transitions in a Paragraph

Read the following paragraph. Circle the transitional words that indicate the details listed, and answer the questions that follow.

Memory involves more than taking in information and storing it in some mental compartment. In fact, psychologists probing the workings of memory have had to grapple with three enduring questions. First, how does information get *into* memory? Then, how is information *maintained* in memory? And finally, how is information pulled back out of memory? These three questions correspond to the three key processes involved in memory: *encoding* (getting information in), *storage* (maintaining it), and *retrieval* (getting it out).

—Adapted from Wayne Weiten, *Psychology*

a. The topic is

1. Information in the memory

2. The memory

3. Psychologists' questions about memory

b. Rewrite the main-idea sentence in your own words.

_____

_____

c. Write the three major details that develop the main idea.

1. _____

2. _____

3. _____

d. Circle the letter of the detail that further explains one of the major details you wrote in item 3.

1. Encoding (getting information in)

2. Three questions psychologists ask

3. Psychologists probe memory

Example Transitions

To explain a general idea more clearly, a writer will often follow the idea with one or more specific examples. Here's a short paragraph with underlined words that signal a coming example.

> All cats are territorial; <u>that is</u>, they stake out their own territory, and other cats know to beware trespassing. Whether it lives indoors or outdoors, a cat needs its own space, including places for sleeping, eating, and playing. To establish their territory, cats mark it. <u>For example</u>, male cats will spray, and all cats have sweat glands between their paws that let them leave their scent. <u>Thus</u>, when a cat rubs against your leg, it is marking its territory.

Did you notice that the transition, *that is* explains the word, territorial. Next, *for example,* introduces a description of how cats mark their territory. Finally *thus,* gives a specific example of a cat marking its territory.

The following transitions signal examples.

for example	for instance	that is
as demonstrated by	to illustrate	
such as	including	

Exercise 4-6   Example Transitions in Sentences

Observe the use of example transitions in the following sentences and circle the transition words.

1. New mothers today often worry about whether to take a job after their babies are born. For example, Heather is worried that a job will interfere with her care of her baby.

2. Some researchers believe that a part-time job is beneficial to mothers. For instance, a regular paycheck can support a mother's self-image.

3. Absentmindedness may be a result of how many projects you are involved in. To illustrate, when you are juggling family, work, and several classes, you can easily forget assignments or miss appointments.

4. Biological science, the study of living things, was much advanced by the studies of Greek and Roman philosophers such as Aristotle, Hippocrates, and Galen.

5. Reform of the nation's probation problems could be hastened if just a few changes were made, including, expanding prison capacity, ending probation for chronic offenders, and punishing probation violators.

6. Bald eagles, our national symbol, are making a comeback; for example, the number of eagles in the United States today is about 16,000.

7. Manuel likes to bend the truth a little in talking about his new van. Once, he told Esteban that he could stop the van so suddenly that the paint slid right off, but that wasn't a problem because the startup was so swift that the paint slid right back on.

8. Toni enjoys most sports; that is, as long as she can watch them on TV.

9. Michael is planning a quiet vacation, including resting and spending time in the library.

10. Martha plans to graduate, as demonstrated by the efforts she puts into her assignments.

Exercise 4-7   Example Transitions in a Paragraph

Read the following paragraph. Circle the transitional words that signal an example or illustration, and answer the questions that follow.

During the years of the Great Depression, people could afford few pleasures. One pleasure they could afford was going to a movie since movies cost very little at that time. Families would save for a week to afford this entertainment. As a result, Hollywood turned out happy, optimistic films to help people relax and forget their troubles. For example, Shirley Temple, the sweet, curly-haired child of the Depression years, starred in twenty-one upbeat movies. Another type of movie popular during those years was the lavish musical spectacle. Hundreds of dancers and singers took people's minds from their troubles for the cost of a dime.

a. The topic is

1. Hollywood musicals

2. Depression movies

3. The cost of movies

b. Rewrite the main-idea sentence in your own words.

_____

_____

c. Write the two major details.

1. _____

2. _____

d. Circle the number of the minor detail that supports one of the major details you wrote in item 3.

1. Movies helped people relax.

2. Singers and dancers took people's minds off troubles.

3. Happy, optimistic films

Comparison/Contrast Transitions

Another organizational pattern for paragraphs and essays is *comparison/contrast*. In this order, a writer brings two ideas together to demonstrate either their likenesses or their differences. When the ideas are similar, the writer is making a comparison. For example, cake and candy are similar and can be *compared* because they are both sweet. If the two ideas are quite different, the writer wants you to see the lack of similarity. For example, candy and dill pickles are different and can be *contrasted* because one is sweet and the other is sour. Sometimes these two patterns are used in the same work. The writer shows how two ideas or objects are similar by comparing them. Then, for more emphasis, a contrast is made with something quite different. A short paragraph will illustrate this strategy.

> I like McDougal's hamburgers. They are tasty and filling just <u>like</u> the hamburgers at Bill's. <u>However</u>, the french fries at Bill's are better because they are thin and crispy <u>while</u> the fries at McDougal's are fat and greasy.

The words *just like* prepare you for a comparison. The word *however* prepares you for a change of thought. And *while* prepares you for the contrast of french fries.

Study the comparison/contrast signal words in the following two lists.

Comparison

like	equally	just like	also
as	similarly	just as	likewise

Contrast

but	although	however	even though
yet	instead	while	on the contrary
in contrast			

Exercise 4-8   Comparison/Contrast Transitions in Sentences

Circle the transitions in these sentences and think about the association being made between the ideas or objects. Write the words comparison *or* contrast *on the blank after the sentence according to the relationship shown.*

1. The carpet was a green shag and looked like grass that needed

   to be mowed. _____

2. Those who lie to us harm us just as much as those who steal

   from us. _____

3. When someone hurts you, record the hurt in sand; however, when someone is kind, record the act in marble. _____

4. The desert spread out before us just like a giant pancake sizzling on a griddle. _____

5. Columbus can be admired for his discovery of America although his courage in adventuring into the unknown is perhaps even more admirable. _____

6. We all make mistakes, but only a fool repeats them. _____

7. Achieving success without effort is just as difficult as getting the hot pepper out of a bowl of chili. _____

8. To watch the sun rise at dawn can lift your spirits. Similarly, watching the sun set can be equally inspiring. _____

9. Although you lack experience, intelligence and a good attitude may lead you to success. _____

10. When you are angry, it is as if a wind blows out the light in your mind. _____

Exercise 4-9   Comparison/Contrast Transitions in a Paragraph

Circle the transitions in the paragraph and answer the questions that follow.

News articles in newspapers are very different from nightly television newscasts. Both types of reporting have much to offer in keeping us aware of current events, but there are major differences in their presentations. Newspapers cover events in more detail, while television news items are usually quite brief. Newspaper stories depend primarily on the printed word. At most, one photograph will accompany the story. In contrast, television stories will often have a film clip or an on-the-scene report. Pictures put you at the heart of the action and have great appeal. Another difference is that you can choose to read an entire newspaper article, scan the first paragraph, or turn the page. Television locks you into the story; you can't turn to another one.

a. The topic is

1. Television and newspaper stories

2. Stories in the newspapers

3. The contrast between TV news and newspaper stories

b. Rewrite the main-idea sentence in your own words.

_____

_____

c. Explain the main differences between newspaper stories and television news (major details).

1. _____

2. _____

3. _____

d. Circle the number of the minor detail that supports one of the major details you wrote in item c.

1. Newspapers provide greater depth in coverage.

2. Newspapers provide comics.

3. TV pictures are appealing.

Cause-and-Effect Transitions

Writers, particularly in science, social science, and history texts, often state one idea, a *cause,* and then discuss one or more of its *effects.* Or, just the reverse, they may describe an *effect* and then discuss what *caused* that effect.

Causes explain how or why something occurs.

Effects are the results of what happens.

Study these everyday examples:

1. Because it was raining, I took my umbrella. (The rain caused the effect of my taking an umbrella.)
2. As a result of careful shopping, I was able to save enough for a pizza. (Saving money shopping caused the effect of my having the extra money for a pizza.)
3. Shelia works two jobs; consequently, she has little time for recreation. (Because Shelia works two jobs, the effect is that she has little time for recreation.)

As you can see from these examples, sometimes a writer mentions a cause first, and sometimes the effect or result is mentioned first. It is important to distinguish causes from effects. These questions will be helpful.

1. Is this fact a result of some action? (effect)
2. Does this fact explain how or why something occurred? (cause)

Remember, too, that any particular effect may have one or more causes. For example, you may decide to change your major. That fact or effect may be caused by meeting someone you admire in another field, further study of the benefits derived from a particular vocational choice, and many other causes. Another example of an effect is the Civil War, which had several causes, including slavery and states' rights.

In the same way, a cause may give rise to more than one effect. Consider frequent television viewing (the cause). Such viewing may have several effects, such as less time for reading and other activities or promotion of sexist stereotyping and a tendency to violence.

Here are some frequent cause-and-effect signal words.

because	if–then	accordingly	since	as a result
thus	therefore	consequently	so	in short

Exercise 4-10 Cause-and-Effect Transitions in Sentences

I. Read the following sentences and circle the transition words. Then write the correct cause or reason on the first line and the effect or consequence on the lines following. The first one is done as an example.

1. Fred bought a car because he had saved his money.

   CAUSE: ___Fred saved his money.___

   EFFECT: ___He bought a car.___

2. Phil rode his bike because he liked to exercise.

   CAUSE: _____

   EFFECT: _____

3. Because it was Halloween, we prepared treats for the kids who would be coming to our door.

   CAUSE: _____

   EFFECT: _____

4. Julie has a test tomorrow, so she plans to study tonight.

   CAUSE: _____

   EFFECT: _____

5. People who drive drunk cause accidents.

   CAUSE: _____

   EFFECT: _____

6. I enjoy eating at Taco Bell; therefore, I go there often.

   CAUSE: _____

   EFFECT: _____

7. After the stress of classes, Mario needs to relax by playing basketball for an hour when he gets home.

CAUSE: _____

EFFECT: _____

8. Frank's ability to deal with customers pleasantly earned him a salary increase.

CAUSE: _____

EFFECT: _____

9. The hot, dry weather is causing the lake levels to recede.

CAUSE: _____

EFFECT: _____

10. The lake is receding because of the hot, dry weather.

CAUSE: _____

EFFECT: _____

11. Because Terry continued to ask questions in class, she eventually understood the difficult material.

CAUSE: _____

EFFECT: _____

II. The following sentences are more complex and involve two causes. (Hint: The second cause is always the same as the first effect.) Write the causes and effects on the lines that follow. The first one is done as an example.

1. Because Tammy worked hard all day, she was hungry, so she ate a large dinner.

CAUSE: _Tammy worked hard all day._____

EFFECT: _She was hungry._____

CAUSE: _She was hungry._____

EFFECT: _She ate a large dinner._____

2. Beth was tired after spending the day at the zoo with a four-year-old, so she went to bed early.

   CAUSE: _____

   EFFECT: _____

   CAUSE: _____

   EFFECT: _____

3. Tanya spent the afternoon skiing, which was exhausting, so she took a nap before dinner.

   CAUSE: _____

   EFFECT: _____

   CAUSE: _____

   EFFECT: _____

4. Since Li knew she would be out late, she left the lights burning, so no one would know the house was empty.

   CAUSE: _____

   EFFECT: _____

   CAUSE: _____

   EFFECT: _____

5. Having caught a cold from her friend, Marsha decided not to attend class.

   CAUSE: _____

   EFFECT: _____

   CAUSE: _____

   EFFECT: _____

6. Because David liked good food, he decided to take a gourmet cooking class, where he learned to make special dishes.

CAUSE: _____

EFFECT: _____

CAUSE: _____

EFFECT: _____

7. Feeling elated by an A on his last test, a grade he achieved by good preparation, Morris decided to celebrate by seeing a movie.

CAUSE: _____

EFFECT: _____

CAUSE: _____

EFFECT: _____

8. After Diana ran for two miles, she was gasping for air, so she stopped to take several deep breaths.

CAUSE: _____

EFFECT: _____

CAUSE: _____

EFFECT: _____

9. Paul partied until 2 A.M. which left him tired; consequently, he missed his 8 A.M. class.

CAUSE: _____

EFFECT: _____

CAUSE: _____

EFFECT: _____

10. Because Cheryl was learning to ice skate, she had a few bruises from falling and decided to treat them with ointment

CAUSE: _____

EFFECT: _____

CAUSE: _____

EFFECT: _____

11. Andy is looking for work after graduation so that he can afford to have his own apartment.

CAUSE: _____

EFFECT: _____

CAUSE: _____

EFFECT: _____

III. Sometimes more than one reason or cause is responsible for an effect. Find the two causes for the effects in the following sentences. Write out the two causes followed by the effect. The first one is done for you.

1. Since Todd wanted to go to the beach and his car was not running, he rode the bus.

    CAUSE 1: _Todd wanted to go to the beach._____

    CAUSE 2: _His car was not running._____

    EFFECT: _He rode the bus._____

2. Charles has a high grade-point average in his two-year college and he is a gifted athlete, so he will probably be offered a scholarship to a university.

    CAUSE 1: _____

    CAUSE 2: _____

    EFFECT: _____

3. You study your vocabulary cards each morning and evening; since this repeated study helps you retain information, you will do well on the test.

    CAUSE 1: _____

    CAUSE 2: _____

EFFECT: _____

4. Mr. Coleman, who often traveled to Las Vegas, filed for bankruptcy because of his compulsive gambling habit.

CAUSE 1: _____

CAUSE 2: _____

EFFECT: _____

5. Because the defense lawyer's objection was valid, the judge threw out the evidence and ultimately dismissed the case.

CAUSE 1: _____

CAUSE 2: _____

EFFECT: _____

6. Anne worked the machine carefully because she was unfamiliar with it and wanted a good product.

CAUSE 1: _____

CAUSE 2: _____

EFFECT: _____

7. Lincoln issued the Emancipation Proclamation in 1862 because he was philosophically opposed to slavery, and he believed that freeing the slaves would hasten the war's end.

CAUSE 1: _____

CAUSE 2: _____

EFFECT: _____

8. Marcie decided to buy the red dress, but she had no cash, so she used her charge card.

CAUSE 1: _____

CAUSE 2: _____

EFFECT: _____

9. When she saw the advertised sale, Melanie, who loves sales, rushed to the store.

   CAUSE 1: _____

   CAUSE 2: _____

   EFFECT: _____

10. Steve saved the cat, which had climbed up in the tree after being chased by the dog.

    CAUSE 1: _____

    CAUSE 2: _____

    EFFECT: _____

11. Jim, who hated housework, called his mother for instructions on running the vacuum cleaner before cleaning the rug.

    CAUSE 1: _____

    CAUSE 2: _____

    EFFECT: _____

Exercise 4-11 Cause-and-Effect Signal Words in a Paragraph

Read each paragraph, noting the cause-and-effect transitions, and answer the questions that follow.

Great works of art, once enjoyed, often remain in our memories, bringing continued pleasure. Consequently, once we have read a great novel, a thoughtful essay, or a poem that moves us, we can recollect these experiences and enjoy them again days and weeks later. We may learn a lesson that helps us handle our own daily problems. A powerful piece of music may sing itself repeatedly in our mind. We may be doing some mindless task like scrubbing a floor when the melody floats into our mind and refreshes us. An effective painting like Monet's *Water Lilies* can be recalled, creating again the sense of awe our first sighting inspired. Therefore, treating ourselves to the inspiration offered by great artists is giving ourselves something to enjoy in recollection.

a. The topic is

1. Recalling great music

2. Lasting effects of great art

3. The purposes of art

b. Rewrite the main idea in your own words.

_____

_____

c. List the three major details used to support this main idea.

1. _____

2. _____

3. _____

d. Circle the number of a minor detail that further explains one of the major details you wrote in item 3.

1. Powerful music stays in our memories.

2. Great art brings repeated pleasures.

3. Ideas from literature can help us face problems.

Mixed Transitions

You can expect to find many organizational patterns in material in your texts. Noticing and identifying signal words will aid you in understanding. But did you notice that some transitional words have more than one function? For example, the word *also* can signal something being added, or it may suggest a comparison. Review the lists of transitions in this chapter to note other words that may signal different organizational patterns. It is important to be aware of these shifts because writers will use more than one organizational pattern to develop and explain ideas.

Exercise 4-12 Mixed Transitions in Sentences

Use the transitional words listed here to make the clearest connection in the sentences that follow, then place a check mark beside the kind of transition demonstrated. The first one is completed for you as an example.

for example   however   since   before   furthermore
because   such as   as   as a result   similarly

1. *Before* the invention of computers, people used typewriters more frequently.

    _____ a. listing

    _____ b. cause and effect

    _✓_ c. time

2. We experience a change in seasons _____ the

    earth tilts on its axis as it revolves around the sun.

    _____ a. Example

    _____ b. Cause and effect

    _____ c. Comparison

3. If you're preparing for a dinner date, try to get as much done

    ahead of time as possible; _____, choose your

    outfit and accessories the night before.

    _____ a. Example

    _____ b. Comparison

    _____ c. Contrast

4. Have your children help with household duties _____

    putting silverware on the the table, hanging up their own

    clothes, and helping with the dishes.

_____ a. Time

_____ b. Contrast

_____ c. Example

5. My brother, Gino, is so clumsy that my mother always says,

"You're as clumsy _____ a bull in a china closet."

_____ a. Cause and effect

_____ b. Time

_____ c. Comparison

6. Mario continually ran out of money before his paycheck was

due; _____, he was always borrowing money.

_____ a. Example

_____ b. Comparison

_____ c. Cause and effect

7. Originally, people carried water from an outside well. Today,

_____, we simply turn on a faucet.

_____ a. Contrast

_____ b. Example

_____ c. Cause and effect

8. _____ I have begun to use a computer for assign-

ments, my writing grades have improved.

_____ a. Contrast

_____ b. Time

_____ c. Cause and effect

9. Welfare benefits should be controlled carefully; _____,

they should be offered for a limited time.

_____ a. Contrast

_____ b. Cause and effect

_____ c. Listing

10. A piece of jewelry adds a fresh look to an older outfit;

_____, a colorful new scarf achieves the same

effect.

_____ a. Comparison

_____ b. Cause and effect

_____ c. Listing

Other Organizational Patterns

Sometimes, particularly in writing composed of several paragraphs, you will find other kinds of organization. The writer may suggest a problem and propose one or more solutions for the problem. For example, a writer who is concerned with the overcrowding of our prisons will probably examine several solutions for this problem in the essay. This common pattern of problem/solution is often linked with the cause-and-effect pattern. In this instance, the causes of prison crowding may also be discussed.

Two other forms of organization, *classification* and *division*, are also often found together, particularly in science texts, For instance, within the group or general class of birds, there are about 8,600 different kinds or species. In a passage about birds, you may find a discussion of the general characteristics of birds, such as warm-bloodedness and adaptations for flight, two elements of their classification. This classification might be followed by a division, the details about a particular species such as the pigeon and its parts: beak, feathers, wings, and feet.

Classification begins with a general group like college students and discusses the many qualities they share in common, while division divides a large group such as college students into smaller groups and analyzes the qualities or details that distinguish one group from another.

Finally, written structures may have an overall pattern of *definition*. Your textbooks often define words immediately after their introduction. Sometimes definitions are boldfaced or placed in the margin rather than being placed in a glossary. At other times, a paragraph or more will be required to define a term within the text adequately. A history text discussing types of government may spend several pages beyond the dictionary definition to define *democracy*.

Now that you have worked with different paragraph patterns, use your knowledge of transitions and paragraph organization to read the following paragraphs and answer the questions that follow.

Exercise 4-13   Paragraphs with Different Patterns of Organization

Read each paragraph, determine the organizational pattern, and answer the questions that follow.

1. Simplistic as it sounds, the first thing that environmental scientists—indeed, probably all scientists—should do is get involved. Educating the public should be an integral part of every scientist's career; if something is worth discovering, it is worth communicating. If those of us who are most familiar with the beauty and intricacy of nature, and its essential role in supporting humanity, will not come to nature's—and thus humanity's—defense, who will? How can we complain about the lack of action by politicians or the ignorance of talk show hosts, Sunday morning television pundits, or even brownlash reporters, if we don't help them get the facts straight.

   —Paul R. Ehrlich and Anne H. Ehrlich,
   Betrayal of Science and Reason

   a. The paragraph's organizational pattern is

      1. Cause and effect

      2. Problem/solution

      3. Listing

   b. The topic is

      1. Environmental scientists

      2. Educating about environmental issues

      3. Television talk shows

   c. Rewrite the main idea in your own words.

   _____

   _____

d. What responsibility do the writers suggest that scientists have?

_____

_____

2. In an uncut forest, the leaves, branches, and roots of trees and bushes as well as leaf litter all act like a great sponge, absorbing as much as 90 percent of rainwater and snowmelt. Water is then slowly released into the air as vapor or gradually enters rivers from creeks and streams or from pools of groundwater. As a result, the flow of water in rivers of forested watersheds is relatively steady, although it may fluctuate between dry and wet seasons.

—Michael L. Weber and Judy A. Gradwohl,
The Wealth of Oceans

a. The paragraph's organizational pattern is

1. Comparison/contrast

2. Cause and effect

3. Sequential order

b. The topic is

1. Forests

2. Forested watersheds

3. Water in rivers

c. The paragraph makes an argument for preserving forests.

1. True

2. False

3. Cultural stereotypes have appeared to direct women into fields and careers in which their presumed superiority in helping others, in being more sensitive and more caring, can be usefully applied. Examples include nursing (not medicine), education (not research), social work (not psychiatry), and the like. In fact, some women are very sensitive, caring, and warm, and these helping professions among others are well served by having such persons as members. But some men are also sensitive, caring, and warm; indeed, it is possi-

ble to be sensitive, caring, and warm, and also be highly capable in math, facile with high-tech tools, and analytic.

—Martin Bloom, *Introduction to the Drama of Social Work*

a. The topic is

1. Cultural stereotypes in jobs

2. The caring nature of women

3. Vocational choices

b. According to the writer, only women make good nurses.

1. True

2. False

c. What is suggested by the contrast between nursing and medicine and education and research?

_____

_____

d. The writer suggests that only men are highly capable in math.

1. True

2. False

4. One of the syndromes of development in Greenland is that everything seems to have happened recently. The Danish Navy's new heavily armed, high-speed inspection ships were recently introduced. The vote to join the Common Market and the narrow majority to withdraw as of January 1, 1985. Not long ago the Defense Ministry restricted entry permits to Qaanaaq for military reasons.

—Peter Hoeg, *Smilla's Sense of Snow*

a. The paragraph's organizational pattern is

1. Sequential

2. Cause and effect

3. Listing

b. The topic is

1. Recent development in Greenland

2. The Common Market

3. Danish control

c. Rewrite the main idea in your own words.

_____

_____

5. Two terms often used to define people's religious or political positions are "conservative" and "liberal." Older people are often labeled conservative while the young are often viewed as liberal. What exactly do these terms mean? *Conserve* has the basic meaning of "preserving" or "saving." In political and religious terms, that means to continue with existing conditions. However, *liberal* has the basic meaning of "free," and in a religious and political sense it means favorable to progress and reform. For example, a conservative is most inclined to say, "But we've always done it this way." In contrast, the liberal might say, "It's time for a change." Applying these terms to individuals can be difficult since a person can be conservative on some positions and liberal on others. Further, an action or position once considered liberal may now be considered conservative. For example, when President Franklin D. Roosevelt established Social Security, this was considered an extremely liberal action. Today, however, attempts to preserve Social Security are viewed as conservative.

a. This paragraph contains details of definition, example, and comparison-contrast. The writer's *main* organizational pattern is

1. Examples illustrating the terms

2. Defining the terms

3. Comparing and contrasting the terms

b. The topic is

1. The meaning of the terms *liberal* and *conservative*

2. Social Security

3. The difficulty of defining the terms

c. Rewrite the main-idea sentence in your own words.

_____

_____

6. In sports, very often having too many good players is just as much a negative as having too few. Having too many players often creates jealousies and dissension, cancers that eat at the heart of any group. So I knew that if we didn't find a way to solve this problem as a team, we definitely were not going to be in any position to win a national championship. I wondered what to do about it. Then one day in the fall I met with the team and told them about my problem.

I said, "Here is the problem I have as a coach, and you are either all going to help me solve it or I'm going to solve it myself autocratically. Which one is it going to be?"

The point is, I gave them a chance to be part of the solution. I made them aware of the problem right in the beginning and gave them a big stake in the potential solution of it. This reinforced to those players who didn't figure to see a lot of playing time that it wasn't because I didn't value them as players. It also instantly brought them all closer together as a team. They understood that they were all being asked to sacrifice some of their individual goals in the name of the collective good; and that if we all somehow found a way to solve this problem, they had a chance to become part of basketball history, to become part of something special, which is what ended up happening. The fact that every one of our players understood the goal we had to accomplish resulted in the 1996 NCAA Championship.

—Rick Pitino, *Success Is a Choice*

a. The writer's main pattern of organization is

1. Definition

2. Problem/solution

3. Cause-and-effect

b. The topic is:

1. Jealousy in basketball

2. Winning the NCAA Championship

3. Solving a problem as a team

    c. Rewrite the main idea in your own words.

    _____

    _____

    d. Define the word *autocratically* as used in the second pararaph from context.

    _____

Chapter Review

Fill in the blanks with the correct words.

1. _____ _____ support, explain, and develop the main idea.

2. Minor details support, explain, and develop the _____

   _____.

3. Transitions or signal words help you to understand the writer's _____.

4. The pattern of organization that shows likeness and differences is called _____.

5. If the events or details are listed in a particular order, the pattern is called _____.

6. If the organization is primarily by example, the major details will provide _____.

7. Organization signaled by a phrase like "the three reasons" is called _____.

8. An effect is a result of a _____.

9. An effect may have one or _____ causes.

10. Noting signal words helps you to understand the writer's

_____.

Sentence Completion

Complete the following sentences to show the organization suggested.

1. Because of the thunderstorm, _____

_____. (cause and effect)

2. The thunderstorm was like _____

_____. (comparison)

3. First, the thunder rolled _____

_____

_____. (time order)

4. Thunder seemed to shake the house; in addition, _____

_____

_____. (listing)

5. The thunder frightened us; however, _____

_____

_____. (contrast)

6. The thunder was not the worst thing that could happen. For

example, _____

_____. (example/detail)

Reading Selection 1

Purpose

Television is an important element in many people's lives today. The following article, adapted from a text on human development, discusses the effects of televison on school-age children and adolescents. Read to learn some of the effects of television, according to the authors.

Preview

1. Preview the article by considering the heads and subheads, which suggest the areas to be considered.
2. Check the vocabulary and questions that follow the article.

Anticipate/Associate

1. Think about stereotypes you have seen on television. Have these stereotypes influenced your thinking in any way?
2. Can you remember as a child wanting something because you had seen it advertised on television?
3. Do you believe that television violence has an influence on young people's behavior?
4. In your opinion, is there any value to be found in television programing?

Television's Influence on Attitudes, Behavior, Creativity, and Cognition

Robert V. Kail and John C. Cavanaugh

Influence on Attitudes and Social Behavior

Back in 1954, the Chairman of the U.S. Senate Subcom-   1
mittee on Juvenile Delinquency, Estes Kefauver, was concerned about the amount of violence in television programming. At that time, only about half of the households in the United States had television sets, yet the public was already aware of the frequent portrayal of violence in TV programs and worried about its effect on viewers, especially young ones. Anecdotes suggesting a link were common. A 6-year-old fan of

Hopalong Cassidy (a TV cowboy of the 1950s) asked his father for real bullets for his toy gun, because his toy bullets didn't kill people the way Hopalong's did.

More than 40 years later, citizens remain concerned about violence on TV—with good reason. Children's cartoons typically have one violent act every three minutes (The term *violence* here refers to use of physical force against another person.) The average North American youngster will see several thousand murders on TV before reaching adolescence. 2

What is the impact of this steady diet of televised <u>mayhem</u> and violence? According to Bandura's (1986) social learning theory, children learn by observing others; they watch others and often imitate what they see. Applied to TV, this theory predicts more <u>aggressive</u> behavior from children who watch violent TV. This prediction was supported by laboratory studies conducted in the 1960s. Children watched specially created TV programs in which an adult behaved violently toward a plastic "Bobo" doll; the adult kicked and hit the doll with a plastic hammer. When children were given the opportunity to play with the doll, those who had seen the TV program were much more likely to behave aggressively toward the doll than were children who had not seen the program. 3

Critics noted many limitations in this and other early studies and doubted that viewing TV violence in more realistic settings would have such pronounced effects on children. Today, however, we know that viewing TV violence "hardens" children, making them more accepting of interpersonal violence. Suppose, for example, a child is baby-sitting two youngsters who begin to argue and then fight. Baby-sitters who are frequent viewers of TV violence are more inclined to let them "slug it out," because they see this as a normal, acceptable way of resolving conflicts. 4

Is this increased <u>tolerance</u> for aggression reflected in children's behavior? The answer from research is clear. Frequent exposure to TV violence causes children to be more <u>aggressive</u>. One of the most compelling studies examined the impact of children's TV viewing at age 8 on criminal activity at age 30. Eight-year-olds exposed to large doses of TV violence had the most extensive criminal records as 30-year-olds. The link was found for both males and females, although females' level of criminal activity was much lower overall. Thus, children who are frequent viewers of TV violence learn to resort to aggression in their interactions with others. For many, their aggression eventually puts them behind bars. 5

Of course, violence is only one part of what children see   6
on TV. Let's examine other ways in which TV is an important
influence on children as they develop.

Stereotypes

TV is said to provide a "window on the world." Unfor-   7
tunately, the view is distorted, particularly when it comes to
minorities, women, and the elderly. In the early days of TV,
African Americans almost never appeared in programs. When
they did appear, they were limited to minor roles such as the
gentle buffoon.

The situation is much the same for women and the el-   8
derly. Their portrayal on TV bears little resemblance to reality. No more than one-third of all TV roles are for women.
When women are shown on TV, they are often passive and
emotional. Most are not employed; those who have jobs are
often in stereotypical female careers such as teachers or secretaries. Also, the land of television evidently has a fountain
of youth, because older Americans are grossly underrepre-
sented. Although nearly 20% of the U.S. population is 60 or
older, less than 5% of the characters in prime-time TV are
that age. Ironically, older adults on TV are usually men, despite the fact that women far outnumber men at this point in
the life span.

Surprisingly, we know relatively little about the effects   9
of these stereotyped portrayals on children's attitudes toward
minorities or the elderly. However, the impact of the stereotyped presentation of females is clear. As you can imagine,
children who watch TV frequently end up with more stereotyped views of males and females. Sex-role stereotypes were
studied in a small Canadian town that was located in a valley
and could not receive TV programs until a transmitter was
installed nearby in 1974. Two years later, views of personality traits, behaviors, occupations, and peer relations were
measured in the town's children. . . . For example, girls had
more stereotyped views of peer relations. Now they believed
that boasting and swearing were characteristic of boys but
that sharing and helping were characteristic of girls. The boys
in the town had acquired more stereotyped views of occupations, now believing that girls could be teachers and cooks,
whereas boys could be physicians and judges.

Findings like these indicate that TV viewing causes   10
children to adopt many of the stereotypes that dominate television programming. For many children and adolescents,
TV's slanted depiction of the world *becomes* reality.

Consumer Behavior

Sugary cereals, hamburgers and french fries, snack 11 foods, toys, clothing. . . . These products are the focus of a <u>phenomenal</u> amount of TV advertising that is directed toward children. A typical youngster may see more than 50 commercials a day! As early as 3 years of age, children distinguish commercials from programs. However, preschool children often believe that <u>commercials</u> are simply a different form of entertainment—one designed to inform viewers. Not until 8 or 9 years of age do most children understand the persuasive intent of commercials. At the same time that children grasp the aim of commercials, they begin to realize that commercials are not always truthful.

Commercials are effective sales tools with children. 12 Children grow to like many of the products advertised on TV. Like the youngster in the photograph, they may urge parents to buy products that they have seen on television. In one study, more than 75% of the children reported that they had asked their parents to buy a product they had seen advertised on TV. More often than not, parents had purchased the product for them!

The selling power of TV commercials has long con- 13 cerned advocates for children, because so many ads focus on children's foods that have little nutritional value and that are associated with problems such as obesity and tooth decay. The U.S. government once regulated the amount and type of advertising on children's TV programs, but today the responsibility falls largely to parents.

Prosocial Behavior

TV is clearly a <u>potent</u> influence on children's aggression 14 and on the stereotypes they form. Can this power be put to more prosocial goals? Can TV viewing help children learn to be more generous, to be more cooperative, and to have greater self-control? Yes, according to early laboratory studies. In these experiments, children were more likely to act <u>prosocially</u> after they watched brief films in which a peer acted prosocially. For example, children were more likely to share or more likely to resist the temptation to take from others when they had seen a filmed peer sharing or resisting temptation.

An early study by Bryan and Walbek typifies this sort of 15 experimentation. Third- and fourth-grade children received a prize for playing a game, then watched a film about another child who had received the same prize and was asked to donate some of the prize to charity. In one version of the film, the child donated part of the prize; in another version, the child did not. The children in the study were then given the opportunity to donate a portion of their winnings to the same charity shown in the film. Children were much more likely to donate when they had seen the film about the generous child than when they had seen the film about the stingy one. Thus, from watching others who were generous, children themselves learned to be generous.

Research with actual TV programs lead to the same con-   16
clusion. Youngsters who watch TV shows that emphasize prosocial behavior, such as *Mister Rogers' Neighborhood*, are more likely to behave prosocially. In fact, a comprehensive analysis revealed that the impact of viewing prosocial TV programs is much greater than the impact of viewing tele-vised violence. Boys, in particular, benefit from viewing prosocial TV, perhaps because they are usually much less skilled prosocially than girls are.

Although research indicates that prosocial behavior *can*   17
be influenced by TV watching, two important factors restrict the actual prosocial impact of TV viewing. First, prosocial be-haviors are portrayed on TV programs far less frequently than aggressive behaviors; opportunities to learn prosocial behav-iors from televison are limited. Second, in the real world of TV watching, the relatively small number of prosocial pro-grams must compete with other kinds of televison programs, as well as other activities, for children's time. Children sim-ply may not watch the few prosocial programs that are tele-vised. Clearly, we are far from harnessing the power of televi-sion for prosocial uses.

Influences on Creativity

During the 1930s and 1940s, radio included adventure,   18
comedy, music, sports, and news programs. When TV was in-troduced, many of these programs were transported (with minor changes) into the new medium. Some early critics noted that radio programs required listeners to generate their own mental images of the activity depicted in the program, but TV provided viewers with ready-made images. Would this difference stifle viewers' creativity? Years later, we know the answer is yes. Although some studies find no link be-tween the amount of TV viewing and creativity, about half find a negative relation. As children watch more TV the ten-dency is for them to be less <u>creative</u> on measures of <u>divergent</u> thinking.

What explains this negative relation? Perhaps, as the   19
early critics observed, frequent TV viewers do not develop skill in creating their own images because TV provides ready-

made images. Another possibility is that children who watch TV frequently have less time for other activities that do stimulate creative thinking, such as reading. . . . Whatever the explanation, it is clear that creativity can be added to the list of developmental phenomena that can be harmed by excessive TV viewing.

Influences on Cognition

1969 was a watershed in the history of children's television. That year marked the appearance of a program produced by Children's Television Workshop that was designed to use the power of video and animation to foster such skills as recognizing letters and numbers, counting, and vocabulary in preschool children. Evaluations conducted in the early years of *Sesame Street* showed that it achieved its goals: Preschoolers who watched the show regularly were more proficient at the targeted academic skills than were children who watched less often. Frequent viewers also adjusted to school more readily, according to teachers' ratings. . . .   20

Building on the success of *Sesame Street*, Children's Television Workshop has developed a number of other successful programs. *Electric Company* was designed to teach reading skills, *3-2-1 Contact* focused on science and technology, and *Square One TV* aimed at mathematics. More recent programs have included *Reading Rainbow, Where in the World Is Carmen Sandiego?*, and *Bill Nye the Science Guy*. Programs like these leave little doubt that TV's socializing influence need not be limited to the learning of aggression and stereotypes. Children *can* learn academic skills and useful social skills, if parents insist that their youngsters be good viewers, and if they insist that TV improve the quality and variety of programs available for children and adolescents.   21

Check Your Understanding

Review

1. The article discusses six areas where television viewing influences behavior and attitudes. List these. (*Hint:* The first six paragraphs are concerned with one topic, suggested by the title.)

   1. _____

   2. _____

     3. _____

     4. _____

     5. _____

     6. _____

2. Of the six areas in item 1, the writers note that only two areas have some positive impact on behavior and attitudes. Write down these areas.

     1. _____

     2. _____

Fill in the Blanks

Use the words from the list to complete the sentences that follow. Cross out each word as you use it.

stereotyped   creative   aggressive   commercials   far less

1. Frequent exposure to television violence causes children

   to be more _____.

2. Women and the elderly are often _____

   on television.

3. _____ on television are effective

   sales tools with children.

4. Prosocial behavior is shown on television _____

   than aggressive behavior.

5. Listening to radio programs is a more _____

   activity than watching television.

Multiple Choice

Select the letter of the answer that best completes the statement.

_____ 1. The main idea of the entire article is:
   a. Television has great influence on the behaviors of the young.
   b. Television viewing should be restricted.
   c. No beneficial behavior results from television viewing.

_____ 2. Women on television are often portrayed as
   a. aggressive.
   b. passive and emotional.
   c. housewives.

_____ 3. The article is primarily supported by
   a. examples.
   b. research studies.
   c. personal opinion.

_____ 4. According to the article, television commercials frequently focus on
   a. cars.
   b. clothes.
   c. children's foods.

_____ 5. Which of the following is not an effect of frequent television viewing?
   a. Stereotyping minorities
   b. Increased creativity
   c. Increased aggressive behavior

True/False

Label the following statements as true or false according to the article.

_____ 1. Television bears a responsibility for tolerance of the increased aggression in children's behavior.

_____ 2. Television's view of the world is sometimes distorted.

_____ 3. Stereotyped television presentations may influence children's views.

_____ 4. Commercials are not effective sales tools with children.

_____ 5. Parents often buy a product children have seen on TV and consequently request.

_____ 6. Television can be used to promote healthy social behavior.

_____ 7. Radio is a more effective instrument for fostering creativity than televison.

_____ 8. The program *Sesame Street* is the only worthwhile program for developing children.

_____ 9. Children can learn useful social skills from watching television.

_____ 10. Parents have a responsibility to monitor the programs that children view.

Vocabulary

Circle the letter of the best synonym for the following words. Refer to their use in the article and use a dictionary as needed.

1. *portrayal*
   a. sketch
   b. characterization
   c. entrance way

2. *anecdote*
   a. short story
   b. joke
   c. medicine to counteract poison

3. *mayhem*
   a. crime
   b. mutilation
   c. killing

4. *aggressive*
   a. boss
   b. hostile
   c. assertive

5. *tolerance*
   a. charity
   b. acceptance of
   c. patience

6. *depiction*
   a. representation
   b. portrait
   c. drawing

7. *phenomenal*
   a. factual
   b. fantastic
   c. extraordinary

8. *divergent*
   a. differing
   b. contrary
   c. opposite

9. *potent*
   a. big
   b. powerful
   c. poisonous

10. *buffoon*
    a. a stupid person
    b. amusing fool
    c. character

Writing

1. Describe the benefits you derived from a televison program you watched as a youngster.
2. Write a paper defending or condemning the influence of a program currently shown on television.

Critical Thinking

1. Describe how you think televison programming could be improved. How might you bring your ideas into reality?
2. Should the government place more controls on television programming? Why or why not?

Reading Selection 2

Purpose

Read this article, which provides another point of view about television viewing. Pete Hamill, the author, was a newspaper reporter who wrote many news stories about drug-related crimes. He was troubled with the question of why the use of drugs continues to ruin so many lives. Finally, a possible answer occurred to him. Hamill wrote this article in 1990, when George Bush was President, and mentions other people in the news at that time, such as William Bennett, then Secretary of Education; Manuel Noriega, former president of Panama; the Sandinistas, the drug-connected former ruling party of Nicaragua; and the Medellin cartel, drug suppliers in Colombia. Plan to look for effects mentioned by Hamill.

Preview

1. Take a minute to skim the article for general content.
2. Check the questions and vocabulary that follow the selection.

Anticipate/Associate

1. A jack-in-the-box is a children's toy. When it is opened, a clown figure pops up. Television is sometimes referred to as the "box," and crack is a drug. What associations can you make between this toy and the title of the article?
2. What do you think are some of the reasons that people use drugs?

Crack and the Box

Pete Hamill

One sad rainy morning last winter, I talked to a woman who was addicted to crack cocaine. She was twenty-two,   1 stiletto-thin, with eyes as old as tombs. She was living in two rooms in a welfare hotel with her children, who were two, three, and five years of age. Her story was the usual tangle of human woe: early pregnancy, dropping out of school, vanished men, smack and then crack, tricks with johns in parked cars to pay for dope. I asked her why she did drugs. She shrugged in an empty way and couldn't really answer beyond "makes me feel good." While we talked and she told her tale of squalor, the children ignored us. They were watching television.

Walking back to my office in the rain, I brooded about   2
the woman, her zombielike children, and my own callous indifference. I'd heard so many versions of the same story that I almost never wrote them anymore; the sons of similar women, glimpsed a dozen years ago, are now in Dannemora or Soledad or Joliet; in a hundred cities, their daughters are moving into the same loveless rooms. As I walked, a series of homeless men approached me for change, most of them junkies. Others sat in doorways, staring at nothing. They were additional casualties of our time of plague, demoralized reminders that although this country holds only 2 percent of the world's population, it consumes 65 percent of the world's supply of hard drugs.

Why, for God's sake? Why do so many millions of Amer-   3
icans of all ages, races, and classes choose to spend all or part of their lives stupefied? I've talked to hundreds of addicts over the years; some were my friends. But none could give sensible answers. They stutter about the pain of the world, about despair or boredom, the urgent need for magic or pleasure in a society empty of both. But then they just shrug. Americans have the money to buy drugs; the supply is plentiful. But almost nobody in power asks, Why? Least of all, George Bush and his drug warriors.

William Bennett talks vaguely about the heritage of six-   4
ties permissiveness, the collapse of Traditional Values, and all that. But he and Bush offer the traditional American excuse: It Is Somebody Else's Fault. This posture set the stage for the self-righteous invasion of Panama, the bloodiest drug arrest in world history. Bush even accused Manuel Noriega of "poisoning our children." But he never asked *why* so many Americans demand the poison.

And then, on that rainy morning in New York, I saw an-   5
other one of those ragged men staring out at the rain from a doorway. I suddenly remembered the inert postures of the children in that welfare hotel, and I thought: television.

Ah, no, I muttered to myself: too simple. Something as   6
complicated as drug addiction can't be blamed on television.

Come on . . . but I remembered all those desperate places I'd visited as a reporter, where there were no books and a TV set was always playing and the older kids had gone off somewhere to shoot smack, except for the kid who was at the mortuary in a coffin. I also remembered when I was a boy in the forties and early fifties, and drugs were a minor sideshow, a kind of dark little rumor. And there was one major difference between that time and this: television.

We had unemployment then; illiteracy, poor living conditions, racism, governmental stupidity, a gap between rich and poor. We didn't have the all-consuming presence of television in our lives. Now two generations of Americans have grown up with television from their earliest moments of consciousness. Those same American generations are afflicted by the pox of drug addiction.   7

Only thirty-five years ago, drug addiction was not a major problem in this country. There were drug addicts. We had some at the end of the nineteenth century, hooked on the cocaine in patent medicines. During the placid fifties, Commissioner Harry Anslinger pumped up the budget of the old Bureau of Narcotics with fantasies of reefer madness. Heroin was sold and used in most major American cities, while the bebop generation of jazz musicians got jammed up with horse.   8

But until the early sixties, narcotics were still marginal to American life; they weren't the $120-billion market they make up today. If anything, those years have an eerie innocence. In 1955 there were 31,700,000 TV sets in use in the country (the number is now past 184 million). But the majority of the audience had grown up without the dazzling new medium. They embraced it, were diverted by it, perhaps even loved it, but they weren't *formed* by it. That year, the New York police made a mere 1,234 felony drug arrests; in 1988 it was 43,901. They confiscated ninety-seven *ounces* of cocaine for the entire year; last year it was hundreds of pounds. During each year of the fifties in New York, there were only about a hundred narcotics-related deaths. But by the end of the sixties, when the first generation of children *formed* by television had come to maturity (and thus to the marketplace), the number of such deaths had risen to 1,200. The same phenomenon was true in every major American city.   9

In the last Nielsen survey of American viewers, the average family was watching television seven hours a *day*. This has never happened before in history. No people has even been entertained for seven hours a day. The Elizabethans didn't go to the theater seven hours a day. The pre-TV generation did not go to the movies seven hours a day. Common   10 sense tells us that this all-pervasive diet of instant imagery, sustained now for forty years, must have changed us in profound ways.

Television, like drugs, dominates the lives of its addicts.   11
And though some lonely Americans leave their sets on without watching them, using them as electronic companions, television usually absorbs its viewers the way drugs absorb their users. Viewers can't work or play while watching television; they can't read; they can't be out on the streets, falling in love with the wrong people, learning how to quarrel and compromise with other human beings. In short, they are asocial. So are drug addicts.

One Michigan State University study in the early eight-   12
ies offered a group of four- and five-year-olds the choice of giving up television or giving up their fathers. Fully one third said they would give up Daddy. Given a similar choice (between cocaine or heroin and father, mother, brother, sister, wife, husband, children, job), almost every stoned junkie would do the same.

There are other disturbing similarities. Television itself   13
is a consciousness-altering instrument. With the touch of a button, it takes you out of the "real" world in which you reside and can place you at a basketball game, the back alleys of Miami, the streets of Bucharest, or the cartoony living rooms of Sitcom Land. Each move from channel to channel alters moods, usually with music or a laugh track. On any given evening, you can laugh, be frightened, feel tension, thump with excitement. You can even tune in *MacNeil/Lehrer* and feel sober.

But none of these abrupt shifts in mood is *earned*. They   14
are attained as easily as popping a pill. Getting news from television, for example, is simply not the same experience as reading it in a newspaper. Reading is *active*. The reader must decode little symbols called words, then create images or ideas and make them connect; at its most basic level, reading is an act of the imagination. But the television viewer doesn't go through that process. The words are spoken to him by Dan Rather or Tom Brokaw or Peter Jennings. There isn't much decoding to do when watching television, no time to think or ponder before the next set of images and spoken words appears to displace the present one. The reader, being active, works at his or her own pace; the viewer, being passive, proceeds at a pace determined by the show. Except at the highest levels, television never demands that its audience take part in an act of imagination. Reading always does.

In short, television works on the same imaginative and   15
intellectual level as psychoactive drugs. If prolonged televi-

sion viewing makes the young passive (dozens of studies indicate that it does), then moving to drugs has a certain coherence. Drugs provide an unearned high (in contrast to the earned rush that comes from a feat accomplished, a human breakthrough earned by sweat or thought or love).

And because the television addict and the drug addict are alienated from the hard and scary world, they also feel they make no difference in its complicated events. For the junkie, the world is reduced to him and the needle, pipe, or vial; the self is absolutely isolated, with no desire for choice. The television addict lives the same way. Many Americans who fail to vote in presidential elections must believe they have no more control over such a choice than they do over the casting of *L.A. Law.*   16

The drug plague also coincides with the unspoken assumption of most television shows: Life should be *easy.* The most complicated events are summarized on TV news in a minute or less. Cops confront murder, chase the criminals, and bring them to justice (usually violently) within an hour. In commercials, you drink the right beer and you get the girl. *Easy!* So why should real life be a grind? Why should any American have to spend years mastering a skill or a craft, or work eight hours a day at an unpleasant job, or endure the compromises and crises of a marriage? Nobody *works* on television (except cops, doctors, and lawyers). Love stories on television are about falling in love or breaking up; the long, steady growth of a marriage—its essential *dailiness*—is seldom explored, except as comedy. Life on television is almost always simple: good guys and bad, nice girls and whores, smart guys and dumb. And if life in the real world isn't that simple, well, hey, man, have some dope, man, be happy, feel good.   17

The doper always whines about how he *feels;* drugs are used to enhance his feelings or <u>obliterate</u> them, and in this the doper is very American. No other people on earth spend so much time talking about their feelings; hundreds of thousands go to shrinks, they buy self-help books by the millions, they pour out intimate confessions to virtual strangers in bars or discos. Our political campaigns are about emotional issues now, stated in the simplicities of adolescence. Even alleged statesmen can start a sentence, "I feel that the Sandinistas should . . . " when they once might have said, "I *think* . . . " I'm convinced that this <u>exaltation</u> of cheap emotions over logic and reason is one by-product of hundreds of thousands of hours of television.   18

Most Americans under the age of fifty have now spent their lives absorbing television; that is, they've had the   19 structures of drama pounded into them. Drama is always about conflict. So news shows, politics, and advertising are now all shaped by those structures. Nobody will pay attention to anything as complicated as the part played by Third World debt in the expanding production of cocaine; it's much easier to focus on Manuel Noriega, a character right out of *Miami Vice,* and believe that even in real life there's a Mister Big.

What is to be done? Television is certainly not going 20 away, but its addictive qualities can be controlled. It's a lot easier to "just say no" to television than to heroin or crack. As a beginning, parents must take immediate control of the sets, teaching children to watch specific television *programs,* not "television," to get out of the house and play with other kids. Elementary and high schools must begin teaching television as a subject, the way literature is taught, showing children how shows are made, how to <u>distinguish</u> between the true and the false, how to recognize cheap emotional <u>manipulation</u>. All Americans should spend more time reading. And thinking.

For years, the defenders of television have argued that 21 the networks are only giving the people what they want. That might be true. But so is the Medellin cartel.

Check Your Understanding

Review

Study the organization of the article by answering these questions.

1. Hamill considers a problem in the first five paragraphs.

   What is the problem? _____

   What is Hamill's answer? _____

2. Paragraphs 6–10 note comparisons and contrasts between the past (the 1940s and 1950s, when he was growing up) and the present. List a few of the contrasts.

   1940s–1950s   Present

   _____   _____

   _____   _____

_____	_____
_____	_____
_____	_____

3. In paragraphs 11–19, Hamill makes at least eight comparisons between television watching and drug use to support his answer as to why so many people are addicted to drugs. List the five you consider most important as support.

  1. _____

  2. _____

  3. _____

  4. _____

  5. _____

4. What three suggestions does Hamill make in paragraph 20 for changing television habits?

  1. _____

  2. _____

  3. _____

Fill in the Blanks

Fill in the blanks below with the word or words that best completes the meaning.

1. Hamill believes that drug _____ and

   television _____ are similar.

2. The traditional American excuse for doing something

   harmful is that it "_____ _____

   _____ _____."

3. The average American family watches television

   _____ hours a day.

4. Watching television is a passive experience, while read-

ing is an _____ one.

5. Americans, according to Hamill, are more interested in

feeling than in _____.

Multiple Choice

Select the letter of the answer that best completes the statement.

_____ 1. The main idea is:
    a. Drug addiction ruins lives.
    b. Television viewing should be controlled by the government.
    c. Television is a major factor in creating a drug culture.
    d. a and b above.

_____ 2. The article is primarily organized by
    a. Definition
    b. Comparison/contrast
    c. Examples
    d. Cause and effect

_____ 3. You can conclude from this article that Hamill
    a. is opposed to television viewing.
    b. believes that reading is more important than watching television.
    c. believes that drug users live wasted lives.
    d. b and c above.

_____ 4. Hamill's primary type of support for the points he makes is
    a. examples.
    b. authorities.
    c. statistical facts.
    d. opinions.

_____ 5. Hamill believes that
    a. television is the only cause of drug addiction.
    b. drug users should be sent to prison.
    c. controlling television viewing can help solve the drug problem.
    d. a and c above.

True/False

Label the following statements as true or false according to the article.

_____ 1. Drug users are stupid.

_____ 2. There is a connection between Third World debt and drug production.

_____ 3. Millions of Americans use drugs.

_____ 4. Solving our drug problem is simply a matter of controlling television use.

_____ 5. In the 1940s and 1950s, no one used drugs.

_____ 6. In the 1940s and 1950s, the United States faced the same problems that exist today, except for drug use.

_____ 7. Television dominates most people's lives.

_____ 8. Television requires considerable thinking.

_____ 9. Television leads people to believe that life should be easy.

_____ 10. The government should place controls on television viewing.

Vocabulary

Use the following words from the article to complete the sentences. First, check the words in context, then use the dictionary for unfamiliar words.

stupefied   demoralized   manipulation   exaltation
distinguish   diverted   obliterate   addiction
pervasive   dominate

1. The man was _____, whether by drugs

   or drink was not known.

2. A tornado can _____ an entire city

   block.

3. Sometimes a young man's thoughts are _____

   by a pretty girl.

4. Completing the Triathalon gave Sheila a feeling of

   _____.

5. People can suffer a(n) _____ to many

   substances.

6. Attempting to get others to submit to your ideas some-

   times requires _____.

7. A person or thing that controls us is said to

   _____ us.

8. The odor of perfume can be _____.

9. The team was _____ after their fifth

   defeat.

10. It is difficult to _____ between identi-

    cal twins.

Writing

1. Describe a kind of "addiction" you or someone you know
   may have had to something such as food, a physical activity,
   or video games.
2. Write a paragraph or essay to agree or disagree with Hamill's
   belief that considerable television viewing can lead to drug
   addiction. Support your idea with examples.

Critical Thinking

1. In the last paragraph Hamill says that television networks
   argue they are giving people what they want. Give reasons
   for agreeing or disagreeing with the networks' view.
2. What ideas do you have for controlling drug use in our country? You might want to brainstorm this question and then
   evaluate the ideas for cost and potential for success of your
   proposed solutions.
3. Are Hamill's suggestions for controlling television viewing practical? Why or why not? How is television watching
   controlled in your home? What suggestions do you have for
   controlling widespread television addiction?

Strategies for
Critical Reading

PART II

Chapter 5

Inference and Implied Main Ideas

Inspector Gregory to Sherlock Holmes: "Is there any point to which you would wish to draw my attention?"

Sir Arthur Conan Doyle

Sometimes writers don't make their point or clearly state their main idea in a topic sentence included in the paragraph. Like Inspector Gregory in the quotation above, you must learn to look closely at the details to determine the point or main idea. In the case of longer selections consisting of two or many more paragraphs, you will always need to grasp the central idea or main point by the process of drawing together major ideas and supporting details.

This chapter will help you:

- use the skills of analysis and synthesis to make valid inferences
- sequence ideas and place ideas in order
- work with transitions and key words to order paragraphs
- use analysis and synthesis to complete word analogies.

An old story tells of six blind men who approach an elephant. One grabs the elephant's trunk and cries, "The elephant is very like a snake." The second runs into the broad side of the elephant and declares, "No, you are mistaken. The elephant is very like a brick wall." The third blind man feels the elephant's tail and says, "You are both wrong. The elephant is like a thin rope." The fourth, grabs the elephant's ear and shouts, "You're all wrong. An elephant is like a huge fan." And the fifth, who has touched

the elephant's tusk, says, "The elephant is like a thin slippery rock." Finally the sixth, who has placed his arms around one of the elephant's legs, exclaims, "Surely, the elephant is like a tree trunk."

Whose conclusion is correct? They based their judgments of the elephant on their preview and perceptions, the information they received from their sense of touch. In addition, they each added information from associations, things experienced in the past. Unfortunately, each of the blind men held only a single part of the true picture of the elephant. Paying attention to and thinking about all the parts, then putting the parts together to see the whole picture, is important in making inferences and drawing conclusions about a writer's main idea or central point. This process of looking at parts and then putting the parts together in order to draw conclusions is called analysis and synthesis.

Analysis and Synthesis

You have been using the skills of analysis and synthesis all your life, even though you may not have used those terms. Analysis is the process of separating a thing or an event into its different parts. Each of the blind men focused on only one part of the whole elephant, and the judgments or inferences they made about the part they examined were correct as far as they went. The process of analysis requires that you look at *all* the separate parts. No wonder their judgments were incomplete and inaccurate.

Synthesis is the combining of parts, usually to make a new element, something not immediately evident from looking at the separate parts. If the six blind men had combined their observations of the parts of the elephant, they could have reached a more valid, but still incomplete, conclusion or synthesis about what an elephant is. They still needed more analysis to realize they had examined only one side of the elephant. Further analysis would have revealed that an elephant has two sides with one tail and trunk and two ears and tusks. When you are analyzing, be sure you have all the separate parts necessary to make a valid judgment.

Study this saying: "If it is bright and sunny after two cold and rainy days, it is probably Monday." You probably are not even aware of the analysis you bring to understanding this saying. No doubt you have had the experience of miserable weather ruining your weekend plans followed by wonderful weather on Monday when you have to return to work, the classroom, or both. Thus, your lightning-quick analysis, followed by a synthesis, brings a smile. You, too, have experienced what the writer has described.

We could not survive in daily life if we did not synthesize, draw conclusions, and make *inferences*. Consider the following situations:

1. Your friend says, "What do you think of my new outfit?"

You must decide whether to say that purple dots mixed with orange stripes make a striking outfit or to give your honest opinion that the outfit, particularly on your friend, is something less than flattering. You have to make an inference about the best response to make in the situation.

2. A friend or spouse asks, "Would you like to go to a movie tonight?"

You may want to consider whether the person really wants to go to a movie or would prefer, as you do, to stay home with popcorn and the VCR. A judgment is called for.

3. The college's star baseball pitcher asks you, "What did you think about my pitching in that game?"

Since your team lost, primarily because of his pitching, you will need to weigh whether to tell him exactly what you think or to encourage him by telling him, "Tomorrow's another day."

4. You're driving and see an icy patch in the road ahead.

Does the driver in front of you see the problem? If he does, will he slow down, slam on his brakes and slide, or decide to switch lanes? You need to be prepared to make some quick judgments.

5. Should you go out with friends tonight to celebrate someone's birthday or stay home and review for an important test tomorrow?

What things might you consider before making a decision?

To Celebrate   To Study

_____   _____

_____   _____

_____   _____

_____   _____

You are accustomed to making these kinds of inferences daily. You look beneath the surface of what is said, consider the situation, synthesize, and make an inference about the best response.

Here's another example to illustrate how you use the skills of analysis and synthesis every day. Pretend you're flipping the pages of a magazine and you see the ad on page 189. As you read about the qualities of the Heavenly Express, you are given some facts from the manufacturer's information. Given this information, you can synthesize—put together the claims made—to form a personal conclusion. Any of the following conclusions could be your synthesis because you are adding your personal experiences. All are valid conclusions for different people.

1. I would like more information.
2. Sounds like a car I would like.
3. This car is too expensive for me.
4. Is this for real?

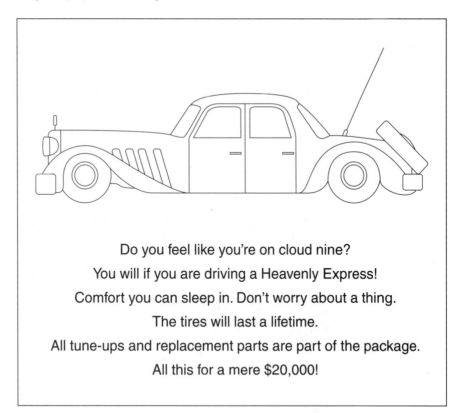

Do you feel like you're on cloud nine?
You will if you are driving a Heavenly Express!
Comfort you can sleep in. Don't worry about a thing.
The tires will last a lifetime.
All tune-ups and replacement parts are part of the package.
All this for a mere $20,000!

Analysis, then, is looking at the separate parts of the whole (in this case, the facts given about the advertised car) and attempting to see the relationship of the parts to the whole, your synthesis. Thus, you used the individual facts to arrive at a personal judgment about how the facts related to your interests. One of the difficulties in making inferences from reading material is that you should not, as you did with the car, bring in your own personal knowledge, background, and experience. You must develop your synthesis, your inference, only from the facts presented.

Inferring a Main Idea from Supporting Details

Develop the process of making inferences about the main idea sentence by thinking about the supporting details given in the paragraph. Putting the details together, you can get a good idea of the general topic and make up your own main-idea sentence to cover the details. Locating key words will assist your thinking. Use the first set of supporting details in the paragraphs that follow as an example.

Exercise 5-1   Using Supporting Details to Create a Main-Idea Sentence

For each list of supporting ideas, write a topic or subject, then a main-idea sentence to cover all the details given. The first set is completed as an example.

1. Details:
   a. Americans eat an average of 12 pounds of chocolate a year.
   b. Soldiers at war carry at least three chocolate bars in their packs.
   c. Chocolate has gone into outer space with the astronauts.
   d. More than 90 percent of Americans eat some chocolate every day.

   Topic: ___American chocolate eaters___

   Main-idea sentence: ___Chocolate is an important part of___

   ___American life.___

2. Details:
   a. Cigarettes contain nicotine, an addictive drug, which means that if you start smoking it is extremely difficult to stop.
   b. If the body absorbs too much nicotine at one time, the poison can kill immediately.
   c. Cigarettes also contain tar that coats the lungs, making it hard to breathe.

   Topic: _____

   Main-idea sentence: _____

   _____

3. Details:
   a. Gabby Street, an early catcher with the Washington Senators, once caught a ball that had been dropped 555 feet from the top of the Washington Monument.
   b. Jimmy Piersall, who played for the New York Mets, was so happy when he hit his 100th homer that he ran all the way around the bases backward.
   c. The St. Louis Browns once brought in a player who was only 43 inches tall. The pitcher couldn't pitch low enough for a strike, so the short player walked.

Topic: _____

Main-idea sentence: _____

_____

4. Details:
   a. Frederick Douglass, a former slave, worked hard for the Abolitionist cause before and after the Civil War and influenced eight presidents to improve conditions for African Americans.
   b. Major Martin Delany, one of the first African American commissioned officers in the Civil War, was a descendant of African royalty.
   c. Harriet Tubman, an escaped slave, returned to the South fifteen times to help lead others to freedom by the Underground Railroad.

   Topic: _____

   Main-idea sentence: _____

   _____

5. Details:
   a. Robots were first put to work in 1961, assembling cars in the Ford company plants.
   b. Robots pour hot metal and weld, sort and deliver mail; in Japan, robots make other robots.
   c. Farmers can use robots to sort and pack fruit and vegetables.
   d. Washing buildings, painting bridges, building dams, removing bombs before they explode, and handling radioactive material are other useful functions robots perform.

   Topic: _____

   Main-idea sentence: _____

   _____

6. Details:
   a. The longest tornado traveled 293 miles over a seven-hour period.
   b. Once in Missouri a railroad coach weighing 83 tons was carried 80 yards off its track by a tornado.

c. The most tornados ever recorded in a day was 138; they swooped through thirteen states in 1974.
d. In 1925, Missouri, Illinois, and Indiana were struck by the deadliest tornado, which killed 689 people, injured 2,000, and left 11,000 homeless.

Topic: _____

Main-idea sentence: _____

_____

_____

Supplying Implied Causes

In Chapter 4 you looked at the paragraph organization relating causes and effects. Sometimes there is an implied cause not mentioned by the writer. Use the strategy for making an inference to supply the missing cause.

Exercise 5-2   Supply the Missing Cause

In the following sentences, one cause and one effect are mentioned, but a missing cause is implied. The first example is completed for you.

1. Tom's bicycle tire was flat, so he filled it with air.

   CAUSE: _Tire was flat_____

   IMPLIED CAUSE: _He wanted to ride the bike._____

   EFFECT: _He filled the tire._____

Perhaps you thought of other possible implied causes, such as that someone else wanted to ride the bike or Tom was preparing to sell the bike. Given the facts in the sentence, all of these are possible implied causes.

2. Baseball season started today, so many people called in sick.

   CAUSE: _____

IMPLIED CAUSE: _____

EFFECT: _____

3. Because I had twisted my ankle, I went to the doctor.

   CAUSE: _____

   IMPLIED CAUSE: _____

   EFFECT: _____

4. José missed the party because he had a biology test the next day.

   CAUSE: _____

   IMPLIED CAUSE: _____

   EFFECT: _____

5. We didn't have cleaning materials in the house, so I went to the store.

   CAUSE: _____

   IMPLIED CAUSE: _____

   EFFECT: _____

6. The refrigerator was empty; Karen went to a restaurant.

   CAUSE: _____

   IMPLIED CAUSE: _____

   EFFECT: _____

7. Since she was unhappy with chances for promotion in her present occupation, Ms. Smedley recently returned to college to complete her baccalaureate degree.

   CAUSE: _____

   IMPLIED CAUSE: _____

   EFFECT: _____

8. Kenneth lost his contact lenses, so he bought a new pair.

CAUSE: _____

IMPLIED CAUSE: _____

EFFECT: _____

9. The rainstorm was violent, so drivers turned on their car lights.

CAUSE: _____

IMPLIED CAUSE: _____

EFFECT: _____

10. Helen tried out for the volleyball team hoping to get an athletic scholarship.

CAUSE: _____

IMPLIED CAUSE: _____

EFFECT: _____

11. Since real estate prices are good right now, Sandra is looking at homes.

CAUSE: _____

IMPLIED CAUSE: _____

EFFECT: _____

Making Valid Inferences

In the exercise on finding implied causes, you saw that several answers were possible from the stated facts. In paragraphs and longer passages, the details will help you to limit your choices and to make correct inferences based on the details provided. Try some analysis and synthesis to make an inference about the main idea in the following paragraph.

Regular exercise has been proven to lower high blood pressure because exercise relaxes the vascular system. Further, exercise increases the capacity of the heart's coronary arteries and increases the blood flowing to the heart. Moreover, dangerous blood clots are broken down by exercise, leading to a decrease in heart attacks. One expert says that those who improve their fitness through exercise have a better than 50 percent chance of reducing the risk of death from heart disease.

To analyze this paragraph, identify the particular facts related. (This paragraph has a basic listing organization, so a list is a good way to analyze and look at the parts.)

1. _____

2. _____

3. _____

4. _____

Looking at the separate parts you have listed, decide which of the following inferences are valid. Place a V in the blank beside those conclusions that can be correctly inferred from the paragraph as a whole.

_____ 1. Couch potatoes are risking heart problems.

_____ 2. A regular exercise program improves the heart.

_____ 3. Health benefits result from regular exercise.

_____ 4. I should jog a mile every day.

_____ 5. Regular exercise will help me lose weight.

_____ 6. All couch potatoes will have an early death.

The first three are valid conclusions or inferences to be drawn from the paragraph. The last three are not. Sentence 4 is too specific. Jogging might be good for you but dangerous for someone who has not been exercising regularly. Sentence 5 has been proven by other studies and may be a fact known to you, but it is not suggested by the facts given. Sentence 6 assumes too much; it jumps to a conclusion not suggested or implied. Jumping to conclusions is an exercise not recommended for careful readers.

Exercise 5-3   Making Valid Inferences

Read the following paragraphs and mark the valid inferences and conclusions with a V.

1. People once feared that shipbuilding would be hampered by the scarcity of tall trees for sailing masts, that railroads would be crippled by a shortage of timber for railroad ties, and the U.S. economy would grind to a halt with the exhaustion of coal. Yet people figured out how to switch to metal masts (and then steam power); they invented concrete railroad ties and built superhighways; and they found better ways to extract coal, as well as oil, gas, and other fuels. But these solutions brought new problems such as acid rain, dramatically rising atmospheric carbon dioxide, stripped lands and oil spills. Still technological optimists argue that industrial society will go on solving problems as they arise.

   —Joel E. Cohen, "Ten Myths of Population," *Discover*

   _____ a. Shipbuilders at one time used lumber for sailing masts.

   _____ b. The supply of lumber is limited.

   _____ c. Solutions to problems sometimes bring new problems.

   _____ d. People are resourceful in solving problems.

   _____ e. The writer believes that all technological problems can be solved.

2. Dr. John Morreall, a philosopher and laugh consultant, works with businesses like Kodak and Xerox and even the Internal Revenue to persuade them of the importance of laughter on the job. He believes that laughter helps the workers to be more creative as well as better problem solvers. Laughter can also ease the way during evaluations or whenever criticism is part of the job. Giving employees the freedom to laugh may be even more important than salary raises in keeping employees satisfied with the work environment.

   —Adapted from Natalie Angier,
   "A Universal Language," *The New York Times*

   _____ a. Many companies are encouraging laughter in the workplace.

   _____ b. Laughter can be healthy.

_____ c. Job evaluations should be laughing matters.

_____ d. Some connection can be made between the ability to laugh and the ability to think of creative solutions.

_____ e. Dr. Morreall is a successful businessman.

_____ f. Dr. Morreall is a creative consultant.

The ability to make inferences, as you have done in this exercise, will help you grasp the central point or main idea from written material.

Identifying an Unstated or Implied Main Idea

In a paragraph or longer passage with no stated main idea, the writer will have implied the main idea. You will need to study the details, look at the organization, and make an inference to determine the main idea. Evidence is provided that suggests something beyond what is stated. Use this important skill to face the challenge of finding unstated but implied ideas in a paragraph. Study the two following paragraphs and the explanations that follow.

1. Insects outnumber people 200 million to one. Ever wonder why we are so dreadfully outnumbered by these pests, who dine with us at a picnic and dine on us if they're mosquitoes? For one thing, plants and flowers would die out if they were not fertilized by insects. Some insects burrow in the ground, breaking up the hard ground and making it easier for plants to grow. If plants didn't grow and flourish, animals that feed on plants would also die. Without insects, birds that feed on insects would also die.

Analysis: The topic is clearly insects, and although one sentence talks about some annoying qualities of insects, the rest of the sentences point out how insects are helpful to plants, animals, and birds. The implied main idea is: Insects are beneficial to life on earth (or have some good points, or are necessary for the survival of life).

Before reading the next paragraph, recall that Amelia Earhart was an early woman pilot who was lost attempting to be the first woman to fly around the world at the equator.

2. When Amelia Earhart was a young girl, she, her sister, and her cousins built a homemade roller coaster. They nailed together wooden planks to reach from the top of the woodshed to form a kind of slide to the bottom. Then they put roller skate wheels on a box. When they got in the box at the top of the woodshed, the box flew down the slide. Earhart also enjoyed riding horses and playing baseball and football. These were not the usual sports for young girls at that time.

Analysis: The topic is Amelia Earhart. The paragraph is not about her whole life, but about some of the things she enjoyed doing as a young girl. The sports she enjoyed and the building of the roller coaster suggest that she liked adventure and doing things differently than other young girls. The paragraph tells nothing about her school or her family. The implied main idea is: As a young girl Amelia Earhart enjoyed being different (or being adventurous, or taking risks).

You may have written the implied ideas for these two paragraphs a little differently, as the words in parentheses suggest, but your sentence should express the same basic idea. We can risk conclusions and inferences if we think carefully about all the information given.

Exercise 5-4   Choosing the Best Implied Main Idea

The following paragraphs are followed by two possible implied main-idea sentences. Put a check mark before the sentence that best expresses the main idea.

1. On D-Day, June 6, 1944, Allied forces crossed the English Channel to begin the invasion of the German-held French coast of Normandy. Paratroopers were dropped behind the German lines at both ends of the 50-mile stretch of beach. Royal Air Force bombers attacked the area with bombs to distract the Germans from the coast and destroy some of their weapons. Small boats carried a few thousand American, British, and Canadian soldiers to attack the beach. Even though the soldiers had pills for seasickness, the sea was so rough that many were sick. Jumping over the sides of the boats, the men waded through shallow water, carrying their rifles over their heads.

    _____ a. On D-Day, June 6, 1944, the Allied forces attacked the Germans at Normandy.

    _____ b. The Allies used many tactics to arrive at Normandy on D-Day.

2. Genetic engineers have been working with DNA for more than fifty years. DNA, or deoxyribonucleic acid, is unique in every one of the 6 billion people in the world, unless they are identical twins. When human life begins as a tiny cell, that cell contains forty-six chromosomes, twenty-three each from the male and female donors of the sperm and egg. This original cell grows and multiplies until the body is made up of millions of cells, each containing forty-six chromosomes and the unique DNA.

_____ a. Scientists experiment with DNA contained in all living cells.

_____ b. Each of the millions of cells in a human body contains the same unique DNA.

3. The smallest mammal on land, and also the fiercest, eats all day. The short-tailed shrew and the least shrew are smaller than mice. A toothbrush or a ballpoint pen may weigh as much an one of these adult shrews. The pigmy shrew weighs about as much as a penny. But whatever its weight, the shrew must eat about its own weight in food each day. With its poisonous bite, sharp, pointed teeth, and huge appetite, the shrew tackles its weight in insects, spiders, snails, worms, and mice.

_____ a. The shrew is a small, fierce mammal.

_____ b. The shrew, though the smallest mammal, eats its weight in food each day.

4. An ancient fort was recently discovered at Parris Island, South Carolina The fort was built in 1562, well before the settlement in Jamestown in 1607. The French explorer Jean Ribault named the fort Charlesfort, left twenty-seven men there, and returned to France for supplies. But he faced many problems at home and could not return with more settlers and supplies. Eventually, the fort was abandoned, and the original settlers returned home to France.

_____ a. Early settlers faced many hardships in the New World.

_____ b. Charlesfort, founded in 1562, was abandoned for lack of supplies and settlers.

5. What we call "gender" encompasses biological sex but goes beyond it to the socially prescribed roles deemed appropriate for each sex by the culture in which we live. Complicating the issue is that only the broad outlines of gender roles are

drawn by the larger society. The gender roles we each carry out are highly individualistic, built on our biological and physical makeup, appearance and personality, life experiences such as work and education, and history of sexual and romantic interactions. Each element influences how others perceive us as a man or a woman and how we perceive other's intentions and expectations for us.

—Mark B. White and Kirsten J. Tyson-Rawson, "A Peace Plan for the Gender Wars," *Psychology Today*

_____ a. Gender is not just biological; it is influenced by society and the characteristics of the individual.

_____ b. Gender involves others' perceptions of the individual.

Supplying an Implied Main Idea

A more difficult step is to write your own idea of the main idea of the paragraph. Use these questions to help your discovery process.

1. Does the organization of the paragraph suggest the topic?
2. What is the topic of the paragraph?
3. What details support this topic?

Exercise 5-5   Writing an Implied Main Idea Sentence

Use the three questions to guide you in identifying the paragraph organization, determining the topic, and using the details to determine the main idea of the paragraphs that follow.

1. In Alaska, bears have been known to walk 15 miles to find ripe blueberries. The red-backed vole that also lives in Alaska likes blueberries so well that its teeth remain blue all summer. Birds like the cedar waxwing can eat all the berries on a single bush. Native Americans liked wild blueberries, too. They not only ate them fresh, they also dried the berries in the sun, mashed them into powder, and flavored stews and puddings with them.

Topic: _____

Implied main idea: _____

Supporting details: _____

_____

_____

2. Scientists who study the arrangement of the atoms that make up crystals are called crystallographers. They study the crystals that make up salt, sugar, sand, rocks, jewels, and snowflakes. In fact, most nonliving substances in solid form are made of crystals. The atoms or molecules in a crystal are arranged in a particular pattern that is repeated over and over throughout the whole crystal. For one thing, the study of crystals has led to the development of synthetic, or artificial, rubies and diamonds.

Topic: _____

Implied main idea: _____

Supporting details: _____

_____

_____

3. A strong, intelligent wolf is the leader of a wolf pack. His mate for life is the second most important member. She is the only female in the pack allowed to have pups. She may have as many as six pups, which she doesn't leave for at least two weeks after birth. Other members of the pack bring food to leave outside the den. Once the pups' eyes are open, other members of the pack help the mother watch and feed the pups. They even show great patience in playing games with the young wolves.

Topic: _____

Implied main idea: _____

Supporting details: _____

_____

_____

4. More than 200,000 different species of fungi exist in the world. The most familiar forms of fungi are mushrooms, toadstools, mold, mildew, and rust. Fungi do not need light like plants, nor do they eat food like animals. Instead, they subsist on dead or living materials. Fungi help dead trees and leaves to decay and add nourishment to the soil. Living plants like orchids, strawberries, corn, tomatoes, and apple trees grow better with the help of fungi feeding on their roots, producing foods that the plants absorb. However, fungi can also destroy trees like the birch and elm and food crops like wheat, rye, and potatoes.

Topic: _____

Implied main idea: _____

Supporting details: _____

_____

_____

5. The island of Madagascar, 1000 miles long and about the size of Texas, is located just below the equator in the Indian Ocean. The island was formed about 95 million years ago when it broke off and floated away from Africa. On Madagascar you can find grasslands, rain forests, mountain forests, and dry brush. With this variety of ecosystems, the island is home to 150,000 plants and animals that are not found elsewhere in the world. A few years ago, fishermen in Madagascar caught a fish that scientists thought had become extinct 70 million years ago.

Topic: _____

Implied main idea: _____

Supporting details: _____

_____

_____

Discuss with group members the answers to the preceding exercises. Group members will not always have written the implied main idea in exactly the same way. Analyze the different responses to be sure they are reasonable.

The Sequence or Order of Ideas

Chapter 4 introduced the different ways of ordering ideas. Sorting out the order of ideas is often important to understanding complex textbook material. You have done some work with sequential order, which may be by alphabet; by numbers; by procedure, as in directions; by position, necessary for reading maps; and by size or weight, as well as by time, place, importance, and process, as discussed in Chapter 4. Three vocabulary words frequently used in textbooks are helpful in understanding order:

Precede   Remember that the suffix *pre-* means before.

Cede, a Latin root, means to go.

When one thing precedes another, it goes or comes before the other.

Example: Numerically, one precedes two.

Subsequent   The prefix *sub-* means "under," "below," or "beneath."

Sequ, another Latin root, means to follow, as one event follows another in sequence.

The root and prefix together, *subsequ*, mean something that follows another, or is after another.

Example: Numerically, two is subsequent to one.

Respectively   This word has little to do with the respect we give to figures of authority. It has a special meaning of its own, and that is "in the order given."

Example: "For dinner I ate ice cream, some vegetables, and a lamb chop, respectively."

The speaker is making clear that, strangely enough, dessert was eaten first.

One more technique will help you in working out problems of order. Look at these two sentences.

In alphabetical arrangement, A is followed by B, which is
followed by C.

In alphabetical arrangement, C follows B, which follows A.

Both sentences describe the same order, but the letters being discussed are in reverse order. Notice the construction *is followed by*
in the first sentence and *follows* in the second sentence. This
change of the verb, from what is called passive voice, to active
voice, makes a difference in the order of the objects mentioned, but
not in their actual, or real order. Look at these two sentences using
the verb *preceded.*

In alphabetical arrangement, A precedes B, which precedes C.

In alphabetical arrangement, C is preceded by B, which is
preceded by A.

Again the use of the passive verb form *is preceded by* and the
active form *precedes* changes the order in which the letters are
mentioned. Look for various forms of the verb *to be* (such as *is,*
was, are, or *were*) followed by the preposition *by.* Noticing the passive construction should alert you to items listed in what you
might consider reverse order.

Exercise 5-6   Understanding Confusing Order

*Each of the items that follows contains a description of some
kind of order. Put the ideas in the appropriate order or sequence.
Making a chart will help you order the items. Sometimes a first,
temporary chart will help with more complicated orderings with
more than three items. Study the two examples that follow:*

I. Mary is taller than Sandra but shorter than Cassandra.

Arrange the girls with the tallest first.

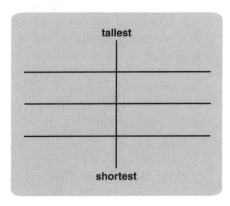

The first information is that Mary is taller than Sandra, so you would make a sketch showing this fact:

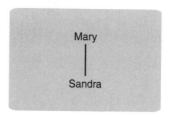

Next, you know that Mary is shorter than Cassandra, so you complete the figure as follows:

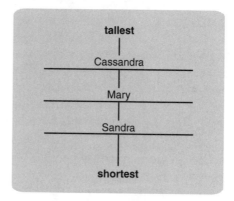

II. The Civil War, which began in 1861, preceded the Emancipation Proclamation by two years and the Alaska Purchase by six years.

Since *preceded* means "came before," you know that the Civil War began before the Emancipation Proclamation was issued. Since the second part of the sentence does not have a verb, you know that *preceded* is understood. With this information, you can not only sequence but date the events as follows:

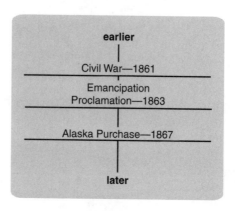

Work the following problems by yourself, then check them with your group. The examples will get increasingly more difficult, so work slowly and thoughtfully. Underline key ideas, draw lines, and make first sketches of relationships that are clear, as in example A earlier.

1. The planet Venus is closer to the sun than Earth but not as close as Mercury.

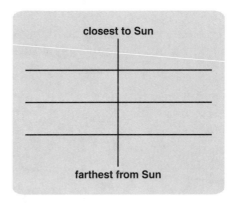

2. In the dictionary the word *halo* precedes *harbor*, and *handle* precedes *harbor*.

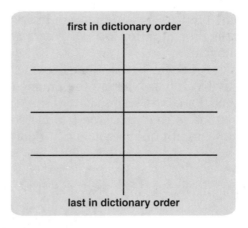

3. James Buchanan was the fifteenth U.S. President. Following him were Abraham Lincoln, Andrew Johnson, and Ulysses S. Grant, respectively.

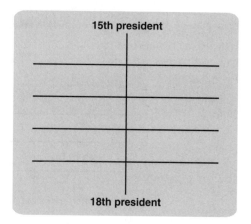

4. The state court structure consists of four courts, ranging from the highest court to the lowest. A case might enter the lowest court, the municipal court, and proceed to the State Supreme Court after passing through the circuit or county court and the appeals court, respectively.

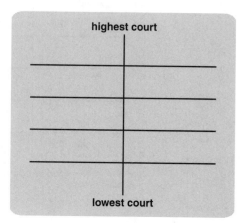

5. In 1961, the first American man in space was Alan Shepard, who was preceded by the Russian cosmonaut, Yuri Gagarin. They were followed in 1969 by the first men on the moon, Neil Armstrong, Edwin Aldrin, and Michael Collins.

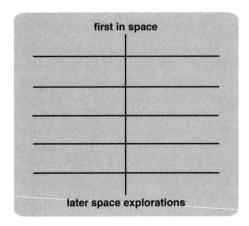

6. Brazil, whose capital is Brasília, is the largest country in square miles on the continent of South America. The Republic of Colombia is smaller than the country of Argentina, whose capital is Buenos Aires. The Republic of Peru is larger than Colombia but smaller than Argentina.

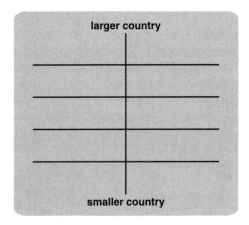

7. Amelia Earhart was the first woman to fly solo over the Atlantic ocean. Earlier, Charles Lindbergh made a nonstop, solo flight across the Atlantic in 1927. Leonardo da Vinci, the famous painter, actually designed an airplane in the fifteenth century. But it was not until the Wright brothers, Orville and Wilbur, made the first powered and controlled flights in 1903 that flying an aircraft became a reality.

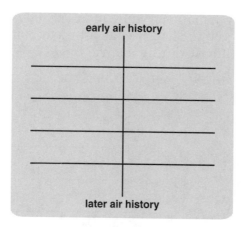

8. Because of family moves, Angelo has attended many colleges. In 1991, he went to school in New York City. Several years before that, he attended schools in Dallas and then successively in Miami, Boston, and Los Angeles. However, the year before he was in Los Angeles was the year he spent in New York City.

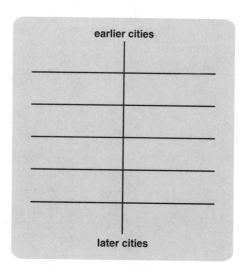

9. Hung in the Museum of American History in Washington in 1907, the 48-foot flag called the "Star-Spangled Banner" was made by Mary Young Pickersgill and her 13-year-old daughter, Caroline. They finished it just a month before it flew over Baltimore's Fort McHenry. Subsequently, Francis Scott Key wrote

our national anthem, "The Star-Spangled Banner" when he saw the flag after an all-night bombardment of the fort by the British during the War of 1812. Write the four events in order.

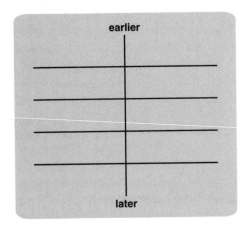

10. In an opinion survey grading the qualities of presidents, Abraham Lincoln received the highest rating. Lincoln was succeeded by Franklin Delano Roosevelt. Ranked at the end of the list was Richard Nixon. In the middle were Ronald Reagan, George Bush, and Bill Clinton. Reagan succeeded Clinton, who was preceded by Bush.

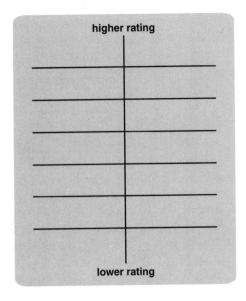

Working with Transitions and Key Words to Order Paragraphs

Transitions and key words are important in connecting ideas and making sense of the ideas in a paragraph. Sometimes the arrangement of the paragraph by chronology, examples, listing, cause-and-effect, and other kinds of order is useful in sorting out ideas. Put together the skills you have learned in Chapters 3 and 4 to reorder the following sentences so that they form a logical, ordered paragraph.

Exercise 5-7 Ordering Ideas

First, read all the sentences in each group carefully and locate the sentence that appears to be the main idea, and then underline supporting words and ideas. Link ideas by drawing lines between sentences to show connections. Then number the sentences in the order they should appear in a paragraph. The following example is marked for you.

___3___ For example, family members should practice crawling through the house in the event the rooms are filled with smoke.

___2___ These routes should be planned and practiced periodically.

___1___ Every family should plan and practice escape routes from their house in the event of fire.

___4___ They should also learn how to move through the house in darkness because every minute spent in a burning house means extra danger.

You might find other key words that are important to linking the ideas, but those underlined are essential to understanding the order of the sentences.

Group 1

_____ Finally, pictures of Thanksgiving and Christmas holidays are wonderful, but sometimes it is hard to tell one year from another.

_____ Looking at photograph albums is a real trip down memory lane.

_____ I remember events from the lives of the children as I see them grow from album to album.

_____ Next, pictures of family vacations recall for me places we've been, things we've seen, and the seemingly end-less complaints of tired children.

Group 2

_____ Such programs often ignore alcohol, a substance that is addictive and even more likely to harm.

_____ Drug awareness programs for the young often focus on illegal drugs like cocaine, heroin, and marijuana.

_____ For example, suicide and automobile crashes cause more than 10,000 deaths of young people each year.

_____ In fact, alcohol is a contributing factor in the deaths of many young people.

Group 3

_____ A unit of measure for the amount of energy we obtain from food is called a calorie.

_____ In contrast, each time your body uses an extra 3,500 calories in exercise, you lose a pound.

_____ Each time you eat 3,500 more calories than your body needs to maintain weight, you gain a pound.

_____ Each pound of body fat contains about 3,500 calories.

Group 4

_____ The exercise course allows the dogs to use a variety of muscles.

_____ The club includes treadmills, a lap pool, massage facili-ties, and an outdoor exercise course.

_____ Would you believe an exercise club for dogs?

_____ A fitness center for dogs called The Total Dog is located in Los Angeles.

Group 5

_____ So she decided to tutor students having difficulty in school.

_____ She had majored in education and psychology.

_____ A year ago, Melanie graduated from college.

_____ However, this fall she couldn't find an opening in the local school district.

_____ She finds the work enjoyable, and it provides an adequate income.

Group 6

_____ As a result, you will find landscapes with features of varying ages produced by forces that are no longer active.

_____ These landforms were created by different forces acting on the earth's surface.

_____ The earth's surface consists of many different landforms.

_____ Scientists in the past believed that large landforms, such as mountains, were created suddenly as a result of cataclysmic events.

_____ Now the theory is that these landforms evolved very slowly.

Group 7

_____ First of all, the cockroach is a survivor.

_____ How has the cockroach managed to survive for millions of years?

_____ It has survived longer than man and may well outlive the human race.

_____ The cockroach you just crunched under your heel is no ordinary bug.

_____ For one thing, it has adapted and continues to adapt to changing conditions.

_____ In fact, eating a cockroach would probably make anyone sick.

_____ Also, it has few natural enemies; birds and mammals get sick from eating cockroaches.

Group 8

_____ Even after the lights go out and the house has quieted down, the puppy continues to moan.

_____ Every night when the puppy is placed in its box, it begins to howl, yip, and whine.

_____ Since it is impossible to sleep while listening to a heartbreaking "woo-wooo," the family begins to suffer from loss of sleep.

_____ Buying a new puppy can have drastic effects in a quiet household.

_____ As a consequence, everyone becomes hostile, short-tempered, depressed, and irritable.

_____ For one thing, the puppy keeps the entire family awake for at least two solid weeks.

Group 9

_____ First of all, don't go to a popular restaurant where your service might be rushed.

_____ And finally, bringing a book to read will make the experience more pleasurable.

_____ Dining alone at a restaurant occurs more frequently than you might believe.

_____ Instead, try a small restaurant where the service is more personal and lone diners are a more common sight.

_____ Many lone diners note that the dining experience was not always pleasant.

_____ Several things can be done to make the experience more enjoyable.

_____ You could even call ahead to ask whether the restaurant encourages solo dining.

Group 10

_____ "For the third time, John," she said, "roast beef and mashed potatoes."

_____ When he heard no reply, he walked into the dining room and repeated the question.

_____ The story is told of a man who was convinced his wife had a hearing problem.

_____ Again, there was no reply, so he went to the kitchen, where his wife, at the stove, had her back to him.

_____ "What's for dinner, honey?" he said in a loud voice.

_____ She turned around to face him.

_____ Arriving home from work, he decided to test her, and asked quite loudly, "What's for dinner, honey?"

When you have completed ordering the preceding paragraphs, read them over to yourself to be sure you are satisfied that the order makes good sense. Discussing your order with group members may give you additional clues in finding order.

Inferring Word Relationships: Analogies

You have already used your skills of inferring when you determine the meaning of a word from context. Now, continue to use the concepts of analyzing and synthesizing to see the relationships between pairs of words. Analogies are often used for test items and in sentences that make comparisons. Seeing relationships and making associations are skills we use every day. If you check the weather before going out in the morning, you might say, "If it is raining, I will take an umbrella; or if the sun is shining, I'll wear a hat." You have just made an analogy. An *analogy* is an unstated (implied) similarity between two pairs of unlike things. In this example you related rain to umbrella and sun to hat. By analogy, you associate rain with the need for protection with an umbrella. You associate sun with the need for protection with a hat.

Analogies can be written in two forms. The first uses words and the second uses symbols to stand for words. Look at the two examples.

1. Rain is to umbrella as sun is to hat. (Umbrellas and hats provide protection in different kinds of weather.)
2. Rain:umbrella::sun:hat.

The symbol: stands for the words *is to* and the symbol :: stands for *as*, which suggests that a relationship between the two pairs of words can be made.

You synthesize the relationship between the pairs by noting that though the weather is different, it influences a choice of clothing in both cases. Many different kinds of relationships between the pairs of words can exist. Examples of the most common types follow.

1. courage:bravery::charity:love

   Each word in each pair is a *synonym* of the other. The pairs of words are related because they are both pairs of synonyms.

2. tall:short::thin:fat

   Each word in the pair is opposite in meaning or an *antonym* of the other. The pairs of words are related because they are both pairs of antonyms.

3. finger:hand::toe:foot

   The relationship within the pairs is that of a part to the whole. The pairs of words are related because they both describe the relationship of a part to the whole.

4. week:weak::hear:here

   The relationship is that each pair of words sounds alike but is spelled differently; they are *homonyms.* The pairs of words are related because they are both pairs of homonyms.

Exercise 5-8   Working with Analogies

Now try analyzing and synthesizing the following analogies. Remember to study each pair first to see the relationship between the two words in the pair. Then see if that same relationship exists between the pairs. (The relationship could be something other than those in the examples just given.) Write the relationship you find on the line before the analogy. You should recognize some vocabulary words from earlier chapters.

_____ 1. quiet:silent::twist:turn

_____ 2. one:won::sail:sale

_____ 3. principal:school::captain:ship

_____ 4. courage:fear::hate:love

_____ 5. guitarist:band::citizen:nation

_____ 6. tentative:uncertain::retain:keep

_____ 7. exhaust:refresh::isolate:bring together

_____ 8. expect:anticipate::permit:allow

_____ 9. unique:unusual::erupt:explode

_____ 10. ambiguous:clear::feasible:impossible

Now use your skills to complete the following analogies. The first one is completed as an example.

1. brush:paint::hammer:_____nail_____

   You use a brush to paint and you use a hammer to nail something.

2. bear:mammal::robin:_____

3. decay:growth::failure:_____

4. rose:dandelion::flower:_____

5. duet:quartet::two:_____

6. dominate:outdo::potent:_____

7. precede: before::subsequent:_____

8. word:sentence::sentence:_____

9. analysis:synthesis::separate:_____

10. trivial:important::responsible:_____

Chapter Review

Label the following statements as true or false.

_____ 1. Analysis is the cognitive process of taking ideas apart.

_____ 2. Synthesis involves putting ideas together to form a unity.

_____ 3. The details of a passage are of no help in determining in implied main idea.

_____ 4. All inferences are equally valid.

_____ 5. An analogy is an unstated relationship between two dissimilar things.

_____ 6. Making inferences requires making associations.

_____ 7. Finding an unstated main idea requires making inferences.

_____ 8. Identifying the topic of a passage is of no help in determining an unstated main idea.

_____ 9. Finding the main idea of paragraphs will help in understanding difficult reading material.

_____ 10. *D* precedes *A, B,* and *C* in the alphabet.

Reading Selection 1

Purpose

Drinking on college campuses remains a problem. In this selection from a psychology text, the author examines the effects of drinking on the mind and body. Read for information about the effects of alcohol.

Preview

Before reading this selection, first preview the headings, the underlined vocabulary, and the questions at the end of the selection.

Are any of the vocabulary words familiar? Read the context around the word for clues to the word's meaning.

Anticipate/Associate

1. What do you think are some of the social effects of alcohol?
2. What might be some of the medical effects of alcohol?
3. What do you suppose is the difference between a problem drinker and an alcoholic?
4. Have you had any experiences yourself, or with others, in the consumption of alcohol?

Alcohol

Lester Lefton

The students at my daughters' high school wore black   1
arm bands to show they mourned the death of their sopho-
more friend Mark Smock. At 15 years of age, with a learner's
permit to drive, Mark Smock crashed into a telephone pole on
a poorly lit street just two miles from his home. It was later
learned that his blood alcohol level was exceedingly high. A

high school student crashing a car, getting killed and maybe even killing or seriously injuring a friend in the front seat is a tale told all over this country, every year in every community.

Alcohol consumption in the United States has been at an all-time high for more than a <u>decade</u>. According to the U.S. Department of Health and Human Services, about 80 percent of <u>urban</u> U.S. adults report having used alcohol at some time; it is estimated that 10 million people over age 18 in the United States are problem drinkers or alcoholics (defined and discussed shortly). Each year, surveys show that about one-fourth of eighth-grade students and more than one-third of tenth-grade students reported having had five or more drinks on at least one occasion during the previous two weeks.

Alcohol is the most widely used sedative-hypnotic. A **sedative-hypnotic** is any class of drugs that relax and calm people and, in higher doses, induce sleep. Because alcohol is readily available, relatively inexpensive, and socially accepted, <u>addiction</u> to this drug is easy to establish and maintain. In fact, most Americans consider some alcohol consumption appropriate; they often consume alcoholic beverages before, during, and after dinner, at weddings and funerals, at religious events and during sports events.

Effects of Alcohol

Alcohol is a depressant that decreases <u>inhibitions</u> and thus increases some behaviors that are normally under tight control. For example, it may <u>diminish</u> people's social inhibitions and make them less likely to restrain their <u>aggressive</u> impulses. . . . The <u>physiological</u> effects of alcohol vary, depending on the amount of alcohol in the bloodstream and the gender and weight of the user. . . . After equal amounts of alcohol consumption, women have higher blood alcohol levels than men do, even allowing for differences in body weight; this occurs because men's bodies typically have a higher percentage of fluid than do women's. With less blood and other fluids in which to <u>dilute</u> the alcohol, women may end up with higher blood alcohol concentrations with fewer drinks than men. . . .

With increasing amounts of alcohol in the bloodstream, people typically exhibit progressively slowed behavior; often they exhibit severe motor disturbances, such as staggering. A blood alcohol level greater than 0.10 percent (0.1 milligram of alcohol per 100 milliliters of blood) usually indicates that the person has consumed too much alcohol to function responsibly. In most states, a 0.10 percent blood alcohol level legally defines intoxication; police officers may arrest drivers who are found to have this level of blood alcohol.

The nervous system becomes less sensitive to, or ac-   6
commodates, alcohol with increased usage. After months or
years of drinking, drug tolerance develops and a person has to
consume ever-increasing amounts of alcohol to achieve the
same effect. Thus, when not in a an alcoholic state, a heavy
drinker develops anxiety, cravings, and other withdrawal
symptoms. . . .

Problem Drinkers Versus Alcoholics

Alcohol-related problems are medical, social, or psycho-   7
logical problems associated with alcohol use. A person who
shows an alcohol-related problem such as missing work occasionally because of hangovers, spending a paycheck to buy
drinks for friends, or losing a driver's license because of
drunk driving is abusing alcohol. Alcohol-related problems
caused by <u>chronic</u> (repeated) alcohol abuse may include liver
<u>deterioration</u>, memory loss, and significant mood swings. . . .
A person with alcohol-related problems, a problem drinker,
who also has a physiological and <u>psychological</u> need to consume alcohol and to experience its effect is an **alcoholic.** All
alcoholics are problem drinkers, but not all problem drinkers
are alcoholics. Without alcohol, alcoholics develop physiological withdrawal symptoms. In addition, they often develop tolerance; a single drink or even a few will not affect them. . . .

Social and Medical Problems

From both a medical and a psychological standpoint, al-   8
cohol abuse is one of the greatest social problems in the
United States. Between 30 and 40 percent of the homeless are
people with alcohol problems. . . . Drunkenness is the biggest
law enforcement problem today, accounting for millions of
arrests each year. The Department of Transportation has estimated that alcohol is involved in more than 39,000 automobile deaths each year. Although the number of deaths caused
by alcohol-related accidents has decreased in the last few
years, the number in the next three years will still exceed the
American death toll of the Vietnam War. In addition people
involved in violent crimes and suicide are often found to have
been drinking.

Although alcoholism is seen as a social disease because   9
of its <u>devastating</u> social consequences, it is also a medical
problem. Biomedical researchers look for the effects of alcohol on the brain, as well as anything about the brains and
basic genetics of alcoholics that may predispose them to alcoholism. . . . Researchers know that chronic excessive drink-

ing is associated with loss of brain tissue, liver <u>malfunctions</u> and <u>impaired</u> <u>cognitive</u> and motor abilities.

Check Your Understanding

Review

Paragraph 1

    1. What was the effect of Mark Smock's drinking? _____

    2. What three causes contributed? _____

                                              _____

                                            _____

Paragraphs 2 and 3

    1. Using your experience and facts in both paragraphs, make some inferences about what causes people, young and old, to drink.

        Causes: _____

                _____

                _____

    2. List three effects of alcohol consumption.

        _____

        _____

        _____

Paragraphs 4–7

    1. What are two psychological effects of drinking?

        _____

        _____

2. What physiological effects are mentioned?

_____   _____

3. What causes women to reach higher blood alcohol levels when they drink the same amount of alcohol as men?

_____

Paragraphs 8–9

1. What are the social effects of heavy drinking?

_____   _____

_____   _____

2. What are the medical effects of alcohol abuse?

_____   _____

_____   _____

Multiple Choice

Select the letter of the answer that best completes the statement.

_____ 1. The main idea of the article is that
   a. alcoholism is a social disease.
   b. alcoholism causes many problems.
   c. alcohol consumption is at an all-time high.

_____ 2. The writer is
   a. opposed to drinking.
   b. concerned about problems caused by alcohol consumption.
   c. overstating the case against alcohol.

_____ 3. In paragraph 2, the topic sentence is
   a. sentence 1
   b. sentence 2
   c. sentence 3

_____ 4. You can infer that
   a. the writer's daughters drink.
   b. the writer has been a problem drinker.
   c. alcoholism is an expensive social and medical problem.

_____ 5. The purpose of paragraph 7 is
   a. to discuss the problems associated with abusing alcohol.
   b. to explain the difference between problem drinkers and alcoholics.
   c. to warn against drinking.

True/False

Mark the following statements as true or false.

_____ 1. The story of the high school student in paragraph 1 is intended as a typical example.

_____ 2. All problem drinkers are alcoholics.

_____ 3. An inference from the article is that you should never take a drink.

_____ 4. One cannot become addicted to alcohol.

_____ 5. Alcoholics cause problems to others as well as to themselves.

_____ 6. Alcohol has no effect on the brain.

_____ 7. Men are better drinkers than women.

_____ 8. One who abuses alcohol is always an alcoholic.

_____ 9. Someone with a blood alcohol level of 0.10 does not function responsibly.

_____ 10. Drunk driving is the only law enforcement problem related to alcohol consumption.

Vocabulary

Use the ten words listed here and introduced in this reading to complete the sentences that follow. You may need to change the endings of some words to use them correctly in the sentences.

inhibitions   malfunctions   cognitive   deterioration
devastating   addiction   dilute   physiological
diminish   psychological

1. I plan to take my car to my mechanic since the engine appears to be _____.

2. Alicia found the death of her pet bird a(n) _____

   experience .

3. Terry _____ his coffee with water so that he doesn't get too much caffeine.

4. A(n) _____ effect is one that affects our bodies.

5. Some people suffer from drug _____.

6. A(n) _____ problem relates to the functioning of our minds.

7. Marsha had no _____ about questioning things she did not understand.

8. Someone with _____ hearing can still function effectively with a hearing aid.

9. Her _____ skills were improved as she improved her ability to analyze.

10. Since the house had had no improvements made since 1970, its _____ had been rapid.

Complete the following analogies:

1. decade: ten::century:_____

2. city:farm::_____:rural

3. habitual:continuing::_____:long lasting

4. love:hate::passive:_____

5. damage:ruin::weakness:_____

Writing

1. Write a paragraph about the social effects of alcohol. Give specific examples of some of the problems.
2. Write a paragraph comparing and contrasting problem drinkers with alcoholics.

3. Describe the worst problem, as you see it, that problem drinkers cause for themselves and for others.

Critical Thinking

1. What can be done to stop alcohol consumption by teenagers?
2. What do you believe causes people to begin drinking?

Reading Selection 2

Purpose

The following article examines the issue of conformity, both its good and bad aspects. The selection is taken from *Beyond Feelings: A Guide to Critical Thinking*. The author, Vincent Ryan Ruggiero, first defines conformity, then discusses how conformity is both necessary and dangerous. Read to consider conformity in your life.

Preview

Read the headings, then review the questions and the vocabulary at the end of the selection for a road map of the article's direction.

Anticipate/Associate

1. What do you expect to learn about the good and bad features of conformity?
2. Do you conform, that is, behave as others do? Think about how you dress, act, and even think.

Examining Conformity

Vincent Ryan Ruggiero

Conformity is behaving the way others around us do. In   1
many ways conformity is good. A child is conforming when
he stays away from the hot stove or looks both ways before
crossing the street. An automobile driver is conforming when
he obeys traffic signs. And signals. So is a hospital worker
when he sterilizes the operating room. These cases of conformity make living safer. Conformity can also make daily
activities more productive. When the employees of a department store arrive at their work places at the specified time

each day, the store can open promptly without inconveniencing its customers. When supermarket stock clerks stock the various items in their <u>designated</u> places, customers can shop more efficiently.

Similarly, in a hundred different ways, from using the "up"   2
escalator to go up, to not parking by a fire hydrant, to using the right door to enter a building and the left to exit, conformity makes life less confusing for ourselves and others. And by conforming to the rules of etiquette, we make it more pleasant.

Without a measure of conformity people would never   3
learn to hold a pencil, let alone write. And more complex skills, like flying a plane or operating a computer, would be impossible to acquire. How much nonconformity, after all, does the job of driving a car permit? Can we drive facing sideways or to the rear? Can we <u>accelerate</u> with our left hand and blow the horn with our <u>right foot</u>? Certainly not without some frustration. Yet these limitations are hardly cause for complaint. The safety and comfort such conformity brings us far outweigh the <u>crimp</u> in our creativity.

Not Always Beneficial

Unfortunately conformity does not always work to our   4
advantage. Sometimes going along with others does not so much increase our safety or serve our convenience as it reinforces our dependency on others. There are situations which require careful evaluation and judgment. In such situations, to conform with the views or actions of others out of conviction, after we have thought and decided, is responsible. But to conform *instead* of thinking and deciding is irresponsible.

As human beings, we are social creatures. We must live   5
with others and relate to them. From our earliest moments of consciousness, we learn the importance of getting along with others. Few things are more painful to a child than separation from the group. Parents sending us to our room, teachers keeping us in while friends went out to play—these were hard punishments to bear. And even more difficult was the rejection of the group itself.

As we grow older, the desire to be included does not go   6
away. It merely takes different forms. We still yearn for the recognition, acceptance, and approval of others. And that yearning is intensified by the <u>bombardment</u> of thousands of advertisements and TV commercials. "Join the crowd—buy this." "Don't be left out—everyone who is someone has one." Young teenagers trying to be sophisticated, and middle-aged people trying to be "cool" and "<u>relevant</u>" have in common the urge to fit some <u>prefabricated</u> image. Conformity promises them *belonging*.

External Pressure

In addition to the urge to conform which we generate   7
ourselves, there is the external pressure of the various formal
and informal groups we belong to, the pressure to endorse
their ideas and attitudes and to imitate their actions. Thus
our urge to conform receives continuing, even daily reinforcement. To be sure, the intensity of the reinforcement,
like the strength of the urge and the ability and inclination to
withstand it, differs widely among individuals. Yet some
pressure is present for everyone. And in one way or another,
to some extent, everyone yields to it.

It is possible that a new member of a temperance group   8
might object to the group's rigid insistence that all drinking
of alcoholic beverages is wrong. He might even speak out, reminding them that occasional, moderate drinking is not
harmful. That even the Bible speaks approvingly of it. But the
group may quickly let him know that such ideas are unwelcome in their presence. Every time he forgets this, he will be
made to feel uncomfortable. In time, if he values their fel-
lowship, he will refrain from expressing that point of view.
He may even refrain from *thinking* it.

This kind of pressure, whether spoken or unspoken, can   9
be generated by any group, regardless of how liberal or conservative, formal or casual it may be. Friday night poker
clubs. Churches. Political parties. Committees. Fraternities.
Unions. The teenage gang that steals automobile accessories
may seem to have no taboos. But let one uneasy member re-
mark that he is beginning to feel guilty about his crimes and
their <u>wrath</u> will descend on him.

Similarly, in high school and college, the crowd a stu-   10
dent travels with has certain (usually unstated) expectations
for its members. If they drink or smoke, they will often make
the member who does not do so feel that he doesn't fully
belong. If a member does not share their views on sex, drugs,
studying, cheating, or any other subject of importance to
them, they will communicate their displeasure. The *way*
they communicate, of course, may be more or less direct.
They may tell him he'd better conform "or else." They may
launch a teasing campaign against him. Or they may be even
more subtle and leave him out of their activities for a few
days until he asks what is wrong or decides for himself and
resolves to behave more like them.

<u>Ironically</u>, even groups pledged to fight conformity can   11
generate strong pressure to conform. As many young people
in the 1960's learned to their dismay, many "hippie" com-
munes were as <u>intolerant</u> to dissenting ideas, values, styles of
dress and living as the "straight" society they rebelled against.

The urge to conform on occasion clashes with the ten-   12
dency to resist change. If the group we are in <u>advocates</u> an
idea or action that is new and strange to us, we can be torn between seeking their acceptance and maintaining the security
of familiar ideas and behavior. In such cases, the way we turn
will depend on which tendency is stronger in us or which
value we are more committed to. More often, however, the
two tendencies do not conflict but reinforce each other. For
we tend to associate with those whose attitudes and actions
are similar to our own.

Check Your Understanding

Review

Write five ideas you want to recall from the article.

1. _____

2. _____

3. _____

4. _____

5. _____

Fill in the Blanks

Complete the statements by writing the best word in the blank

1. _____ helps us learn many skills.

2. Conformity can be both _____

   and _____.

3. Conformity can lead you to _____ too

   much on others.

4. Groups you belong to can pressure you to _____.

5. _____ pressure from others can

   be spoken or unspoken.

Multiple Choice

Select the letter of the answer that best completes the statement.

_____ 1. The main idea of the selection is that
   a. conforming helps us live safer, happier lives.
   b. you should think carefully before deciding to conform.
   c. you must never conform.
   d. groups are harmful to independent thinking.

_____ 2. You can infer that the desire to conform
   a. lessens as you grow older.
   b. is strongest when you are young.
   c. comes from internal pressure alone.
   d. is a desire that needs thoughtful consideration.

_____ 3. The main idea of paragraph 5 is:
   a. Getting along with a group is important.
   b. Belonging to a group is a natural desire of humans.
   c. Parents should not send children to their rooms.
   d. It's better not to depend on others.

_____ 4. According to the author, conformity
   a. helps us learn many skills.
   b. makes us better thinkers.
   c. encourages us to join groups.
   d. is dangerous.

_____ 5. Paragraphs 9 and 10 are primarily organized by
   a. cause-and-effect.
   b. comparison/contrast.
   c. example.
   d. sequence.

Valid/Invalid

Mark the following statements as valid (V) or invalid (I) according to the article.

We can infer that

_____ 1. belonging to groups is dangerous.

_____ 2. advertising can pressure us to conform.

_____ 3. conformity is a sign of weakness.

_____ 4. we should learn never to conform.

_____ 5. conformity can lead to poor decision making.

_____ 6. conformity is unimportant when learning to write.

_____ 7. we should all conform more.

_____ 8. some conformity is unavoidable.

_____ 9. it requires thinking and will power not to conform.

_____ 10. the groups we belong to always share our values.

Vocabulary

Read the sentence and select the best meaning for the italicized vocabulary word from the three choices offered. Write the letter of the best choice on the blank. Check the italicized word in the text and use a dictionary if necessary.

_____ 1. Because he did not drink, we *designated* Ramon to drive us home from the party.
   a. demanded
   b. asked
   c. selected

_____ 2. At term's end, deadlines seemed to *accelerate* activity in the library.
   a. increase
   b. reduce
   c. hasten

_____ 3. Buying a new car can put a *crimp* in your budget.
   a. hole
   b. wrinkle
   c. constriction

_____ 4. Our ears are subject to a *bombardment* of noise every day.
   a. attack
   b. increased
   c. variety

_____ 5. The instructor found the student's answer extremely *relevant.*
   a. disturbing
   b. important
   c. appropriate

_____ 6. She obviously *prefabricated* the reason for her behavior.
   a. made up before hand
   b. explained
   c. prepared

_____ 7. Some politicians *advocate* abortion; others do not.
   a. hate
   b. accept
   c. support

_____ 8. Some people are *intolerant* of others' disabilities.
   a. understanding
   b. unsympathetic toward
   c. reject of

_____ 9. *Ironically,* his plans to make tons of money failed when he lost his original investment.
   a. tragic
   b. surprising
   c. opposite to what was expected

_____ 10. A father's *wrath* affects his family.
   a. anger
   b. power
   c. apparel

Writing

Write about some experience when you either conformed or didn't conform. Why was it a good or bad experience? What, if anything, did you learn from the experience? Some examples of experiences might be trying a new style or product, going along with something a group decided to do or not do.

Critical Thinking

1. Discuss with your group some of the specific difficulties you might face in deciding not to conform with a group's decision about fraternity practices or simply drinking at a party.
2. Is there more or less pressure to conform in college than there was in high school? Why or why not?
3. Think of examples when a group's decisions might be helpful and/or harmful.

Chapter 6

Reading to Evaluate

'Tis with our judgments as our watches, none
Go just alike, yet each believes his own.

Alexander Pope

The quotation suggests that we trust our own judgment about facts and events in spite of the opinions others might hold. When you apply this thought to reading materials, you can see a problem. In Chapter 5 you noticed that not all inferences you can make are valid. The writer writes to convey a message. If your reasoning about what you read leads you to a faulty conclusion or an incorrect judgment about the message, the fault may be yours. In other words, your watch may not have the correct time. Our judgment can be inaccurate when we neglect to evaluate all aspects of a situation. Critical, evaluative thinking is a skill that can be developed.

This chapter will consider:

- how to distinguish fact from opinion
- how to recognize common propaganda devices
- how to detect bias in a writer's choice of words
- how to make logical inferences in order to evaluate arguments objectively

Distinguishing Fact from Opinion

To critically evaluate, it is important to be able to tell when writers are presenting you with facts and when they are giving you opinions. Here are some strategies to help you recognize and identify information as factual.

Facts are pieces of information based on evidence and personal observations.

Facts can be checked or proven by using other resources.

Facts frequently contain numbers and dates.

For example, it is a fact that gold was discovered at Sutter's Mill in the territory of California in January 1848. Further, during the year 1849 almost 80,000 people emigrated to California. If you didn't know those facts, you could easily check them in an encyclopedia.

In another example, suppose your friend told you she had attended a baseball game yesterday in which the Pittsburgh Pirates played the Cleveland Indians. She said, "The final score was 6–4 for the Indians. I think the game would have had another outcome if the Pirates had used a better pitcher." The first sentence is a fact and could be easily checked in the newspaper. The last sentence is your friend's personal opinion.

The following are some strategies for recognizing opinions.

Opinions are expressions of personal feelings, attitudes, or judgments.

Opinions are based on a person's value system.

Almost any statement about a future event is an *opinion.*

People express many different opinions. If you can think of another point of view about a statement, that means the statement is an opinion that cannot be proved true or false. In the preceeding example there is no way to replay the game with another pitcher and prove that your friend's opinion is fact.

Two kinds of word clues are helpful in determining whether a statement is an opinion. *Value words* and *qualifiers* almost always signal an opinion.

The first list contains a few value words, words that indicate the worth or status of something. When you see these words, you can immediately recognize the statement as an opinion. These words are just a sample of the many value words. Can you add to the list?

best	good	valuable	worthwhile
great	poor	worthless	beautiful

_____ _____ _____ _____

Another set of words, called qualifiers, also suggests that a statement is an opinion. Phrases like: *I believe, I suggest, I feel, I think,* or *in my view* are clear markers for an opinion. The words *in fact* and *actually* often come before an opinion; don't be tricked by these words into accepting an opinion as a fact. Finally, certain other qualifiers also suggest that a statement is an opinion. Some of these words are in the following list.

apparently   presumably   probably   perhaps
sometimes   usually   possibly   it would seem

Although these word clues will help you to distinguish fact from opinion, sometimes they appear when the statement is not an opinion and sometimes no word clues are apparent. For example, if someone says, "Sometimes it rains," obviously the word *sometimes* is not a clue to an opinion. You must engage in active thinking to detect the difference between a fact and an opinion.

Exercise 6-1   Distinguishing Fact from Opinion

Put an (F) before those statements that are facts and an (O) before those that are opinions. Underline any words in the statements that are clues or helpful in deciding your answer.

_____ 1. It rained heavily last July 4th.

_____ 2. President John Kennedy was killed by gunshots in Dallas on November 22, 1963.

_____ 3. Blondes have more fun.

_____ 4. Medical statistics prove that smoking is harmful to your health.

_____ 5. Football is the most dangerous sport.

_____ 6. I think tennis is the best exercise.

_____ 7. More than 60 percent of adults do not perform a minimum 30 minutes of moderate exercise daily.

_____ 8. Almost 16 million Americans have adult diabetes.

_____ 9. Tom believes that riding his motorbike is the best exercise.

_____ 10. Capital punishment should be abolished.

Answers with explanations:

1. *Fact:* This information could be checked in a newspaper or by calling a weather station. The date is a clue.

2. *Fact:* An encyclopedia would support this statement. Date and specific place are clues.

3. *Opinion:* An often-quoted cliché, but many redheads and brunettes would not agree.

4. *Fact:* The statement correctly indicates that medical statistics are available to support the harmful effects of smoking. Research could provide such statistics.

5. *Opinion:* This one is tricky. Many might agree, and research might reveal statistics to support the idea that football is dangerous, but as it is written this statement is an opinion. Remember that soccer and ice hockey are also dangerous.

6. *Opinion:* Others have other favorite sports.

7. *Fact:* As the numbers suggest, this statement is a fact that can be verified.

8. *Fact:* Numbers again suggest that you could find proof of this statement.

9. *Fact:* It is a fact that in Tom's opinion riding his motorbike is the best exercise.

10. *Opinion:* Many people support capital punishment as a way to deter criminals.

Exercise 6-2   Discussion of Fact and Opinion

Consider the preceding sentences again and discuss the following questions.

1. What if the numbers used in sentences 1 and 2 were changed? Are the statements still facts?

2. Sentence 4 is a fact, but tobacco companies do not all agree. Is it still a fact?

3. Sentence 5 is an opinion. Do you think you could find some statistics to support this opinion?

4. When Columbus set out on his voyage, it was considered a fact that the world was flat. What is the fact now?

5. What conclusions about facts and opinions can you draw from your discussion?

Conclusions:

_____

_____

_____

_____

From your discussion, you should have arrived at the conclusion that even once you have identified a statement as a fact or an opinion, you still need to consider how reliable the source of the statement is. Do the facts need to be checked further? Is the person giving the opinion an expert source, one who has conducted studies or experiments to support the opinion? On the other hand, is the opinion given by someone whose self-interest is furthered by it? For example, the tobacco companies have a vested interest in resisting the many studies indicating the harmful effects of tobacco.

Be aware that facts and opinions often are found together in a single paragraph and even in a single sentence. The next exercise will give you some experience in sorting the facts from the opinions.

Exercise 6-3   Fact and Opinion in Paragraphs

Consider the following short paragraphs. Indicate on the lines following the paragraph whether a sentence is a fact (F), an opinion (O), or both (B).

1. (a) Abraham Lincoln was the greatest U.S. President. (b) The sixteenth president of the country, he saved the United States and freed the slaves. (c) Former President Harry S. Truman has called him "a decent man, a good politician, and a great President." (d) Today's leaders could learn from Lincoln's political skills, which were based on his moral principles. (e) However, he was too homely to have become president in this television age.

a. _____   b. _____   c. _____   d. _____   e. _____

2. (a) Gun-control legislation has both supporters and opponents. (b) Actually, laws restraining ordinary citizens from purchasing guns will have little effect on the illegal use of guns because most handguns used by criminals are stolen, borrowed, or bought privately. (c) For example, only about 2 percent of the 65 million privately owned handguns are employed to commit crime. (d) That means 98 percent of the guns used in crimes have been illegally obtained. (e) What is needed more than legislation is metal detectors like those in airports that would detect the presence of a handgun as a person enters a building.

a. _____   b. _____   c. _____   d. _____   e. _____

3. (a) Today, some 55 percent of credit cards come with no annual fees. (b) However, getting a credit card with no annual fees may not be as good a deal as it seems. (c) Late payment fees have gone up from $15 to as much as $20, and some companies charge if you are only one day late. (d) Charging over your credit limit can now cost you $15 to $20. (e) In the past, credit card companies used to raise your available credit to cover your purchases. (f) Using a credit card with no annual fee has become a risky business.

a. _____   b. _____   c. _____   d. _____   e. _____   f. _____

4. (a) Walking can be hazardous to your health. (b) Every year more than 90,000 pedestrians are hit by cars, and nearly 5,500 die. (c) The number of pedestrian deaths is greater than the number of deaths from plane, train, and ship accidents combined. (d) Obviously, there's a lot of reckless driving going on in our streets. (e) Perhaps that's because drivers who hit pedestrians receive light punishments.

a. _____   b. _____   c. _____   d. _____   e. _____

Exercise 6-4   Drawing Conclusions

With your group members, discuss your answers to the preceding paragraphs. Then discuss the following questions for each paragraph.

Paragraph 1

What ideas in sentence (a) could be open to opinion?

_____

_____

Sentence (d) is an opinion, but what facts could you look for to support this opinion?

_____

_____

Paragraph 2

Sentence (b) by itself appears to be an opinion. What might influence you to agree with that opinion?

_____

_____

Do you feel as sure about accepting sentence (e) dealing with metal detectors? Why or why not?

_____

_____

Paragraph 3

Give your opinion about sentence (f). Is the view expressed correct or incorrect? Be sure to back up your opinion with facts from personal experience or the experience of someone you know.

_____

_____

Paragraph 4

Discuss the facts that may have been ignored or overlooked in the opinions expressed in sentences (d) and (e).

_____

_____

Recognizing Common Propaganda Techniques

Writers and speakers sometimes consciously and other times unconsciously use *invalid,* or faulty, reasoning in attempting to persuade others to believe as they do. You have probably done this yourself. Do you remember trying to convince your parents to let you attend some event or buy some faddish product? Did you support your request with something like, "But everyone else has. . . ." You can probably complete this statement with something from your memory. If so, you were using a familiar propaganda technique.

When invalid reasoning is used deliberately, it is called *propaganda.* Propaganda is information given to persuade you to believe something, support something, or frequently to buy some product. When you are trying to analyze or synthesize information, it is important to be aware of invalid reasoning, whether it is intentional or not. As a child, you were unknowingly making use of a propaganda technique when you tried to convince your parents of something on the grounds that "everyone else has or does" whatever. Your parents may have responded with something like, "I suppose if everyone were going to jump off the cliff, you would, too." This is as good a response as any to the propaganda technique called *bandwagon appeal.* Others among the many common faulty reasoning techniques to be considered include *transfer, "plain folks," name calling,* and *testimonial.*

Bandwagon Appeal

The appeal to your reasoning here is that if everyone else is doing something, supporting something, or buying something, you should too. The technique takes its name from an old practice. During parades in small towns, folks would race to jump onto the bandwagon, to be one of the crowd. Today children and young adults who need to feel part of a group will often use this argument. Notice that "everyone does it" does not address the merits of the action. It is faulty reasoning because there is no reasoning, just the emotional appeal to be like everyone else. Here are some examples:

Come to Mazie's Deli. You'll find all your friends there.

(Is the food good? Are the prices right? This argument doesn't give any facts, except the statement that all your friends are there.)

Drink Flipzi, the drink of the "now" generation.

(The only information given is that the "now" generation
drinks Flipzi. There isn't even any evidence to support the
statement as true. Perhaps there is a picture of members of
the happy "now" generation, but that doesn't prove that
Flipzi is the drink of the "now" generation.)

Transfer

Transfer is a kind of reasoning that asks you to transfer your
positive feelings about one thing to something that has nothing to
do with the first thing—usually a product or idea that someone
wants you to accept. As in the preceeding example, happy people
are pictured and you would like to be like them. Car advertisements often show the car surrounded by spectacular scenery. The
transferred idea is that you will find yourself in that beautiful environment when you buy the car. Politicians seldom appear in photographs without an American flag somewhere in the background.
That's to help you transfer the idea that the politician is a real pa-
triot with the country's interest at heart.

Here are some more examples of transfer. A telephone book
shows more than twenty businesses that are A-1 something. The
colors of red, white, and blue appeal to your feelings of patriotism.
Because most people like small children, cute dogs and cats, and
beautiful natural scenes, you will find them pictured in many advertisements. Think, too, about the names given to automobiles. Positive feelings aroused by these words and images are unconsciously
transferred to the product. Consider the following examples.

The American Insurance Company is ready to serve you.
(Because the company is American, it's got to be good.)

Want a soft touch? Try Velvet, the toilet paper with class.
(There are two appeals here. The transfer of your feelings
about the softness of velvet, and the suggestion that this
paper is special.)

"Plain Folks"

Most people consider themselves average and identify with
and trust those who are also average, just regular people. That's why
plain folks appeal can cloud objective reasoning. For example,

politicians tell us about their ordinary backgrounds, such as having attended a public high school rather than a private one. One politician currently spends many days working side by side with ordinary workers in all kinds of jobs. His purpose, he says, is to know more about working conditions. An unstated purpose is to get us to identify with him, to see him as just like other ordinary workers. Here are two more examples:

> An ordinary homemaker in a TV commercial exclaims, "My wash gets three times cleaner with Splash detergent."

(Who doesn't want clean laundry, and this ordinary homemaker certainly appears to be a trustworthy model.)

> If you want a safer place for your children to grow up, join the Community Action Group.

(Of course, you want a safe environment for your children, but is this group the only way or even the best way to achieve it?)

Name Calling

You may have used the technique of *name calling* as a child. When all else fails in an attempt to win an argument, you may have resorted to calling your opponent names. Your attack was direct and may have sent your opponent running away in tears. When this emotional, rather than logical, technique is used, it distracts people from considering the facts. Some years ago, a person in politics who was labeled a "card-carrying communist" was easily discredited. Today, a U.S. president accused of smoking marijuana has to defend himself. A large company labeled as one that discriminates against any group may have difficulty hiring or selling its product. Consider these examples:

> The Blank Company uses animals for experimentation.

(Many people are offended by the use of animals for experimentation, but this use may be humane and necessary for the development of a product safe for human consumption.)

> Aspirex is the only pain reliever that can reduce the risk of heart attack.

(Here, the name calling is almost hidden. The suggestion is that other aspirin-based pain relievers cannot reduce heart attack risk.)

Testimonial

To testify means to "speak for," and *testimonials* muddy our thinking by using famous people and supposedly expert witnesses to speak for products and ideas. Think first about famous people. You have often seen and heard movie stars, sports figures, and others tell you the benefits of doing something or buying something. Golfers, tennis stars, football players, and others will attest to their use of a product, but you must remember that such testimonials are done for money. Famous people are paid for recommending products; often they endorse political candidates as well. Because you recognize the name of the famous person, you may accept their endorsement. The testimony of experts is very much like this. Experts in their own field are sometimes used to testify or support ideas far removed from their area of specialty. You may not recognize their names, but they may influence your thinking simply because they are important in their own field. Here are two examples:

Dr. Hava Notion, a famous surgeon,
prefers Bright toothpaste.

(The faulty reasoning assumes that because the doctor is a great surgeon, she surely must know the best toothpaste to use.)

President Hambone is supported for re-election
by Spring Star, winner of an Academy Award.

(The fact that Spring Star is supporting the President should be nothing more than interesting. Her support does not make Hambone a good candidate even though you love her movies.)

Exercise 6-5   Recognizing Propaganda Techniques

Many more traps exist on the road to clear, objective, unemotional thinking, but the five just discussed should help you be more alert in analyzing what you hear and read. Decide what is wrong with the following statements by selecting the letter of the propoganda technique that best identifies it.

a. transfer   b. testimonial   c. "plain folks"
d. name calling   e. bandwagon

——— 1. "I can exercise more comfortably in No Corn Shoes," says marathon runner Carl Callus.

——— 2. Don't believe a word he says. He's a Republican.

——— 3. All good students spend several hours in the library every day.

——— 4. The post office uses red, white, and blue packaging for priority mail.

——— 5. The famous anthropologist Dr. Digger buys Super Burgers for his dog.

——— 6. The average college student knows that Pick-Pen writes more clearly.

——— 7. Trust One-Shot Grocery, the preferred stop for millions of shoppers.

——— 8. How could she know the best car deal? She believes in abortion!

——— 9. Senator Rocket grew up in the slums; he knows how hard we have to work for our money.

——— 10. I believe in Sturdy Insurance Company because their symbol is a strong oak tree.

Answers with Explanations

1. (b) Remember that Carl Callus was probably paid to make this testimonial statement.

2. (d) Naming a person's political party is not always name calling, but in this case it is.

3. (e) These "good students" might be talking about last night's party, but nevertheless they are plain folks like us; and, of course, that's a good bandwagon to get on.

4. (a) The post office is reminding us with this transfer element that it is a part of our government.

5. (b) Although Dr. Digger is famous, we can't accept his testimony that the burgers are good for his dog.

6. (e) Pick-Pens seem to be used by plain folks (average students). You could also see this as an invitation to get on the bandwagon with other students.

7. (e) Don't you want to get on the bandwagon with millions of other shoppers?

8. (a) or (d) A person's knowledge about buying a car has nothing to do with his or her position on abortion. This one could be labeled *transfer* if you transfer a negative feeling about her feeling on abortion, or a kind of *name calling* for the same reason. Even if you agree with the abortion position, you can see that the two facts have no relationship with each other.

9. (c) Senator Rocket may be "plain folks" like us, but that doesn't mean he's the candidate to vote for.

10. (a) The strong oak tree suggests you transfer the idea of strength to the insurance company. It is strong and will be in business for a long time.

Exercise 6-6   Discussion of Propaganda Techniques

Consider the ten sentences in Exercise 6–5 and discuss the following questions. Recall that the purpose of propaganda techniques is to persuade you to believe something, support something, or buy something.

1. Sentences 2, 4, 8, and 9 use different techniques but share a common purpose. What is the purpose of a person making these statements?

   _____

   _____

2. What is the shared purpose of sentences 1, 5, 6, 7, and 10?

   _____

   _____

3. Discuss why it is important to be alert to propaganda techniques in your reading.

   _____

   _____

Detecting Bias

Bias is another technique that can interfere with your ability to analyze reading material. *Bias* means to have a subjective or personal point of view. You can be biased toward chocolate ice cream as opposed to strawberry. That point of view is not particularly important unless, of course, someone wants to buy you a treat that you will like. Important biases are those about important issues, ideas people hold because of their individual value systems. Writers do not necessarily write to deceive, but they often write to convey ideas based on their value system. It is important to recognize that everyone in the world is biased. Newspaper editorials and political speeches are always biased. You can reveal a person's bias directly by simply saying or writing, "I oppose that," or "I support that."

The following paragraphs consider four warning signs to be considered in detecting bias presented in information. First, you need to consider word choice. *Connotative words,* words that are surrounded by the feelings we bring to them beyond their dictionary meaning, can reveal a bias. Second, the use of *stereotypes,* general images of people not based on fact, suggests that a person may be prejudiced either for or against a particular group. Third, *omitted information* may also be the result of bias. Ask yourself what was not presented that might be important to understanding an issue. Finally, it is often necessary to consider the *writer's background.* The age, race, sex, and political and religious background of writers may influence their value system and therefore their biases.

Connotative Words

A dictionary may provide similar definitions for the words *student, scholar,* and *egghead.* You can test your feelings about these words by asking yourself which you would rather be called. Similarly, a rat catcher and an exterminator may do the same work, but if this were your job, which title would you prefer? You must be alert to noticing connotative words. Look at these examples.

1. Capital punishment is an extreme punishment.
2. Capital punishment is murder.
3. Capital punishment is the law in some states.

The first sentence suggests that the writer may be opposed to capital punishment, but you can't be sure. You would have to read the sentence in context to be certain. The second sentence shows that the writer condemns capital punishment because it is called "murder." The third sentence makes a simple statement of fact with no emotion. Becoming sensitive to and recognizing the tone that words convey is important in detecting bias.

Stereotypes

Sometimes bias is revealed by the use of stereotypes. Remember that stereotypes are the images we have of groups of people or of people in particular professions. An African-American professor likes to challenge his class about their stereotypes. He tells them that he is going to introduce them to a coal miner, a truck driver, a jazz musician, a writer, and a gourmet cook and asks them to imagine what these people will look like. He leaves the room and then returns to announce that he has been all of these people. Stereotypes are sometimes like the propaganda technique noted earlier, name calling. If a father holds the stereotype that all Irish people drink too much, he may say to his daughter, "I don't want you dating that Irish kid. The Irish are all drunkards."

Omitted Information

A writer may also show bias by omitting important information. Writers have to make choices in the information they present. Sometimes the information is deliberately omitted as a result of bias. Consider the following paragraph.

> We pay for the things we want not with money, but with time: that is, the time it takes to earn the money to afford whatever it is we think we want. For example, buying a home can cost thirty years. Those years may represent all of your working life. Before we buy, we need to consider the investment of time.

This seems like a straightforward paragraph. But consider the following details, which were not mentioned.

a. Although it may take thirty years to pay for your home, you have an investment that usually increases in value.
b. Renting a place to live also costs money and a similar investment of time.
c. Your income tax may be reduced by the interest paid on your mortgage loan.

Why do you think the writer omitted these details? The writer's purpose is to make you aware of the time you invest to earn the possessions you feel you want. The details, which are true, do not add weight to his argument; instead, they detract from the idea that buying things costs us time. Consequently, the writer omitted them from his argument.

The Writer's Background

Frequently, it is helpful to know something about the background of a writer. This information helps you determine the bias. The writer of the preceeding paragraph is obviously not a real estate agent. Since the writer is asking you to consider the weighty question of the value of your time, you could guess that he or she is a philosopher of some kind.

Exercise 6-7   Detecting Bias

All of the following groups of sentences show some bias, a reason for you to question the information given. Choose a letter from the following list to label the kind of bias on the line before the sentence. Use the lines below each sentence to explain the bias.

a. Connotative words
b. Stereotypes
c. Omitted information
d. The writer's background

_____ 1. Tony is a real cheapskate; he never takes me to a decent restaurant on a date.

_____

_____

_____ 2. As president of Flimflam products, I can assure you that you won't find a better product on the market.

_____

_____

_____ 3. Women shouldn't become truck drivers. That's an occupation for men.

_____

_____

_____ 4. This diet based on sunflower seeds will have you shedding pounds in weeks.

_____

_____

_____ 5. The Democratic party is filled with flaming liberals who won't even try for a balanced budget.

_____

_____

_____ 6. Don't ask Hernando to join our basketball team. He spends hours playing chess.

_____

_____

_____ 7. The car salesperson says, "Buy this beauty today. A bargain like this won't last."

_____

_____

_____ 8. The use of animals for medical experimentation is both horrifying and abominable.

_____

_____

_____ 9. After damaging the front fender in an accident, the son tells his father, "I left the car in the driveway with a full tank of gas."

_____

_____

_____ 10. I wouldn't leave my baby in that day care center. Several of the assistants are men, and you know they can't care for children as well as a woman can.

_____

_____

Exercise 6-8   Discussion of Bias

With your group members, discuss your answers about the bias in the preceding statements. Some of you may have labeled the type of bias differently. Discuss possible different answers. Talk about which statements could be changed to remove the bias. What kind of bias is most difficult to correct?

Evaluating Arguments and Making Logical Inferences

Now you can pull together all the information you have gained about main ideas, facts and opinion, propaganda devices, and bias to evaluate the following pieces and make good inferences. Read and study the paragraphs and answer the questions that follow.

Exercise 6-9   Putting It All Together

I. (a) Have you watched television news lately? (b) We worry about rating the sit-coms and cop shows to protect our children, but no one rates the nightly news. (c) The violence, murder, and general mayhem offered for our consumption each night is far worse than any offering during prime time. (d) The Oklahoma City bombing and subsequent trial, and the murder of a six-year-old beauty queen are just two examples. (e) In a recent survey, 65 percent of the children interviewed had watched a television news program the day before, and more than half were sad, depressed, or angry after the program. (f) The money-hungry producers of the nightly news programs violate our sense of decency. (g) It's time to forget about freedom of the press and fight for control of the kinds of images projected for our children on our television screens.

1. Mark the following expressions of the main idea as (B) too broad, (N) too narrow, and (C) comprehensive.

   _____ a. Television should be tightly censored.

   _____ b. Television news producers are at fault.

   _____ c. Television news programs are too violent.

2. Which sentences express opinions rather than facts?

   _____

3. Can you find any biased words? If so, list them.

   _____

4. List any propaganda devices that were used.

   _____

   _____

5. Which of the following are valid inferences to be made from the paragraph? Mark (V) for valid.

   _____ a. The writer is a woman.

   _____ b. The writer believes that news programs harm children.

   _____ c. The writer has no respect for the Bill of Rights.

   _____ d. An agency to supervise the content of news programs is desirable in the writer's view.

   _____ e. The writer wants television news off the air.

   _____ f. Children are the focus of the writer's concern.

   _____ g. The writer would support rating television news.

   _____ h. The writer has children.

6. Discuss with group members what can be done to solve the problem that the writer discusses.

II. (a) A woman looks in her cupboard and announces, "It's dry as a bone." (b) Your friend just lost 30 pounds, and someone declares, "She's just a bag of bones." (c) Someone asks you to finish mowing the lawn for him because he is "bone tired." (d) Where did we get these weird, unflattering ideas about bones? (e) The expression "dry as a bone" probably comes from the book of Ezekiel in the Bible. (f) Ezekiel is asked by God to prophesy to some bones in the desert, calling upon the bones to rise up and "hear the word of the Lord." (g) Fact is, bones are not dry. (h) They are composed of a matrix of fibers of protein and collagen and are filled with marrow. (i) As far as being a "bag of bones" is concerned, we all are. (j) But if we didn't have this internal structure, we would creep along like a slug or an earthworm. (k) And finally, "bone tired"—don't let anyone pull this one on you. (l) Bones cannot get tired. (m) Our brains send us messages of fatigue received from our muscles, not our bones. (n) So give your bones a break. (o) Whoops! Not literally, of course.

1. Mark the following expressions of the main idea as (B) too broad, (N) too narrow, and (C) comprehensive.

    _____ a. Bones are composed of many substances.

    _____ b. Familiar sayings about bones are not always correct.

    _____ c. Our internal skeleton is complex.

2. Which sentences express opinions? _____

3. What biased words are used? _____

4. What fact does sentence (g) omit or ignore? (Think about Ezekiel's dry bones.)

    _____

5. Which of the following are valid inferences? Mark (V) for valid.

    _____ a. The writer knows a lot about bones.

    _____ b. Bones are an essential part of our organism.

    _____ c. Expressions of speech like "bag of bones" should not be taken literally.

    _____ d. Bones break easily.

    _____ e. The expression "dry as a bone" comes from Ezekiel.

III. (a) Education that involves only the gathering, processing, and assimilating of knowledge for its own sake ignores the need of all people to learn to ask questions and find solutions. (b) People who acquire a wealth of individual facts—a pile of unrelated names, dates, formulas, structures, and equations—may be well prepared for *Jeopardy* or Trivial Pursuit. (c) But if they are unable to apply their knowledge to issues of more significance, they are not educated. (d) For example, it is interesting to know that more than half the population of the U.S. is female. (e) The question beyond the fact is this: Why do women still play a subordinate role in a society where they are the majority? (f) Another example: It is a fact that the infant death rate in the U.S. is 13 in every 1,000 births. (g) This death rate is higher than that of twelve other countries. (h) Beyond this, we should be asking: Why, with our country's wealth and advanced technology, should these conditions exist? (i) True education should lead us not to a knowledge of facts alone, but to the questions and solutions beyond the facts.

1. Mark these possible main ideas as (B) too broad, (N) too narrow, and (C) comprehensive.

    _____ a. Education involves the gathering of knowledge.

    _____ b. True education goes beyond facts.

    _____ c. Education should be never-ending.

2. In which sentences are opinions expressed?

    _____

3. What biased words were used?

    _____

4. Mark the following valid inferences with a (V).

    _____ a. The writer believes that women have no chance of advancement in today's society.

    _____ b. Education today consists of learning facts.

    _____ c. The infant death rate in the United States is too high, according to the writer.

    _____ d. The writer is an educator.

    _____ e. Learning facts is a waste of time.

    _____ f. Finding solutions to the problems of society should be the goal of education.

IV. (a) Keith Campbell, a scientist at The Roslin Institute laboratory in Scotland, knew that according to the textbooks cloning an adult mammal was impossible. (b) But against all odds, he and his colleagues worked to clone a lamb from a single cell. (c) The ewe, Dolly, was born in July 1996, but her birth was not announced to the world by the journal *Nature* until March 1997. (d) Dolly's birth raised ethical and moral questions around the world. (e) If sheep can be cloned, why not human beings? (f) Should human cloning be regulated or banned? (g) Many countries such as Britain, Denmark, Germany, Belgium, the Netherlands, and Spain ban experimentation. (h) Questions arise. (i) Should human beings take over the role of Creator? (j) Will cloning humans have positive or negative results? (k) If cloning should become legal, will it therefore be moral?

1. Mark the main ideas as (B) too broad, (N) too narrow, and (C) comprehensive.

    _____ a. Human cloning raises moral questions.

    _____ b. Dolly, a ewe, was cloned.

    _____ c. Human cloning will soon be a reality.

2. Which sentences express opinions? _____

3. What biased words can be found?

    _____

4. Mark the following valid inferences with a V.

    _____ a. Human cloning is immoral.

    _____ b. Dolly's birth has had more than scientific effects.

    _____ c. Scientists should stop experimenting with cells.

    _____ d. The writer is a scientist.

    _____ e. Campbell worked alone to create Dolly.

    _____ f. Cloning of humans is possible.

Chapter Review

Label the following statements as true or false based on your study of this chapter.

_____ 1. A fact is something that can be proved.

_____ 2. Opinions are good support if they are offered by an unbiased expert in the subject field.

_____ 3. An inference is usually a fact.

_____ 4. Reasoning is a process of drawing a conclusion from evidence.

_____ 5. Opinions frequently contain value words.

_____ 6. Propaganda is a kind of invalid reasoning.

_____ 7. A bias indicates a subjective or personal point of view.

_____ 8. Using stereotypes is an indication of bias.

_____ 9. Transfer is a propaganda device used when famous people promote an idea or product.

_____ 10. Connotative words carry emotional feelings attached to their literal meaning.

Vocabulary

Show your understanding of the words recently introduced by selecting the correct word from the list to complete the sentences that follow. Some of the words were used in the paragraphs in Exercise 6-9. Cross out each word as you use it.

analysis	synthesis	propaganda	stereotype
bias	mayhem	consumption	subsequent
projected	matrix	prophesy	subordinate
fatigue	literally	assimilate	technology
significance	cloning	colleagues	ethical

1. Labeling someone because of imagined characteristics of a group is using a _____.

2. A bull in a china closet could cause _____.

3. The _____ of fiber is important for a healthy diet.

4. He resigned _____ to the charge that he had stolen the firm's money.

5. Many ads use _____ to convince the public to buy a product.

6. Putting ideas together to form a new idea is called _____.

7. It is _____ many new jobs will be developed in the next decade.

8. Strenuous effort sometimes causes _____.

9. Try to _____ your notes before an exam.

10. Your value system can be the basis for _____.

11. Those who work together may be called _____.

12. The Ten Commandments are the basis for a Christian's _____ decisions.

13. _____ of humans raises moral questions.

14. Arranging rows and columns into a rectangular arrangement forms a _____.

15. Boris is working his way up in the company from his _____ position.

16. Police do a careful _____ of a crime scene.

17. Clues are studied to determine their _____.

18. If someone exaggerates, it's best not to take their words _____.

19. You live in an age when some knowledge of _____

   is essential.

20. Some people use decks of cards to _____

   the future.

Critical Thinking

First, write out your position on the following situations that might justify the cloning of humans. Then give reasons to support your positions. Finally, discuss decisions with your group. (Remember that in decisions of an ethical nature each individual is entitled to his or her own judgment.)

1. Should cloning be allowed for exceptional people like Einstein, Mozart, and Lincoln?

   Opinion _____

   Reason _____

   _____

2. Should cloning of a child be allowed as a means of producing bone marrow to save the child's life?

   Opinion _____

   Reason 1 _____

   Reason 2 _____

3. Would cloning eliminate the need for sexual reproduction since cells would reproduce artificially?

   Opinion _____

   Reason 1 _____

   Reason 2 _____

4. Should cloning be permitted for infertile couples?

Opinion _____

Reason 1 _____

Reason 2 _____

5. Should a woman be allowed to have her dead father cloned in order to use his cells to give birth to a child like her father?

Opinion _____

Reason 1 _____

Reason 2 _____

Writing

Write a paragraph expressing your ideas about one of the issues raised by the paragraphs in Exercise 6-9.

1. What do you think is important in a good education?
2. Should scientists experiment with the cloning of humans?
3. What suggestions would you make about how to control violence on television?

Reading Selection 1

Purpose

You have learned that you must consider bias when reading persuasive material. Sometimes printed matter is biased by omitting facts or simply by recounting events from a particular point of view. Newspapers show bias, even in objective news stories, by the placement of the article on the page and the amount of coverage given to it. Read this short article, which examines some issues about bias.

Preview

1. Read the first sentence or two of each paragraph in the article. What ideas are suggested?
2. Check the questions and the vocabulary at the end.

Anticipate/Associate

1. Think about why people present biased views.
2. Is a biased view one that is different from yours?
3. How can omitting or ignoring facts create bias?

Whose History?

James M. Henslin

Consider the Battle of Little Bighorn. U.S. history books   1
usually recount the massacre of an outnumbered, brave band
of cavalrymen, with Gen. George Custer going down to a sad
but somehow glorious defeat. When Joe Marshall, a Lakota
Sioux, heard this version as a fourth-grader, he mustered all
the courage he could, raised his hand, and told the class the
version he had heard from descendants of the battle's survivors. This version refers to an armed group invading Native
American lands. When the young boy finished, his teacher
smiled indulgently and said, "That's nice, but we'll stick to
the real story."

The U.S. history books say that there were no survivors   2
of this battle. Think about this for a moment, and the point
about perspectives in history will become even more obvious. For the Native Americans, there were *many* survivors.
Indeed, it is those survivors who used a technique called "oral
tradition" to recount what took place during that battle.
Their descendants have written a book that recounts those
events, but the white officials who head the Little Bighorn
Battlefield National Monument won't let the book be sold
there—only books that recount the event from the European-
American perspective may be sold.

This issue of perspective underlies the current contro-   3
versy surrounding the teaching of history in U.S. schools.
The question of *what* should be taught was always assumed,
for the school boards, teachers, and textbook writers were
united by a background of similar expectations. It was un-
questioningly assumed, for example, that George Washington
was the general-hero-founder of the nation. No question was
raised about whether school curricula should mention that
he owned slaves. In the first place, most white boards, teachers, and textbook writers were ignorant of such facts, and,
secondly, on learning of them, thought them irrelevant.

But no longer. The issue now is one of balance—how to   4
make certain that the accomplishments of both genders and
our many racial and ethnic groups are included in teaching.

This issue, called <u>multiculturism</u>, is now central to school districts around the nation. Teachers, administrators, school boards, and publishers are wrestling with a <u>slew</u> of difficult questions. How much space should be given to Harriet Tubman versus George Washington? Is enough attention paid to discrimination against Asian Americans? to Latinos? Is the attempted <u>genocide</u> of Native Americans sufficiently acknowledged? What about the contributions to U.S. society of women? How about those of white ethnics—Poles, Russians, and so on?

No one knows the answers. What is certain at this point   5
is that the image of U.S. society has changed—from a melting pot to a tossed salad. At the heart of the current issue is the fact that so many groups have retained separate identities, instead <u>fusing</u> into one as was "supposed" to happen. The question being decided now is how much emphasis should be given to the salad as a whole, and how much to the cucumbers, tomatoes, lettuce, and so on.

The answers to such questions will give birth to new   6
images of history, which, rather than consisting of established past events, as is commonly supposed, is a flowing, winding, and sometimes twisted perception that takes place in the present.

Check Your Understanding

Review

List at least five issues mentioned in the article that are a source of concern in the teaching of history.

1. _____

2. _____

3. _____

4. _____

5. _____

Fill in the Blanks

Complete the following statements by writing the best words in the blank.

1. General Custer was defeated at the Battle of _____

   _____ .

2. History books tell us there were _____ survivors.

3. In the past it was assumed that everyone shared the same

   _____ .

4. In the past the U.S. society was called a _____

   _____ .

5. The writer suggests calling U.S. society a _____

   _____ .

Multiple Choice

Select the letter of the answer that best completes the statement.

_____ 1. The main idea is:
   a. The United States is a melting pot.
   b. Native Americans have been overlooked.
   c. New perspectives must be considered in telling history.
   d. b and c above.

_____ 2. The writer's purpose is to
   a. inform.
   b. persuade.
   c. entertain.
   d. inform and persuade.

_____ 3. The writer believes that in the past history teaching was
   a. distorted.
   b. untrue.
   c. deliberately prejudiced.
   d. a and b above.

_____ 4. According to the article, readjusting history texts will be
   a. a source of controversy.
   b. a simple matter of telling the truth.
   c. a matter of balance.
   d. a and c above.

_____ 5. The writer implies that
   a. written history is a pack of lies.
   b. history writers have deliberately omitted facts.
   c. we all see things from our own point of view.
   d. we owe the Native Americans an apology.

True/False

Label the following statements as true or false according to the article.

_____ 1. Studying history is a matter of learning facts.

_____ 2. Multiculturalism is a central issue today.

_____ 3. Native Americans preserved their history in tribal record books.

_____ 4. The writer implies that a melting pot is better than a tossed salad.

_____ 5. It is a simple matter to avoid bias and prejudice in writing.

_____ 6. The imagery or picture of the United States has changed.

_____ 7. Early settlers almost erased the Native American population.

_____ 8. Gender and race have nothing to do with accurate history.

_____ 9. The writer implies that finding balance in retelling history will be difficult.

_____ 10. The story of the Battle of Little Bighorn is an illustrative detail.

Vocabulary

Select the best meaning for the italicized word and write its letter on the blank.

_____ 1. *mustered* all his courage
   a. gathered as if for battle
   b. discharged from service
   c. met a certain standard

_____ 2. *descendants* of the survivors
   a. tribal leaders
   b. children and grandchildren
   c. those coming down

_____ 3. teacher smiled *indulgently*
     a. giving in to the wishes of another
     b. forgiving someone's sins
     c. being long suffering

_____ 4. *perspectives* in history
     a. clear views
     b. different points of view
     c. the view before

_____ 5. underlies the current *controversy*
     a. idea for control
     b. disagreement
     c. state of affairs

_____ 6. facts were considered *irrelevant*
     a. unimportant
     b. very revealing
     c. unnecessary

_____ 7. this issue, called *multiculturalism*
     a. many cultures
     b. different ideas
     c. segregation

_____ 8. a *slew* of difficult questions
     a. a killing
     b. a variety
     c. a large number

_____ 9. attempted *genocide* of Native Americans
     a. differences in generations
     b. destruction of germs
     c. murder of a race

_____ 10. *fusing* into one
     a. confusing
     b. blending together
     c. making separate

Writing

Describe one of your prejudices. Do you have a point of view about an issue such as affirmative action, feminism, Native American gambling places, illegal immigrants, abortion, the death penalty? Explain your point of view in a paragraph. Try not to use connotative words or bias in your paragraph.

Critical Thinking

1. Discuss the difference, if any, between having an opinion on an issue, having a perspective, or a bias.

2. What are the problems you foresee in trying to achieve balance in multicultural issues in history or in daily life?
3. Do you agree with the description of our society as formerly a "melting pot" and now a "tossed salad"? Discuss your understanding of these terms. Assuming that these are valid metaphors, what are some advantages and disadvantages of both of these conditions?

Reading Selection 2

Purpose

Even when you have read and understood a passage, it is important to remember that you can't believe everything you read. Keep in mind that the writer, because of his or her bias, may knowingly or unknowingly present the facts to make you believe as he or she does.

You have undoubtedly read about or have seen television presentations or movies about the death of President John F. Kennedy in 1963. Many people still don't believe we know all the facts about his death. Bookshelves are filled with different writers' theories. Read the following passage to learn some of the views.

Preview

Take a minute to read the questions that follow the reading to help you focus on the subject.

Anticipate/Associate

Recall anything you have read or heard about the assassination of President Kennedy. Where, when, and by whom was he killed?

The Assassination of President Kennedy

Jeffrey Waggoner

On Friday, November 22, 1963, just southwest of the intersection of Elm and Houston streets in Dallas, Texas, hundreds of people witnessed one of the most famous murders in recent history. The victim was the president of the United States. The assassination lasted between six and eight seconds. But by the time those few seconds were over, John Fitzgerald Kennedy, the thirty-fifth president of the United

States, had received two gunshot wounds. One of them was fatal. The first shot hit Kennedy in the region of his lower neck or upper back. Doctors said he could have survived this first wound if he had <u>sustained</u> no others. The second, though, was fatal. It caused massive damage to Kennedy's skull and brain.

Doctors at Dallas's Parkland Hospital pronounced President Kennedy dead at 1:00 that afternoon. Almost two hours later, at 2:48, Vice President Lyndon B. Johnson was sworn in aboard Air Force One as the nation's new chief executive. 2

One week later, President Johnson created the President's Commission on the Assassination of President Kennedy. He appointed Earl Warren, chief justice of the United States Supreme Court, to head the commission, known simply as the Warren Commission. 3

In September 1964, just ten months after its creation, the Warren Commission issued its report on the assassination. The Warren Report appeared to be an <u>exhaustive</u>, thorough inquiry into Kennedy's death. The published report was more than 800 pages long. The commission and its staff had heard testimony from 489 people who were or might have been involved with the assassination. An additional twenty-six volumes of "Hearings and Exhibits" accompanied the report for anyone interested enough to examine the commission's research. 4

The Warren Commission's most significant conclusion was that one man, Lee Harvey Oswald, acted alone and pulled the trigger behind every shot fired in Dealey Plaza on November 22, 1963. 5

After his arrest, <u>circumstantial</u> evidence accumulated against Oswald rapidly. The Warren Commission examined such evidence and combined it with its own <u>psychological</u> profile of Oswald. The commission concluded that Oswald was Kennedy's lone assassin. Oswald was <u>depicted</u> in the Warren Report as a frustrated, confused political <u>zealot</u> who would have killed a U.S. president just to increase his own tortured self-esteem. This was the official theory of John F. Kennedy's assassination. According to it, the assassination resulted from forces that no one could have predicted or prevented. To the Warren Commission, it was simply an outcome of Oswald's unstable childhood and his attraction to "un-American" philosophies. 6

The circumstantial evidence against Oswald was strong; it would have been difficult to deny in any court of law. But ever since the official theory was published in the Warren Report, independent researchers have insisted that Oswald—if he was involved at all—probably had help with the assassination. 7

In 1978, the House Select Committee on Assassinations   8
agreed with such conclusions. The committee thoroughly
researched the assassination for two years. The committee
concluded "that President John F. Kennedy was probably
assassinated as a result of a <u>conspiracy</u>."

Which conclusion is correct? The official theory? Or one   9
of the conspiracy theories formulated in the decades following the assassination? Did Oswald, acting alone, kill President Kennedy? Or does the circumstantial evidence only hide
the more <u>tantalizing</u> evidence of a conspiracy?

The most damaging charge leveled against the Warren   10
Commission was that it did not conduct its inquiry with an
open mind. Critics concluded that the commission had assumed from the outset that Oswald was the lone assassin. Such
an assumption would have greatly affected its investigation.

When critics compared the published Warren Report   11
with the available evidence, they found a multitude of con-
tradictions. The report left little doubt that the Warren Commission thought Oswald had killed Kennedy. The available
evidence, however, often sharply contradicted such a conclusion. Even much of the evidence in the commission's
own "Hearing and Exhibits" either clouded the certainty of
Oswald's guilt or indicated a conspiracy.

The commission's final report was written as if every   12
shred of evidence proved that Oswald shot Kennedy. The
commission ignored even its own evidence if it contradicted
the conclusion that Oswald was the lone assassin. One
<u>discrepancy</u> between the Warren Report and the available ev-
idence involved Oswald's marksmanship. The Warren Commission partly based its conclusion on a belief that Oswald
was an accomplished marksman. The men who trained with
Oswald in the marines, though, remembered him as an unsure, uncoordinated individual who showed little <u>aptitude</u> for
firearms. Contrary to such testimony, the Warren Commission found Oswald so skillful with a rifle that he could perform feats of marksmanship that no expert has since been
able to duplicate. The marines who served with Oswald
laughed at the suggestion.

Another discrepancy concerned Oswald's precise loca-   13
tion at the time of the shooting. He undeniably was in the de-
pository when the shots were fired. But was he on the sixth
floor, where the rifle and empty shells were recovered? The
Warren Commission was satisfied that Oswald was the gun-
man seen on the sixth floor at 12:15—even though it heard
testimony that he very likely was not on that floor immediately before or during the assassination.

Check Your Understanding

Review

The first six paragraphs present information in chronological order. List the most significant facts from those paragraphs in the order they are given. Sift out the details and list one main idea for each paragraph.

1. _____

2. _____

3. _____

4. _____

5. _____

6. _____

Fill in the Blanks

Complete the statements by writing the best word or phrase in the blank.

1. Kennedy was assassinated on _____.

2. He was the _____ President of the United

   States.

3. The President who succeeded Kennedy was _____.

4. The name of the commission that first studied the assassination was the _____.

5. The commission's published report was _____

   pages long.

Multiple Choice

Select the letter of the answer that best completes the sentence.

_____ 1. The main idea of the entire article is that
   a. the Warren Report settled the matter of who was responsible for the assassination.

    b. the Warren Report ignored available evidence.

    c. new evidence has been uncovered since the Warren Report was published.

_____ 2. This article

    a. is almost entirely factual.

    b. contains many opinions.

    c. proves that Oswald was the sole assassin.

_____ 3. The writer cites evidence to prove that

    a. Oswald was an excellent marksman.

    b. Oswald was not in the depository at the time of the assassination.

    c. the Warren Report ignored available evidence in writing the report.

_____ 4. A reader can conclude that reports from reliable sources

    a. must be accepted as true.

    b. may contain invalid conclusions.

    c. are deliberately misleading.

_____ 5. The Warren Report concluded that

    a. the assassination was the result of a conspiracy.

    b. Oswald was the lone assassin.

    c. there wasn't enough evidence to draw a conclusion.

True/False

Label the following statements as true or false.

_____ 1. The writer does not support the conclusions of the Warren Report.

_____ 2. The Warren Report concluded that the assassination was the result of a conspiracy.

_____ 3. The writer gives evidence to prove that the Warren Report ignored evidence.

_____ 4. President Kennedy was shot three times.

_____ 5. More than 400 people were interviewed to obtain the facts presented in the Warren Report.

_____ 6. According to the article, Oswald was convicted in the report on the basis of circumstantial evidence.

_____ 7. The Warren Report was accompanied by twenty-six more volumes of evidence.

_____ 8. The House Select Committee on Assassinations agreed with the conclusions of the Warren Report.

_____ 9. At one time, Oswald served as a marine.

_____ 10. Critics of the Warren Report suggest that the commission failed to keep an open mind.

Vocabulary

Match each of the words in column A, which were underlined in the text, with a synonym from column B. If you have difficulty after looking at the context, consult your dictionary.

Column A	Column B
_____ a. sustained	1. incidental
_____ b. exhaustive	2. considering all elements
_____ c. circumstantial	3. fanatic
_____ d. psychological	4. illustrated
_____ e. depicted	5. undergone
_____ f. zealot	6. mental
_____ g. conspiracy	7. difference
_____ h. tantalizing	8. ability
_____ i. discrepancy	9. teasing
_____ j. aptitude	10. plot

Critical Thinking

A few of the theories Jeffrey Waggoner refers to are presented in the following brief excerpts from various books about the assassination. Match the theory with the paragraph by placing the number of the theory in the blank beside the paragraph.

1. Lee Harvey Oswald was a lone killer.
2. Lee Harvey Oswald was completely innocent.
3. The President was a victim of a CIA plot.
4. The President was innocently shot by a Secret Service Agent.

_____ Why should Oswald wish to assassinate the President; and after firing at the President, how did he plan to escape? Did he wish to flee from the building? If so, why did he remain in the lunchroom sipping a soda? Was he in a hurry? If so, why did he take a ride on a bus?

—Mark Lane, *Plausible Denial: Was the CIA Involved in the Assassination of JFK?*

_____ Agent Hickey had picked up his automatic rifle and was preparing to return the sniper's fire. Numerous witnesses had seen him with the gun in his hands. Hickey's actions, in fact, showed remarkable presence of mind and considerable courage. Pointing this out would have certainty [sic] put the Secret Service in a better light.

—Bonar Menninger, *Mortal Error: The Shot That Killed JFK*

_____ Lee Oswald has been repeatedly identified here as the President's slayer. He is never "alleged" or "suspected" or "supposed" or "surmised"; he is the culprit. . . . The evidence pointing to his guilt is far more incriminating than that against Booth, let alone Judas Iscariot. [John Wilkes Booth was the assassin of President Lincoln. Judas Iscariot was the Apostle who betrayed Jesus Christ.]

—William Manchester, *The Death of a President*

_____ [A summary of *They've Killed the President* by Robert Sam Anson] Anson's thesis is that there was a conspiracy in the assassination of President Kennedy, most probably involving the CIA and also probably involving organized crime, the FBI, and anti Castro elements, Jimmy Hoffa or his supporters, and/or "right-wing elements."

—David W. Belin, *Final Disclosure: The Full Truth about the Assassination of President Kennedy*

Points for Discussion

1. Using the following facts about each of the authors, describe the biases each appears to have.

Mark Lane, an author, lawyer, teacher, lecturer, and film-maker, was a campaign manager for JFK in 1960. He also wrote *Rush to Judgment*, a book criticizing the Warren Report.

Bias: _____

Bonar Menninger, a journalist, tells the story of Howard Donahue, a ballistics expert and firearms examiner.

Donahue presents evidence that the fatal shot came from Special Agent Hickey's gun.

Bias: _____

William Manchester is a journalist, researcher, observer of the Warren Commission, and close friend of the Kennedy family. In researching for this book, he gathered more than forty-five volumes of material.

Bias: _____

David W. Belin served as a lawyer, counsel to the Warren Commission, and a key investigator of the assassination.

Bias: _____

2. What conclusions can you draw from this exercise about the validity of what you read, even in books by experts?

_____

3. Share your conclusions with your group.

Chapter 7

Interpreting Purpose, Tone, and Figurative Language

There would seem to be almost no limit to what people can and will misunderstand when they are not doing their utmost to get at a writer's meaning.

Ezra Pound

Sometimes getting meaning from the written word is complicated by not understanding the writer's tone, purpose, and use of figurative language. For example, Jonathan Swift, author of *Gulliver's Travels,* wrote an essay called "A Modest Proposal" suggesting that Irish infants would make an excellent meat stew for the starving British and at the same time solve the problem of overpopulation. His purpose was to shame the British for the mistreatment of the Irish and the Irish for their passive acceptance. His tone was bitterly ironic. Many of his readers were horrified because they thought his suggestion was meant seriously. They did not get his meaning because they misunderstood his purpose and his tone. Figurative language can also be a stumbling block in the way of clear understanding because what is written is not meant to be read or understood literally.

This chapter will consider:

- how to determine a writer's purpose
- how to understand the writer's tone
- how to interpret figurative language

The Writer's Purpose

To fully understand the message a writer is delivering, it is not enough to recognize and understand main ideas, locate details, and make inferences for understanding. Inferences can be invalid if you are not aware of the purpose the writer hopes to achieve. Because writers want you to respond to what is written, they carefully select their words so that you can make the correct response. Writers usually have one of three major purposes:

1. To inform
2. To persuade
3. To entertain

The Purpose of Informing

The purpose most frequently found in your textbooks is probably to *inform*, that is, to share facts and ideas with you. Informative writing consists of sentences and paragraphs of explanation, definition, example, cause-and-effect, and comparison/contrast. Additionally, quotations from experts may be given to support the information presented. Newspapers, magazines, and the Internet are easily accessible sources of informational writing. Here is a paragraph example of informative writing about political action committees (PACs) adopted from a text on American government. The context of the paragraph is a larger discussion of political campaign financing supported by figures and facts from the Federal Election Commission.

Of all these forms of spending, probably the most controversial is that involving PAC money. Some PACs, due to the amount of money they are able to raise and their ability to get their supporters to the polls on Election Day, are more influential than others; but there are few poor, noninfluential PACs. Some observers claim that PACs are the embodiment of corrupt special interests that use campaign donations to buy the votes of legislators. Furthermore, they argue that the less affluent and minority members of our society do not enjoy equal access to these political organizations.

The paragraph indicates that PACs are controversial and gives a few reasons to support this generalization. The purpose is clearly to inform rather than persuade. It is important to remember that a selection may include paragraphs of information although the major purpose of the entire piece is to persuade. Careful reading of the entire selection is necessary to determine a writer's purpose.

The Purpose of Persuading

When writers present ideas in order to *persuade* you, they want to change your opinion or your actions. Their purpose is to make you think as they do, and they will make appeals to your reason and your emotions. Writers may use quotations from experts that support the view that they want you to accept. Persuasive writing in itself is neither good nor bad, but as you saw in Chapter 6, there are many ways to appeal to the reader with faulty or unsupported reasoning. Advertisements, editorials in newspapers, and letters to the editor usually have the purpose of persuading the reader. Jonathan Swift's modest proposal was intended to persuade his readers to take action to solve the problems of famine and overpopulation, not to make infant stew. Because readers misunderstood his purpose, they were horrified.

Read the following paragraph from an essay in which the writer presents his opinion that the habit of reading is declining and further argues that this decline will affect our ability to reason logically.

> Young people have been losing the newspaper habit even faster than their parents. "We are developing a generation that has no interest in reading except insofar as it is assigned in school," concludes Daniel Kevles, professor of humanities at Caltech. "They don't read newspapers or magazines. I sense a general lack of interest in public affairs among my students." A recent *Times Mirror* survey found that only 30% [of] Americans under the age of 35 said they had read a newspaper the previous day, compared to 67% in 1965.
>
> —Mitchell Stephens, "The Death of Reading,"
> *Los Angeles Times*

The writer has quoted an expert in the field and cited a survey to support his argument that people are no longer reading very much.

The Purpose of Entertaining

The primary purpose of many writers is to *entertain*. Don't confuse entertainment with something that makes you laugh, however. Laughter is the response to something humorous. Entertaining writing may be humorous, but it can also be descriptive, bringing a place or object or person vividly alive for you, or it can stir feelings or emotions in you through vivid anecdotes. We are also entertained by words and images that make chills run up and down our backs. Think of the movies you go to see that frighten you or even make you cry. Writers of novels, short stories, or poems write with the purpose of entertaining, as do many nonfiction writers. However, a writer whose main purpose is to inform or persuade may also use entertaining narratives, anecdotes, and descriptions to develop and support major ideas. Read the following paragraph from an essay by Dave Barry. If you are familiar with Barry's writing, you know that he intends to entertain you. If you have not read Barry's work before, you may think he intends to inform you because he seems to be presenting factual material.

> You may be interested to learn that thanks to a Used Gum Tracing procedure developed by the FBI, school authorities can now analyze the DNA in the dried-spit molecules, and by cross-referencing with your Permanent Record, determine *exactly who was chewing every single wad* [of gum]. This means that someday in the future—perhaps at your wedding—burly officers of the Gum Police will come barging in and arrest you and take you off to harsh prisons where you will be forced to eat food prepared by *the same people who ran your high-school cafeteria.*
>
> —Dave Barry, *Dave Barry Is Not Making This Up*

Barry's paragraph uses the FBI and DNA testing to suggest the possibility that someday you may be arrested for the gum wads you secretly deposited under desk tops and classroom seats in high school. At what point were you first sure that Barry was being funny?

It is important to be able to determine the writer's purpose so that you derive the messages intended. Use the following exercise to practice determining the writer's purpose.

Exercise 7-1   Determine the Purpose

Read the following sentences and label each according to the writer's purpose using these letters: (I) to inform, (P) to persuade, or (E) to entertain.

_____ 1. Fall was the smell of cherry pies baking in the oven of the wood stove, the smell of hams hanging in the smokehouse, the dry smell of fodder in the fields, and the pungent smell of apples.

_____ 2. The fall day was dark and dreary, promising snow before nightfall.

_____ 3. Encourage, but don't force, your child to exercise.

_____ 4. By the ninth century, many monks copied essays, histories, plays, and Bibles by hand on parchment to preserve these important works.

_____ 5. As darkness approached, the distant hill seemed to melt into the horizon and disappear.

_____ 6. *Roe v. Wade*, the Supreme Court decision allowing abortions, should be reversed. Abortions are legalized murder.

_____ 7. Talking computers have been possible for years, but the technology has been expensive and, for now, the applications are limited.

_____ 8. Talking about his early career as a boxer, Bob Hope says he was called "Rembrandt Hope" because he spent so much time on the canvas.

_____ 9. Every college student must have access to a computer even if it is only in a lab.

_____ 10. Well-rested people are awakened by their biological clocks at about the same time the alarm would usually go off.

The Writer's Tone

Closely related to the writer's purpose is the tone of the writing. In fact, mistaking the tone can cause a reader to misunderstand the purpose—for example, informing readers of a problem can be misread as persuading someone to commit a wrongdoing. Swift's "Modest Proposal" is an example. In the paragraph about a plan to solve the problem of gum wads under desks, we saw the purpose reflected by tone. *Tone* is easier to detect from speakers, whose facial expression, and voice often convey a special meaning. Try saying the following sentence to convey the three different meanings that follow.

"Sure, you can borrow my car tonight."

1. As if you are happy to oblige (sincerely)
2. As if you would never lend your car to this person under any condition (ironically)
3. As if speaking to your boss because you are secretly hoping for a raise (enthusiastically)

In writing, the tone and therefore the purpose of this statement are not so apparent. Tone reveals the feelings of the writer or the speaker and can change the message being given. The major clues to tone are the words the writer has chosen; consequently, it is important to pay attention to the words writers use. Another way to think about tone, as in the car example, is to see it as the attitude of the writer toward the ideas presented. What is the attitude of the following students toward test taking? Choose the feeling that describes the attitude from these tone words:

angry optimistic ironic cheerful depressed

_____ 1. I am excited about this test because I have studied hard, and I usually do well on essay tests.

_____ 2. I don't like taking tests, but I have prepared for this one and feel fairly comfortable about it.

_____ 3. Tests are a joke. I don't bother preparing because I can't guess what is in the professor's mind.

_____ 4. I didn't do well on the last test, and I probably won't do well this time, either.

_____ 5. I hate tests. I'd like to organize a protest in favor of abolishing tests.

Irony

A tone that is frequently used but sometimes easy to miss is called *ironic*. (You may remember that the word was introduced in Chapter 5.) The tone is ironic when what is presented is the opposite of what is intended. Similarly, a situation is ironic when it is the opposite of what is expected. For example, the situation is ironic when someone who doesn't study does extremely well on an exam. The tone is ironic when someone says, after admiring a sensational new car, "I wouldn't have that old heap if someone gave it to me." (As a further example, sentence 1 above could possibly be ironic if the speaker has difficulty with essay tests.)

To help yourself detect tone in writing, study the following list of tone words. You may need to use the dictionary and make vocabulary cards for some of the words. Words that express similar attitudes or feelings are grouped together, but they are not always exact synonyms.

angry	*ironic*	*sorrowful*
vindictive	sarcastic	distressed
indignant	cynical	depressed
malicious	mocking	uneasy

happy	*objective*	*sympathetic*
optimistic	formal	compassionate
humorous	matter-of-fact	tolerant
amused	serious	patient

Exercise 7-2 Becoming Familiar with More Tone Words

Using a thesaurus, a dictionary of synonyms, find more synonyms for the tone words in the following list. (If you don't have a thesaurus, a dictionary will be helpful, but it won't give you as many possible synonyms.) Think about the synonyms that you find. Could a writer use this tone in writing? If you think not, don't include the word. Could any of these words be grouped under the headings given in the preceding list?

excited   critical   vengeful   melancholy   sentimental

_____   _____   _____   _____   _____

_____   _____   _____   _____   _____

_____   _____   _____   _____   _____

Exercise 7-3 Finding Purpose and Tone in Paragraphs

Read the following passages to determine the purpose of the writer and the tone used. Use the two lists of words given on pages 276–77 and recall that the writer's purpose is either to inform, to entertain, or to persuade. Write your answers below the paragraphs with purpose first, followed by tone.

1. What do cats eat? Usually, cats are pretty fussy about their menu. But one cat, call him Herman, chose a really strange menu. He ate an entire watermelon and promptly died. Cats rarely eat fruit, and certainly not an entire watermelon. Herman's human caretakers were filled with grief, so they gave Herman a proper cat funeral and buried him in the backyard. Fall passed into winter, followed by spring. Herman's owners went to check on his gravesite. Lo and behold, a watermelon patch was sprouting on the spot!

_____   _____

2. Many smokers think about quitting. Thinking doesn't cut it. Look at the good things that occur once a smoker throws away the weed. Shortly after quitting, a smoker begins to look and feel better. Coughs disappear. The odor of cigarettes in the smoker's hair and clothes is gone. A nonsmoker runs far less chance of dying of lung cancer, stroke, or heart attack. These are facts. If you're a smoker, face facts and start to be good to yourself.

---

3. Fifty years ago, kids got their culture from comics, a few movies, and radio, with boundaries supplied by religious, family, and educational structures. Today some of those structural boundaries are weakened. At the same time youngsters sit at the center of vast entertainment and informational resources. They are bombarded by cable channels, videos, Nintendo, and the Internet. Once there was a trickle of information coming to kids from outside the borders of healthy structures. Today the trickle has become a flood. You may consider this flood a miracle or a nightmare, but you must be aware that it is reality.

---

4. I hate blind dates. You never know what kind of a dud your best friend will dig up for you. "Dig up" is the right expression. Some of the characters I've met on a blind date should be returned immediately to the cemetery. That's why I was very reluctant to take a chance on the date my roommate insisted was a perfect match for me. Would you believe, after a whirlwind courtship, we were married last week? Proves there's an exception to every rule.

---

5. When you study mathematics, it is important to develop a spirit of independence. Try to do all assigned problems without assistance. If it's necessary to discuss your difficulties with a classmate or instructor, you will not gain the most from your efforts. Don't, however, hesitate to ask questions when a problem arises. If you have tried to work with a concept and have not been successful, it is important to ask for help. You need to develop the good sense to know the difference between asking for help too soon and waiting too long to ask for help.

_____   _____

Exercise 7-4   For Discussion

Discuss your answers to the exercise on tone and purpose with others in your group. There is only one right answer for the purpose blank. But you may have some different answers for the tone blank. Discuss what in the paragraph led you to determine the tone. In discussion, you may find that group members have chosen different words to describe tone but that the words are synonyms.

Figurative Language

Reading that involves understanding the exact meaning of the words and ideas presented is called *literal reading.* For some academic reading, particularly in literature and composition courses where you will read much narrative and descriptive material, you will need to read and interpret figurative language.

Figurative language requires you to understand more than the literal or exact words. You do a kind of mental translation of the words. For example, you have heard someone say or said yourself, "I've told you a thousand times." This statement is not to be taken literally. The speaker is using *exaggeration* to make the point that they have said something before. Exaggeration, or *hyperbole,* is usually easy to detect. When you detect figurative language, you must read and think beyond the words, visualize, and use your other four senses. Doing this will help you appreciate the ideas and the emotions conveyed by what is written. There are a number of other figures of speech besides hyperbole. Four are considered here: *idioms, similes, metaphors, and symbols.* Study the following examples.

Idioms

Example: Has anyone ever asked you if you got up on the wrong side of the bed?

Explanation: An *idiom* is a set expression with a special meaning. The meaning here is that someone thinks you are unusually moody or grumpy today.

Idioms can be tricky. On the one hand, if you have not heard the expression before, you may not understand what the idiom means. On the other hand, idioms can be overused, tired expressions, called *clichés.* Many idioms have colorful backgrounds that add to their meaning when you are aware of the story behind the expression. If someone tells you "your name is mud," you have two reasons for being upset. It's clear that mud is unpleasant, but long ago "mud" was a slang expression for "fool."

If your brother suggests that a good apartment is available at a reasonable rate, he might tell you to "strike while the iron is hot." You do not take him literally; instead, you understand that you should take advantage of the opportunity immediately. This expression developed from the work of blacksmiths who heated metal to repair horseshoes. When the metal was glowing red, the blacksmith pounded the metal into shape. If he waited too long, the metal would cool and have to be heated again.

If you have ever seen a possum, you understand that the idiom "to play possum" means to pretend to be asleep or unaware. If a possum senses danger, it becomes limp and appears dead. When the danger is past, the possum scurries away. Ever have to "shell out" money for an unexpected expense? This expression comes from colonial days when Indian corn was used for money. The corn was left on the cob until the purchase was completed, when the buyer would shell out the corn to pay for the item. Try translating the idioms in the exercise that follows.

Exercise 7-5   Working with Idioms

Explain the intended meaning of the underlined idiom. Write the intended meaning on the line below the expression. If you have not heard the expression before, make your best guess. You may want to discuss your answers with others in your group. The first one is done as an example.

1. The senator didn't answer the question directly; instead, he <u>beat around the bush</u>.

     He evaded the question.

2. The juror found the accused guilty <u>beyond a shadow of a doubt</u>.

3. Having lost her job, Sabrina was advised by friends to <u>keep a stiff upper lip</u>.

   _____

4. When Sara was angry at Scot's comment, he said, "I wasn't serious. I was just <u>pulling your leg</u>."

   _____

5. Angela wanted the stereo, but decided against buying because it <u>cost an arm and a leg</u>.

   _____

6. The test was a <u>piece of cake</u>.

   _____

7. Learning to use the computer is as <u>easy as pie</u>.

   _____

8. Taking more courses than you can handle is having <u>too many irons in the fire</u>.

   _____

9. When Sandy called to Ricco to hurry up, he said, "<u>Keep your shirt on</u>."

   _____

10. When you want to repeat gossip, it is best to <u>hold your tongue</u>.

   _____

Similes

Example: Did anyone ever tell you that they could read you like an open book?

Explanation: A *simile* is a comparison of two unlike things using "like" or "as." Writers use similes to add meaning and color beyond the actual written words. In this case, the speaker is saying that she knows you, your feelings, and your intentions as if she had read all about them. When the poet William Wordsworth wrote, "I wandered lonely as a cloud," he compares himself to a cloud alone in a blue expanse of sky. The simile lets the reader visualize and feel his loneliness. When the poet Langston Hughes asks if a dream deferred (put off) is "like a raisin in the sun," he suggests that the dream has dried up or died. Work with the similes that follow.

Exercise 7-6   Similes

Remember that a simile helps the reader to visualize the comparison being made by using like *or as to direct attention to the comparison. Study the following similes and write the two things that are compared. The first one is done for you.*

1. The barber's scissors clacked around my head like a pair of castanets.

   sound of scissors, clacking of castanets

2. Wearing high heels, she was as graceful as a newborn calf stumbling after its mother. (Note the irony in this comparison.)

   _____

3. The angry woman sounded like she was fastening each word with a thumbtack.

   _____

4. The shoppers, having stood in line for an hour waiting for the store to open, advanced on the open door like an avenging army.

   _____

5. The apples hung like Christmas ornaments on the loaded trees.

   _____

6. The morning after the big party, she felt like all the symptoms on her aspirin bottle.

   _____

7. While he waited for his date to answer the door, his heart chugged like a jalopy trying to climb a steep hill.

---

8. She was as thin as a soda straw.

---

9. The red poppies waved in the breeze like a matador's cape.

---

10. White clouds trailed across the sky like wisps of smoke.

Metaphors

Example: Elephants in the wild are mighty battleships surging across the plains.

Explanation: A *metaphor,* like a simile, is a comparison of two unlike things used to paint a word picture and enhance your pleasure in reading. The only difference is that in a metaphor the comparison is made without using the words *like* or *as.* We know that an elephant is not a battleship, but we form a picture of an elephant's movement. Have you ever seen geese flying south in V formation? One poet saw them as "pulling in winter," that is, their formation seems to pull winter behind them. Try working with some metaphors.

Exercise 7-7   Metaphors

Although metaphors sometimes directly state that one thing is another, often the comparison is implied. In these cases, you will need to think creatively to find the comparisons being made. Ask yourself what is being compared to what, or what is like some other object. Write the comparisons on the line below the statement. The first one is completed for you.

1. Hawks sliced the evening sky looking for carrion.

   <u>Hawks cut through the sky like knives</u>

2. His shirt was covered with polka dots of spilled coffee.

   _____

3. Her eyes were big blue question marks.

   _____

4. The school bus gobbled up the children waiting in front of their homes.

   _____

5. His ramrod-straight back gave him the appearance of dignity.

   _____

6. After the instructor's question, the students sat with zippered mouths.

   _____

7. He was only a little man, but he was starched with self-esteem.

   _____

8. The old woman spent hours wandering through the fields of memory.

   _____

9. The threads of the sad tale were finally woven.

   _____

10. Tossed by the wind, the broken swing creaked eerily.

    _____

Exercise 7-8   Creating Similes and Metaphors

Try making your own similes and metaphors for extra practice in recognizing them. Take any two activities from the following list and compare them—for example, Dancing and Skydiving.

When I'm dancing, I feel like I'm floating free in the blue sky.

Building a bridge	Playing cards
Cleaning house	Ice skating
Swimming	Dancing
Taking a test	Skydiving
Eating a steak	Going to the dentist

Symbols

Example: A politician might say, "I stand for motherhood, apple pie, and freedom."

Explanation: A *symbol* is similar to a metaphor except that the comparison is even more hidden because the object being compared is omitted. Symbols stand for other things. Apple pie, for example, stands for home. Sometimes it is clear to everyone what a symbol means. A heart symbolizes love and a dove symbolizes peace. We are familiar with many symbols in our daily lives and, in fact, take them for granted. Sometimes, however, a symbol is more complex, with a circle of meaning. In the discussion following the next exercise, you will see that you and your classmates may have different associations for the same symbol.

Exercise 7-9   Thinking about Symbols

The following are some familiar symbols. In the blank after each symbol, note the associations you make with it. Some symbols will have more than one idea associated with them.

Symbol	**Associations**
1. four-leafed clover	_____
2. black cat	_____
3. elephant	_____
4. light bulb	_____
5. Uncle Sam	_____
6. a rose	_____
7. diploma	_____

8. clock   _____

9. owl   _____

10. broken heart   _____

In discussion you may have noted that some group members have different answers for these common symbols. The associations you make are a result of your background and experiences. Colors used symbolically are especially confusing. For example, the color red suggests love (valentines), danger (stop sign), and anger (a flushed face.) Symbols depend for their meaning on context (just as vocabulary words do) and change their meaning in a different time and place. How do you know when a word, color, or idea is being used as a symbol? In a story, the symbol will be repeated. Just because a character looks at his watch does not make the watch a symbol. If the writer frequently refers to this watch, it is probably a symbol that will add meaning to the story if you observe it.

Notice how differently two poets use the rose. One uses a rose as a comparison, and the other uses a rose as a symbol.

> O, my luve is like a red, red rose
>   That's newly sprung in June;
> O, my luve is like the melodie
>   That's sweetly played in tune.
>   —Robert Burns, "A Red, Red Rose"

> 'Tis the last rose of summer
>   Left blooming alone;
> All her lovely companions
>   Are faded and gone.
>   —Thomas Moore, "'Tis the Last Rose"

In the first selection the poet's loved one is compared to a rose, which suggests her beauty. The tone is light and happy. In the second selection, the rose symbolizes not only the end of summer but also death. The tone is one of sadness.

Exercise 7-10 Understanding a Short Paragraph

Read the following short paragraph, which uses several kinds of figurative language to describe the difficulties of being the father of teenage daughters, and answer the questions that follow.

The worst time for a father comes when his daughter is fifteen. I have now had three daughters pass through the treacherous waters of fifteen and I'm not sure I'll be strong enough to man the lighthouse for the fourth. I have heard the long phone conversations full of mournful sounds, conversations that have left my daughters looking a little less balanced than Scarlett O'Hara. I have seen them trying to learn about love, the only subject that no one has ever been able to study for.

—Bill Cosby, *Love and Marriage*

1. Label the following topics or subjects as too broad (B), too narrow (N), comprehensive (C).

   _____ a. Raising daughters

   _____ b. Daughters on the phone

   _____ c. Daughters at fifteen

2. What is the meaning of "treacherous" underlined in the passage?

   _____ difficult

   _____ disloyal

   _____ dark

3. What does Cosby mean by the idiom "man the lighthouse"?

   _____

4. Scarlett O'Hara is the romantic and troubled heroine of the book and movie *Gone with the Wind*. What do you think Cosby is implying when he compares his daughters to Scarlett?

   _____

   _____

Exercise 7-11 Understanding a Poem

A poem does not require the same kind of prereading activities that you usually do. It does, however, require rereading. Reading the poem aloud is also helpful. Look for vivid images and comparisons. Langston Hughes was an important African American poet during the Harlem Renaissance when African American culture flourished in New York City. What difficulties might an African American have encountered some sixty years ago?

MOTHER TO SON

Well, son, I'll tell you:
Life for me ain't been no crystal stair.
It's had tacks in it,
And splinters,
And boards torn up,
And places with no carpet on the floor—
Bare.
But all the time
I'se been a-climbin' on,
And reachin' landin's
And turnin' corners,
And sometimes goin' in the dark
Where there ain't been no light.
So, boy, don't you turn back.
Don't you set down on the steps
'Cause you finds it kinder hard.
Don't you fall now—
For I'se still goin' honey,
I'se still climbin'
And life for me ain't been no crystal stair.

Questions About the Poem

1. To what does the mother compare her life?

   _____

2. What specific words are symbols for the difficulties of her life?

   _____

3. Write below some actual or literal problems that the image words in your answer to item 2 might represent.

   _____

   _____

4. In your own words, write the mother's message to her son.

   _____

_____

5. Why would this mother's message be taken seriously by her son?

_____

_____

_____

Chapter Review

Fill in the blanks with the correct answers from the reading.

1. What are the three purposes a writer may have for writing?

   1. _____   2. _____   3. _____

2. What were the four kinds of figurative language noted in the chapter?

   1. _____   2. _____   3. _____   4. _____

Label the following statement as true or false.

_____ 1. A writer may have different purposes for individual paragraphs in a selection.

Reading Selection 1

Purpose

We often hear from others and sometimes feel ourselves that we are not working hard enough, being productive enough, using our time well enough. You learned as a child to be "busy as beaver." Perhaps you read Aesop's animal fables and learned of the industry and cleverness of certain animals. Scientists in many fields have recently looked more closely at animals. Their studies, used as a source for this article, suggest some new ideas about animals, rest, and laziness. You will also notice some figurative speech used in the article.

Preview

1. Read the first paragraph and quickly skim the rest of the article by reading the first sentences of paragraphs.
2. Look over the questions and the vocabulary at the end.

Anticipate/Associate

1. Have you ever watched any animals or insects closely? What habits of some creatures do you admire?
2. What do you think scientists might have learned from close observance of different species?

As Lazy As a Beaver

Natalie Angier

In these <u>languid</u> mid-summer days, people who feel the urge to take it easy but remain burdened by a <u>recalcitrant</u> work ethic might do well to consider that laziness is perfectly natural, perfectly sensible and shared by nearly every other species on the planet.

Contrary to fables about the <u>unflagging</u> industrious of ants, bees, beavers and the like, field biologists engaged in a new specialty known as time budget analysis are discovering that the great majority of creatures spend most of their time doing nothing much at all.

They eat when they must or can. They court and breed when driven by seasonal impulses. Some species build a makeshift shelter now and again, while others fulfill the occasional social obligation, like picking out fleas from a fellow creature's fur.

But more often than not, animals across the <u>phylogenetic</u> spectrum will thumb a <u>proboscis</u> at biblical injunctions to labor—and proceed to engage in any number of inactive activities: sitting, sprawling, dozing, rocking back and forth, ambling around in <u>desultory</u> circles.

"If you follow an organism in the field for extended periods of time, and catalog every type of activity for every moment of the day, you can't help but come to the conclusion, by George, this organism isn't doing much, is it?" said John Herbers, a zoologist at the University of Vermont, who has written comparative reports of laziness in animals. "Being lazy is almost universal."

In fact, compared with other creatures, human beings spend anywhere from two to four times as many hours working, particularly if family, household and social duties are taken into account.

But lest people feel <u>smug</u> about their <u>diligence</u>, evolutionary biologists are discovering that animal inactivity is almost never born of aimless <u>indolence</u>, but instead serves a broad variety of purposes.

Some animals sit around to conserve precious calories,   8
others to improve digestion of the calories they have consumed. Some do it to stay cool, others to keep warm.

Predators and prey alike are best camouflaged when they   9
are not fidgeting or fussing.

Some creatures linger quietly in their territory to guard   10
it, and others stay home to avoid being cannibalized by their
neighbors.

So while there many not be a specific gene for laziness,   11
there is always a good excuse.

"When you just see an animal that looks like it's in re-   12
pose, you may be looking at any number of very adaptive features," said Paul Sherman of Cornell University in Ithaca,
N.Y. "You can't say it's simply doing nothing, and you can't
always predict from common sense alone what the apparent
rest is all about."

So diverse are the possible reasons for laziness that some   13
biologists are beginning to shift the focus of their research.
Rather than observing the behavior of animals in action, as
field researchers historically have, they are attempting to understand the many factors that lie behind animal inertia.

They hope that by learning when and why an animal   14
chooses inactivity, they can better understand key mysteries
of ecology, like the distribution of different species in a particular environment and how animals survive harsh settings
and lean times.

"In the past, field biologists focused on movement,   15
foraging, mating behavior," said Herbers. "Now they're worrying about why animals sit still."

Animals certainly give their researchers much to fret over.   16

Craig Packer and Anne Pusey, zoologists with the Uni-   17
versity of Minnesota in Minneapolis, have studied lions in
the Serengeti since the 1970s. They say nearly all of that time
has been spent staring through binoculars at tawny heaps of
fur, the pride's collective immobility broken only by the
intermittent twitch of an ear.

"A lion can lie in the same spot, without budging, for 12   18
hours at a stretch," said Pusey. "They're active on their feet
maybe two or three hours a day." In that brief spate of effort,
they are likely to be either hunting or devouring the booty of
that hunt, which is one reason they need so much downtime.

"A lion can eat an enormous amount in one sitting,"   19
maybe 70 pounds of meat," said Pusey. "Their bellies get extremely fat, and they look incredibly uncomfortable and incredibly immobile, lying on their backs and panting in the heat.

Monkeys are commonly thought of as nature's indefati-   20
gable acrobats, but many species sit around as much as three-

quarters of the day, not to mention the 12 hours of the night they usually spend sleeping.

Frans de Waal, a primatologist at the Yerkes Regional Primate Center in Atlanta and author of "Peacemaking among Primates," said that he was amused to discover the lax habits of the woolly spider monkey, which he observed in Brazil with Karen Stryer.   21

One morning the two researchers awoke before dawn to get out to a distant observation site by 7 A.M., when they assumed the monkeys would begin their day's foraging.   22

"We were sitting there and sitting there," said de Waal. "By 11 o'clock, the monkeys were still sleeping, at which point I fell asleep myself."   23

Hummingbirds are the world's most vigorous and energy-intensive fliers—when they are flying. The birds turn out to spend 80 percent of their day perched motionless on a twig; at night, they sleep.   24

Beavers are thought to bustle about so single-mindedly that their name is often used as a synonym for work. But beavers emerge from the safe haven of their lodge to gather food or to patch up their dam for only five hours a day, give or take a few intermissions.   25

"Even when they're supposed to be most active, they'll retreat back into the lodge for long periods of time, and rest," said Gerald E. Svendsen, a zoologist at Ohio University in Athens who studies beavers.   26

Even the busy bees or worker ants of Aesopian fame dedicate only about 20 percent of the day to doing chores like gathering nectar or tidying up the nest. Otherwise, the insects stay still.   27

"They seem to have run out of work to do," said Gene E. Robinson, an entomologist at the University of Illinois in Urbana-Champaign. "They really do look lazy."   28

Biologists studying animals at rest turn to sophisticated mathematical models resembling those used by economists, which take into account an animal's energy demands, fertility rate, the relative abundance and location of food and water, weather conditions and other factors.   29

They do extensive cost-benefit analyses, asking questions like: How high is the cost of foraging compared to the potential calories that may be gained?   30

Such a calculation involves not only a measure of how much more energy an animal burns as it rummages about relative to what it would spend resting, but also a consideration of, for example, how hot it will become in motion, and how much of its stored water will then be needed to evaporate away heat to cool the body.   31

Overheating can be a deadly threat for many animals.   32

When they complete their computations, biologists usu-   33
ally end up respecting an animal's decision to lie low.

"Let's say a moose spends so much time foraging that its   34
body temperature rises close to the lethal maximum," said
Gary E. Belovsky, associate professor of wildlife ecology at
the University of Michigan in Ann Arbor.

"And let's say a wolf comes along and chases it. Well,   35
that raises the moose's body temperature further, and it's
likely to drop over dead. The moose must stay cool if it is to
survive."

And perhaps biologists who study inactivity can even   36
lend luster to the much-<u>maligned</u> creature that gave laziness
its most <u>evocative</u> term: the sloth.

Found throughout Central and South America, the sloth   37
hangs from trees by its long rubbery limbs, sleeping 15 hours
a day and moving so infrequently that two species of algae
grow on its coat and between its claws.

A newborn sloth sits atop its mother's belly and is so   38
loath to move that it freely defecates and urinates onto her
fur, which she will only intermittently bother to clean.

But lest such sluggishness seem almost perverse, the   39
sloth is suited to its niche. By moving so slowly, it stays re-
markably inconspicuous to predators. Even its fungal coat
serves a camouflaging purpose.

With the algae glinting greenish-blue in the sunlight, the   40
sloth resembles the hanging plant it has very nearly become.

Check Your Understanding

Review

*List five animals mentioned in the article and give a reason for
their laziness.*

1. _____

   _____

   _____

2. _____

   _____

   _____

3. _____

   _____

   _____

4. _____

   _____

   _____

5. _____

   _____

   _____

Fill in the Blanks

Complete the statements by writing the best word in the blank.

1. Many reasons are given for the apparent _____ of animals.

2. A new type of study done by biologists is called _____ _____ analysis.

3. Animals and insects have a variety of _____ for their indolence.

4. A lion can eat _____ pounds of meat in at one feeding.

5. Even hummingbirds spend _____ percent of their day resting.

Multiple Choice

Select the letter of the answer that best completes the statement.

____ 1. The main idea is:
  a. Many animals spend time doing nothing at all.

      b. Humans are more hard-working than animals.

      c. We may have the wrong idea about animals.

      d. Studies show that animals are lazy for a purpose.

_____ 2. We can infer that

      a. animals' laziness has a purpose.

      b. scientists are studying animal behavior.

      c. we know all there is to know about animals.

      d. none of the above.

_____ 3. Animals rest a lot

      a. to avoid becoming prey to another animal.

      b. because they are naturally lazy.

      c. to avoid becoming chilled or overheated.

      d. a and c above.

_____ 4. The facts in the article are supported by

      a. statistical facts.

      b. observations made by experts.

      c. opinions.

      d. examples.

_____ 5. The writer's main purpose is to

      a. inform.

      b. persuade.

      c. entertain.

      d. a and c above.

True/False

Label the following statements as true or false.

_____ 1. The writer sometimes uses words like *proboscis* for "nose" to create a humorous effect.

_____ 2. The sloth moves so slowly that it collects moss.

_____ 3. Scientists are discovering that animals, seemingly lazy, are really resting for good reasons.

_____ 4. Aesop, the ancient fable writer, must have spent a lot of time observing animals.

_____ 5. Animals do nothing just because they feel like doing nothing.

_____ 6. People can learn some valuable lessons from the animals.

_____ 7. Scientists have learned all they can from the habits of animals.

_____ 8. Apparent laziness in animals is often a means of survival.

_____ 9. You can infer from the article that studying animal behavior is a waste of time.

_____ 10. You can conclude that animals learn to adapt to their environment.

Vocabulary

I. The suffix -ist *indicates a noun form, and the suffix* -ologist *means "one who studies." Using that information, complete these statements. Consult the article and the dictionary for help if necessary.*

1. A economist is one who studies the _____.

2. A primatologist is one who studies _____.

3. One who studies animals is a _____.
   (*Hint:* Where are caged animals kept?)

4. One who studies plant and animal life is a _____.

5. An entomologist studies _____.

Matching

II. Put the matching letter from Column B before its synonym in Column A.

Column A   Column B

_____ 1. languid   a. of evolutionary history

_____ 2. unflagging   b. calling forth

_____ 3. phylogenetic   c. spoken badly about

_____ 4. proboscis   d. inactivity

_____ 5. desultory   e. varied

_____ 6. predators   f. nose

_____ 7. maligned   g. aimless

_____ 8. diverse   h. tireless

_____ 9. evocative   i. relaxed

_____ 10. inertia   j. animals that prey on others

Vocabulary

III. Complete the sentences using the following words.

recalcitrant   diligent   indolence
ecology   smug   intermittently
immobility   indefatigable   spate
foraging

1. Even the ants are not as _____ as we thought.

2. When your car won't run, it's in a state of _____.

3. Sometimes the car runs, but only _____.

4. Teenagers are often found _____ in the fridge.

5. The unexpected death caused a _____ of emotions.

6. The study of organisms within their environment is called _____.

7. You can learn habits of _____ from the animals.

8. Perhaps humans are too inclined to _____.

9. One successful attempt can lead you to be _____.

10. The prisoner was punished for his _____ behavior.

Writing

1. Write a paragraph explaining three reasons that animals apparently spend so much time at rest. Use a specific animal to illustrate each reason.
2. Write a paragraph summarizing the main ideas of this article. (Remember, no details, just main ideas.)
3. Write a paragraph describing the activity of an animal or insect that you have observed.
4. Write a paragraph discussing the tone of this article. Give details in your paragraph to support your conclusion about the writer's tone.

Critical Thinking

1. What value to humans is there in the extensive study of animals described in the article?
2. Should animals be used for human experimentation, such as testing perfume, face powder, or medicines? Give reasons for or against.

3. Do you think most humans work too hard compared with other animals? Why do humans work so hard? What is gained, and what is lost, by humans' diligence at work?

Reading Selection 2

Purpose

Your first purpose for reading a short story like the one that follows is for entertainment—pleasure or enjoyment. However, since you know you will be answering questions about the story, a careful rereading will be necessary.

Preview

1. Since this selection is a story, reading first sentences is not a helpful way to preview. Instead, read the questions carefully and glance at the vocabulary at the end of this chapter.
2. As you read, try to place yourself in the story by imagining you are the main character, the old woman named Phoenix. Consider that her name relates her to the phoenix, a mythological bird that lived in the desert. Every 500 years it would fly into an altar fire, and be completely destroyed, then arise from the fire renewed.

Anticipate/Associate

1. Have you known any older persons who have shown great strength in dealing with the problems of daily living?
2. Ask yourself in your reading why the old woman is making this difficult trip.

A Worn Path

Eudora Welty

It was December—a bright frozen day in the early morn-   1
ing. Far out in the country there was an old Negro woman with her head tied in a red rag, coming along a path through the pinewoods. Her name was Phoenix Jackson. She was very old and small and she walked slowly in the dark pine shadows, moving a little from side to side in her steps, with the balanced heaviness and lightness of a pendulum in a grandfather

clock. She carried a thin, small cane made from an umbrella, and with this she kept tapping the frozen earth in front of her. This made a grave and <u>persistent</u> noise in the still air, that seemed <u>meditative</u> like the chirping of a solitary little bird.

She wore a dark striped dress reaching down to her shoe tops, and an equally long apron of bleached sugar sacks, with a full pocket: all neat and tidy, but every time she took a step she might have fallen over her shoelaces, which dragged from her unlaced shoes. She looked straight ahead. Her eyes were blue with age. Her skin had a pattern all its own of number-less branching wrinkles and as though a whole little tree stood in the middle of her forehead, but a golden color ran un-derneath, and the two knobs of her cheeks were <u>illuminated</u> by a yellow burning under the dark. Under the red rag her hair came down on her neck in the <u>frailest</u> of ringlets, still black, and with an odor like copper.

Now and then there was a <u>quivering</u> in the thicket. Old Phoenix said, "Out of my way, all you foxes, owls, beetles, jack rabbits, coons and wild animals! . . . Keep out from under these feet, little bob-whites. . . . Keep the big wild hogs out of my path. Don't let none of those come running my di-rection. I got a long way." Under her small black-freckled hand her cane, limber as a buggy whip, would switch at the brush as if to rouse up any hiding things.

On she went. The woods were deep and still. The sun made the pine needles almost too bright to look at, up where the wind rocked. The cones dropped as light as feathers. Down in the hollow was the mourning dove—it was not too late for him.

The path ran up a hill. "Seem like there is chains about my feet, time I get this far," she said, in the voice of argument old people keep to use with themselves. "Something always take a hold of me on this hill—pleads I should stay."

After she got to the top she turned and gave a full, <u>severe</u> look behind her where she had come. "Up through pines," she said at length. "Now down through oaks."

Her eyes opened their widest, and she started down gen-tly. But before she got to the bottom of the hill a bush caught her dress.

Her fingers were busy and intent, but her skirts were full and long, so that before she could pull them free in one place they were caught in another. It was not possible to allow the dress to tear. "I in the thorny bush," she said. "Thorns, you doing your appointed work. Never want to let folks pass, no sir. Old eyes thought you was a pretty little *green* bush."

Finally, trembling all over, she stood free, and after a mo-ment dared to stoop for her cane.

"Sun so high!" she cried, leaning back and looking, while the thick tears went over her eyes. "The time getting all gone here."   10

At the foot of this hill was a place where a log was laid across the creek.   11

"Now comes the trial," said Phoenix.   12

Putting her right foot out, she mounted the log and shut her eyes. Lifting her skirt, leveling her cane fiercely before her, like a <u>festival</u> figure in some parade, she began to march across. Then she opened her eyes and she was safe on the other side.   13

"I wasn't as old as I thought," she said.   14

But she sat down to rest. She spread her skirts on the bank around her and folded her hands over her knees. Up above her was a tree in a pearly cloud of mistletoe. She did not dare to close her eyes, and when a little boy brought her a plate with a slice of marble-cake on it she spoke to him. "That would be acceptable," she said. But when she went to take it there was just her own hand in the air.   15

So she left that tree, and had to go through a barbed-wire fence. There she had to creep and crawl, spreading her knees and stretching her fingers like a baby trying to climb the steps. But she talked loudly to herself: she could not let her dress be torn now, so late in the day, and she could not pay for having her arm or her leg sawed off if she got caught fast where she was.   16

At last she was safe through the fence and risen up out in the clearing. Big dead trees, like black men with one arm, were standing in the purple stalks of the withered cotton field. There sat a buzzard.   17

"Who you watching?"   18

In the furrow she made her way along.   19

"Glad this not the season for bulls," she said, looking sideways, "and the good Lord made his snakes to curl up and sleep in the winter. A pleasure I don't see no two-headed snake coming around that tree, where it come once. It took a while to get by him, back in the summer."   20

She passed through the old cotton and went into a field of dead corn. It whispered and shook and was taller than her head. "Through the maze now," she said, for there was no path.   21

Then there was something tall, black, and skinny there, moving before her.   22

At first she took it for a man. It could have been a man dancing in the field. But she stood still and listened, and it did not make a sound. It was as silent as a ghost.   23

"Ghost," she said sharply, "who be you the ghost of? For I have heard of nary death close by."   24

But there was no answer—only the ragged dancing in the   25
wind.

She shut her eyes, reached out her hand, and touched a   26
sleeve. She found a coat and inside that an emptiness, cold
as ice.

"You scarecrow," she said. Her face lighted. "I ought to   27
be shut up for good," she said with laughter. "My senses is
gone. I too old. I the oldest people I ever know. Dance, old
scarecrow," she said, "while I dancing with you."

She kicked her foot over the furrow, and with mouth   28
drawn down, shook her head once or twice in a little strutting
way. Some husks blew down and whirled in streamers about
her skirts.

Then she went on, parting her way from side to side   29
with the cane, through the whispering field. At last she came
to the end, to a wagon track where the silver grass blew between the red ruts. The quail were walking around like pul-
lets, seeming all dainty and unseen.

"Walk pretty," she said. "This the easy place. This the   30
easy going."

She followed the track, swaying through the quiet bare   31
fields, through the little strings of trees silver in their dead
leaves, past cabins silver from weather, with the doors and
windows boarded shut, all like old women under a spell sitting there. "I walking in their sleep," she said, nodding her
head <u>vigorously</u>.

In a ravine she went where a spring was silent flowing   32
through a hollow log. Old Phoenix bent and drank. "Sweet-gum
makes the water sweet," she said, and drank more. "Nobody
know who made this well, for it was here when I was born."

The track crossed a swampy part where the moss hung   33
as white as lace from every limb. "Sleep on, alligators, and
blow your bubbles." Then the track went into the road.

Deep, deep the road went down between the high green-   34
colored banks. Overhead the live-oaks met, and it was as dark
as a cave.

A black dog with a lolling tongue came up out of the   35
weeds by the ditch. She was meditating, and not ready, and
when he came at her she only hit him a little with her cane.
Over she went in the ditch, like a little puff of milkweed.

Down there, her senses drifted away, A dream visited   36
her, and she reached her hand up, but nothing reached down
and gave her a pull. So she lay there and presently went to
talking. "Old woman," she said to herself, "that black dog
come up out of the weeds to stall you off, and now there he
sitting on his fine tail, smiling at you."

A white man finally came along and found her—a   37
hunter, a young man, with his dog on a chain.

"Well, Granny!" he laughed. "What are you doing there?"   38

"Lying on my back like a June-bug waiting to be turned   39
over, mister," she said, reaching up her hand.

He lifted her up, gave her a swing in the air, and set her   40
down. "Anything broken, Granny?"

"No, sir, them old dead weeds is springy enough," said   41
Phoenix, when she had got her breath. "I thank you for your
trouble."

"Where do you live, Granny?" he asked, while the two   42
dogs were growling at each other.

"Away back yonder, sir, behind the ridge. You can't even   43
see it from here."

"On your way home?"   44

"No sir, I going to town."   45

"Why, that's too far! That's as far as I walk when I come   46
out myself, and I get something for my trouble." He patted
the stuffed bag he carried, and there hung down a little closed
claw. It was one of the bob-whites, and its beak hooked bitterly to show it was dead. "Now you go home, Granny!"

"I bound to go to town, mister," said Phoenix. "The   47
time come around."

He gave another laugh, filling the whole landscape. "I   48
know you old colored people! Wouldn't miss going to town to
see Santa Claus!"

But something held old Phoenix very still. The deep   49
lines in her face went into a fierce and different <u>radiation</u>.
Without warning, she had seen with her own eyes a flashing
nickel fall out of the man's pocket onto the ground.

"How old are you, Granny?" he was saying.   50

"There is no telling, mister," she said, "no telling."   51

Then she gave a little cry and clapped her hands and   52
said, "Git on away from here, dog! Look! Look at that dog!"
She laughed as if in admiration. "He ain't scared of nobody.
He a big black dog." She whispered, "Sic him!"

"Watch me get rid of that cur," said the man. "Sic him,   53
Pete! Sic him!"

Phoenix heard the dogs fighting, and heard the man run-   54
ning and throwing sticks. She even heard a gunshot. But she
was slowly bending forward by that time, further and further
forward, the lids stretched down over her eyes, as if she were
doing this in her sleep. Her chin was lowered almost to her
knees. The yellow palm of her hand came out from the fold of
her apron. Her fingers slid down and along the ground under
the piece of money with the grace and care they would have
in lifting an egg from under a setting hen. Then she slowly
straightened up, she stood erect, and the nickel was in her
apron pocket. A bird flew by. Her lips moved. "God watching
me the whole time. I come to stealing."

The man came back, and his own dog panted about them. "Well, I scared him off that time," he said, and then he laughed and lifted his gun and pointed it at Phoenix.   55

She stood straight and faced him.   56

"Doesn't the gun scare you?" he said, still pointing it.   57

"No, sir, I seen plenty go off closer by, in my day, and for less than what I done," she said, holding utterly still.   58

He smiled, and shouldered the gun. "Well, Granny," he said, "you must be a hundred years old, and scared of nothing. I'd give you a dime if I had any money with me. But you take my advice and stay home, and nothing will happen to you."   59

"I bound to go on my way, mister," said Phoenix. She inclined her head in the red rag. Then they went in different directions, but she could hear the gun shooting again and again over the hill.   60

She walked on. The shadows hung from the oak trees to the road like curtains. Then she smelled wood-smoke, and smelled the river, and she saw a steeple and the cabins on their steep steps. Dozens of little black children whirled around her. There ahead was Natchez shining. Bells were ringing. She walked on.   61

In the paved city it was Christmas time. There were red and green electric lights strung and criss-crossed everywhere, and all turned on in the daytime. Old Phoenix would have been lost if she had not distrusted her eyesight and depended on her feet to know where to take her.   62

She paused quietly on the sidewalk where people were passing by. A lady came along in the crowd, carrying an armful of red-, green- and silver-wrapped presents; she gave off perfume like the red roses in hot summer, and Phoenix stopped her.   63

"Please, missy, will you lace up my shoe?" She held up her foot.   64

"What do you want, Grandma?"   65

"See my shoe," said Phoenix. "Do all right for out in the country, but wouldn't look right to go in a big building."   66

"Stand still then, Grandma," said the lady. She put her packages down on the sidewalk beside her and laced and tied both shoes tightly.   67

"Can't lace 'em with a cane," said Phoenix. "Thank you, missy. I doesn't mind asking a nice lady to tie up my shoe, when I gets out on the street."   68

Moving slowly and from side to side, she went into the big building, and into a tower of steps, where she walked up and around and around until her feet knew to stop.   69

She entered a door, and there she saw nailed up on the wall the <u>document</u> that had been stamped with the gold seal and framed in the gold frame, which matched the dream that was hung up in her head.   70

"Here I be," she said. There was a fixed and <u>ceremonial</u>   71
stiffness over her body.

"A charity case, I suppose," said an attendant who sat at   72
the desk before her.

But Phoenix only looked above her head. There was sweat   73
on her face, the wrinkles in her skin shone like a bright net.

"Speak up, Grandma," the woman said. "What's your   74
name? We must have your history, you know. Have you been
here before? What seems to be the trouble with you?"

Old Phoenix only gave a twitch to her face as if a fly were   75
bothering her.

"Are you deaf?" cried the attendant.   76

But then the nurse came in.   77

"Oh, that's just old Aunt Phoenix," she said. "She does-   78
n't come for herself—she has a little grandson. She makes
these trips just as regular as clockwork. She lives away back
off the Old Natchez Trace." She bent down. "Well, Aunt
Phoenix, why don't you just take a seat? We won't keep you
standing after your long trip." She pointed.

The old woman sat down, bolt upright in the chair.   79

"Now, how is the boy?" asked the nurse.   80

Old Phoenix did not speak.   81

"I said, how is the boy?"   82

But Phoenix only waited and stared straight ahead, her   83
face very solemn and withdrawn into <u>rigidity</u>.

"Is his throat any better?" asked the nurse. "Aunt   84
Phoenix, don't you hear me. Is your grandson's throat any better since the last time you came for the medicine?"

With her hands on her knees, the old woman waited,   85
silent, erect and motionless, just as if she were in armor.

"You mustn't take up our time this way, Aunt Phoenix,"   86
the nurse said. "Tell us quickly about your grandson, and get
it over. He isn't dead, is he?"

At last there came a flicker and then a flame of compre-   87
hension across her face, and she spoke.

"My grandson. It was my memory had left me. There I   88
sat and forgot why I made my long trip."

"Forgot?" The nurse frowned. "After you came so far?"   89

Then Phoenix was like an old woman begging a <u>dignified</u>   90
forgiveness for waking up frightened in the night. "I never did
go to school, I was too old at the Surrender," she said in a soft
voice. "I'm an old woman without an education. It was my
memory fail me. My little grandson, he is just the same, and
I forgot it in the coming."

"Throat never heals, does it?" said the nurse, speaking   91
in a loud, sure voice to old Phoenix. By now she had a card
with something written on it, a little list. "Yes. Swallowed
lye. When was it?—January—two-three years ago—"

Phoenix spoke unasked now. "No, missy, he not dead,   92
he just the same. Every little while his throat begin to close
up again, and he not able to swallow. He not get his breath.
He not able to help himself. So the time come around, and I
go on another trip for the soothing medicine."

"All right. The doctor said as long as you came to get it,   93
you could have it," said the nurse. "But it's an <u>obstinate</u>
case."

"My little grandson, he sit up there in the house all   94
wrapped up, waiting by himself," Phoenix went on. "We is
the only two left in the world. He suffer and it don't seem to
put him back at all. He got a sweet look. He going to last. He
wear a little patch quilt and peep out holding his mouth open
like a little bird. I remembers so plain now. I not going to forget him again, no, the whole <u>enduring</u> time. I could tell him
from all the others in creation."

"All right." The nurse was trying to hush her now. She   95
brought her a bottle of medicine. "Charity," she said, making
a check mark in a book.

Old Phoenix held the bottle close to her eyes, and then   96
carefully put it into her pocket.

"I thank you," she said.   97

"It's Christmas time, Grandma," said the attendant.   98
"Could I give you a few pennies out of my purse?"

"Five pennies is a nickel," said Phoenix stiffly.   99

"Here's a nickel," said the attendant.   100

Phoenix rose carefully and held out her hand. She re-   101
ceived the nickel and then fished the other nickel out of her
pocket and laid it beside the new one. She stared at her palm
closely, with her head on one side.

Then she gave a tap with her cane on the floor.   102

"This is what come to me to do," she said. "I going to   103
the store and buy my child a little windmill they sells, made
out of paper. He going to find it hard to believe there such a
thing in the world. I'll march myself back where he waiting,
holding it straight up in this hand."

She lifted her free hand, gave a little nod, turned around,   104
and walked out of the doctor's office. Then her slow step
began on the stairs, going down.

Check Your Understanding

Review

1. What does the worn path symbolize?

2. How does the old woman resemble the phoenix of ancient mythology mentioned in the introduction to the story?

_____

3. Find at least five examples of metaphors or similes used by Welty to add color to the story. Add the number of the paragraph where you find the comparison. Explain what the figure of speech compares. The first one is done as an example.

Figure of Speech   Paragraph

1. Her tapping cane is "like the chirping of   1

   a solitary little bird."

   Explanation: Her cane tapping is feeble and the only

   sound to be heard.

2. _____   _____

   _____

   Explanation: _____

   _____

3. _____   _____

   _____

   Explanation: _____

   _____

4. _____   _____

   _____

   Explanation: _____

   _____

5. _____   _____

_____

Explanation: _____

_____

6. _____   _____

_____

Explanation: _____

_____

Multiple Choice

Select the letter of the answer that best completes the statement.

_____ 1. The main idea (or theme and message) of the story could be:
   a. Phoenix shows great strength of character in achieving her goal.
   b. Phoenix has a difficult life.
   c. The old woman is treated badly by many people she meets.

_____ 2. The tone of the story can be described as
   a. ironic.
   b. lightly humorous.
   c. inspiring.

_____ 3. You can infer that Phoenix is
   a. white.
   b. African American.
   c. Hispanic.

_____ 4. The attitude of the old woman about making the trip could be described as
   a. joyful.
   b. resigned.
   c. determined.

_____ 5. Nature plays an important part in the story. How does nature treat Phoenix?
   a. more kindly than humans do
   b. harshly
   c. with indifference

True/False

Label the following statements as true or false.

_____ 1. Phoenix and her grandson live with his mother.

_____ 2. Phoenix outwits the hunter.

_____ 3. The reason for Phoenix's journey is not clear until the end of the story.

_____ 4. Phoenix's journey takes about an hour.

_____ 5. Phoenix probably needs glasses.

_____ 6. The story takes place around Christmas.

_____ 7. This is the first time that Phoenix has made this trip.

_____ 8. A snake is on Phoenix's path.

_____ 9. Phoenix has brought along a lunch.

_____ 10. Phoenix's grandson is dying.

Vocabulary

Put a check mark beside the adjectives that accurately describe Phoenix. Use a dictionary to be sure about unfamiliar words.

____ stupid   ____ clever   ____ proud   ____ selfish

____ persistent   ____ crazy   ____ strong willed   ____ brave

____ devoted   ____ loving

Matching

Find a word from column B to match the words in column A. Put the correct letter on the blank before the words in column A.

Column A	Column B
_____ 1. meditative	a. trembling
_____ 2. persistent	b. pattern of lines or rays
_____ 3. illuminated	c. stiffness
_____ 4. frailest	d. celebration
_____ 5. quivering	e. thoughtful

_____ 6. severe   f. record

_____ 7. festival   g. with energy

_____ 8. vigorously   h. ritual

_____ 9. radiation   i. harsh

_____ 10. document   j. weakest

_____ 11. ceremonial   k. perservering

_____ 12. rigidity   l. having a serious manner

_____ 13. dignified   m. stubborn

_____ 14. obstinate   n. lighted

_____ 15. enduring   o. continuing

Writing

1. Write a paragraph about an older person you have known who overcame difficulties as Phoenix did. What did that person overcome? How did that person accomplish his or her goal?
2. Phoenix talks to herself a lot. We all do. Write a paragraph about your self-talk. When, why, and where do you talk to yourself?

Critical Thinking

1. Discuss your answers to the questions on the story. In the Vocabulary section, you may be able to give a good defense for answers other than those given in the Answer section.
2. What does the story say about treatment of the poor and elderly? Talk about specific instances, such as the hunter, the nurses, the need for the trip.

Study Techniques

Chapter 8

Strategies for Study and Active Reading

> Reading maketh a full man; conference a ready man; and
> writing an exact man.
>
> *Francis Bacon*

Reading with comprehension is only the first step to being a successful college reader. In addition, you must be able to retain and
recall the information you have read. You need control of your
reading as a foundation for further understanding of course material, and you need to use the information gained from reading to
pass tests and exams. Discussing or conferring about what you
have read is important, but to gain the most from your reading,
writing is necessary. The study habits, techniques, and strategies
that you use after reading are as important as your original
thoughtful mastery of the meaning of your reading.

This chapter will consider:

- how to plan your time for study
- how to schedule review
- how to take good notes for study
- the value of group study and discussion
- strategies for developing your memory

Review of Strategies for Difficult Reading

In earlier chapters you learned strategies to help you comprehend demanding reading material. Practicing these strategies is the
first step in becoming an effective reader.

1. Before you read, take the time to focus your attention
   by previewing, anticipating the material to be read, and

making associations with what you may already know about the topic.

2. Don't assume that you know a familiar word used in a new context. Remember that words have many meanings.
3. Understand the meaning of new, special words used in context.
4. Use the glossary or a dictionary.
5. Read difficult material slowly, aloud if possible.
6. Break long sentences into key words.
7. Highlight and/or underline key concepts.
8. Check details to be sure that meaning is not changed by the details.
9. Rewrite difficult sentences in your own words in the margin or on a separate sheet of paper.
10. Make note of questions that arise from your reading so that you can ask your instructor for clearer understanding.

Practicing these ten strategies is the beginning. Remember that if the textbook material is difficult, it is best to spend study time in slow, focused reading. Reading difficult material quickly, other than the reading you do for a survey overview, is a waste of time. You may have time to read the selection a second time, but the second time probably won't give you a much better understanding.

Finding Study Time

The first step in becoming an effective student—that is, one who understands and remembers what he or she reads—is to plan time for study. People today live busy lives. Perhaps, in addition to your college classes, you work full or part time. Or perhaps you have a family that needs your time, care, and attention. Or perhaps you have become involved in campus activities. Whatever the demands on your time in addition to attending classes, it is important to find time outside class for additional study.

Several strategies for blocking out time for study are recommended. You may want to try them all to see what works best for you.

First, you can chart your week. (Figure 8.1) Make a schedule from the hour you get up until you go to bed. Fill in the hours that are already assigned. For example, you may have reading class from 9 to 10 on MWF and composition from 9:30 to 10:45 on TTH. Be sure to include some specified time to study each subject you are enrolled in. An average of two hours of study time for each class period is recommended. Don't let a half-hour here and there escape. You can do a lot of review in short time periods. Also, when you make a schedule, don't forget to give yourself sufficient time for rest and relaxation. Thinking seriously for a few minutes about how you spend your time will give you more time to spend.

Fill in the blank schedule to give yourself a start on organizing your time. You may want to make a copy of this schedule and monitor your time for a week. That is, make a record of how you actually spend your time for a week. Then review the schedule and plan the best use of your time. Most students discover that planning their time leads to more effective use of their time.

The weekend is not included in the schedule because your weekend time is more flexible, but unless you plan your weekend to include some study time, you may lose valuable time to relatively unimportant activities.

Table 8.1   Weekly Schedule

Time	Mon.	Tues.	Wed.	Thurs.	Fri.
7.00					
8:00					
9:00					
10:00					
11:00					
12:00					
1:00					
2:00					
3:00					
4:00					
5:00					
6:00					
7:00					
8:00					
9:00					
10:00					
11:00					
12:00					

Another technique that works for some students is to plan your tasks at the beginning of each day. When you have listed all the things you have to do, go back and make a priority listing. Number those tasks that must be done with a 1. For example, if you have a test coming up the next day, you will want to be sure to schedule some review time. The next most important tasks should be marked with a 2. You may need to make a dental appointment.

You can put this off for a few days, but eventually this task will become a priority 1 if you value the care of your teeth. A priority 3 is the least important. You may want to watch a football game on television, but you can tape the program for future viewing when you don't have too many 1s. Be sure that finding time to study is a priority 1.

Here's a final strategy. Whenever you have a task that cannot be accomplished in an hour or so, divide the task into manageable parts. In preparing to read, consider how much you can read and absorb in one period. Sometimes you can begin reading with attention, but you will lose your focus if you read too long without stopping to refocus. The strategy is to break your reading into manageable chunks. Read and take a break for some other task, or at least stop to consider what you have just read and to predict and make associations about the next section. A reading assignment of twenty or more pages may be difficult to cover all at once. For example, suppose an assignment for your humanities course is to read the chapter "Ancient Rome: The Spirit of the Empire." In your preview of the pages, as you focus on the headings and illustrations, plan to divide your reading and study. The headings and number of pages are:

Trajan's Triumph (1)
The Drama of Roman History (3)
The Art of an Empire (4)
The Architecture of Rome (7)
Art and Daily Life: Sculpture and Painting (3)
Theater and Music (2)
The Roman Poets (3)
The Roman Character (2)

Consider how much you can read and absorb in one period. As you preview the chapter headings, ask yourself whether some topics seem to be related. Faced with a long reading assignment, you don't want to begin at the beginning and plow through to the end of the assigned pages only to realize at the end that you have no clear idea of what you have read. How might you divide this reading assignment into two reading periods?

You can spend time getting oriented to the chapter by reading just the first two sections. This will allow extra time for the many illustrations that will draw your attention and stimulate you to make associations. Studying the illustrations will make the words of the text more meaningful and memorable for you.

How you plan to schedule your reading of the chapter is as individual as you are. The point is to take the time to plan. Planning your reading time is an additional help in keeping yourself focused on the task.

In scheduling time for study, it is important to find time for more than just completing reading assignments. You need to schedule time for reviewing. Three kinds of review are helpful.

When to Review

Review is not limited to something you do just before a test. In other words, last-minute cramming shouldn't masquerade as review. To be effective and to help store ideas for later use, the first review of your reading should occur within 24 hours. Keep in mind that the more frequently you practice spaced review, the more effectively the material will be stored for later recall.

First: The 24-Hour Review

Maybe you will review after a short break by predicting what the next section of reading will cover. Or maybe you won't go back to a reading assignment for several hours or until the next day. To do this review, look over the material quickly, paying particular attention to your marginal notes. Or you might review before class to refresh your thinking about the topic and help you associate your reading with class lectures or activities. Study experts tell us that without this kind of review you will forget 80 percent of the material you read. What a waste!

Second: The Weekly Review

Schedule time once or twice a week to spend 5 or 10 minutes reviewing your class material, both reading and notes, again. It may help you make new connections to new readings, lectures, and activities. Making connections and associations is one of the best methods for remembering.

Third: Review before a Test

This review can be quick and easy if you have been doing regular 24-hour and weekly reviews. You will already be quite familiar with the material. Just imagine, the night before a test you won't have to be up all night rereading tons of pages in order to prepare! As you look over your notes, you will realize that most of the facts are well-established in your mind. You can get your rest and be fresh for test taking in the morning.

Note Taking to Help You Review

How can you keep repeated reviewing interesting? This section describes several methods for review: three kinds of note taking, writing a summary, and group study. Obviously, you can review by looking over your underlining and marginal notes on a reading selection. Using different techniques, however, will bring variety to your review sessions. You will find some methods more appealing to you than others, and you will find some methods work best in some situations and not so well in others. Note taking and summarizing make you rethink your material. The writing involved in these methods reinforces ideas in your memory. Group study and collaborative learning reviews help you clarify your ideas and give you the opportunity to learn by talking and teaching.

Outlining

If what you have read is well organized, you can get a clear visual picture of the main ideas and supporting ideas by outlining. Start with the marginal notes and the underlining that you have made of the reading material. Use these notes to make an outline that will look something like this:

I. Main idea
   A. Supporting detail
   B. Supporting detail
II. Main idea
   A. Supporting detail
      1. Minor point
      2. Minor point
   B. Supporting detail

As you can see, this kind of note taking requires you to think carefully about the relationship between ideas. If you are making the outline for your own study and not to be given to an instructor, you can be more flexible in your format and add additional notes to clarify points for yourself. How would you outline the following section from the humanities text already mentioned, "Trajan's Triumph"?

> The citizens of ancient Rome lined the streets of their city in A.D. 106 and watched from its splendid buildings. They were gathered to cheer the triumph of their Emperor Trajan, a procession celebrating his victory over a barbarian army. Romans of all classes, from humble laborers to wealthy senators, stirred with satisfaction at the spectacle. They knew that the emperor's conquest would bring taxes to fill Rome's treasury and more slaves to perform its labor.
>
> Passing beneath a triumphal arch, the emperor's chariot led the procession. Following were his proud legions of soldiers, the backbone of the Roman Empire, who quelled rebellion and expanded Rome's borders. Then came the barbarian captives with ropes around their necks: once proud commanders of their own people, they had now unwillingly joined the many peoples of the Roman Empire. The crowd in Trajan's glistening new forum leaned forward to see the laurel wreath of victory placed on the emperor's head. Every Roman citizen was made to feel the power of Rome and take pride in its empire.
>
> —Philip E. Bishop, *Adventures in the Human Spirit*

Exercise 8-1   Outlining

Complete the outline of the two paragraphs above.

I. Trajan's victory procession in A.D. 106

   A. _____ (who attended?)

   B. Victory meant

      1. _____

      2. _____

II. Trajan's chariot followed by

   A. _____

   B. _____

   C. Ceremony concluded with crowning of Trajan

As you can see, you have condensed some two hundred words to just a few. This makes review much easier and is also a good study aid because you will be reviewing as you transfer your notes to this new format. However, this tight structure does not appeal to all note takers and not all material is easily transferred to this formal pattern.

Mapping

Mapping is a note-taking method that allows you to be more creative. You are free of the structure of outlining. You can show the difference in importance between ideas by changing the size of your shapes or by varying the shapes themselves. For example, main ideas can be rectangles with supporting ideas in circles connected to the main ideas with lines. Some students enjoy using color to distinguish between main ideas and details. Relationships are shown by lines drawn between the connecting points. Some students learn more easily from these visual notes and some material adapts itself more easily to a visual map. The map in Figure 8.1 below illustrates a way of mapping the section titled "Trajan's Triumph." Compare this map with the outline you created in Exercise 8-1.

Study the outline you made and the map of "Trajan's Triumph." Which would be more helpful for you in reviewing this material? Which would be easier for you to create as a study aid? There are no right answers to these questions other than the answer that works best for you. Now read the following paragraphs

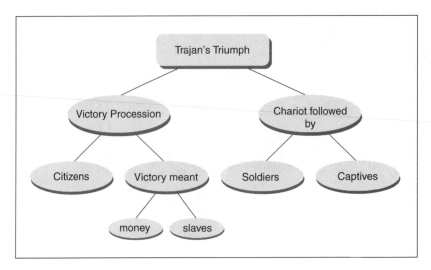

Figure 8.1   Map of Trajan's Triumph

about the two different ways in which people tend to manage their time and prepare to make to map the selection.

Time Management

Psychologist Carl Jung discovered that most people organize their lives in one of two ways. One group composed of individuals who might be called *closure types*, sticks with a task until it's finished ("closure" means "completion"). Many closure types say they feel heavily burdened by unfinished tasks. As one student put it, "I seem to have a cement block on my back until the job is done." The other group, made up of people who might be called *open-ended types*, prefers more flexibility. Members of this group switch easily from one project to another and deadlines do not weigh as heavily on them.

Jung believed that a preference for one style or the other is inborn; he also noted that neither is good or bad. They are simply different. *Closure types* tend to be highly organized and efficient, but they may lack flexibility. For example, they may have trouble scheduling recreation, exercise, and family life when an important deadline is near. Their perfectionism can create stress, since they often pride themselves on following a plan perfectly.

On the other hand, *open-ended types* may have trouble following a set plan. They often feel stifled by lists and schedules, even when an important task is looming. Open-ended types often struggle with procrastination—putting off jobs until their stress levels become intolerable.

Both groups may have trouble overcoming their differences when they work together as a team, committee, or family. Closure types tend to push for swift completion of a job, while open-ended types want more spontaneity and freedom.

Effective time management begins with *self-knowledge* and *self-management*. Be aware of your own preferred style and its advantages and disadvantages as you work on organizing your time.

—Adapted from Jean A. Reynolds, *Succeeding in College.*

Exercise 8-2   Mapping a Selection

To create a map of this selection, first determine the topic and write that in the center block. What are the two types of people discussed? These types will go in the two circles of the map. The points made about the types are noted as advantages and disadvantages. These will be entered in the next level of the map under each type. Finally, there are further supporting details that can be added. Complete the map in Figure 8.2.

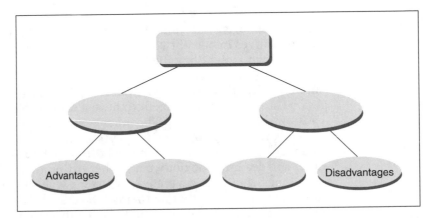

Figure 8.2

Double-Column Note Taking

Double-column note taking is more organized than mapping but not quite as structured as traditional outlining. To prepare for *double-column note taking,* draw a vertical line on your paper—or fold the paper into two sections. You might have equal sections if you wish to place lecture notes on one side and reading notes on the other. Or you might use a smaller side for key points and main ideas and a larger side for details, questions, and special notes. Or if the ideas sort themselves into two main ideas, as you saw in the article "Time Management," you might use double-column note taking. The sample in Table 8.2 shows you the double-column notes you might make on this article.

Table 8.2   Time Management Types

Open-ended Types	Closure Types
Advantages	*Advantages*
Flexible—can switch projects	Highly organized—efficient
Disadvantages	*Disadvantages*
Trouble setting a plan	Burdened by unfinished
Procrastinates	Stressed by change

The following summary of an introductory chapter on American government adapts easily to double-column note taking because the main points are numbered. Make marginal notes of supporting details after a first reading of this selection.

The Political Landscape

1. The Roots of American Government: Where Did the Ideas Come From?

The American political system was based on several notions that have their roots in classical Greek ideas, including natural law, the doctrine that human affairs should be governed by certain ethical principles that can be understood by reason. The ideas of social contract theorists John Locke and Thomas Hobbes, who held the belief that people are free and equal by God-given right, have continuing implications for our ideas of the proper role of government in our indirect democracy.

2. Characteristics of American Democracy

Key characteristics of this democracy established by the Framers [of the Constitution] are popular consent, popular sovereignty, majority rule and the preservation of minority rights, equality, individualism, and personal liberty, as in the Framers' option for a capitalistic system.

3. Characteristics of the American People

Several characteristics of the American electorate can help us understand how the system continues to evolve and change. Chief among these are changes in size, population, ideological beliefs, and composition of the political parties.

4. The Frustrated Public

Americans are a frustrated lot due primarily to dissatisfaction with the economy and unrealistic expectations of government. In the past, each generation has turned over a better America to its children; but many today believe this is no longer the case. While many have legitimate concerns about the economy, job security, and the role of government, it is important to remember that there are many things governments do well and many ways in which Americans are better off today than they were a few decades ago.

5. Changing America

The political, economic, and social climate of the United States is constantly changing. The current negativity about politics is probably just another phase in the evolution of the political process. An understanding of the process, institutions,

and issues of the American government and political system
will help us to meet the challenges that currently face the
system.

—Karen O'Connor and Larry J. Sabato,
American Government: Continuity and Change

Exercise 8-3   Double-Column Note Taking

*This article focused on five major points made in the chapter
"The Political Landscape." As a review technique, copy the
major ideas and then complete the second column with all the
supporting details you can recall for each major idea.*

The Political Landscape

Major Ideas   Supporting Details

1. _____   1. _____

2. _____   2. _____

                              _____

                              _____

                              _____

                              _____

                              _____

                              _____

3. _____   3. _____

                              _____

                              _____

4. _____   4. _____

                              _____

5. _____   5. _____

_____

_____

If you were studying this material for a test, you would be sure that you could complete the supporting details with further details from the chapter. Double-column notes are a good aid to keep available for frequent review.

Summarizing

Writing a *summary* in paragraph form of what you have read is a good method to use to see the "big picture" in the material. If the textbook you are using does not have a summary following each chapter, writing a summary is a good method for reviewing the chapter's main ideas. Use your marginal notes to review the main ideas. After writing your summary, check the reading material to make sure that you have covered all the main ideas. Details and examples are usually not part of a summary. Although a summary does not give you a visual representation of the subject, it does require that you think about and evaluate the material. Unfortunately, it is easy to misrepresent the original source when you create a summary. Study the following paragraph and the summary that follows.

We tend to think of most mothers—no matter what their species—as having some kind of almost-divine "maternal instinct" that makes them love their children and take care of them no matter what the cost or circumstance. While it is true that most females have built into their genetic blueprint the *tendency* to be interested in (and to care for) their offspring, this inborn tendency is always expressed in a given environment. The "maternal instinct" is strongly influenced by the mother's past experiences. Humans seem to have weaker instincts of all kinds than do other animals—since our behavior patterns are more affected by learning than by our genes, we have greater flexibility in what we do and become. But we pay a sometimes severe price for this freedom from genetic control. (133 words)

Summary

Most mothers of all species have an inborn sense that makes them good mothers; however mothers are also influenced by their environment. This influence is strongest in humans where environment can sometimes, unfortunately, overcome the natural instinct to care for our offspring. (41 words)

Commentary

As you can see, four sentences have been reduced to two. Major ideas are reworded so that the summary is about one-third the length of the original paragraph. There is no golden rule about the length of a summary. For example, the chapter summary of "The Political Landscape" summarized thiry-five pages of text in one page. Length of the summary depends on the material and the use you intend to make of the summary.

Exercise 8-4   Evaluating a Summary

Two more summaries of the paragraph on human instincts follow. Read both paragraphs and evaluate how accurately each one summarizes the original paragraph.

Summary 1

It is natural for mothers of all kinds to love and care for their children because of an inborn tendency. Past experiences, however, have an effect on this instinct to care. These past experiences have a stronger effect on human mothers because human instincts are weaker and more easily influenced by environment. Humans learn behaviors from their own experiences. This can have a bad effect on their instinct to care for their children. (75 words)

This is longer than the first summary, but not too long. Does it accurately reflect the content of the original paragraph? Why or why not?

_____

_____

_____

Summary 2

Mothers should care for their children. They have a natural, inborn instinct that helps them care. Human mothers may sometimes not care as much because their instinct to care is weaker. (30 words)

This summary is both inaccurate and incomplete. Which sentence(s) are inaccurate? Why?

_____

_____

_____

What important information is omitted? _____

_____

_____

Now try writing your own summary of the paragraph that follows the one just used as a sample. Do marginal notes and/or highlighting before attempting a summary.

Normal monkey and chimpanzee mothers seldom appear to inflict real physical harm on their own children; human mothers and fathers often do. Serapio R. Zalba, writing in a journal called *Trans-action*, estimated in 1971 that in the United States alone, perhaps 250,000 children suffer physical abuse by their parents each year. Of these "battered babies," almost 40,000 may be very badly injured. The number of young boys and girls killed by their parents annually is not known, but Zalba suggests that the figure may run into the thousands. Parents have locked their children in tiny cages, raised them in dark closets, burned them, boiled them, slashed them with knives, shot them, and broken almost every bone in their bodies. How can we reconcile these facts with the much discussed maternal and paternal "instincts?" (133 words)

—James V. McConnell, "Monkey Love,"
Understanding Human Behavior

_____

_____

_____

_____

_____

_____

Paraphrasing

One important notion to keep in mind in making a summary review is the importance of *paraphrasing* (putting in your own words) the content of the material you are reading. Paraphrasing is a difficult skill, but one well worth the effort of mastering. For one thing, paraphrasing helps you make the ideas of the material more completely your own. If you can restate in your own words, you clearly understand the ideas. Thus, a summary that accurately paraphrases material you have read assures you that you have grasped the main ideas of the reading. Further, if you are taking notes on your reading for a research paper, your notes must follow certain guidelines. If the guidelines are not followed, you risk distorting a writer's ideas or worse still, *plagiarizing* (stealing someone else's words or ideas.)

Distortion occurs when you omit one or more of the ideas the writer is presenting or change the writer's meaning even slightly. Plagiarism occurs not only when you repeat a writer's exact words and phrases but when you use his or her ideas without crediting your source.

Guidelines for Good Paraphrasing:
1. *Read* the material slowing and carefully.
2. *Review* the selection sentence by sentence, thinking of the key meaning.
3. *Think* how sentences can be combined and perhaps presented in a different order.
4. *Decide* what synonyms you can use for words in the passage.

Read the following paragraph that discusses conformity. Then compare the paragraph with the paraphrase that follows.

> The urge to conform on occasion clashes with the tendency to resist change. If the group we are in advocates an idea or action that is new and strange to us, we can be torn between seeking their acceptance and maintaining the security of familiar ideas and behavior. In such cases, the way we turn will depend on which tendency is stronger in us or which value we are more committed to.
>
> —Vincent Ryan Ruggiero,
> *Beyond Feeling: A Guide to Critical Thinking*

Sometimes the desire to conform conflicts with our inclination to have things the same because we want group acceptance, but we also want the comfort of things we know. Our final choices will depend on whichever pressure proves stronger to us.

Notice how the first two sentences of the original were combined without losing the meaning. Circle the vocabulary changes that were made.

Exercise 8-5   Practicing Critical Thinking and Paraphrasing Skills

Read the first statement and then read the paraphrases that follow. If the paraphrases exactly *reflect the idea of the original statement, mark (S) for same on the blank before the statement. If the paraphrase is different, mark (D).*

1. *Taking notes on difficult reading material is a helpful aid to memory.*

    _____ a. Taking notes is a helpful memory aid.

    _____ b. The memory is reinforced by note taking on difficult material.

    _____ c. Taking notes is a helpful exercise.

    _____ d. Remembering difficult reading material is aided by note taking.

    _____ e. Note taking is necessary to achieve passing grades.

    _____ f. Taking notes helps in understanding difficult material.

    _____ g. Difficult material can be remembered more easily by taking good notes.

    _____ h. If you take notes on difficult material, you will recall it more easily.

    _____ i. Instructors recommend taking notes on difficult reading.

    _____ j. Note taking on difficult reading helps your ability to remember the material.

2. *You will improve your reading attention by making associations and previewing before reading.*

    _____ a. Making associations before reading will help you focus your attention.

    _____ b. To improve your attention to reading, preview and make associations with the material to be read.

    _____ c. Previewing is important to help focus your attention on reading material.

    _____ d. Instructors recommend previewing and making associations before reading.

_____ e. Before reading, preview the material and recall anything relating to the subject that you can.

_____ f. Reviewing and making associations relating to the subject to be read will help focus your attention.

_____ g. To better focus on reading material, do a preview or survey.

_____ h. To help focus on reading material, do a preview and think about what you already know about the subject.

_____ i. Associating and previewing before reading are two techniques to help you focus on reading material.

_____ j. Before reading, preview and make associations.

Read the following passage, "The Rise of Reptiles," and make marginal notes on main ideas and important supporting details in preparation for writing an accurate summary of about 100 words.

During the Late Carboniferous, insects began an adaptive radiation into lush habitats on land. At about the same time, the *reptiles* (Reptilia) evolved from amphibians. Like modern species, the amphibious forms probably were carnivores. The huge quantities and selections of edible insects represented a major, untapped food source.

Compared to amphibians, early reptiles pursued prey with greater cunning and speed. Their jaw bones and muscles were better at applying sustained, crushing force. They had well-developed teeth, suitable for securing insects and fellow vertebrates. The limbs of nearly all types were better adapted to support the body on land. The circulatory system of those with a four-chambered heart was more efficient. Early reptiles relied fully on more efficient lungs, and they were the first vertebrates to suck in air rather than force it in by mouth muscles. Their cerebrum's thin surface layer, the cerebral cortex, was more highly developed. This brain region is responsible for the most complex integration of sensory information.

Reptiles were the first vertebrates to escape dependency on standing water. They did so through four adaptations that still distinguish reptiles from fishes and amphibians. *First*, they have tough, scaly skin that limits moisture loss. *Second*, the male fertilizes the female internally. That is, sperm are deposited into a female's body; they do not have to swim through water to reach eggs. *Third*, reptilian kidneys are good at conserving water. . . . *Fourth*, reptiles produce eggs in which the embryo develops to an advanced stage before being hatched.

—Adapted from Cecie Starr and Ralph Taggart,
Biology: The Unity and Diversity of Life

Exercise 8-6   Writing an Accurate Summary

Use your own words to capture the main ideas of the article on reptiles. You will have to write your own main-idea sentence for the first and second paragraphs since the main ideas are implied rather than stated. Write your completed summary on the following lines. Check the original to be sure that your paraphrase is an accurate one.

_____

_____

_____

_____

_____

_____

_____

_____

_____

_____

_____

_____

_____

_____

_____

_____

Note taking has been discussed as a method for reviewing reading material. The four kinds of note taking discussed are also helpful in taking lecture notes in class and in reviewing class notes. In every situation you will need to decide what kind of note taking best suits the material and the situation. Be versatile. You can make an outline, draw a map, make double-column notes, or write a summary. Try to experiment with one of the review types that is less familiar to you.

Group Study or Collaborative Work

Assignments in each chapter of this text encourage you to work with other students in thinking about your reading. Research studies show that students perceive, process, and store information in different ways. You should find it helpful to share the different ways in which you locate and clarify information and the methods you use to remember important material. You can creatively solve problems that might be difficult for one student working alone. You can share the different ways in which you decide the meaning of unfamiliar words.

Thinking aloud with others and exchanging ideas has several advantages. You will clarify your own ideas. You will learn that making mistakes is not as important as learning why an answer or idea can be corrected or improved. Group work is most effective if your group has no more than five members and no fewer than three. Open expression of all points of view in a discussion is important. This requires that you respect the views of all members of the group, have assignments prepared for discussion, and encourage all members of the group to contribute to the discussion.

In a recent survey of 480 companies and public organizations conducted by the National Association of Colleges and Employers, results ranked the ability to communicate first among the personal qualities desired by employers of college graduates. Active participation in group discussions will help you develop this desirable quality.

Group activities will vary. Sometimes group activities will require the group to determine a correct answer. Sometimes the group will want to review important concepts. Being able to teach others about something you have learned is helpful in improving both your understanding and your memory. Sometimes the group will share the individual members' different approaches to assignments as in the next exercise.

Exercise 8-7 Collaborative Learning

Review your sets of notes from Exercises 8-1, 2, 3, 4, and 6 with members of the group. After the group spends a few minutes re-

viewing the different sets of notes presented, discuss these questions. Members of the group may well have different answers to these questions. An important question to ask frequently is, "Why?" Listen to learn, and be sure to add your own ideas.

1. What method of note taking seemed to be most effective for each individual? Why?
2. Which of the articles could have been reviewed by a different method of note taking?
3. Which method seemed to be the most fun to work with?
4. Which method seems to be the best tool to use for quick review?
5. Which method would be good to use to prepare for an essay test?

The answers to these specific questions are not as important as an evaluation of what your group has learned. Your instructor may ask your group to give the class a summary of your group's learning experience.

Once you have reviewed by means of competent note taking and have discussed your understanding of the material with others, the next step for effective study is to activate your memory.

Strategies for Developing Your Memory

Several useful strategies will help you activate your long-term memory so that information you have studied will remain with you for future use.

Tips for Effective Memorizing

Remember—you never forget
Use mnemonics (memory aids)
Visualize
Use your five senses and your body
Overlearn

Remembering

Much about how the brain operates is still a mystery. Most researchers agree, however, that we have at least two basic kinds of memory: *short-term* memory and *long-term* memory. Once you have experienced something through your senses, usually through your eyes or ears, the experience is registered in your short-term memory. What is registered lasts in your short-term memory for a very short time, just a matter of seconds. If the information you received is important, you will probably store it in your long-term memory. Recalling this information stored in your long-term memory is the trick you want to master.

Have you ever searched for something for hours or days only to find it when you have given up the search? Your memory is something like that. The information is stored if you have put it into long-term memory; getting tense and raising your adrenalin level will not bring it to the surface. First, you have what is called a *forgetting curve.* Within a short period of time, about 24 hours, you will have forgotten 70 percent of anything you have learned. By the end of the month, if you don't review, you will have forgotten or lost the combination to the memory safe of 80 percent of learned material. This points up the importance of spaced reviewing. The good thing is that once you have learned something, dusting the information off in review sessions makes it easier to recall each successive time. Other tricks can also help with recalling stored information.

Mnemonics

Mnemonics are memory aids that can be helpful in recalling pieces of information. You will need to experiment with different kinds of mnemonics to decide which work best for you, using material like lists, words, and dates that need to be memorized. Look these techniques over and work with them to see which you want to use for memory tasks.

Acronyms are letters that stand for a series of words. You are probably familiar with NASA, which stands for National Aeronautics and Space Administration. Perhaps you learned the names of the Great Lakes (Huron, Ontario, Michigan, Erie, and Superior) using the acronym HOMES. Think of some other acronyms you are familiar with.

Acrostics are phrases or sentences made with the first letter of words that you can associate with things to be remembered. If you have ever taken a music class or music lessons of any kind, you may remember the acrostic "*Every Good Boy Does Fine,*" which helped you remember the lines in a treble clef. To remember the names of the Supreme Court justices, the acrostic " *Really Gross Boys Stick Toads On Kids' Swing Sets*" may help you remember Rehnquist, Ginsburg, Breyer, Souter, Thomas, O'Connor, Kennedy, Scalia, Stevens. Try experimenting with either acronyms or acrostics to help you remember the steps in a procedure for another subject like math.

Exercise 8-8 Making Helpful Acronyms and Acrostics

1. The body of an insect typically consists of the following parts: the head, with two antennae; the thorax, with two wings and six legs; and the abdomen. (*Hint:* the three principal parts can form an acronym.)

2. The three branches of the federal government are the executive, the legislative, and the judicial. The legislative branch consists of the Senate and the House of Representatives. (*Hint:* Items don't have to be remembered in any order, though order is another aid to memory.)

3. The parts of speech are noun, pronoun, verb, adjective, adverb, conjunction, preposition, and interjection. Record a way to remember the names of these parts of speech.

4. Make an acrostic or an acronym to help you remember the nine planets.

5. Think of something from another subject area or even a list of things you want to buy or do and make an acronym or acrostic to share with the class.

Visualizing

Some people find that *visualizing,* creating mental pictures, helps them to remember items by the associations they make. You know that you store information in your memory. Imagine a file cabinet with several drawers.

The first drawer contains material you want to use for a speech on how to become an A student. To remember the points you want to make, you could place the ideas in alphabetical order in the file cabinet.

Ask questions	**B**e neat	**D**o more than required
Make priorities	**O**rganize	**S**chedule time
Study anywhere	**T**est yourself	**W**ork with a group

The files in alphabetical order in the file cabinet will help you remember the points you want to make. Or would an acronym or acrostic work better for you in trying to remember these ideas? You want to use the memory aid that is most helpful for you.

You can even use silly or humorous visuals to help you remember. Perhaps you want to remember four sources of protein other than meat. The sources are grains, legumes, seeds/nuts, and vegetables. Visualize a field of wheat growing in the sunshine (grain). A squirrel sits on the edge of the field with a nut in his mouth (seeds/nuts). Next to the wheat field is a farmer's garden. Enter a rabbit hopping to the beans (legumes), where another rabbit is already happily munching on lettuce (green vegetables).

Visualization is also helpful in remembering the meaning of new vocabulary words. Get a mental picture for the word *decapitate,* for example.

Exercise 8-9   Creating Visualizations

1. Try using visualization to help you recall the seven continents: Australia, Europe, North America, South America, Africa, Asia. (*Hint:* You might use geographic placement—where they would be on a map in relationship to each other—or you might use size or some other idea.) Describe your visualization method and order.

_____

_____

_____

2. Study the names of the past six presidents of the United States: Nixon, Ford, Carter, Reagan, Bush, and Clinton. What object could you visualize to recall each of these names? Write the objects here.

_____

_____

Would you find visualization the best way to remember the presidents in the order that they served? What other system might work for you? If you are an auditory learner, perhaps putting the names to a musical tune might work. Know yourself and experiment until you find the mnemonic devices that work best for you. You will find, too, that different memorization devices work better with some items than others.

Using Your Senses and Your Body

All information that goes into the brain arrives there through your senses. You have seen it with your eyes, heard it with your ears, smelled it with your nose, touched it with some part of your body, or tasted it with your taste buds. If you are trying to learn something, it makes sense to involve as many senses as you can in the learning process. For example, if you have a list of vocabulary words to memorize, you will want to write them (touch), read them (see), recite them (hear). Those are the ordinary and somewhat obvious ways. When the learning is difficult, be creative. Write the words in the air while dancing and singing the words to a familiar melody. Close your eyes and visualize the words placed around your bedroom, on the bed, dresser, windowsill, anywhere. Later, visualizing your bedroom will help you remember what is stored in your memory. Study doesn't need to be dull to be productive.

Overlearning

As noted before, anything you want to learn you learn best by *overlearning.* That means repeated review, using as many of your senses as possible and using mnemonic devices that work for you. Using vocabulary words as an example again, keep your vocabulary cards handy at all times for a quick review while waiting for a bus, standing in line, or waiting for commercials to be over on television. Work with five cards at once. When you are comfortable with one or two of the words, put those cards aside and add others to make a pack of five, and so on until you have control of all the cards.

Exercise 8-10 Exchanging Ideas

With your group members, discuss the following:

1. How effectively have you used your memory for past test taking?
2. Discuss your answers for the mnemonic exercises.
3. What memory tricks have you used in the past?
4. For what subjects do you plan to use some of the suggestions?

Chapter Review

1. List four note-taking strategies to use for review.

   a. _____

   b. _____

   c. _____

   d. _____

2. When are the suggested times for review?

   a. _____

   b. _____

   c. _____

3. Describe three techniques or strategies to help you remember.

   a. _____

   b. _____

   c. _____

Reading Selection 1

Purpose

The late African American Olympic athlete Jackie Joyner-Kersee describes in this selection from her autobiography, *A Kind of Grace*, how a personal role model helped her to overcome a childhood of poverty to win six Olympic medals, three of them gold. Read to learn of her experiences and to discover how a role model can give guidance and direction for achieving goals. Take marginal notes for review.

Preview

1. Read the first sentences of paragraphs to skim the selection.
2. Check the vocabulary and questions at the end.

Anticipate/Associate

1. What do you imagine were some of the difficulties Joyner-Kersee experienced in developing her athletic abilities?
2. How has, or how could, a role model help you to achieve your goals?

My Guiding Light

Jackie Joyner-Kersee

People have always assumed I succeeded at sports because I was a natural talent. Not quite. I had talent and determination, but I needed someone to help me develop it. Nino Fennoy was that person. He encouraged me to imagine myself doing great things and worked with me to turn my fantasies into reality.   1

I met Mr. Fennoy on a spring day in 1973. Mr. Ward piled the girls he'd been coaching into his car and drove us to the field at Hughes Quinn Junior High, some eight blocks from my house. Every evening Mr. Fennoy worked with a group of boys and girls from Lilly Freeman Elementary at the Hughes Quinn playground. The two men had decided to divide the coaching duties of the Franklin-Freeman squad, with Mr. Ward taking the boys and Mr. Fennoy the girls.   2

To determine our skill level, they asked us all to run 120 yards, then circle around and run back, and repeat the drill several times. I did it easily. I still wasn't the fastest, but after   3 almost a year of training with Mr. Ward, I had lots of stamina. I stood about 5'5" tall and weighed a lean 120 pounds—all arms and legs.

"What else are we going to do?" I asked the two coaches   4
when we were done. Mr. Fennoy looked at me and smiled.

The longer I worked with him, the stronger and faster I   5
became. But I still wasn't in the front of the pack at the end of the races—my 440 time was well over a minute. In my first race with Mr. Fennoy as my coach, I didn't finish last, but I was well back. I hoped he wouldn't be disappointed and drop me from the team.

"I tried," I said, shrugging my shoulders apologetically   6
afterward.

He responded with a reassuring smile: "That's all I   7
ask." . . .

Mr. Fennoy was only about 5'7", but his ideas were lofty.   8
The skin beneath his Afro, mustache and beard was the color of parchment and he dressed like many of the thirty-some-thing men in town. But he spoke like a wise, old man—a com-bination sociologist, philosopher and motivational speaker. With his index finger jabbing the air and his hazel eyes staring intently at us, he peppered his speeches at team meetings with phrases like "making maximum use of <u>minimal</u> re-sources" and "the <u>parameters</u> of acceptable behavior."

He had a broad vision of what he wanted to accomplish   9
through the track program. He encouraged us to work hard in practice, as well as in class. With a solid foundation in athlet-ics and academics, he told us, the possibilities were unlim-ited—college scholarships, graduate school, good-paying jobs and productive lives.

In one of his first speeches to us after practice when we   10
were still in elementary school, he explained that success in sports could open doors for us and set us on the path to broader success. "Doing well in sports is fine. But in order to compete and get any portion of what this country has to offer, you have to have an education. You can't get a job if you can't fill out an application."

Like my parents, he stressed that there was a world be-   11
yond East St. Louis and that life in that world wouldn't be a struggle if we were properly prepared. "You have alterna-tives," he said. "You don't have to just be housewives. You don't have to settle for staying here."

Other than my parents, Mr. Fennoy was the major influ-   12
ence on my attitudes and outlook. He inspired me to make the most of my talent, to withstand peer pressure and to avoid the traps into which others fell. . . .

When it was time to travel to meets out of state or across   13
country, we sometimes raised the money for travel expenses
by holding bake sales and raffles. But Mr. Fennoy often turned
down huge donations from people in town, even though expenses could run as much as $5,000 when several of us and a
coach had to travel out of town. We heard about some of the
offers and asked why he'd refused them. "You never want
anyone to think you owe them something," he said. Also, he
reminded us, <u>eligibility</u> rules prohibited gifts to high school
and college athletes. . . .

On one of the first trips I took with the Railers, I didn't   14
have money for lunch. My father wasn't working and my
mother said she just didn't have anything to give me. If I went,
she said I'd have to wait until I got back home that night to eat.
When the van carrying us pulled into the McDonald's parking
lot at lunchtime, my mouth watered and my stomach gurgled.
I'd <u>exerted</u> myself all morning and I was starving. But when it
was time to get off the bus, I was too embarrassed to say I did-
n't have any money, so I told everyone I wasn't hungry.

While my teammates rushed inside with bills clutched   15
in their hands, I waited on the bus. No sense torturing myself
by going inside and smelling the french fries. Mr. Fennoy
walked back to the bus and asked why I wasn't inside. I told
him I wasn't hungry. Without inquiring further, he said,
"Come on inside with me and order what you want."

"Thanks!" I said, flashing a big, grateful grin. We walked   16
in side by side. . . .

During the <u>preliminary</u> round of an AAU meet in Poplar   17
Bluff, Missouri, in 1976, when I was fourteen, I landed a jump
in my last turn during the qualifying round, which should
have been long enough to put me in the final round. But the
official failed to record it. As a result, I was out of the competition. At the time I thought it was a deliberate oversight. The
disappointment was all the more bruising because I had to
finish in one of the top three spots to advance to the AAU Regional competition, and to have a chance at <u>ultimately</u> competing in the AAU National meet. When the official told me
I'd failed to qualify, tears welled up in my eyes and my body
stiffened. I was ready to yell at someone. Mr. Fennoy saw my
face and called me over.

"It's not fair, . . . " I started to rant.   18

"Don't say another word," he ordered, pointing his fin-   19
ger at me. "Let me handle it. And you better not cry, either. . . . Rather than looking for someone to blame or to be
mad with, let's learn from this," he said. The idea of blame
and anger appealed to me more, but I listened.

"From now on, after every jump, always make sure that 20
the judges have recorded your mark. And let's work harder on
your jumping so that next time, one jump won't mean the difference between qualifying and not qualifying."

The lessons stuck with me. Watching Mr. Fennoy, I 21
learned to handle controversy and adversity calmly. And at
each long-jump competition I enter, I walk by the judges after
every jump and, while pretending to look at the standings,
make sure they've recorded the result.

Check Your Understanding

Review

*From your marginal notes and underlining, prepare a set of
notes on another sheet of paper using a map, outline, summary,
or double-column notes to review the passage.*

Multiple Choice

Select the letter of the answer that best completes the statement.

_____ 1. The main idea of the selection is
   a. Sports can be rewarding.
   b. Mr. Fennoy taught more than sports skills.
   c. One can overcome poverty.
   d. Preparation is important.

_____ 2. The author's purpose is to
   a. inform.
   b. entertain.
   c. persuade.
   d. a and c above.

_____ 3. You can infer that the writer
   a. needed to learn to accept injustice.
   b. hated being poor.
   c. wanted to stay in East St. Louis all her life.
   d. was always a superior athlete.

_____ 4. The writer believes that
   a. she succeeded with natural talent.
   b. everyone should participate in sports.
   c. she owes her success, in part, to Mr. Fennoy.
   d. school is a waste of time.

_____ 5. The writer has strong feelings about
   a. unfair judging.
   b. trying to do her best.

  c. being poor.

  d. a and b above.

True/False

Label the following statements as true or false.

_____ 1. Joyner-Kersee was always a superior athlete.

_____ 2. Mr. Fennoy paid for the team's out-of-town trips.

_____ 3. He accepted donations from others to support the student athletes.

_____ 4. On one trip Joyner-Kersee was too proud to admit that she had no money for lunch.

_____ 5. Mr. Fennoy was an inspirational speaker.

_____ 6. Mr. Fennoy believed in fighting for fair judging.

_____ 7. Joyner-Kersee learned to stand up against peer pressure from Mr. Fennoy.

_____ 8. Joyner-Kersee grew up without a father.

_____ 9. Mr. Fennoy believed crying over losses was unacceptable.

_____ 10. Joyner-Kersee's parents were also an influence in her life.

Vocabulary

Read the following sentences to determine whether the italicized phrases are correctly defined. Mark (C) if the definition is correct and (I) if it is incorrect.

_____ 1. To turn *fantasies into reality* means to make facts become real.

_____ 2. His *ideas were lofty* means Fennoy had high aspirations.

_____ 3. *Minimal resources* means to have all that one could expect or hope for.

_____ 4. *Parameters of acceptable behavior* are the boundaries of good actions.

_____ 5. *Eligibility rules* are the rules dictating who can participate in an event.

_____ 6. When Joyner-Kersee says she *exerted herself*, she means she was tired.

_____ 7. A *preliminary round* is the final round or event.

_____ 8. A chance at *ultimately competing* means a last chance at competing.

_____ 9. When Joyner-Kersee says she learned to *handle controversy calmly*, she means she could handle arguments calmly.

_____ 10. When she says she could *handle adversity calmly*, she means she could handle difficulties calmly.

Writing

1. Describe an occasion when you felt you were treated unjustly. How did you react? What were you able to do to right the injustice?
2. Describe someone who has been a role model in your life, or describe someone for whom you try to be a role model.

Critical Thinking

1. Do you think Mr. Fennoy should have accepted donations rather than making the athletes work to pay for their trips?
2. Are sports overemphasized in school, particularly elementary schools?
3. Compare your note taking for this article with the notes of others in your group. Are the results accurate? Did one method of note taking seem to work better than another for recalling content?

Reading Selection 2

Purpose

This selection from a text on public speaking describes problems that interfere with the important study skill of listening. Being a competent reader is not enough for a successful college experience. Listening in group discussions and in lecture classes is also important. Listening is a skill to be added to your study skills. Some students are better listeners because they learn most easily by listening, but many can improve their listening skills by considering some of the things that interfere with listening attentively.

Preview

1. Read and think about the first sentence of each paragraph in the article.
2. Review the questions and vocabulary that follow the article.

Anticipate/Associate

1. When has your failure to listen well resulted in a personal or academic problem?
2. How do you think effective listening would enhance your study efforts?
3. Think of an occasion when you have not been able to listen well. What caused the interference to your listening powers?

Overcoming Barriers to Effective Listening

Michael and Suzanne Osborn

The first step in developing effective listening skills is to become aware of what may keep us from being good listeners. Some <u>barriers</u> to good listening arise from external sources of interference such as a noisy room. But the most <u>formidable</u> barriers to effective listening are internal, based in the listener's own attitudes. At best, these barriers present a challenge; at worst, they may completely block communication. They form the listener's side of Interference Mountain—we must climb above them before we can join speakers in participative communication. To become better listeners, we must recognize and understand our listening problems. 1

One of the most common barriers to effective listening is simply not paying attention. How many times have you found yourself daydreaming, even when you know you should be listening to what is being said? One reason for this problem is that our minds can process information far faster than people usually speak. Most people speak at about 125 words per minute in public, but can process information at about 500 words per minute. This time lapse provides an opportunity for listeners to drift away to more delightful or difficult personal concerns. Too often daydreamers will smile and nod encouragingly even though they haven't heard a thing the speaker has said. This <u>deceptive</u> feedback is a major cause of failed communication. Both personal reactions to words and distractions can set off such reactions. . . . 2

Many listening problems are simply the result of bad   3
habits. You may have watched so much television that you
expect all messages to be fast moving and entertaining. You
may have learned how to pretend you are listening to avoid
dull or difficult materials. Your experiences as a student may
have conditioned you to listen just for facts. You may jump to
conclusions before hearing a complete message. Such habits
can interfere with effective listening.

Some poor listening habits stem from heavy television   4
viewing. Television messages are characterized by fast action
and the presentation of short bits of information. Habitual
television viewing may lead us to want all messages to follow this format. William F. Buckley has commented that
"the television audience . . . is not trained to listen . . . to 15
uninterrupted minutes." Our television-watching experiences may also lead us into "the entertainment syndrome," in
which we demand that speakers be lively, interesting, funny,
and charismatic to hold our attention. Unfortunately, not all
subjects lend themselves to such treatment, and we can
miss much if we listen only to those who put on a "dog and
pony show."

Although honest feedback is important to speech effec-   5
tiveness, we all have learned how to pretend we are paying attention. We may sit erect, gaze at the speaker, even nod or
smile from time to time (although not always at the most appropriate times), and not listen to one word that is being said!
You are most likely to feign attention when you are daydreaming or when a message is difficult to understand. If
the speaker asks, "Do you understand?" you may nod brightly,
sending false feedback just to be polite or to avoid seeming
dimwitted.

Our fear of failure may cause us to avoid listening to dif-   6
ficult material. If we are asked questions later, we can always
say "I wasn't really listening" instead of "I didn't understand." We may believe that asking questions would make us
look less than intelligent—that our questions may be
"dumb," when the truly "dumb question" is the one that is
not asked. Additionally, our desire to have things simplified
so that we can understand them without much effort makes
us susceptible to "snake oil" pitches, those oversimplified
remedies for everything from fallen arches to failing government policies.

Your experiences as a student may contribute to another   7
bad habit: listening only for facts. If you do this, you may
miss the forest because you are so busy counting the leaves
on the trees. Placing too much emphasis on facts can keep

you from attending to the nonverbal aspects of a message. Effective listening includes <u>integrating</u> what you hear and what you see. Gestures, facial expressions, and tone of voice communicate <u>nuances</u> that are vital to the message of the speech.

Overcoming bad habits requires effort. When you find yourself feigning attention, remember that honest feedback helps speakers, but that inappropriate feedback deceives them. Don't try to remember everything or write down all that you hear. Instead, listen to the main ideas and identify supporting materials. Paraphrase what you hear so that it makes sense to you. Try to build an overall picture of the meaning in your mind. Attend to the nonverbal clues as well. Does the speaker's tone of voice change the meaning of the words? Are the gestures and facial expressions <u>consistent</u> with the words? If not, what does this tell you?

8

Check Your Understanding

Review

1. Select one of the methods of note taking to organize essential ideas from this article based on your marginal notes.
2. Write a paraphrase of paragraph 3.

Multiple Choice

Select the letter of the answer that best completes the statement.

_____ 1. The main idea of this selection is that
   a. a number of influences interfere with our ability to be good listeners.
   b. listening is a difficult skill to master.
   c. it is important to respond to speakers while we listen.

_____ 2. Becoming good listeners is difficult because
   a. a noisy environment can interfere.
   b. we watch too much television.
   c. we need to overcome our own bad habits.

_____ 3. When we listen to others, it is important to
   a. nod and smile.
   b. ask questions when we don't understand.
   c. at least pretend to pay attention.

_____ 4. Deceptive feedback can cause
  a. daydreaming.
  b. failed communication.
  c. bad feeling.

_____ 5. The author thinks that
  a. many students do not listen effectively.
  b. you should turn off your television set.
  c. speakers talk too fast.

True/False

Label the following statements as true or false.

_____ 1. There are both external and internal barriers to our ability to listen.

_____ 2. The article focuses primarily on external barriers.

_____ 3. There is little you can do to improve your listening ability.

_____ 4. You can infer that good listening improves group communication.

_____ 5. Appearing to listen is almost as important as really listening.

_____ 6. You should listen only for facts.

_____ 7. Asking questions of a speaker is a sign of real ignorance.

_____ 8. Poor listening habits may stem from television viewing.

_____ 9. Building new habits of listening will require effort.

_____ 10. Appearing to listen will improve your ability to listen.

Vocabulary

The author uses several examples of phrases that help us visualize. Write your interpretation of the following phrases and discuss them with your group.

  1. "Dog and pony show" _____

_____

2. "Snake oil" pitches _____

_____

3. Interference Mountain _____

_____

4. Dimwitted _____

_____

Now define the following words as they are used in context. If necessary, consult your dictionary.

1. *Barriers* to good listening _____

2. Most *formidable* barriers _____

3. *Deceptive* feedback _____

4. Entertainment *syndrome* _____

5. Interesting, funny, and *charismatic* _____

6. To *feign* attention _____

7. Makes us *susceptible* _____

8. *Integrating* what you hear and what you see _____

_____

9. Tone of voice communicates *nuances* _____

_____

10. Facial expressions *consistent* with the words _____

_____

Critical Thinking

1. In groups, compare your methods of note taking. Is one method more effective than another for this assignment?

2. Using your written paraphrase of paragraph 3 and the rules for effective paraphrasing on page 328, evaluate this paraphrase:

> Listening problems are the result of bad habits. Some of the bad habits are watching television, pretending to listen, and listening just for facts.

3. Discuss times when you have used one of the barriers mentioned. How would you now counteract this barrier?
4. Why do you think listening is a difficult skill to master?

Chapter 9

Reading Visuals

Difficult, difficult, difficult . . .
Easy, easy, easy . . .
Neither difficult nor easy.

Zen Buddhism

When you read this saying, you probably asked yourself what on earth it meant. It doesn't seem to make much sense until you think about it. Many of the reading tasks you have in special subjects will seem difficult at first. After you work with the assignments using the special skills you are learning, you should be able to exclaim, "Easy, easy, easy." So the conclusion you can draw is that the assigned reading is neither difficult nor easy because it is both.

One of the special study skills that may seem difficult for you the first time you try it is the skill of reading and understanding *graphic*, or visual, material. If you read graphics successfully, they will often give you helpful additional insights to the written text. In this chapter you will acquire special skills for reading and interpreting visuals.

The chapter will consider:

- how to read and follow directions
- how to follow directions for making grids
- how to read visuals
- guidelines for reading visuals

Finding Your Way Around

Following directions is an important part of living, and it can be essential to success in college. First, you must find your way to the buildings and rooms where your classes are located. Next, you need to follow directions for homework and class assignments. In order to complete your assignments, you need to be able to read and understand the directions and then follow them accurately. Sometimes you might think that being close is good enough. Read the following examples to see the problems that result from being only 99.9 percent correct.

2 million documents would be lost by the IRS each year.

22,000 checks would be deducted from the wrong bank account in the next 60 minutes.

1,314 telephone calls would be misplaced by your phone service each minute.

12 newborn babies would be given to the wrong mother each day.

2,488,200 books would be shipped with the wrong cover on them each year.

Over 5½ million cases of soft drinks would be produced in the next 12 months that will be flatter than a bad tire.

20,000 incorrect prescriptions would be written in the next 12 months.

This 0.1 percent may seem insignificant, but, as these examples illustrate, inaccuracy can be costly and dangerous.

Understanding and following directions is important in all courses, but it is particularly helpful in mathematics courses. The exercises that follow should help you improve your ability to read and follow directions skillfully and to refine your sense of spatial relationships. You don't have to be a skillful artist; you just need to follow directions and become familiar with some mathematical terms. Underlining key words and numbering the steps to follow will help you analyze these directions.

Exercise 9-1   Drawing from Directions

Read the directions below and draw the object described. The first one is completed for you as an example.

1. Draw a half circle with a vertical (north–south) line drawn through the center.

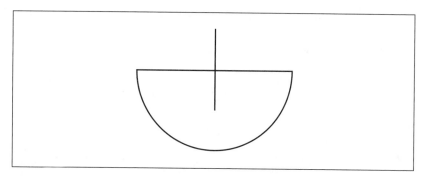

Figure 9.1

2. Draw three separate circles, each with two smaller circles enclosed. (There is more than one way to follow these directions. Does that tell you something about directions?)

3. Draw a patriarchal cross. Begin with a vertical line intersected (crossed) by two horizontal (east–west) lines above the halfway mark of the horizontal line. The top horizontal line is half the length of the horizontal line at the center of the vertical line.

4. Draw an equilateral triangle. This is a three-sided figure with all three sides equal in length.

5. Draw a hexagram, also called the Star of David. A hexagram is two equilateral triangles with one placed on top of the other to form a six-pointed star.

6. Draw two parallel lines, lines that are equally distant at all points. On the left side of the parallel lines, draw two lines beside each other that, are *not* parallel (lines that, if they were drawn to some point in the distance, would meet.)

7. Draw a trapezoid. This is a four-sided figure having two parallel sides and two that are not parallel.

8. Draw a trapezium. This is a four-sided figure with no two sides parallel.

9. Draw an insect that is circular in shape. It has six legs equally distant around its body. Two eyes are on the right top of its

head. A straight line is in the center of its body behind the eyes. Two lines branch out on either side of the straight line.

10. A biology experience: Draw an *ovate* leaf. The leaf itself is shaped like the bowl of a spoon. It is divided by a vein running from the tip to the stem. Branching from the center vein are six veins on each side that point from the vein toward the tip of the leaf.

Exercise 9-2   Discussion of Drawings

Discuss your drawings with other group members and make any adjustments that you think are necessary before checking the answer key. Some drawings may be slightly different but still correct. The group needs to determine whether directions were followed accurately.

Following Directions for Making Grids

In Exercise 9-2 you met some mathematical terms and used the terms *horizontal* and *vertical*. In courses such as psychology, sociology, government, and others, you will use these terms to read graphs and tables. Use your skills of analysis to read the following directions and create your own graph of the activity described.

Exercise 9-3   Making Grids

Work with pencil until you feel your drawing is correct. Underline key words and number the steps described to complete the activity. In some cases, it will be helpful to draw the directional symbols for North, South, East, and West beside your grid. The first grid is prepared as an example.

1. *One square on the grid is equal to two feet.*
   Jackson has a large backyard. He has decided to place the garden along the back 16 feet of the yard 2 feet from the lot line on the back and 4 feet from each side. The garden will be 8 feet long and 6 feet wide. Draw the outline of the garden on the grid.

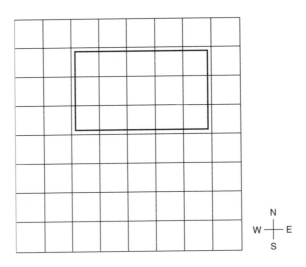

Grid 9.1

2. *A square equals 20 miles.*
   A search plane leaves its base (marked by a star) looking for a ship that has radioed in a distress call. The pilot first flies 80 miles due east, then 60 miles north. Seeing nothing, the pilot turns west for 40 miles and then north for 60 miles. At this point the pilot knows he is out of the range of the ship's call, so he turns west for 40 miles and then south for 80 miles. Here he sights the ship 20 miles west. He radios the position to rescuers and returns to his base. Trace the plane's flight and mark the position of the ship with a star.

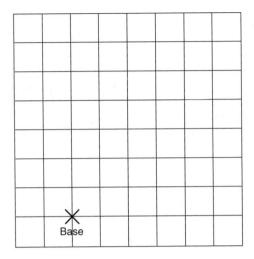

Grid 9.2

Base

3. *Each diagonal line through a square is 30 feet.*
   A baseball diamond is ninety feet square. Starting at home plate
   (marked with a star), draw the diamond. Make a diagonal line
   northeast for 90 feet, northwest for 90 feet, southwest for 90
   feet, and southeast for 90 feet. The pitcher's mound is 60 feet
   north of home plate. Mark it with a circle. The pitcher throws
   a ball to Sammy Sosa. Sosa returns the ball for a home run.

   How far did Sosa run? _____ feet

Grid 9.3

4. *Each square is equal to 30 feet.*

Manuel loves to surf. He slips into the water from the rock, paddling 90 feet north waiting for the "big one." While waiting, he drifts another 90 feet west. Sighting a big wave coming in, he begins paddling furiously for 30 feet north. He stands up and the wave drives him 120 feet southeast. He hops off the board into the surf and wades 30 feet southwest, back to the rock. Draw his path.

How many feet did he travel altogether?   _____ feet.

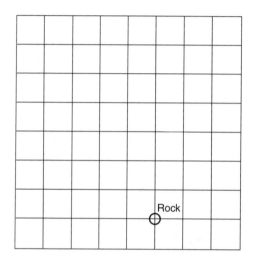

Grid 9.4

Reading Visuals: Is It a Table or a Figure?

Many textbooks use visuals of varying kinds to give information. Pictures, diagrams, tables, graphs, charts, and maps are used to help you understand the text or to add new information. Chapter 1 suggested that one of the important things to preview in a reading selection is the visuals. Visuals consolidate, or back up, information in a smaller space than the text does. The information is presented in an appealing way that can clarify ideas in the text or emphasize those ideas. Most people find it easier to follow a written diagram than an oral explanation. If you can visualize something, you can see the overall pattern more easily. To improve your comprehension of textbook materials, use the visuals to prepare for reading and to help you understand the concepts being presented.

Visuals are first identified as either figures or tabular material. Tabular material is simply a collection of labeled numbers and is called a *table*. The visual is identified by name as a figure or a table in the text, followed by two numbers. The first indicates the chapter in which the visual is found and the next number indicates the visual's number in that chapter. For example, a visual titled Figure 1.1 is the first figure in Chapter 1. As you read along in the text, reference may be made to a particular figure or table by putting its identification in parentheses like this (Fig. 1.1). The figure will probably be on a nearby page in the text. You may even have previewed the figure's important information when you previewed the selection.

A modern version of the story of Goldilocks and the Three Bears will illustrate some of the visuals you will meet in your texts. In the folktale, a golden-haired girl enters the bears' house in their absence and tries their porridge, their chairs, and finally their beds. When the bears return, she jumps out of the window in alarm. In an updated version, imagine Goldy suing the bears for a sprained ankle she received from the jump. Her lawyer has prepared several different kinds of visuals to use in her case against the bears.

Photographs, Sketches, and Pictographs

Photographs, sketches, and pictographs add interest, but more important, they help you visualize an event, idea, or circumstance. For example, after drawing the insect in Exercise 9-1, you can see an insect and remember its parts more easily. Your drawing was a *pictograph*. Pictographs use symbols to represent ideas.

In the case of Goldilocks, the lawyer might prepare a pictograph to show how outnumbered poor Goldilocks was. (See Figure 9.2).

Tables

Tables list facts and numbers in columns for easy reading of complicated information. Often the columns will be labeled. Tables are the visual form closest to standard prose. Instead of sentences

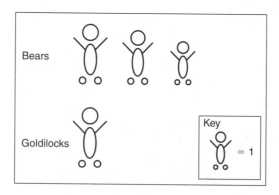

Figure 9.2   Goldilocks Outnumbered

Table 9.1   Bears' Assets Versus Expenses

	January	February	March	Totals
Wage income	$1000	1000	1000	$3,000
Room rental	$100	100	100	$300
Sale of honey	$50	50	50	$150
			Total income	$3,450
Living expenses	$450	450	450	$1,350
			Income – expenses	$2,100

and paragraphs, however, tables present information in columns or rows. This arrangement makes the numbers or facts presented easier to see; consequently, it is easier to make comparisons and show relationships.

Goldilocks's lawyer wanted to show that the bears would well be able to pay Goldilocks's medical and emotional expenses. The lawyer will point out that the bears earn at least $2,100 in a three-month period that could help with Goldy's living and medical expenses. (See Table 9.1).

Graphs

Graphs are visuals that show the relationships between different pieces of information. Three principal kinds of graphs are used. The *line graph* compares one or more lines, usually over a period of time so that you can see increases and decreases. Line graphs, a frequently used visual, are easy to read because you can usually see general trends from the direction of the lines. The lawyer has prepared a line graph of Goldy's loss of income as a restaurant server in the months since the accident. Notice that Goldy's initial monthly income of $500 plunges to nothing (Figure 9.3)

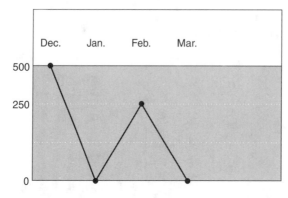

Figure 9.3   Goldy's Income

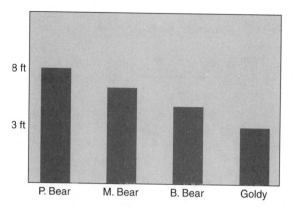

Figure 9.4   Intimidation by Size

after the accident. She tries to return to work in February but, according to her lawyer, cannot handle the physical and emotional stress.

A *bar graph* shows columns or bars arranged either in horizontal or vertical comparison to each other. Both can be divided to show parts of the whole, two or more wholes, more than one effect, and various other kinds of information. The lawyer has prepared a bar graph to show how Goldy was frightened by the size of the bears. (See Figure 9.4).

A *pie graph,* one of the easiest visuals to read, is a circle divided like a pie into sections. Each section represents a percentage of the whole. Usually each section is labeled with a number or percentage, but even without the numbers you can easily see who or what has the bigger share of the "pie." The lawyer's two pie graphs (Figure 9.5) show how little damage Goldy did to the bears' porridge holdings.

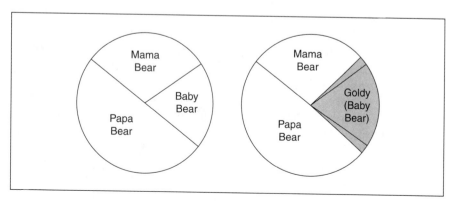

Figure 9.5   What Goldy Ate

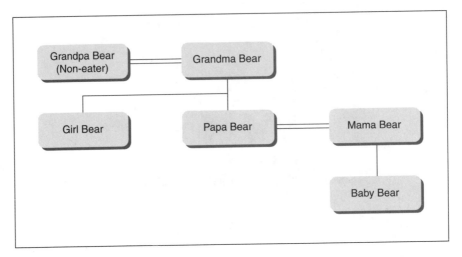

Figure 9.6   The Bears' Forebears

Charts

Charts are often used to show information about relationships and connections. Flow charts might show the steps you would take to accomplish a particular task in a sequential pattern, for example, or the relationships of positions in a company and who reports to whom. Goldy's lawyer has prepared a chart showing the Bear family relationships. You will see (Figure 9.6) that Grandpa Bear was a man-eater. This family history was the cause of Goldy's fear and consequent jumping from the window.

Maps

Even if you don't plan to take a geography course, reading a *map* is an important skill in developing your ability to follow spatial directions. As the world grows smaller with our ability to communicate instantly with anyone anywhere, it is important to know more about world locations as well as the location of the nearest deli.

The *legend*, usually a corner box on a map, is important in understanding what the map is showing—physical features such as elevations, the scale or size of what is presented, and codes and symbols used on the map. The lawyer has prepared a map of the area involved in the Goldilocks episode. (See Figure 9.7).

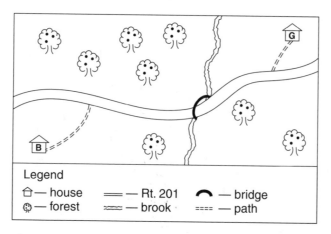

Figure 9.7   Map of Involved Area

Guidelines for Reading Visuals

Many kinds of visuals are presented in textbooks to aid in your understanding of the text material. To read and use visuals successfully, some general guidelines are helpful.

1. First, get an overview. Is there a title or caption? Read it carefully.

2. Look for footnotes or explanatory material. Is the information up to date? Who collected the information? (Look for authority and bias.) How many people, countries, examples, etc., were used as information for the visual?

3. Be sure that you understand the numbers presented. Are the figures in hundreds, thousands, millions?

4. What general conclusions can you draw from the information presented? Your conclusions can be important in understanding such things as trends, increases, and averages. The simple figures and tables in the preceeding sections will serve as a guide as you read visuals.

Exercise 9-4   Reading Visuals

Each example of a visual is followed by questions to help you interpret the message of the visual.

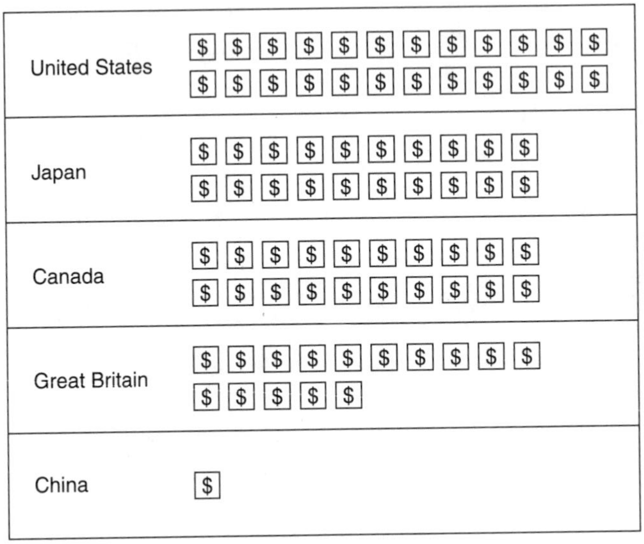

*Each symbol represents approximately $1,000. [$]

Figure 9.8 Yearly Income per Person in Selected Nations

Pictograph

1. *Read the pictograph in Figure 9.8 to answer the following questions true, false, or CT for "can't tell."*

_____ a. Japan has a higher per-person income than China.

_____ b. The United States has the highest per-person income (PPI) in the world.

_____ c. Little difference exists between the PPI of Canada and Japan.

_____ d. The standard of living is higher in Great Britain than in Russia.

_____ e. The United States has the highest per-person income of those countries mentioned on the graph.

2. *In the blank, write the approximate per-person income for each nation listed in the graph.*

United States	Japan	Canada	Great Britain	China
________	________	________	________	________

Birth Rates over a Decade

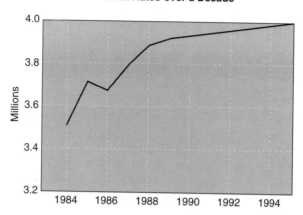

Figure 9.9

Line Graph

1. Read the line graph in Figure 9.9 and answer the following questions using true, false, or CT.

_____ a. 1994 is the last year represented on the graph.

_____ b. The birthrate in 1984 was approximately 3,500,000.

_____ c. The birthrate in 1988 was higher than the preceding year.

_____ d. The graph represents birthrates for the United States.

_____ e. The birthrate has increased each year since 1984.

2. Write the birthrate in millions for the following years.

1987   1989   1996

_____   _____   _____

Flowchart

People often play many different roles as they relate to other people and to the events of daily living. Many business

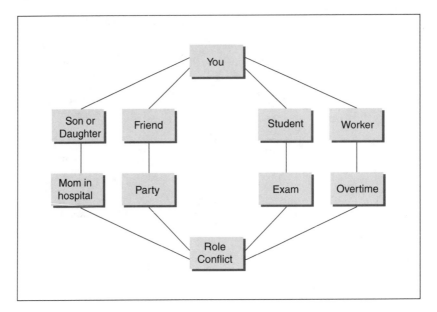

Figure 9.10   Role Conflict

organizations provide flow charts of managers and employees so that people can see who reports to whom and who has responsibility for various functions in the organization. See Figure 9.10 for an illustration of a flow chart that may show a real situation for you.

1. Read the flow chart in Figure 9.10 and answer the following questions using true, false, or CT.

_____ a. "You" are shown playing four different roles.

_____ b. "Your" friend wants you to help prepare for tomorrow's exam.

_____ c. "You" will resolve the conflict by visiting your mother in the hospital.

_____ d. If "you" had a spouse, this would add another role conflict.

_____ e. Different roles are always the source of conflicts.

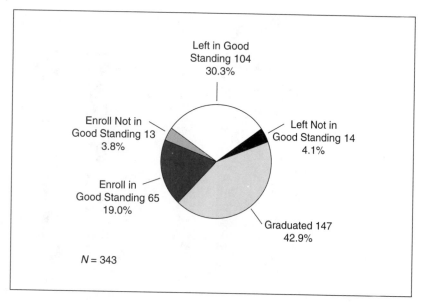

Figure 9.11   Progress of Full-Time Community College Students
after Four Years

Pie Graph

1. *Read the pie chart in Figure 9.11 and answer the following questions using true, false, or CT.*

_____ a. The study is limited to 343 students.

_____ b. After four years, 65 students are still working on their degrees.

_____ c. Because they were displeased with the college, 104 students left.

_____ d. In four years more than 40 percent of the entering students graduate.

_____ e. All students take four years to acquire a degree.

Bar Graph

Read the bar graph in Figure 9.12 and answer the following questions using true, false or CT.

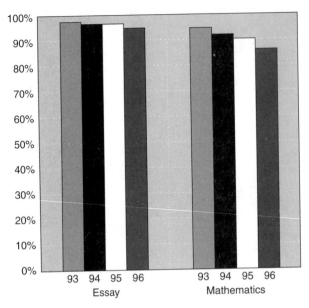

Figure 9.12   Percent of College Students Passing Final Tests

_____ 1. Overall, students have better achievement on the essay test than the mathematics test.

_____ 2. The best rates in both subjects were achieved in 1996.

_____ 3. Teaching preparation for the essay test is superior to teaching preparation for the mathematics test.

_____ 4. The percentage of students passing the mathematics test has decreased each succeeding year.

_____ 5. The best essay test results were in 1995.

Table

Read Table 9.2 and write out true, false or CT for "can't tell."

_____ 1. HSG stands for high score group.

_____ 2. In 1993–94 the greatest number of Hispanics enrolled in college.

Table 9.2   Area High School Graduates and College Enrollment*

Ethnicity	White Non-Hispanic		Black Non-Hispanic		Hispanic	
	Number	*Percent of Total*	*Number*	*Percent of Total*	*Number*	*Percent of Total*
Number of high school graduates (HSG)						
1991–92	2,156	74.60%	583	20.17%	105	3.63%
1992–93	2,345	74.85%	629	20.08%	101	3.22%
1993–94	2,148	73.81%	557	19.14%	146	5.02%
1994–95	2,095	73.79%	546	19.23%	158	5.57%
Number of HSG enrolled in college and % of total HSG enrolled						
1991–92	748	80.86%	138	14.92%	27	2.92%
1992–93	769	79.85%	146	15.16%	29	3.01%
1993–94	675	78.58%	126	14.67%	38	4.42%
1994–95	623	78.76%	119	15.04%	31	3.92%

*The numbers and percentages do not total 100%.

_____ 3. The number of white students graduating each year increased.

_____ 4. The greatest number of black students enrolled in college in 1992–93.

_____ 5. Graduates who did not enter college in the year following graduation never entered college.

Map

Mark the map in Figure 9.13 with the North, South, East, and West directional signals. The symbol in the upper lefthand corner will get you started.

N
W ─┼─ E
S

Preview the map carefully before answering the questions that follow; then put a checkmark by the best answer. You will need to know that the word contiguous *in the context of a map means "having a common boundary." Also note the different types and sizes of print used for the names of countries, cities, and rivers.*

Figure 9.13   Western Europe

© 1991 Facts on File, Inc.

Questions about the Map of Europe

1. In relation to Finland, Romania is:

   _____ north   _____ east   _____ south   _____ southwest

2. Which river runs through Hungary?

   _____ Danube   _____ Euro   _____ Tigris

3. Norway is contiguous to

   _____ Finland   _____ Sweden   _____ England

4. Sicily is _____ of Italy.

   _____ north   _____ east   _____ south   _____ west

5. To go from Berlin to Milan, you would travel

   _____ northeast   _____ southeast   _____ northwest

   _____ southwest

6. France is contiguous to

   _____ Switzerland   _____ Poland

7. Driving from Lisbon to Barcelona, you would travel

   _____ southeast   _____ southwest   _____ northeast

8. The Po River flows into the Adriatic Sea.

   _____ True   _____ False

9. Which of the following pairs of countries are contiguous?

   _____ Albania/Bulgaria   _____ Norway/Finland

   _____ Romania/Bulgaria

10. Algeria is contiguous to Spain.

    _____ True   _____ False

Chapter Review

Fill in the blanks with the correct words.

1. Reading _____ is an important aid in understanding the written text.

2. Tables and figures have the _____ number as the chapter in which they occur.

3. In a table numbered 7.2, you know that the table is the _____ one in Chapter _____.

4. Circle graph is another name for a _____ graph.

5. Graphs present facts visually with bars, circles, and _____.

6. When you study a _____, examining the title, caption, and explanations is important.

7. A _____ organizes material into rows and columns.

8. A symbol, or _____, graph uses symbols to show information.

9. A circle graph shows _____ the whole of something divided into sections.

10. Flow charts are often used to show relationships in _____.

Reading Selection 1

Purpose

Read the following short selection from a sociology text for some surprises. Study Table 9.3 carefully before answering the questions.

Preview

Skim Table 9.3, which follows the article, to see the kinds of information presented.

Anticipate/Associate

1. Who do you think is most likely to be unemployed: whites, Asian Americans, African Americans, or Latinos?

2. Have you or anyone you know ever been unemployed? Think about experiences of unemployed persons you are familiar with.

Who Is Unemployed?

James M. Henslin

It is hard to believe that Amy and Peter are not offi-   1
cially part of the unemployed. After all, they have no jobs.
In fact, they have no home. They are among the many
homeless and jobless Americans sleeping in alleys and shelters
for the destitute. That, however, is *not* enough to count them
as unemployed.

To see how the calculation works, let us suppose that   2
you lose your job. After six months' frustrating search for
work, you become so discouraged that you stay home and
stare blankly at the television. Amazingly, you no longer are
counted as unemployed. As far as official statistics are concerned, to be unemployed you must be *actively* seeking work.
If not, the government leaves you out of its figures. People
without jobs who are so discouraged that they have not
looked for work during the previous four weeks are simply
not included in the government's unemployment figures.

Now, suppose that you do keep on looking for work, and   3
you remain part of the government's count. But if your neighbor pays you to clean out her garage and rake the leaves, and
if you put in fifteen hours and report them, you won't be
counted, for the government figures that you have a job. Now
assume that you keep on looking for work, don't rake leaves
for a few hours' pay, but can't pay your telephone bill. Again,
you won't show up in the totals, for the Bureau of Labor Statistics counts only people it reaches in a random telephone
survey. To get an accurate idea of how many are unemployed,
then we need to add about 3 percent to the official unemployment rate. If the Labor Department says it is 8 percent,
the true rate is actually about 11 percent—a difference of

about 8 *million people.* This is a conservative figure, for some estimate that 6 million people who want to work have only part-time jobs or are so discouraged that they no longer look for work.

Table 9.3   The Official U.S. Unemployment Rate

Category	Percentage	Category	Percentage
Sex		*Ethnic Background*	
Male	6.2%	*of Latinos*	
Female	6.0	Puerto Rican	
		Men	11.0%
Marital Status		Women	12.4
of Women[a]		Mexican	
Married	4.5	Men	9.5
Single	10.0	Women	11.1
Divorced,	7.4	Cuban	
widowed,		Men	7.9
and separated		Women	8.4
		Other[c]	
		Men	8.9
		Women	9.4

Category	Percentage	Category	Percentage
Race and Ethnicity		*Education*	
African Americans		High school dropouts	
Men	12.0%	Men	13.4%
Women	11.0	Women	10.7
Latinos		High school graduates	
Men	9.4	Men	7.7
Women	10.7	Women	5.5
Whites		1–3 years of college	
Men	5.4	Men	5.2
Women	5.2	Women	4.8
Asian Americans[b]		College graduates	
Men	6.5	Men	3.2
Women	6.5	Women	2.5

[a]Source does not list totals for men.
[b]Source does not list employment of Asian Americans by sex, and this is the overall total listed for both men and women.
[c]Refers primarily to people from Central or South America.

Source: Statistical Abstract 1995: Tables 50, 628, 634, 638, 640, 662.

Check Your Understanding

Since this selection is brief and the purpose of the exercise is to study the table carefully, questions on the text are brief.

True/False

Label the following statements as true or false.

_____ 1. Unemployment figures from the U.S. Bureau of Labor Statistics are reliable.

_____ 2. The main idea presented in the selection is that more people are unemployed than the figures indicate.

_____ 3. The writer supports his information with examples, facts, and authorities.

_____ 4. If you stop actively looking for work, you are not considered unemployed.

_____ 5. If you report working for 15 hours, you may be considered employed for statistical purposes.

_____ 6. The difference between an unemployment rate of 8% and 11% is about 8 million people.

_____ 7. If you are homeless, you are not counted among the unemployed.

_____ 8. Part-time workers are counted among the unemployed.

_____ 9. Random telephone surveys give an accurate count of the unemployed.

_____ 10. You can infer that the government wants to keep the unemployment figures low.

Vocabulary

Circle the letter of the best synonym for each of the following words as used in the selection.

destitute	*calculation*	*statistics*
a. extremely poor	a. forethought	a. mathematics
b. deprived	b. scheming	b. numerical facts
c. criminal	c. estimate based on facts	c. numbers

Questions about Table 9.3 and Figures 9.14 and 9.15.

1. Write the four categories listed in Table 9.3.

    1. _____

    2. _____

    3. _____

    4. _____

2. Why is the marital status for women given and not the marital status for men? (Footnotes often contain important information.)

    _____

3. Which ethnic category is least likely to be unemployed?

    _____

4. Which category of women is least likely to be unemployed?

    _____

5. Which education level has the greatest unemployment?

    _____

6. Why can you not be certain about the unemployment rates for Asian American women?

    _____

7. Which group of Latino women has the highest unemployment?

    _____

8. Which group of men has the highest unemployment rate, including all Latinos?

_____

9. Which group of women has the highest unemployment rate, including all Latinos?

_____

10. Return to the text to explain why the author suggests that these figures are not realistic.

_____

_____

Figure 9.14 looks at employment rather than unemployment and shows the percentage of change in the labor force between 1996 and projected (or estimated) figures for 2006. Study the figure and answer the questions that follow. (The first bar to the left is for 1996 and the second is for 2006.)

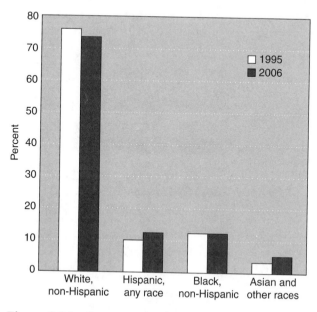

Figure 9.14   Percent of Labor Force by Race, 1996 and Projected 2006

1. Which races will increase their numbers in the labor force between 1996 and 2006? _____

2. Which race will maintain its figures in the labor force?

   _____

3. What is projected to happen to the number of whites in the labor force? _____

4. Which race will still make up the vast majority of workers in the labor force? _____

5. What reasons can you infer for the changes noted in the answers to the first four questions? _____

   _____

   _____

The reasons behind employment and unemployment are another part of an analysis of this subject. Read Figure 9.15 to

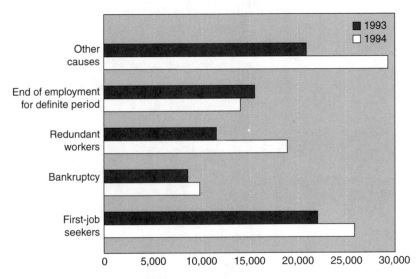

Figure 9.15   Newly Registered Unemployed, by Causes
of Unemployment

answer questions about why people are unemployed. (The top bar represents 1993 and the second bar represents 1994.)

1. What was the greatest cause of unemployment in 1994?

   _____

2. Approximately how many people were unemployed in 1994? _____

3. What was the second greatest cause of unemployment in 1994? _____

4. What was the greatest cause of unemployment in 1993?

   _____

5. Approximately how many people were unemployed in 1993? _____

6. Approximately how many workers were dispensable or nonessential in 1993? _____

Writing

1. You have just read and studied a great deal of information about employment and unemployment. Write a paragraph about some issue that interested you. What facts can you cite? Why is this information personally interesting to you?
2. Make a list of five pieces of information about this topic that you could share with others.

Critical Thinking

1. Look again at Figure 9.14. What do you think would account for the changes in projected employment for the racial categories?
2. Look again at Figure 9.15. What do you suppose are some of the "other causes" for unemployment?
3. What could account for the significant changes in figures between 1993 and 1994?

Reading Selection 2

Purpose

Read to discover the best and the worst jobs. You may be surprised. You may also learn information that will be helpful to you in evaluating your job choice.

Preview

The following article summarizes information rating 250 jobs as the best and worst in our country. The visuals that follow are not directly related to the article. However, they provide additional information about various aspects of the job market.

Anticipate/Associate

1. You probably have some career goal in mind. What aspects of that career appeal to you?

2. Would the fact that the career is labeled one of the worst stop you from preparing for it? Would the fact that the career is not expected to develop by 2005 stop you?

Nerds Get Best Jobs—Tough Guys Finish Last

Perri Capell

Lumberjacks, cowboys, and construction workers may symbolize rugged America. But these occupations rank among the worst jobs in the U.S., according to the *Jobs Rated Almanac* (John Wiley & Sons, New York, NY). 1

The ten worst jobs all involve heavy physical labor. They also include dancer, roustabout, taxi driver, fisherman, roofer, auto painter, and seaman. Chicago author Les Krantz, who prepared the listings, used six criteria to rank 250 common U.S. occupations: day-to-day working conditions, income, employment outlook, physical requirements, security, and inherent stress. The worst jobs did poorly in all categories. Poor working conditions, severe health risks, and bleak futures make the ten worst occupations especially unappealing, says Krantz. 2

The nerds get their revenge in Krantz's book. The ten best jobs are mostly computer or information-oriented positions 3 with good employment growth potential and clean environments. Computer-systems analysts rank third among good jobs and first in job security and future outlook.

Who has the best jobs? <u>Actuaries</u>, due to their relatively high incomes, excellent working environments, high job security, low stress, and almost nonexistent physical demands. After seven to eight years of study to pass required exams, experienced actuaries can earn at least $150,000 a year, says Linda Delgadillo, a spokeswoman for the Society of Actuaries in Schaumburg, Illinois. Moreover, until recent downsizings affected the insurance industry, the society's members suffered virtually no unemployment, she says.

Software engineers, accountants, mathematicians, and computer programmers also fall on the top-ten job list. While decidedly less technical, parole officers make the cut because growing prison populations are expected to increase the number of jobs 44 percent in the next decade, according to Bureau of Labor Statistics projections. The ranks of paralegals, another top-ten contender, will also grow as Americans seek less expensive ways to pursue <u>litigation</u>. Medical secretaries and records technicians round out the top-ten list because they have low-stress jobs that will remain secure in a growing health-care industry.

If you can't handle stress, don't run for the highest office in the land. The position of President of the United States scores high on almost every emotionally demanding factor, such as hazards faced, amount of public contact, and degree of peril facing others. Despite the money and <u>prestige</u>, the President's job ranks 227th overall, barely beating out that of nuclear plant <u>decontamination</u> technicians.

Firefighters' jobs rank second highest in stress, after the President. Third place goes to corporate executives whose seemingly plush jobs aren't all they're cracked up to be. "The people I work with frequently complain about the endless hours they put in and not having time for their families," says Betsy Jaffe, a New York City career counselor who often advises executives in the <u>throes</u> of burn-out.

Many who choose occupations based on earnings potential or prestige don't enjoy them because of the stress, says Arlene Hirsch, a Chicago psychotherapist and author of the forthcoming *Love Your Work* (John Wiley & Sons). She advises people to choose jobs they're passionate about, even if they might seem undesirable to others. "Career satisfaction is based on <u>integrating</u> financial goals with nonmaterial goals, such as creativity, growth, service, meaning, or contribution," she says. Even the worst-ranked jobs can offer high levels of satisfaction to people who enjoy physical activity, don't mind getting cold or wet, and plan to retire before they become <u>obsolete</u>. Sitting in a clean, quiet office all day is not a cowboy's idea of heaven.

Check Your Understanding

Review

1. Map the six criteria used to rank the various occupations (see paragraph 2). You may wish to extend the map by adding detailed criteria mentioned later in the article.

2. List the ten best and ten worst jobs mentioned in the article.

10 Best	10 Worst
_____	_____
_____	_____
_____	_____
_____	_____
_____	_____
_____	_____
_____	_____
_____	_____
_____	_____
_____	_____

Multiple Choice

Select the letter of the answer that best completes the statement.

_____ 1. The main purpose of the article is to
    a. rank all jobs according to the best and the worst.
    b. discuss criteria used to evaluate jobs.
    c. encourage you to seek a particular job.

_____ 2. Paragraph 5 is developed by
    a. comparison/contrast.
    b. examples.
    c. definition.

_____ 3. The tone of the article is
    a. ironic.
    b. serious.
    c. light hearted.

True/False

Label the following statements true or false according to the article.

_____ 1. The article is a kind of summary of information from another source.

_____ 2. Firefighters suffer worse stress than the President of the United States.

_____ 3. Earning potential and prestige are among the best reasons for seeking a particular job.

_____ 4. You should feel passionate about your job choice.

_____ 5. Parole officers are on the top ten job list.

_____ 6. Actuaries require little job preparation.

_____ 7. The amount of public contact the job requires is a factor in job stress.

_____ 8. One criteron used to evaluate jobs is their physical requirements.

_____ 9. Corporate executives have easy jobs.

_____ 10. The insurance industry has excellent working conditions.

Vocabulary

Match the vocabulary words in column A with their definition in column B by placing the letter from column B before the word in column A.

Column A	Column B
_____ 1. actuary	a. wide recognition and distinction
_____ 2. litigation	b. purification
_____ 3. prestige	c. type of suffering
_____ 4. decontamination	d. one who figures insurance rates
_____ 5. throes	e. out of date
_____ 6. integrating	f. legal proceeding
_____ 7. obsolete	g. bringing parts into a whole

Another way of looking at various occupations is using the criteria of job requirements, work requirements, and occupational characteristics. Read Table 9.4 to answer the questions based on these criteria. The letters H, M, and L in the last column (number 14) stand for high, medium and low.

1. Which two occupations might receive a low ranking because of dangerous working conditions?

_____

2. Which occupation requires the least job preparation?

_____

3. Why is it important to know that some occupations provide part-time opportunities?

_____

4. Which occupation would be most appealing for someone who enjoys working outdoors?

_____

5. If someone were seriously interested in one of these occupations, what important information might they need that is missing from the table?

_____

Table 9.4

	Job Requirements								Work Environment			Occupational Characteristics		
	1. Leadership/persuasion	2. Helping/instructing others	3. Problem solving/creativity	4. Initiative	5. Work as part of a team	6. Frequent public contact	7. Manual dexterity	8. Physical stamina	9. Hazardous	10. Outdoors	11. Confined	12. Geographically concentrated	13. Part time	14. Entry requirements
Teachers, Counselors, Librarians and Archivists														
Kindergarten and elementary school teachers	•	•	•	•	•	•	•	•						H
Secondary school teachers	•	•	•	•	•	•		•						H
Adult and vocational education teachers	•	•	•	•	•	•	•	•					•	H
College and university faculty	•	•	•	•	•	•		•					•	H
Counselors	•	•	•	•	•	•								H
Librarians	•	•	•	•	•	•		•					•	H
Archivists and curators			•	•	•									H
Health Diagnosing and Treating Practitioners														
Chiropractors	•	•	•	•	•	•	•	•						H
Dentists	•	•	•	•	•	•	•	•						H
Optometrists	•	•	•	•	•	•	•	•						H
Physicians	•	•	•	•	•	•	•	•					•	H
Podiatrists	•	•	•	•	•	•	•	•						H
Veterinarians	•	•	•	•	•	•	•	•	•	•				H
Registered Nurses, Pharmacists, Dietitians, Therapists, and Physician Assistants														
Dietitians and nutritionists	•	•	•	•	•	•								H
Occupational therapists	•	•	•	•	•	•	•	•						H
Pharmacists	•	•	•	•	•	•					•			H
Physical therapists	•	•	•	•	•	•	•	•						H
Physical assistants	•	•	•	•	•	•	•							M
Recreational therapists	•	•	•	•	•	•				•				M
Registered nurses	•	•	•	•	•	•	•	•	•				•	M
Respiratory therapists	•	•	•	•	•	•	•							L
Speech pathologists and audiologists	•	•	•	•	•	•								H
Health Technologists and Technicians														
Clinical laboratory technologists and technicians		•		•		•					•			
Dental hygienists		•			•	•	•	•					•	M

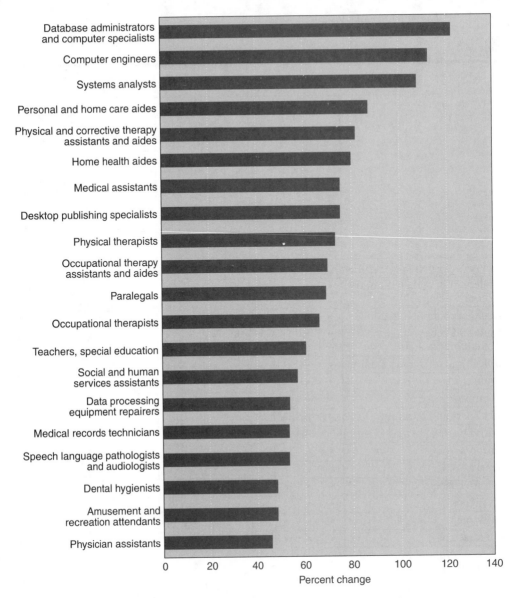

Figure 9.16 Occupations Projected to Grow the Fastest, 1996–2006

When you are making career choices, it is important to consider whether there will be jobs in your career area when you graduate. Figure 9.16 addresses the question of growth, listing the twenty occupations that are projected to have the greatest growth from 1996 to 2006. Read the chart and answer the questions that follow.

1. How many different health-care positions are in the top

   ten occupations for projected growth? _____

2. How many education-related positions are in the top

   twenty? _____

3. What two inferences about population can you make
   from these two projections?

   _____

   _____

4. What is the projected percentage of growth for the occu-

   pation of systems analyst? _____

   Figure 9.17 offers a view of educational background and
projected job openings. You can see that jobs requiring a college degree show an average of 15 percent employment growth.
These occupations also offer above-average wages. Read the
figure to answer specific questions.

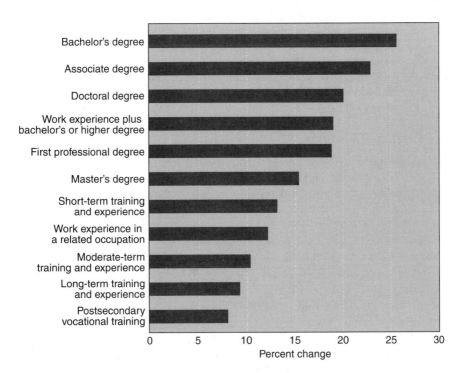

Figure 9.17   Growth Rates by Most Significant Source of Education
and Training, Projected 1996–2006

1. Is it true in general that jobs requiring more education and training will grow faster than jobs requiring less education and training? _____

2. What is the approximate percentage of difference in the growth rate between jobs requiring a master's degree and those requiring a doctorate? _____

3. What approximate percentage of growth is projected for jobs requiring only work experience? _____

4. Why does this bar graph provide a better visual presentation of this information than a pie (or circle) graph would?

   _____

Writing

1. Write a paragraph describing your career goals.
2. Describe what you have learned about your employment future from the two readings and from the figures and tables. Be specific, relating facts to your particular career goal.
3. Identify three criteria mentioned in the text or the visuals and write about why they are or are not important to your career decisions.

Critical Thinking

1. What additional information would you like to know about your planned career?
2. Where can you find more detailed information about your prospective career?

Chapter 10

Test-Taking Tips and Tricks

I tried and failed. I tried again and I succeeded.

Gail Borden Jr.

Reading is an essential skill for taking tests in all subjects. Knowing how to prepare for tests and how to read tests is important to being successful. Keeping a positive attitude about test taking is also important. Knowing some tips, tricks, and techniques about how to read and answer test questions can help give you control and mastery of tests and help you control your anxiety. Once I had a student who had dyslexia, a learning disorder that makes reading difficult. Casey told of an experience he had had in the first grade. Since he was the only child in his class who could not read, he was convinced that the teacher was sharing tricks about reading with the other students that he wasn't being given. Later, after his difficulty with reading was discovered, Casey realized that no tips or tricks had been hidden. Just so, no tricks about test taking are meant to be hidden. This chapter will discuss tips, tricks, and techniques that will help you be a successful test taker.

The chapter will consider:

- how to prepare for tests
- how to handle fear of test taking
- how to read and answer specific kinds of test questions
- how to profit from test results

Preparing for a Test

If you have been practicing the three-step review discussed in Chapter 8 on study techniques, you are well on your way to completing a test with confidence and success. You have been reviewing text material and class notes within 24 hours of class. You have been doing a weekly review of your notes and text. Now you are ready for the final preparation before a test. This study session should occur several days before test day.

Assemble Your Materials

First, assemble all of the materials you will need to study:

Your class notes

Your textbook containing underlining and marginal notes

Your summaries, mind maps, and vocabulary cards

Important class handouts

Tests you have taken previously in the course

Copies of tests the instructor may share

Be sure you have all needed material. If you missed a lecture class, have you borrowed and copied the missing notes from a classmate? Do you have all the handouts that support, clarify, or further develop the text and lecture notes? If you must review five chapters, organize your materials for each chapter. Make a quick overview of your materials. Note particularly the facts and ideas that have been repeated and stressed by the instructor. Is some particular item covered in class notes, mentioned on a handout, and discussed in the text? If so, this is material the instructor feels is important. Study it. Which sections do you feel that you understand fairly well? Which sections are still unclear or need more review?

Past tests are important. If you have chapter tests that you have already taken, you will be able to see the kinds of questions to expect. You will see the points that the instructor previously emphasized as well as points or questions that proved difficult for you in the past. Don't hesitate to ask the instructor for a copy of a test on the material from an earlier semester. The worst thing that can happen is that the instructor will tell you no tests are available.

Review the material carefully, section by section. Doing this with a study group is usually most helpful. Others in the group can explain difficult material for you, and you can reinforce your own learning by explaining and reviewing something for another study group member.

Prepare possible questions of the type expected on the test. Practice on preparing questions is considered later in this chapter. Determine which facts or concepts need to be memorized. If you have been doing the spaced reviewing discussed in Chapter 8, you have already begun the task of memorizing before a final study session. Now this final review session will be more effective.

Overcoming a Fear of Failure

Many students are their own worst enemies when they take a test. They allow anxiety and fear of failure to hinder them from making their best effort. They have prepared adequately, but the sight of a blue book or white test papers being passed to them causes perspiration on a cold day and stomach pains any day. These reactions hinder the brain cells from functioning properly, and all early preparations might just as well not have been made. By the time anxiety-prone students are in college classes, they think these reactions are normal and that all students experience them—or, at least, they think nothing can be done to overcome these feelings. Wrong! This kind of unreasoned response to tests is a learned behavior. Since it has been learned, with practice it can be unlearned. Use this quiz to evaluate your responses to test taking.

Exercise 10-1 Multiple Choice

Circle the letter of the answer that best describes your feelings.

1. I look forward to taking tests.

   a. never   b. sometimes   c. always

2. After a test, I feel good about the experience.

   a. never   b. sometimes   c. always

3. My emotions interfere with my test-taking ability.

   a. always   b. sometimes   c. never

4. I prepare well before taking a test.

   a. never   b. sometimes   c. always

5. During a test, I think about the possibility of failing.

   a. always   b. sometimes   c. never

6. I consider tests to be opportunities for learning.

   a. never   b. sometimes   c. always

7. The sight of a test causes me to forget what I know.

   a. always   b. sometimes   c. never

8. I can control my test anxiety.

   a. never   b. sometimes   c. always

9. I feel ready for a test when the day arrives.

   a. never   b. sometimes   c. always

10. I worry about time when taking a test.

   a. always   b. sometimes   c. never

Scoring: *a* answers are worth 1 point, *b* answers 2 points, and *c* answers 3 points. Add your score and note the comments.

10–15   You are letting anxiety control your test results. This chapter may be just what the doctor ordered.

16–30   Plan to use some of the tips that follow to control your anxiety and improve your test scores.

31–40   You have a healthy anxiety level. A little anxiety can pump you up for a test.

41–50   Are you sure? Maybe you need to develop a little healthy anxiety.

Discussing Test Results

If your overall score on the test was low and your answer to statement 4 was "a," you could probably lower your anxiety level by better test preparation, to be discussed later in this chapter. After all, if you fail to prepare, you prepare to fail.

You may wonder why a fairly high anxiety level is considered healthy. Whenever you are in a stressful situation, and taking a test (even one you have prepared for) is stressful, your adrenal glands release the hormone adrenalin into your bloodstream. Adrenaline increases your breathing and your heartbeat. A little adrenaline stimulates your brain for clearer thinking. Too much can be harmful, causing your muscles to tense and raising your blood pressure. The trick is to keep the stress and anxiety of test taking at a healthy level.

Tricks for Coping with Test Anxiety

Before the Test

Before test time, particularly the night before, there are a number of things to do to prepare yourself for a test—that is, assuming you have made preparations by spaced reviewing.

1. *Relax.* This is easy to say, but not always easy to do. One way to relax is to meditate. Get yourself in a comfortable position in a place where you will not be disturbed. Focus your mind on a word like *flower* or *tree*. Repeat the word without moving your lips. Just concentrating on repeating the unspoken word relaxes tension. If you are primarily a visual learner, you can focus on a picture or a candle. Just keep your attention focused. If you are primarily an auditory learner, you can play soft music and imagine yourself in some happy, peaceful environment. Using one or more of these techniques will help to free your mind of worry.

2. *Talk to others.* Talking to someone about your concerns about a test can lessen the burden. But be sure to talk to someone who will listen to you and give comfort. Don't talk to someone who also has test anxiety. This will not lessen your worry but more likely increase it.

3. *Distract yourself.* Do something that you enjoy—play a computer game, go to a movie with friends, treat yourself to dinner out, play music that you enjoy, watch television, go for a walk. The possibilities are endless. Just don't do anything that will create more stress for you, like watching a horror movie that you will dream about later.

4. *Avoid cramming.* If you have been reviewing material to be included in the test at regular intervals, there is no need for prolonged study the night before a test. A quick review should do. Cramming puts information into your short-term memory, where it is easily forgotten by morning. Cramming can also increase your tension because it shows you how much you should have been learning in the course.

5. *Visualize success.* Think about what a great job you are going to do on the test. Talk to yourself about how well you are going to do. Henry Ford, who barely made it through high school but later perfected the gasoline engine and introduced assembly-line production, has said, "The person who thinks he can, and the person who thinks he can't, are both probably right." Virgil, an early Roman poet, said, "They can because they think they can." Don't let past poor performances stand in the way of success today. You can triumph. Triumph is *umph* added to try. Have the "umph" to try. You can be a successful test taker. On a 3 × 5 card, write out three reasons why you know you will be successful on the test. Memorize these ideas by looking at the card frequently. When you get the

test, write at least one of the ideas on the edge of the test paper to keep your thinking positive.

6. *Make a summary card.* As part of a final review, write the most important things you want to remember on a 3 × 5 card. You will be surprised at how much information you can get on the card by writing small and using both sides. Sometimes instructors allow students to use their cards during the test. Afterward, students often report that they didn't even look at their cards. Preparing the card the night before had helped them summarize the main points they wanted to remember. Having the card on their desk added to their confidence, but preparation was the real key to success.

7. *Face past failures.* One huge stumbling block to being successful is allowing past failures to haunt you. Face the possibility of failure head on. What happens if you fail an important test? Will you fail the course? You can take the course again. Will you fail to graduate? You might delay graduation, but you will graduate if you wish to. Failure is not the end of your personal world unless you fail to get up and try again. Thomas Edison, who invented the light bulb, failed at least 2,000 times before his experiment was successful. He didn't view the 1,999 previous experiments as failures; he saw the invention as a 2,000-step process. Repeating a course may be a part of your successful graduation process.

Practice these techniques to ease your tension the night before a test.

On Test Day

What can you do on test day and during the test to keep your stress level under control? Again, there are tricks to stop an unhealthy flow of adrenalin.

1. *Be prepared.* Get to class in plenty of time with all the materials you will need, such as paper, pencils, pens. It is not a good practice to talk to other students about the test. This is a time when tensions can increase as they are shared.

   Some students find it helpful to arrive in time to review their summary cards. Others find a final review stressful. You have to know what works best for you.

2. *Breathe deeply.* Take a few deep breaths before test time. This is a good, fast relaxer. If you feel yourself getting tense

during the test, stop and breathe deeply again. This takes only a few seconds to do and exhaling deeply gets rid of bad feelings.

At the same time, sit up and stretch your muscles. Students often hunch over their test papers, cramping the muscles in their necks, which restricts the blood flow to the brain. Just don't stretch in a way that will distract your test-taking neighbors.

3. *Look over the test carefully.* Many students jump right into a test without making a helpful survey. Jumping into cold water can be a shock to your nervous system, and so can jumping into a test and running into a difficult question. Take the time to jot a few notes about important dates or formulas that you expect to use in the test. Surveying the test will be a good review. Something on the last page may help you answer a question on the first page. You don't have to begin the test with the first question; find a question or a section that you feel comfortable with and begin working there. You will build your confidence and dispel some tension.

4. *Make notes.* Immediately write any formula or necessary material that you think you might forget in taking the test. Write out at least one reason for knowing that you are going to be successful on this test. In large letters, write out the reminder to READ CAREFULLY AND COMPLETELY. That will remind you to read directions, reading material, and questions slowly and carefully.

5. *Manage your time.* As you survey the test, determine how much time you will need to devote to each section of the test. For example, essay questions require more time than answering ten true or false questions. As you figure your time for each section, be sure to allow a few minutes for a final review of your paper. You may have omitted filling in some answers to difficult questions. You want time to fill in an answer even if it is only a guess. Don't be disturbed by students who complete the test before you. No reward is given for papers turned in early. Often, early papers are hastily done, or the student has not prepared well and consequently guessed at most of the questions.

6. *Ask questions.* Don't hesitate to ask questions. Many times a good question will set you on the right track for an answer. Most instructors are happy to answer your questions; if you ask something they can't answer, they will simply tell you that.

Now that you know some tricks for handling test anxiety, it's time to talk about preparing for a test.

Reading and Answering Specific Kinds of Test Questions

With test jitters under control, and having learned some specific techniques to help you remember difficult material, the next step is knowing how to prepare for and answer the different kinds of test questions. The most common kinds of test questions are:

True or false   Multiple choice   Matching   Short answer   Essay

It helps to know before the test what kinds of questions will be used. Usually, instructors will give you this information if you ask, even if no past test samples are available. Look first at the tips for reading and answering true or false questions.

True or False Questions

Some students like true or false questions because they feel they have a 50–50 chance of being right. Other students hate true or false because they read too much into the questions and debate the questions in their minds endlessly. If you are using good time management for your test, you won't spend too much time debating about a true or false question.

First, you should read the entire statement carefully. If any part of the statement is not true, the statement is false. Sometimes a phrase or a clause can make what appears to be a true statement false.

Clue words can also be a help. If you are in doubt about a true or false statement, look for these clue words: *always, never, every, only, all.* These words, and others with similar meanings, are often a clue that the statement is false. On the other hand, words like: *usually, frequently, often, some,* and *few* are examples of qualifying key words suggesting that the statement may be true.

Exercise 10-2 Using Clue Words

Read the following true or false questions on topics you may not know about and underline the clue words (if any). Then answer the question by writing the words true *or* false.

_____ 1. Most presidents have kept pets in the White House.

_____ 2. Men usually weigh more than women.

_____ 3. The line-item veto allows presidents to eliminate "fat" from the budget.

_____ 4. All violence in society has its roots in the violence seen in movies and on television.

_____ 5. Experiencing passionate love, a person thinks constantly of the loved one.

The first three answers are true and the last two are false. Notice that three of the five answers are true. When all else fails and you must resort to guessing, mark the answer as true. You have a better than 50–50 chance with true. However, some test makers build in a penalty for guessing. If this is the case—and the directions will tell you—it is better not to answer.

As you have learned, complicated sentences can cause problems unless you read carefully. In addition, some short sentences can be complicated because of negative expressions, particularly double negatives. For example to say that someone is *not unskillful* is to say that the person *is* skillful. The negatives *not* and *un-* cancel each other out. You need to rethink such sentences and restate them in your mind without the negatives.

Another difficulty in reading questions is eliminating unnecessary information given in phrases and clauses so that you have the main idea. Be careful here because some phrases and clauses are necessary qualifiers and can change the sentence from a true statement to a false one.

Exercise 10-3 Complicated True or False

Rewrite the statements before writing out the true or false answers. Sometimes you will need to change negative statements to positive, and sometimes you will need to eliminate unnecessary information.

_____ 1. Most U.S. presidents are not inconsiderate of visiting heads of state.

_____ 2. Building the Panama Canal was a not impossible task.

_____ 3. Congress never overrides a presidential veto unless sufficient votes can be found.

_____ 4. The causes of the Civil War are not unclear.

_____ 5. It was not totally unexpected by most of the nations in the world when the United States entered World War II.

Remember, when in doubt, don't toss a coin and disturb your neighbor. Instead, guess that the statement is true.

Multiple Choice Questions

The first rule for answering multiple choice questions is to read the question carefully and try to think of the answer before looking at the choices. Then read all the answers before making your choice. The last answer may be something like: *All of the above.* If you choose the first answer quickly because you know it is correct, you are partially correct, but your answer will be marked wrong.

One of the difficult things about multiple choice is that there are often two good answers, but only one is the best answer. To cut down your choices from four or five to two, use these strategies.

Cross off incorrect answers.

Watch for clues in modifiers.

Know that the longest answer is likely to be correct.

Look for similar answers. One is probably correct.

When the answer is a number, the lowest and the highest are usually incorrect.

If you still can't determine the answer, don't waste time and stir up tension. Simply put a mark in the margin and leave it blank. Something else in the test might unlock the file in your brain where the answer is stored. Before you hand in the test, be sure to return to these unanswered questions. If the answer has not come to you, now is the time to take a guess.

Use these tricks to answer the following multiple choice questions.

Exercise 10-4 Answering Multiple Choice

Select the letter of the answer that best completes the statement. Use the strategies for multiple choice questions.

_____ 1. Which of the following techniques should be used to prepare for tests?
  a. Save all quizzes, past tests, notes, and homework.
  b. Study with a group of students.
  c. Make up your own test questions.
  d. Relax.
  e. All of the above.

_____ 2. Flash cards are effective for learning which of the following?
  a. Names of events and dates.
  b. Scientific or mathematical formulas.

    c. Vocabulary words and their definitions.
    d. Key words for items in a list.
    e. All of the above.

_____ 3. What is the product of $322{,}614 \times 14$?
    a. 562,726
    b. 10,628,786
    c. 4,516,596
    d. 3,642,218

_____ 4. Answers to difficult questions on a test can sometimes be figured out by
    a. eliminating obviously wrong answers.
    b. finding clues from other test questions.
    c. simplifying the phrasing of the test question.
    d. all of the above.

_____ 5. For a negatively phrased question, a student should *never*
    a. change the wording to positive phrasing for better understanding.
    b. eliminate obviously wrong answers.
    c. be careful and reread the question.
    d. choose the first response without reading the others.
    e. Both a and b above.

Matching Questions

When material is presented in columns and the directions ask you to match information, several techniques are helpful. First, read both columns slowly and carefully. Next, match those answers you know, crossing off the answers you have used. Finally, use logical thinking, analysis, and the process of elimination to select the final answers. Use these clues to match some previously introduced vocabulary words. (If you have not yet met these words, do the best you can and then use your dictionary and make vocabulary cards that will be helpful later.)

Exercise 10-5 Practicing Matching Strategies

Match the words in column A with their synonyms from column B by placing the letter of column B before the number in column A.

Column A   Column B

_____ 1. hazardous   a. make up for

_____ 2. subsequent   b. rational

_____ 3. consequence   c. following

_____ 4. depict   d. lessen

_____ 5. compensate   e. forceful

_____ 6. impaired   f. represent

_____ 7. cognitive   g. dangerous

_____ 8. diminish   h. water down

_____ 9. dilute   i. effect

_____ 10. aggressive   j. damaged

Fill-in-the-Blank Questions

Fill-in-the-blank questions require you to use your long-term memory in order to complete sentences with missing information. Sometimes grammatical clues are helpful. For example if *an* precedes the blank, you know you are looking for a word that begins with a vowel. Reading slowly and looking for key words in the statement will help you to recall the required answer. The length of the empty blank is *not* a clue to the length of the missing word or words.

Exercise 10-6 Using Key Words

Complete the statements by writng the best word in the blank. (These statements will help you review concepts from earlier chapters.)

1. You develop your vocabulary by using _____,

   a _____, and by analyzing the _____ of the

   word.

2. _____ are words with the same meaning.

3. Words that are opposite in meaning are called _____.

4. Words often have both a dictionary meaning, or _____,

   and an implied meaning or shaded meaning, called the word's

   _____.

Essay Questions

Some students fear essay questions for many reasons. Try to view these questions as an opportunity to show what you know. When you are faced with an essay question, first restate the idea as an introduction to your essay. This will clarify your thinking and give you a good starting point. Using this restatement, make some rough notes of the points you will want to include. Try to use specific facts like dates and names. Check your restatement to be sure it includes all important parts of the original statement. If you have missed a point, you may lose five or ten points because of a faulty restatement. Consider the following example.

Statement: Discuss the two learning approaches to language acquisition—conditioning and imitation.

Restatement: One learning approach to acquiring language is conditioning.

It is clear that if you stop with this restatement, half of what the instructor wants you to discuss will be omitted.

Be sure you understand the verbs that are most frequently used for essay questions. If the question asks you to discuss and you simply make a list, you have not followed directions and your grade will reflect this fact. Some of the most frequently used words in essay questions are

compare	discuss	describe	list
contrast	define	explain	argue
trace	analyze	summarize	illustrate

Study the following examples:

1. *Contrast the creation of mountains and glaciers.*

   This question wants you to talk about the *differences* between the ways mountains and glaciers are created. Differences is the point to emphasize in your answer. How are mountains and glaciers created differently?

2. *Describe in-line skating and compare it to roller skating.*

   Notice that you are asked to *describe* in-line skating *and* then *compare* it to roller skating. You could first describe and then compare, or you could describe and make comparisons within your description. Just be sure to do both.

3. *Explain the difference between macrosociology and microsociology.*

   This question requires you to define *sociology* and then explain the difference between *macro* and *micro* in the context of sociology.

4. *Certain factors have an influence on your stress levels. Explain how social support, self-esteem, and personality make you more or less susceptible to stress.*

   First, you must understand and explain the three terms. Then, in your explanation, you must note how each can either contribute to your stress or lessen it. You would need to keep in mind that each factor could, in some cases, work both to increase or to decrease stress.

5. *Mass media people should use certain moral principles to guide them in thorny ethical questions. Sometimes these principles are in conflict. List and illustrate three of the conflicts that can arise.*

   A "thorny" question! You must identify some moral principles and instances when these principles come in conflict with news reporting. Then you must *list* three and *illustrate*. In this case, *illustrate* does not mean draw; it means to give specific examples.

You can see that taking time both to understand the question stated and to think of the main points you want to make is fundamental to writing a good essay answer. Further, keep your answer brief, but complete. Your prewriting notes will help you. Conclude your essay with a sentence that restates the idea of the original question without repeating your opening statement or the original question.

Exercise 10-7 Working with Essay Questions

Write an opening or thesis statement for these essay questions by restating the question. You do not, in this case, need to be able to answer the question. You just need to write an opening statement that prepares to address the topic of the required essay.

1. Discuss the effectiveness of any recent U.S. president in handling foreign policy.

   _____

   _____

   _____

2. Analyze the role of movies and television in contributing to the rising violence in our society.

   _____

   _____

3. List and briefly describe the events leading to the American Revolution.

   _____

   _____

   _____

Exercise 10-8 Evaluating Essay Questions

Perhaps the most difficult thing about essay questions is understanding why certain answers failed to receive full credit. To gain an insight into the grading process, evaluate the following responses to an essay question.

You will want to note

> *the opening and concluding sentences*
> *the use of specific details*
> *whether the question asked was answered*

Grade the answers according to the following scale:

> *8–10 = Good to excellent*
> *5–7 = Fair to just passing*
> *0–4 = Inadequate to not passing*

In addition to giving the answer a numerical grade, write a short comment to support the grade you assigned.

The Question:

Describe in five separate sentences five (5) helpful techniques used for taking specific kinds of tests. Be sure to mention the type of test for each technique is appropriate.

Answer 1

I always try to arrive a few minutes early for a test so that I can be both relaxed and organized. With true/false tests, I look for specific, key words. In taking multiple choice tests, I try to eliminate wrong answers. Essay tests frighten me because I'm afraid of making spelling and grammatical errors. Taking tests is stressful, but I try to make them easier by using helpful techniques.

Grade and Comment: _____

_____

_____

Answer 2

1. Read the directions carefully.
2. Match the items you know first.
3. Reword negative statements.
4. Watch for qualifying modifiers like *every* and *always*.
5. Outline your ideas before you begin to write.

Grade and Comment: _____

_____

_____

Answer 3

Learning some techniques for successful test taking has been helpful to me. The five I use most successfully are: (1) Reading the questions carefully for all kinds of tests. (2) Watching out for key words like *always* and *never* in true/false tests. (3) Being sure to answer all the parts of an essay question. (4) Leaving difficult questions in true/false, multiple choice, matching and short answer until I have completed the rest of test in the hope that I will find some clues later. Finally, in any kind of test I know it is important to look over the test carefully to be sure I have answered all the questions.

Grade and Comment: _____

_____

_____

Answer 4

I hate tests, particularly essay tests. Everything I thought I had learned goes out of my head. I can't think of even one thing that I could use to make test taking easier. If I could, I would use it to answer this question.

Grade and Comment: _____

_____

_____

Answer 5

Tes taken is ezy if you no some tips one thing is to read both colums in matching. Another is get an anser ready for multile choice before you look at the ansers. In ture/fasle tests you shud know if one part is fasle, the answer is fasle. Also, study with your group that helps alot.

Grade and Comment: _____

_____

_____

Exercise 10-9 Essay Question Discussion

After you have completed the grading exercise, meet with your group members to discuss the grades assigned. Your group members' grades should be similar but not necessarily the same. Discuss the grades and the reasons for assigning those grades. Feel free to change grades as you listen to the reasons given by group members. This exercise should help you see that instructors are looking for the same kinds of things in essay answers and will usually assign grades much as you have done.

The Value of Returned Tests

As you could tell from the comments about using past tests to help you prepare for an upcoming test, previous tests are valuable. Use your own previous tests to help you understand your own test-taking skills. Too often students glance at the grade, rejoice or mourn, and forget to look carefully at the test. *When a test is returned, it is time to make a careful analysis of the questions you have missed. You need to understand why you missed the questions you missed. Use the following questions for your own careful test analysis.*

1. Did I answer all the questions, or did I accidentally leave blanks?
2. Did I change a correct answer to an incorrect one? (On debatable questions, questions where you are unsure, your first answer is more likely to be correct.)
3. Did I forget to use one of the test tips?
4. Did I misread the directions?
5. Were any errors the result of carelessness?
6. Did I misread a question?

Now take a look at your overall performance and answer these questions. It is important to understand whether your test time was well spent, and your study time was used effectively. What do you know now about taking this particular kind of test that will be helpful to you in the future?

1. Did I manage my time well by allowing enough time for all parts of the test?
2. During test preparation time, did I study the right things, emphasizing what the instructor used in the test? (Or did I study main ideas when details were needed?)
3. Did I keep my tension under control?
4. What can I do next time to make my efforts more successful? Take better class notes? Do more spaced review?

Chapter Review

Label the following statements as true or false.

_____ 1. The most important way to prepare for a test is to do spaced review.

_____ 2. Being too tense can defeat your best efforts in test taking.

_____ 3. You should not waste time looking over a test before beginning.

_____ 4. When in doubt about an answer to a test question, go with your first response.

_____ 5. Planning your response to an essay question is a waste of time.

_____ 6. Always leave a question unanswered when you are not sure.

_____ 7. Read all questions slowly and carefully.

_____ 8. Never change an answer to a test question.

_____ 9. Failing a test is probably not the worst thing that can happen to you.

_____ 10. Never ask questions of the instructor during a test.

Reading Selection 1

Purpose

The following article from a health text offers some ideas about how to handle stress in test taking and in other aspects of your life. Read it for ideas to help you have less stress in your life.

Preview

Before reading this article, first think carefully about the headings. Read the questions and note the vocabulary that follow the selection. Plan to make marginal notes and some form of note taking.

Anticipate/Associate

1. What have you already learned about controlling stress?

2. When have you suffered from stress?

3. How have you tried to handle stress in the past?

Stress Management

Rebecca J. Donatelle and Lorraine G. Davis

Stress can be challenging or defeating depending upon how we learn to view it. The most effective way to avoid defeat is to learn a number of skills known collectively as stress management. Stress management consists primarily of finding balance in our lives. We balance rest, relaxation, exercise, nutrition, work, school, family finances, and social activities. As we balance our lives, we make the choice to react <u>constructively</u> to our stressors. Robert Eliot, a cardiologist and stress researcher, offers two rules for people trying to cope with life's challenges: (1) "Don't sweat the small stuff," and (2) remember that "it's all small stuff."   1

Dealing with Stress

The first step of stress management is to examine thoroughly any problem involving stress. Figure 10.1 on page 410 shows a decision-making model for stress reduction. As the model shows, dealing with stress involves assessing all <u>aspects</u> of a stressor, examining how you are currently responding to the stressor and how you may be able to change your response, and evaluating various methods of coping with stress. Often we cannot change the requirements at our college, unexpected distressors, or accidents. <u>Inevitably</u>, we will be stuck in classes that bore us and for which we find no application in real life. We feel powerless when a loved one has died. The facts themselves cannot be changed; only our reactions to the distressors in our lives can be changed.   2

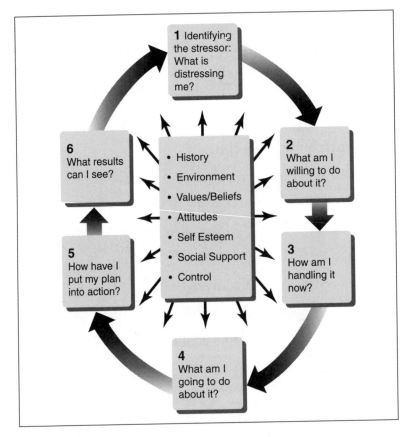

Figure 10.1

Assessing Your Stressors

After recognizing a stressor, you need to <u>assess</u> it. Can
you <u>alter</u> the circumstances in any way to reduce the amount
of distress you are experiencing, or must you change your behavior and reactions to the stressor to reduce your stress levels? For example, if five term papers for five different courses
are due during the semester, you will probably quickly assess
that you cannot alter the circumstances: your professors are
unlikely to drop their requirements. You can, however, change
your behavior by beginning the papers early and spacing them
over time to avoid last-minute stress. If your boss is vague
about directions for assignments, you cannot change the boss.
You can, however, ask the boss to <u>clarify</u> in writing the things
that are expected of you.

Changing Your Responses

Changing your responses requires practice and emotional control. If your roommate is habitually messy and this

causes you stress, you can choose among several responses. You can express your anger by yelling, you can pick up the mess and leave a nasty note, or you can defuse the situation with humor. The first response that comes to mind is not always the best response. Stop before reacting to gain the time you need to find an appropriate response. Ask yourself, "What is to be gained from my response?"

Many people change their response to potentially stress- 5 ful events through cognitive coping strategies. These strategies help them prepare for stressors through gradual exposure to increasingly higher stress levels.

Learning to Cope

Everyone copes with stress in different ways. For some 6 people, drinking and taking drugs helps them to cope. Others choose to get help from counselors. Still others try to keep their minds off stress or to engage in positive activities such as exercise or relaxation techniques. . . . Regardless of how you cope with a given situation, your conscious effort to deal with this situation is an important step in stress management.

Managing Emotional Responses

Have you ever gotten all worked up about something 7 you thought was happening only to find that your perceptions were totally wrong or that a communication problem had caused a *misinterpretation* of events? If you're like most of us, that has probably happened to you. We often get upset not by realities but by our faulty perceptions.

Stress management requires that you examine your self- 8 talk and your emotional response to interactions with others. With any emotional response to a distressor you are responsible for the emotion and the behaviors elicited by the emotion. Learning to tell the difference between normal emotions and those based on irrational beliefs can help you either to stop the emotion or to express it in a healthy and appropriate way. Admitting your feelings and allowing them to be expressed through either communication or action is a stress-management technique that can help you get through many difficult situations.

Learning to Laugh and Cry

For some people, learning to express emotions freely is a 9 difficult task. However, it is a task worth learning. Have you ever noticed that you feel better after a good laugh or cry? It wasn't your imagination. Laughter and crying stimulate the heart and temporarily rev up many body systems. Heart rate and blood pressure then decrease significantly allowing the body to relax.

Taking Mental Action

Stress management calls for mental action in two areas. 10 First, positive self-esteem, which can help you cope with stressful situations, comes from learned habits. Successful stress management involves mentally developing and practicing self-esteem skills.

Second, because you can't always <u>anticipate</u> what the 11 next distressor will be, you need to develop the mental skills necessary to manage your reactions to stress after they have occurred. The ability to think about and react quickly to stress comes with time, practice, experience with a variety of stressful situations, and patience. Rather than seeing stressors as <u>adversaries</u>, learn to view them as exercises in life.

Changing the Way You Think

Once you realize that some of your thoughts may be ir- 12 rational or <u>overreactive</u>, making a conscious effort to refrain or change the way you've been thinking and focus on more positive ways of thinking is a key element of stress management. Here are more specific actions you can take to develop these mental skills. *Worry constructively.* Don't waste time and energy worrying about things you can't change or things that may never happen. *Look at life as being fluid.* If you accept that change is a natural part of living and growing, the jolt of changes may hold much less stress for you. Consider alternatives. Remember that there is seldom only one appropriate action. *Anticipating* options will help you plan for change and adjust more rapidly. *Moderate expectations.* Aim high, but be realistic about your circumstances and motivation. *Weed out trivia.* Don't sweat the small stuff, and remember that most of it is small stuff. *Don't rush into action.* Think before you act.

Taking Physical Action

Adopting the attitudes necessary for effective stress 13 management may seem to have little effect. However, developing successful emotional and mental coping skills is actually a satisfying accomplishment that can help you gain confidence in yourself. Learning to use physical activity to <u>alleviate</u> stress helps support and complement the emotional and mental strategies you employ in stress management.

Exercise

Exercise is a significant contributor to stress manage- 14
ment. Exercise reduces stress by raising levels of endorphins,
mood-elevating, pain-killing hormones, in the blood stream.
As a result, exercise often increases energy, reduces <u>hostility</u>,
and improves mental alertness.

Relaxation

Like exercise, relaxation can help you cope with stress- 15
ful feelings. . . . Relaxation also helps you to refocus your en-
ergies and should be practiced daily until it becomes a habit.
. . . When you begin to feel your body respond to distress,
make time to relax, both to give yourself added strength and
to help alleviate the negative physical effects of stress. . . .

Eating Right

Whether foods can calm us and nourish our psyches is a 16
controversial question. . . . But what is clear is that eating a
balanced, healthful diet will help provide you with the stamina needed to get through problems and may stress-proof
you in ways that are not fully understood

Check Your Understanding

Review

After you have reviewed the reading on stress management by underlining, writing marginal notes, making necessary vocabulary cards, and making notes for study, you are
ready for questions on the reading.

Multiple Choice

Select the letter of the answer that best completes the statement.

_____ 1. The main idea of this selection is that
   a. stress can be managed.
   b. everyone has stress.
   c. stress is harmful.

_____ 2. To handle stress, you should
   a. worry constructively.
   b. avoid taking tests.
   c. not sweat the small stuff.
   d. a and c above.

_____ 3. Exercise can
   a. contribute to stress.
   b. increase energy.
   c. increase hostility.
   d. make you less mentally alert.

_____ 4. To react constructively to stressful situations, you should
   a. avoid exercise.
   b. understand what causes stress.
   c. confront the stressor aggressively.
   d. take up drinking.

_____ 5. Which of the following can contribute to stress for a college student?
   a. tests
   b. roommates
   c. jobs
   d. all of the above

True/False

Label the following statements as true or false according to the article.

_____ 1. It is important to know your current responses to different kinds of stress.

_____ 2. It is reasonable to assume that you can change college requirements.

_____ 3. Stress is inevitable.

_____ 4. You can change your response to stress.

_____ 5. Studying what causes stress for you is pointless.

_____ 6. Most stressors can be met with a variety of responses.

_____ 7. We all cope with stress in different ways.

_____ 8. There are no harmful ways of coping with stress.

_____ 9. The writer implies that you cannot cause stress by misunderstanding the situation.

_____ 10. Healthy mental skills will help you to avoid stress.

Vocabulary

Match the vocabulary in column A with a synonym from column B. Place the correct matching letter on the blank before the word. Refer to the context for the word in the text and use your dictionary if necessary.

Column A   Column B

_____ 1. aspect   a. unavoidably

_____ 2. clarify   b. promoting improvement

_____ 3. inevitably   c. draw out

_____ 4. alter   d. enemy

_____ 5. defuse   e. hatred

_____ 6. assess   f. appearance to the eye or mind

_____ 7. elicit   g. lessen

_____ 8. irrational   h. look forward to

_____ 9. adversary   i. responding too strongly

_____ 10. alleviate   j. handle successfully

_____ 11. constructive   k. evaluate

_____ 12. overreactive   l. change

_____ 13. anticipate   m. explain

_____ 14. hostility   n. not reasonable

_____ 15. cope   o. eliminate tension

Read Figure 10.1 on page 410 to answer the questions. Write your answers on the blanks provided.

_____ 1. How many steps are listed to assess a distressing situation?

_____ 2. How many elements are involved in making decisions about changing a stressful situation?

_____ 3. Could you reverse the order of steps 2 and 3 and still do a successful analysis?

_____ 4. Can all the elements affect all the steps in stress assessment?

_____ 5. Could you reverse the order of steps 5 and 6?

_____ 6. Is this figure a pictograph?

7. Explain the difference between step 2 and step 4.

Writing

1. Write about a time when you have experienced stress. How did you react? What techniques have you learned that you could now use to manage stress in a similar situation?
2. If you have never experienced stress, explain how you have avoided it.

Critical Thinking

Discuss these questions with others.

1. What are the major causes of stress in American life?
2. What changes can *you* make in *your life* to decrease stress?
3. What changes should occur in American life to reduce stress?
4. What can *you* do to bring about some of these changes?

Reading Selection 2

Purpose

We all need heroes, people we consider great. Whom do you consider to be great? What qualities make a "great" person different from his or her peers? These questions are examined in the following article, which looks at the achievements of some people considered to be great in the light of history.

Preview

1. Take two minutes to skim the first paragraph and the main headings in the article.
2. Check the questions and the vocabulary that follow the article.

Anticipate/Associate

1. Have you ever thought about becoming great? In what field would you like to make a record for yourself?
2. Who are some of the people you consider to be great?

Who Is Great?

Michael Ryan

As a young boy, Albert Einstein did so poorly in school 1
that teachers thought he was slow. The young Napoleon
Bonaparte was just one of hundreds of artillery lieutenants in
the French Army. And the teenage George Washington, with
little formal education, was being trained not as a soldier but
as a land surveyor.

Despite their unspectacular beginning, each would go 2
on to carve a place for himself in history. What was it that en-
abled them to become great? Were they born with something
special? Or did their greatness have more to do with timing,
devotion and, perhaps, an <u>uncompromising</u> personality?

For decades, scientists have been asking such questions. 3
And, in the past few years, they have found evidence to help
explain why some people rise above, while others—similarly
talented, perhaps—are left behind. Their findings could have
<u>implications</u> for us all.

Who Is Great?

Defining who is great depends on how one measures 4
success. But there are some <u>criteria</u>. "Someone who has made
a lasting contribution to human civilization is great," said
Dean Keith Simonton, a professor of psychology at the University of California at Davis and author of the 1994 book
Greatness: Who Makes History and Why. But he added a
<u>caveat</u>: "Sometimes great people don't make it in the history
books. A lot of women achieved great things or were influential but went unrecognized."

In writing his book, Simonton combined historical 5
knowledge about great figures with recent findings in genetics, psychiatry and the social sciences. The great figures he focused on include men and women who have won Nobel
Prizes, led great nations or won wars, composed symphonies
that have endured for centuries, or revolutionized science,
philosophy, politics or the arts. Though he doesn't have a formula to define how or why certain people rise above (too
many factors are involved), he has come up with a few common characteristics.

A "Never Surrender" Attitude

If great achievers share anything, said Simonton, it is an 6
unrelenting drive to succeed. "There's a tendency to think

that they are <u>endowed</u> with something super-normal," he explained. "But what comes out of the research is that there are great people who have no amazing intellectual processes. It's a difference in degree. Greatness is built upon tremendous amounts of study, practice and devotion."

He cited Winston Churchill, Britain's prime minister   7
during World War II, as an example of a risk-taker who would never give up. Thrust into office when his country's morale was at its lowest, Churchill rose brilliantly to lead the British people. In a speech following the Allied <u>evacuation</u> at Dunkirk in 1940, he inspired the nation when he said, "We shall not flag or fail. We shall go on to the end. We shall never surrender." After the war. Churchill was voted out of office but again demonstrated his fighting spirit when he delivered his famous "Iron Curtain" speech at Westminster College in Missouri in 1946. This time, at the dawn of the Cold War, he <u>exhorted</u> the entire Western world to stand up to communism: "We hold the power to save the future," he said. "Our difficulties and dangers will not be removed by closing out eyes to them."

Can You Be Born Great?

In looking at Churchill's role in history—as well as the   8
roles of other political and military leaders—Simonton discovered a striking pattern: "Firstborns and only children tend to make good leaders in time of crisis: They're used to taking charge. But middle-borns are better as peacetime leaders: They listen to different <u>constituencies</u> better and make the necessary compromises. Churchill, an only child, was typical. He was great in a crisis, but in peacetime he was not effective—not even popular.

Timing is another factor. "If you took George Washing-   9
ton and put him in the 20th century, he would go nowhere as a politician," Simonton declared. "He was not an effective public speaker, and he didn't like shaking hands with the public. On the other hand, I'm not sure Franklin Roosevelt would have done well in Washington's time. He wouldn't have had the radio to do his fireside chats."

Can You Be Too Smart?

One surprise among Simonton's findings is that many   10
political and military leaders have been bright but not overly so. Beyond a certain point, he explained, other factors, like the ability to communicate effectively, become more important than <u>innate</u> intelligence as measured by an IQ test. The

most intelligent U.S. Presidents, for example—Thomas Jefferson, Woodrow Wilson and John F. Kennedy—had a hard time getting elected, Simonton said, while others with IQs closer to the average (such as Warren G. Harding) won by landslides. While political and economic factors also are involved, having a genius IQ is not necessary to be a great leader.

In the sciences, those with "genius level" IQs do have a 11 better shot at achieving recognition, added Simonton. Yet evidence also indicates that overcoming traditional ways of thinking may be just as important.

He pointed to one recent study where college students 12 were given a set of data and were asked to see if they could come up with a mathematical relation. Almost a third did. What they did not know was that they had just solved one of the most famous scientific equations in history: the Third Law of Planetary Motion, an equation that Johannes Kepler came up with in 1618.

Kepler's genius, Simonton said, was not so much in solv- 13 ing a mathematical challenge. It was in thinking about the numbers in a unique way—applying his mathematical knowledge to his observations of planetary motion. It was his boldness that set him apart.

Love Your Work

As a child Einstein became fascinated with the way 14 magnets draw iron filings. "He couldn't stop thinking about this stuff," Simonton pointed out. "He became obsessed with problems in physics by the time he was 16, and he never stopped working on them. It's not surprising that he made major contributions by the time he was 26."

"For most of us, it's not that we don't have the abil- 15 ity," Simonton added, "it's that we don't devote the time. You have to put in the effort and put up with all the frustrations and obstacles."

Like other creative geniuses, Einstein was not moti- 16 vated by a desire for fame, said Simonton. Instead, his obsession with his work was what set him apart. Where such drive comes from remains a mystery. But it is found in nearly all creative geniuses—whether or not their genius is acknowledged by contemporaries.

"Emily Dickinson was not recognized for her poetry 17 until after her death," said Simonton. "But she was not writing for fame. The same can be said of James Joyce, who didn't spend a lot of time worrying about how many people would read *Finnegans Wake*. Beethoven once said when confronting a musician struggling to play some of his new quartets, "They are not for you, but for a later age.' "

Today, researchers have evidence that an <u>intrinsic</u> passion for one's work is a key to rising above. In a 1985 study at Brandeis University conducted by Teresa Amabile, now a professor of business administration at Harvard University, a group of professional writers—none famous—was asked to write a short poem. Each writer was then randomly placed in one of three groups: One group was asked to keep in mind the idea of writing for money; another was told to think about writing just for pleasure; and a third group was given no instruction at all.   18

The poems then were submitted <u>anonymously</u> to a panel of professional writers for evaluation. The poetry written by people who thought about writing for money ranked lowest. Those who thought about writing just for pleasure did the best. "Motivation that comes from enjoying the work makes a significant difference," Amabile said.   19

What Price Greatness?

Many great figures have had poor personal relationships, perhaps a result of their drive to excel, said Simonton. And great people, he added, often can be unbearable: "Beethoven, for instance, was <u>tyrannical</u> with servants and rude to his friends. His personal hygiene was not particularly great either. When working, he would go for days or weeks without bathing."   20

Yet one common belief about greatness—that it often is accompanied by mental imbalance—seems unfounded.   21

"Certain types of <u>psychopathology</u> are more common in some professions than in others," explained Dr. Arnold M. Ludwig, a psychiatrist at the University of Kentucky Medical Center and author of a new book, *The Price of Greatness.* "Poets, for example, have high rates of depression. But architects as a group are very stable. Fiction writers and jazz musicians are more likely to abuse drugs and alcohol. But when you go outside the artistic fields, you find <u>phenomenal</u> creative achievements among scientists, social activists and politicians. It is certainly possible for people to achieve great things without corresponding mental illness."   22

Dr. Ludwig did some personal research on the issue as well. "I have two children who are very creative and artistic," he said. "I decided to find out whether they would have to be crazy if they were to grow up to be geniuses. I was happy to find out that they would not."   23

Check Your Understanding

Review

Write a summary sentence about each of these ideas discussed in the article.

1. What does the phrase "never surrender" mean in this article?

   _____

   _____

2. What does the article mean by "born great"?

   _____

   _____

3. What does time have to do with greatness?

   _____

   _____

4. How important is intelligence?

   _____

   _____

5. How does your attitude toward work affect greatness?

   _____

   _____

6. Are people who are considered great free of problems?

   _____

   _____

Fill in the Blanks

Complete the statements by writing in the best word.

1. The article explains some criteria for _____.

2. Great achievers share an unrelenting desire to _____.

3. _____ _____ was a great British

   leader during World War II.

4. People who _____ their work are more suc-

   cessful.

5. Overcoming _____ ways of thinking is im-

   portant to becoming great.

Multiple Choice

Select the letter of the answer that best completes the statement.

_____ 1. The main idea is that
  a. great people are those who achieve their goals.
  b. greatness is inborn.
  c. anyone can be great.
  d. great people rise above others.

_____ 2. The writer's purpose is to
  a. inform.
  b. persuade.
  c. entertain.
  d. a and b above.

_____ 3. The method of organization is primarily
  a. time order.
  b. listing items.
  c. examples.
  d. cause-and-effect.

_____ 4. You can assume that the writer
  a. believes greatness is impossible for normal people.
  b. values the qualities that make people great.
  c. believes that women cannot achieve greatness.
  d. wants to be great himself.

_____ 5. The writer's tone could be described as
  a. sarcastic.
  b. optimistic
  c. tolerant
  d. straightforward

True/False

From the writer's point of view, label the following statements as true or false.

_____ 1. You need to have a high IQ to be successful.

_____ 2. The writer uses authorities to support his five points.

_____ 3. Most people considered great had a tremendous desire to succeed.

_____ 4. George Washington probably would not be considered a great president if he were to serve today.

_____ 5. Ability to communicate effectively is not usually an important factor in success.

_____ 6. Becoming successful requires time, perseverance, and optimism.

_____ 7. The desire to make money is an important motivation in achieving success.

_____ 8. All great people have slightly unbalanced personalities.

_____ 9. Many great people are unrecognized by history.

_____ 10. Many great people are unrecognized in their lifetimes.

Vocabulary

Use the words from the list to complete the sentences that follow.

constituencies	innate	obsessed
intrinsic	uncompromising	endowed
evacuation	psychopathology	exhorted
criteria	phenomenal	anonymously
implication	caveat	tyrannical

1. Successful people can be said to be _____

   with their work.

2. Motivation should come from within or be _____.

3. A psychiatrist may study cases of _____.

4. Parents often add a(n) _____ to their

   permissions.

5. The article suggests several _____ for

   success.

6. The _____ of the article is that we can all

   be great.

7. When a hurricane heads toward land, a(n) _____

   route is suggested.

8. The instructor _____ the class to review

   frequently.

9. A dictator is often _____.

10. The threatening letter was delivered _____.

11. Politicians usually pay attention to the desires of their

    _____.

12. Raising your grade from a D to an A is a(n) _____

    improvement.

13. The qualities we are born with are considered to be

    _____.

14. If you refuse to accept minimal efforts, you may appear to

    be _____.

15. The college has a(n) _____ chair of

    education.

Writing

1. Write a paragraph describing someone in your personal
   life who has qualities of greatness that you admire.
2. Describe someone from the past who you think should
   have been used as an example in the article. Be sure to give
   at least three supported reasons for including this person.

Critical Thinking

1. What other qualities would you include as marks of greatness?
2. Of the qualities mentioned in the article, which two do you think are the most important to achieving greatness? Be ready to give reasons to support your choice.
3. Make a list of ten great people not included in the article. Evaluate them using the qualities mentioned. How do they measure up to these standards?

Chapter 11

Applying Critical Thinking and Study Skills to Selected Readings

> The life which is unexamined is not worth living.
>
> *Socrates*

Once you have read and comprehended a passage, it is important to evaluate the passage for the validity of the message, particularly if the writer's purpose is to persuade. In the readings in this chapter you will use your strategies for making inferences (Chapter 5), and understanding the writer's use of persuasive techniques (Chapter 6). Understanding the writer's purpose and tone (Chapter 7) will also be important. Plan to use marginal notes and underlining. Some note taking (Chapter 8) will also assist you in thinking about the passage. In addition, you will be examining your own personal value system since the articles raise questions about issues that bear on your personal ethical and moral beliefs. Establishing and thinking about your own ethical standards is important, as Socrates suggested more than 2,000 years ago. Your family, your church, your school, and your peers have all had an effect on the development of your personal moral code. Sometimes, however, you will have to think about situations when two values you hold are brought into conflict. Such a situation should cause you to examine your values and find a way to resolve the conflict.

Reading Selection 1

Purpose

This article from a college text, *The Media of Mass Communication,* introduces you to some conflicts in values that face workers in the field of mass media. Ethics, the moral guides and considerations that govern most people's lives, have a special place in the media. What should be reported in the newspaper? Is the fact that someone died of AIDS necessary information in a death notice? Should television news show violent scenes from crime stories? How much control is exercised by the media to keep movies and television entertainment programs moral? Should important trials be televised? The selection does not answer these questions, but it does explain the difficulties and conflicts that the media face in attempting to be ethical.

Preview

1. Read the first paragraph and the headings to stimulate your thinking on this subject.

2. Check the questions and the vocabulary at the end of the article.

Anticipate/Associate

1. Arthur Ashe, a world famous tennis player who contracted AIDS during surgery, was forced to go public with the news of his disease. He called a news conference to make a personal announcement because he knew that the next day the news was to appear in the press. People who are considered "public figures" have great difficulty keeping their private lives private. Is this lack of privacy right, moral, and ethical?

2. How do you think the media should be controlled?

The Difficulty of Ethics

John Vivian

Prescriptive Ethic Codes

The mass media abounds with codes of ethics. The earliest was adopted in 1923, the Canons of Journalism of the American Society of Newspaper Editors. Advertising, broadcast and public relations practitioners also have codes. Many newcomers to the mass media make an erroneous assumption that the answers to all the moral choices in their work exist in the prescriptions of these codes. While the codes can be helpful, ethics is not so easy.

The difficulty of ethics becomes clear when a mass communicator is confronted with a conflict between moral responsibilities to different concepts. Consider:

Respect for Privacy

The code of the Society of Professional Journalists prescribes that reports will show respect for the dignity, privacy, rights and well-being of people "at all times." The SPJ prescription sounds excellent, but moral <u>priorities</u> such as dignity and privacy sometimes seem less important than other priorities, as many people would argue in the case of Arthur Ashe. The public interest also overrode privacy in 1988 when the *Miami Herald* staked out presidential candidate Gary Hart overnight when he had a woman friend in his Washington townhouse.

Commitment to Timelines

The code of the Radio-Television News Directors Association prescribes that reporters be "timely and accurate." In practice, however, the virtue of accuracy is jeopardized when reporters rush to the air with stories. It takes time to confirm details and be accurate—and that delays stories.

Being Fair

The code of the Public Relations Society of America prescribes dealing fairly with both clients and the general public. However, a persuasive message prepared on behalf of a client is not always the same message that would be prepared on behalf of the general public. Persuasive communication is not necessarily dishonest, but how information is marshaled to create the message depends on whom the PR person is serving.

Conflict in Duties

Media ethics codes are well-intended, usually helpful guides, but they are simplistic when it comes to knotty moral questions. When media ethicians Clifford Christians, Mark Fackler and Kim Rotzoll compiled a list of five duties of mass media practitioners, some of these <u>inherent</u> problems became obvious.

Duty to Self

Self-preservation is a basic human instinct, but is a photojournalist shirking a duty to subscribers by avoiding a dangerous combat zone?

<u>Self-aggrandizement</u> can be an issue too. Many college   8
newspaper editors are invited, all expenses paid, to Hollywood movie premieres. The duty-to-self principle favors going:
The trip would be fun. In addition, it is a good story opportunity, and, as a free favor, it would not cost the newspaper anything. However, what of an editor's responsibility to readers?
Readers have a right to expect writers to provide honest ac-
counts that are not colored by favoritism. Can a reporter write
straight after being wined and dined and flown across the continent by movie producers who want a gung-ho story? Even if
reporters rise above being affected and are true to conscience,
there are the duty-to-employer and the duty-to-profession
principle to consider. The newspaper and the profession itself
can be tarnished by suspicions, no matter whether they are
unfounded, that a reporter has been bought off.

Duty to Audience

Television programs that reenact violence are popular   9
with audiences, but are they a disservice because they frighten
many viewers into inferring that the streets are more dangerous than they really are?

Tom Wicker of the *New York Times* tells a story about   10
his early days as a reporter in Aberdeen, North Carolina. He
was covering a divorce case involving one spouse chasing the
other with an axe. Nobody was hurt physically, and everyone
who heard the story in the courtroom, except the divorcing
couple, had a good laugh. "It was human comedy at its most
<u>ribald</u>, and the courtroom rocked with laughter," Wicker re-
called years later. In writing his story, Wicker captured the
darkly comedic details so skillfully that his editor put the
story on Page One. Wicker was proud of the piece until the
next day when the woman in the case called on him. Worn
out, haggard, hurt and angry, she asked, "Mr. Wicker, why did
you think you had a right to make fun of me in your paper?"

The lesson stayed with Wicker for the rest of his career.
He had unthinkingly hurt a fellow human being for no better
reason than evoking a chuckle, or perhaps a belly laugh, from
his readers. To Wicker, the duty-to-audience principle never
again would transcend his moral duty to the dignity of the
subjects of his stories. Similar ethics questions involve
whether to cite AIDS as a contributor to death in an obituary,
to identify victims in rape stories and to name juveniles
charged with crimes.

Duty to Employer

Does loyalty to an employer transcend the ideal of pur-   11
suing and telling the truth when a news reporter discovers

<u>dubious</u> business deals involving the parent corporation? This is a growing issue as the mass media become consolidated into fewer gigantic companies owned by <u>conglomerates</u>. In 1989, for example, investigative reporter Peter Karl of Chicago television station WMAQ broke a story that General Electric had manufactured jet engines with untested and sometimes defective bolts. Although WMAQ is owned by NBC which in turn is owned by General Electric, Karl's exclusive, documented and accurate story aired. However, when the story was passed on to the network itself, Marty Ryan, executive producer of the *Today* show, ordered that the references to General Electric be edited out.

Duty to the Profession

At what point does an ethically motivated advertising-agency person blow the whistle on misleading claims by other advertising people?   12

Duty to Society

Does duty to society ever transcend duty to self? To audience? To employer? To colleagues? Does ideology affect a media worker's sense of duty to society? Consider how Joseph Stalin, Adolf Hitler and Franklin Roosevelt would be covered by highly motivated communist, fascist, and libertarian journalists.   13

Are there occasions when the duty-to-society and the duty-to-audience principles are <u>incompatible</u>? Nobody enjoys seeing the horrors of war, for example, but journalists may feel that their duty to society demands that they go after the most grisly photographs of combat to show how horrible war is and, thereby, in a small way, contribute to public pressure toward a cessation of hostilities and eventual peace.   14

Check Your Understanding

Review

On notebook paper, map or outline the main ideas presented. There are two major ideas, each with several important subpoints.

Fill in the Blanks

Complete the statements by writing the best word in the blank.

1. The mass media have many codes of _____.

2. The first media code, written in 1923, was written for

   _____.

3. Respect for _____ is an element of the journalism code.

4. Radio and television news must be both timely and

   _____.

5. A problem of ethics can come from a _____

   in duties.

Multiple Choice

Select the letter of the answer that best completes the statement.

_____ 1. The main idea is that
   a. the media should follow their codes of ethics.
   b. the media deal with conflicting issues in making moral choices.
   c. there is no point in having a code of ethics.
   d. a and c above.

_____ 2. The writer's purpose is to
   a. inform.
   b. entertain.
   c. persuade.
   d. a and c above.

_____ 3. The writer implies that
   a. newspapers are often unethical.
   b. it takes time to confirm details and be accurate.
   c. codes of ethics sometimes present dilemmas.
   d. a and c above.

True/False

Label the following statements as true or false according to the article.

_____ 1. Respect for privacy is a common element in ethical codes.

_____ 2. The writer implies that government should control the media.

_____ 3. It is also implied that sometimes media people need to ignore some ethical principles to fulfill their duties.

_____ 4. The writer suggests that the public interest sometimes overrides respect for privacy.

_____ 5. Newscasters always delay their stories to assure accuracy.

_____ 6. Persuasive communication in the media is necessarily dishonest.

_____ 7. According to the writer, television shows that reenact violence are a disservice to the public.

_____ 8. Media codes serve only as guides.

_____ 9. According to the writer, showing horrible war pictures may be a duty for a reporter.

_____ 10. Media morality would be simple if everyone were ethical.

Vocabulary

I. Use the words from the list to complete the sentence. Think about the part of speech required. Use a dictionary if necessary.

1. erroneous   erroneously   erroneousness

   He was identified _____.

2. imperiled   peril   perilous

   The adventure was filled with _____.

3. haggard   haggardly   haggardness

   Her _____ was a result of overwork.

4. transcend   transcendent   transcendently

   The _____ generosity of the public

   aided the flood victims.

5. cessation   ceasing   ceaseless

   The _____ of the loud knocking was a

   relief.

II. On the blanks below each sentence, write a definition of the underlined word.

1. His hesitant reply left me <u>dubious</u> about his honesty.

   _____

2. General Electric is an example of a <u>conglomerate</u>.

   _____

3. Divorce often results when the two parties find themselves <u>incompatible</u>.

   _____

4. The comedian's jokes were <u>ribald</u>.

   _____

5. Sometimes there are conflicting <u>priorities</u>.

   _____

6. With any complex duty there are <u>inherent</u> difficulties.

   _____

7. Politicians accepting honorary degrees often do so for reasons of <u>self-aggrandizement</u>.

   _____

Writing

1. Explain in a paragraph why ethics in the media are difficult to maintain. Give at least three reasons.
2. Imagine you are a reporter and learn that the President has a contagious disease like tuberculous. Being able to file this story would give you a raise and improve your reputation. Explain the actions you would take and your reasons for doing so.

Critical Thinking

Think about these questions raised in the article and discuss with your group or class.

1. Should a photojournalist go into a dangerous military combat zone to satisfy readers? What would you do? Why?
2. Are reporters influenced by gifts and favors? Would you be influenced by receiving free game tickets from a baseball star? What might the star expect?
3. How would you suggest drawing the line between respect for privacy and the public's right to know? Which do you think is more important? Why? Can you think of a situation in which you might change your values?
4. Should audiences be subjected to scenes of starving children because the media thinks it has a duty to inform the world of the children's suffering? Discuss what good could come from this coverage.

Reading Selection 2

Purpose

If you keep a well-manicured lawn and extol the talents of the popular rock star Bruce Springsteen, are you exhibiting conformity? According to social psychologists, it depends on whether your behavior is the result of group pressure. Conformity occurs when people yield to real or imagined social or authoritarian pressure. Because of the decimation of the Jewish people by Adolf Hitler's commands to bureaucrats under his authority, many social psychologists have wanted to test how much human beings are affected by peer pressure and the commands of authority.

Preview

The most famous, or infamous (depending on your point of view), of these experiments were conducted by Dr. Solomon Asch and Dr. Stanley Milgram. The Milgram experiment is described in this article, taken from a sociology text.

1. Read the first sentence of each paragraph.
2. Check the questions and the vocabulary at the end of the article.

Anticipate/Associate

1. How much are you influenced by what others think and do? For example, if all the students in the room agreed on one answer, would you change your answer to match theirs?

2. If your boss told you to steal some money from the company for both of you to share, would you do it?

If Hitler Asked You to Execute a Stranger, Would You? The Milgram Experiment

James M. Henslin

Imagine that you are taking a course with Dr. Stanley   1
Milgram, a former student of Dr. [Solomon] Asch's. Assume
that you did not take part in Dr. Asch's experiment and have
no reason to be <u>wary</u> of these experimenters. You appear in
the laboratory to participate in a study on punishment and
learning. A second student arrives, and you draw lots for the
roles of "teacher" and "learner." You are to be the teacher, he
the learner. You are glad that you are the teacher when you
see that the learner's chair has <u>protruding</u> electrodes and resembles an electric chair. Dr. Milgram shows you the machine you will run. You see that one side of the control panel
is marked "Mild Shock, 15 volts," the center says "Intense
Shock, 350 Volts," while the far right side reads, "DANGER:
SEVERE SHOCK."

"As the teacher, you will read aloud a pair of words," ex-   2
plains Dr. Milgram. "Then you will repeat the first word, and
the learner will reply with the second word. If the learner
can't remember the word, you press this lever on the shock
generator. The shock will serve as punishment, and we can
then determine if punishment improves memory." You nod,
now extremely relieved that you haven't been <u>designated</u> a
learner.

"Every time the learner makes an error, increase the   3
punishment by 15 volts," Dr. Milgram says. Then, seeing the
look on your face, he adds, "The shocks can be extremely
painful, but they won't cause any permanent tissue damage."
He pauses, and then adds, "I want you to see." You then follow him to the "electric chair," and Dr. Milgram gives you a
shock of 45 volts. 'There. That wasn't too bad, was it?" "No,"
you mumble.

The experiment begins. You hope for the learner's sake   4
that he is bright, but unfortunately he turns out to be rather
dull. He gets some answers right, but you have to keep turning up the dial. Each turn of the dial makes you more and
more uncomfortable. You find yourself hoping that the
learner won't miss another answer. But he does. When he received the first shocks, he let out some moans and groans,
but now he is screaming in agony. He even protests that he

suffers from a heart condition. *How far do you continue turning that dial?*

By now, you probably have guessed that there was no electricity attached to the electrodes and that the "learner" was a stooge, only pretending to feel pain. The purpose of the experiment, of course, was to find out at what point people refuse to participate. Does anyone actually turn the lever all the way to DANGER: SEVERE SHOCK?

Milgram was motivated to do this research because the slaughter of so many Jews, gypsies, homosexuals, and others designated by the Nazis as "inferior" required the cooperation of "good people." The fact that millions of ordinary people did nothing to stop the deaths seemed bizarre, and Milgram wanted to see how ordinary, intelligent Americans might react to an analogous situation.

Milgram was upset by what he found. Many "teachers" broke into a sweat and protested to the experimenter that this was inhuman and should be stopped. But when the experimenter, who sat by calmly, supposedly recording how the "learner" was performing, replied that the experiment must go on, this assurance from the "authority" ("scientist, white coat, university laboratory") was enough for most "teachers" to continue, even though the learner screamed in agony and pleaded to be released. Even some "teachers" who were "reduced to twitching, stuttering wrecks" continued to follow orders.

Milgram did eighteen of these experiments. He used both males and females and put some "teachers" and "learners" in the same room, where the "teacher" could clearly see the suffering. In some experiments, he had "learners" pound and kick on the wall during the first shocks and then go silent. No verbal feedback was involved. On other occasions he even added a second "teacher," this one a stooge who refused to go along with the experiment. The results varied from situation to situation. The highest proportion of "teachers" who pushed the lever all the way to 450 volts—65 percent—occurred when there was no verbal feedback from the "learner." Of those who could turn and look at the "learner," 40 percent turned the lever all the way. But only 5 percent carried out the severe shocking when the stooge-teacher refused to comply, a result that bears out some of Asch's results.

Milgram's experiments raised a ruckus in the scientific community. Not only were social researchers surprised, and disturbed, at the results, but they also were alarmed at Milgram's methods. Milgram's experiments became a stormy basis for rethinking research ethics. Associations of social reformers adopted or revised their codes of ethics, and universities began to require that subjects be informed of the nature and purpose of social research. Not only did researchers agree that to reduce subjects to "twitching, stuttering wrecks" was unethical, but almost all <u>deception</u> was banned.

The results of the Asch and Milgram experiments leave   10
us with the disturbing question: "How far would *I* go in following authority?" Truly the influence of the group extends beyond what most of us imagine.

Check Your Understanding

Review

Briefly explain Milgram's experiment by describing the activities of the following people.

Teacher _____

_____

Learner _____

_____

Experimenter _____

_____

What were the results of the experiment? _____

_____

_____

_____

Fill in the Blanks

Complete the statements by writing the best word in the blank.

1. The man who planned the experiments was _____

_____.

2. He was trying to understand why people followed inhuman orders in slaughtering the _____ people.

3. His experiments were later considered _____.

4. Each time the "learner" failed, the teacher _____ the electric shock.

5. Actually, the "learners" only _____ to feel pain.

Multiple Choice

Select the letter of the answer that best completes the statement.

_____ 1. The main idea is that
    a. a high percentage of "teachers" were willing to follow orders and increase the electric shock to dangerous levels.
    b. Milgram's experiments were disturbing.
    c. experiments were conducted using students in Milgram's classes.
    d. professors shouldn't experiment with students without their knowledge.

_____ 2. The writer's main purpose is to
    a. inform.
    b. persuade.
    c. entertain.
    d. inform and persuade.

_____ 3. The subject of the experiment was the
    a. the "learner."
    b. the "teacher."
    c. the experimenter.
    d. none of the above.

_____ 4. The "learners" were
    a. stupid.
    b. shocked.
    c. acting.
    d. guessing.

_____ 5. The experiments used
    a. only males.
    b. only females.
    c. Jewish people.
    d. both males and females.

True/False

Label the following statements as true or false according to the article.

_____ 1. Many "teachers" suffered while conducting the experiments.

_____ 2. The experimenter played the role of authority.

_____ 3. People often act against their own values when the action is requested by someone in authority.

_____ 4. Similar experiments are still being performed.

_____ 5. Milgram enjoyed the results of the experiments.

_____ 6. The "teachers" were told that the experiments were to determine whether punishment improves memory.

_____ 7. Most "teachers" did not want to inflict the electric shocks.

_____ 8. Milgram wanted to see whether ordinary people would cause pain to others just because they were told to do so by an authority.

_____ 9. Other scientists approved of Milgram's experiments.

_____ 10. Using slightly different methods provided different results.

Vocabulary

Write the letter of the word or phrase that best defines the word as it was used in the passage.

_____ 1. wary
    a. unsuspecting   b. tired   c. cautious

_____ 2. protruding
    a. interfering   b. raised   c. mathematical

_____ 3. designated
    a. earmarked   b. signed   c. designed

_____ 4. stooge
    a. actor   b. yes-man   c. comic

_____ 5. bizarre
    a. strange   b. market   c. woman's garment

_____ 6. analogous
    a. same   b. thinking   c. comparative

_____ 7. assurance
    a. promise   b. color   c. explanation

_____ 8. ruckus

  a. knapsack   b. noisy commotion   c. a plant

_____ 9. ethics

  a. principals   b. sketches   c. morals

_____ 10. deception

  a. trick   b. decision   c. change

Writing

Choose one of the following ideas and write a paragraph in response.

1. Give your opinion of the methods of the experiments.
2. Comment on the results of the experiments.

Critical Thinking

1. Do you think that experiments like Milgram's using human subjects are ethical? Why or why not?
2. Was anything useful learned from the experiments?
3. Since we are all subject to authorities, how can we be motivated to resist immoral commands?
4. Is authority, which might be evil, necessary in society? Could the world as we know it survive without authority figures?

Reading Selection 3

Purpose

Probably you have discovered (or soon will) how easy it is to find interesting material on the Internet. However, it is important to evaluate the material you find there as to its timeliness, accuracy, and validity. The article that follows describes an Internet hoax that was believed for a time by many people. Read it as a warning to evaluate Internet sources carefully.

Preview

The article is short. Skim first sentences and check the questions and the vocabulary at the end.

Anticipate/Associate

1. Have you, or has someone you know, ever had problems with material found on the Internet?

2. How can you verify the accuracy of material found on the Internet? What checks might you use before citing an "authority" on the Internet?

Internet Writing Can't Be Believed

Howard Kleinberg

That settles it! If it happened on the Internet, I won't be- 1
lieve it. Someone's going to have to prove to me that anything
on the Internet is true, even the baseball scores and weather
report. If I run across a scientific claim that the sky is blue,
I'm going to think it's green.

It's all because of Ian Goddard, and people like him.   2

If there is an Ian Goddard.   3

See? I don't even believe that.   4

A keystroker who says he is Ian Goddard recently ad- 5
mitted that his earlier claim on the Internet that a U.S. Navy
missile shot down TWA Flight 800 was false. "Reckless and
a mistake" was the language he used in explaining it, and
apologizing.

"<u>Malicious</u> and criminal" are the words I would use in 6
rejecting his apology.

It apparently was a person identifying himself as Ian 7
Goddard who influenced former John Kennedy press chief
Pierre Salinger to make a fool of himself last spring in not
only accepting the missile theory but in claiming he had
<u>irrefutable</u> evidence—which he did not. Salinger's involve-
ment created widespread media coverage and promoted the
theory of a deadly military blunder and subsequent cover-up.

Goddard is a mystery to me and to others with whom I 8
spoke. In seeking anything about him on the Internet, we find
only his <u>conspiracy</u> theories, as well as his <u>hoaxes</u>.

When the Goddard missile theory first found its way to 9
the Internet, CBS's *60 Minutes* belittled it, causing Goddard to
bellow back that whatever he puts out is true and <u>verifiable</u>.

In a March 17, 1997, Internet site report, a man calling 10
himself Goddard boasted: "The portions of the Salinger Report that are derived from my work—hence my status as co-
author—are derived from carefully researched and referenced
reports I have posted publicly on the Internet."

Now, in a written statement to Cable News Network,   11
the alleged Goddard admits to making a reckless and mistaken accusation about the Navy missile and confessed that
he pursued and promoted his claim because he "wanted to
give the government a black eye by any means that looked
<u>opportune</u>."

In doing so, he cost the taxpayers millions of dollars in   12
investigative pursuit of his counterfeit claim, brought greater
<u>anguish</u> to the families of those lost on TWA 800 and ren-
dered <u>implausible</u> anything you might see on the Internet.

The Goddard character certainly is not the sole practi-   13
tioner of electronic treachery; it is widespread throughout the
Internet as well as in television commercials (Fred Astaire
and the vacuum cleaner), in the printed word, and in doctored
photographs, film and graphics that pretend to be truthful but
are, in fact, <u>callous distortions</u>.

Seein' ain't believin' any more.   14

Check Your Understanding

Review

Without further research, you cannot be sure of the
events that caused Howard Kleinberg to distrust the Internet,
but it is helpful to place the following events recounted in the
article in a probable chronological (time) order. Place the following events in their probable sequence by numbering the
first event 1, and so on.

_____ Goddard admits a "reckless and mistaken accusation
about the Navy missile."

_____ Pierre Salinger accepts Goddard's accusation as fact.

_____ CBS's *60 Minutes* discounted Goddard's report.

_____ Goddard wanted to give the government a black eye.

_____ Goddard defends his work as "carefully researched."

Multiple Choice

Select the letter of the answer that best completes the statement.

_____ 1. The main idea of this selection is that
     a. Ian Goddard is a hoax.
     b. you can't believe everything you read on Internet.
     c. you can't believe anything anymore.

_____ 2. The writer's primary purpose is to
   a. entertain.
   b. persuade.
   c. inform.

_____ 3. Kleinberg
   a. exaggerates to make his point.
   b. will never believe anything on Internet.
   c. finds only the Internet guilty of providing misinformation.

_____ 4. The paragraph beginning "In doing so. . . " is organized by
   a. examples.
   b. comparison/contrast.
   c. cause-and-effect.

_____ 5. The writer's tone is
   a. ironic.
   b. angry.
   c. sad.

True/False

Label the following statements as true or false according to the article.

_____ 1. The identity of Ian Goddard remains a mystery.

_____ 2. A Navy missile shot down TWA Flight 800.

_____ 3. Goddard's hoax cost millions of dollars.

_____ 4. Goddard's purpose was to seek the truth about TWA Flight 800.

_____ 5. The program *60 Minutes* exposed Goddard as a fraud.

_____ 6. The cause of the flight's crash was covered up by the military.

_____ 7. The Internet is the only source that presents fantasy as fact.

_____ 8. Goddard finally admitted that his reports on the Internet were false.

_____ 9. Goddard admitted that his false claims were "malicious and criminal."

_____ 10. Sophisticated electronic devices cause misinformation.

Vocabulary

Use the words from the list to complete the following sentences.

malicious   irrefutable   conspiracy   hoax   verifiable
opportune   anguish   implausible   callous   distortion

1. My source of information was an authority, so I knew the information was _____.

2. He had a hardened or _____ indifference to my plea for forgiveness.

3. Usually an encyclopedia is a(n) _____ source for factual information.

4. The death of a great leader is usually the cause for sorrow and _____.

5. It seemed like the _____ moment to request a loan.

6. Spreading false rumors is considered an evil and _____ activity.

7. A political plot to destroy a reputation is called a(n) _____.

8. His misrepresentation of the accident was a(n) _____ of the facts.

9. A(n) _____ is a deliberate attempt to mislead someone.

10. Jerry's excuse for missing the study group was far-fetched and _____.

Writing

1. Write a paragraph defending, condemning, or taking a middle position on the use of electronics to doctor photographs and other data, as mentioned in the next-to-last paragraph of the article. Cite reasons and examples to support your point of view.
2. What do you think would be a just punishment (if there should be one) for Ian Goddard if he is ever identified? Again, defend your point of view in a paragraph.

Critical Thinking

1. Discuss what might be done to control Internet abuse by individuals. Should laws be passed? (Brainstorm this one. It's difficult, but solutions need to be developed.)
2. Discuss whether you think Kleinberg overreacted to this situation. What reasons might he have for overreacting?
3. Are there examples of biased words used in this selection?

Reading Selections 4 and 5

Purpose

The two articles that follow were written by two people with very different views on gun control. J. Warren Cassidy was the executive vice president of the National Rifle Association, a powerful organization in supporting the rights of citizens to own guns. (Charlton Heston is now the president.) Sarah Brady is the wife of Jim Brady, who was wounded when then-President Ronald Reagan was shot in 1981. Mrs. Brady chairs an organization called Center to Prevent Handgun Violence. The articles were printed in 1990, but the positions and issues addressed are much the same today. Read to understand the issues.

Preview

1. Read the first sentence of each paragraph.
2. Read the questions that follow the readings and check the vocabulary for unfamiliar words.

Anticipate/Associate

1. Do you own a gun? What are your opinions about the control of guns?
2. Before you read, consider the bias that each of the writers will have. Anticipate what arguments each might make.

The Case for Firearms . . .

J. Warren Cassidy

The American people have a right "to keep and bear   1
arms." This right is protected by the Second Amendment to
the Constitution just as the right to publish editorial comments in this magazine is protected by the First Amendment.
Americans remain committed to the constitutional right to
free speech even when their most powerful <u>oracles</u> have, at
times, abused the First Amendment's <u>inherent</u> powers. Obviously the American people believe no democracy can survive
without a free voice.

In the same light, the authors of the Bill of Rights knew   2
that a democratic republic has a right—indeed, a need—to
keep and bear arms. Millions of American citizens just as
adamantly believe the Second Amendment is crucial to the
maintenance of the democratic process. Many express this
belief through membership in the National Rifle Association
of America.

Our cause is neither trendy nor fashionable, but a basic   3
American belief that spans generations. The N.R.A.'s
strength has never originated in Washington but instead has
reached outward and upward from Biloxi, Albuquerque,
Concord, Tampa, Topeka—from every point on the compass
and from communities large and small. Those who fail to
grasp this widespread commitment will never understand the
depth of political and <u>philosophical</u> dedication symbolized by
the letters N.R.A.

Scholars who have devoted careers to the study of the   4
Second Amendment agree in principle that the right to keep
and bear arms is fundamental to our concept of democracy.
No high-court decision has yet found grounds to challenge
this basic freedom. Yet some who oppose this freedom want
to <u>waive</u> the constitutionality of the "gun control" question
for the sake of their particular—and sometimes peculiar—
brand of social reform.

In doing so they seem ready, even eager, to disregard a   5
constitutional right exercised by at least 70 million Americans
who own firearms. Contrary to current antigun <u>evangelism</u>,
these gun owners are not bad people. They are hardworking,
law abiding, tax paying. They are safe, sane and courteous in
their use of guns. They have never been, nor will they ever be,
a threat to law and order.

History repeatedly warns us that human character can-   6
not be scrubbed free of its defects through vain attempts to

regulate <u>inanimate</u> objects such as guns. What has worked in the past, and what we see working now, are tough N.R.A. supported measures that punish the <u>incorrigible</u> minority who place themselves outside the law.

As a result of such measures, violent crimes with   7
firearms, like <u>assault</u> and robbery, have stabilized or are actually declining. We see proof that levels of firearm ownership cannot be associated with levels of criminal violence, except for their <u>deterrent</u> value. On the other hand, tough laws designed to <u>incarcerate</u> violent offenders offer something gun control cannot: swift, sure justice meted out with no accompanying <u>erosion</u> of individual liberty.

Violent crime continues to rise in cities like New York   8
and Washington even after severe firearm-control <u>statues</u> were rushed into place. Criminals, understandably, have illegal ways of obtaining guns. Antigun laws—the waiting periods, background checks, handgun bans, et al—only harass those who obey them. Why should an honest citizen be <u>deprived</u> of a firearm for sport or self-defense when, for a gangster, obtaining a gun is just a matter of showing up on the right street corner with enough money?

Antigun opinion steadfastly ignores these realities known   9
to rank-and-file police officers—men and women who face crime firsthand, not police administrators who face mayors and editors. These law-enforcement professionals tell us that expecting firearm restrictions to act as crime-prevention measures is wishful thinking. They point out that proposed gun laws would not have stopped <u>heinous</u> crimes committed by the likes of John Hinckley Jr., Patrick Purdy, Laurie Dann or mentally disturbed, usually addicted killers. How can such crimes be used as examples of what gun control could prevent?

There are better ways to advance our society than to ex-   10
cuse criminal behavior. The N.R.A. initiated the first hunter-safety program, which has trained millions of young hunters. We are the shooting sports' leading safety organization, with more than 26,000 certified instructors training 750,000 students and trainees last year alone. Through 1989 there were 9,818 N.R.A.-certified law-enforcement instructors teaching marksmanship to thousands of peace officers.

Frankly, we would rather keep investing N.R.A re-   11
sources in such worthwhile efforts instead of spending our time and members' money <u>debunking</u> the failed and <u>flawed</u> promises of gun <u>prohibitionists</u>.

If you agree, I invite you to join the N.R.A.   12

. . . And the Case against Them

Sarah Brady

As America enters the next decade, it does so with an   1
appalling legacy of gun violence. The 1980s were tragic years
that saw nearly a quarter of a million Americans die from
handguns—four times as many as were killed in the Vietnam
War. We began the decade by witnessing yet another President, Ronald Reagan, become a victim of a would-be assassin's
bullet. That day my husband Jim, his press secretary, also became a statistic in America's handgun war.

Gun violence is an epidemic in this country. In too   2
many cities, the news each night reports another death by a
gun. As dealers push out in search of new addicts, Smalltown,
U.S.A. is introduced to the mindless gun violence fostered by
the drug trade.

And we are killing our future. Every day a child in this   3
country loses his or her life to a handgun. Hundreds more are
permanently injured, often because a careless adult left within
easy reach a loaded handgun purchased for self-defense.

Despite the carnage, America stands poised to face an   4
even greater escalation of bloodshed. The growing popularity
of military-style assault weapons could turn our streets into
combat zones. Assault weapons, designed solely to mow
down human beings, are turning up at an alarming rate in the
hands of those most prone to violence—drug dealers, gang
members, hate groups, and the mentally ill.

The Stockton, Calif. massacre of little children was a   5
warning to our policymakers. But Congress lacked the
courage to do anything. During the year of inaction on Capi-
tol Hill, we have seen too many other tragedies brought about
by assault weapons. In Louisville an ex-employee of a print-
ing plant went on a shooting spree with a Chinese-made
semiautomatic version of the AK-47, gunning down 21 people, killing eight and himself. Two Colorado women were
murdered and several others injured by a junkies using a
stolen MAC-11 semiautomatic pistol. And Congress votes itself a pay raise.

The National Rifle Association, meanwhile, breathes a   6
sigh of relief, gratified that your attention is now elsewhere.
The only cooling-off period the N.R.A. favors is a postpone-
ment of legislative action. It counts on public anger to fade
before such outrage can be directed at legislators. The N.R.A.
runs feel-good ads saying guns are not the problem, and there
is nothing we can do to prevent criminals from getting guns.

In fact, it has said that guns in the wrong hands are the "price we pay for freedom." I guess I'm just not willing to hand the next John Hinckley a deadly handgun. Neither is the nation's law-enforcement community, the men and women who put their lives on the line for the rest of us every day.

Two pieces of federal <u>legislation</u> can make a difference right now. First, we must require a national waiting period before the purchase of a handgun, to allow for a criminal-records check. Police know that waiting periods work. In the 30 years that New Jersey has required a background check, authorities have stopped more than 10,000 convicted felons from purchasing handguns.   7

We must also stop the sale and <u>domestic</u> production of semiautomatic assault weapons. These killing machines clearly have no <u>legitimate</u> sporting purposes as President Bush recognized when he permanently banned their <u>importation</u>.   8

These public-safety measures are supported by the vast majority of Americans—including gun owners. In fact, these measures are so sensible that I never realized the campaign to pass them into law would be such an uphill battle. But it can be done.   9

Jim Brady knows the importance of a waiting period. He knows the living hell of a gunshot wound. Jim and I are not afraid to take on the N.R.A. leaders, and we will fight them everywhere we can. As Jim said in his congressional <u>testimony</u>, "I don't question the rights of responsible gun owners. That's not the issue. The issue is whether the John Hinckleys of the world should be able to walk into gun stores and purchase handguns instantly. Are you willing and ready to cast a vote for a commonsense public-safety bill endorsed by experts—law enforcement?"   10

Are we as a nation going to accept America's bloodshed, or are we ready to stand up and do what is right? When are we going to say, "Enough"? We can change the direction in which America is headed. We can prevent the 1990s from being bloodier than the past ten years. If each of you picks up a pen and writes to your Senators and Representatives tonight, you would be surprised at how quickly we could collect the votes we need to win the war for a safer America.   11

Let us enter a new decade committed to finding solutions to the problem of gun violence. Let your legislators know that voting with the gun lobby—and against public safety—is no longer acceptable. Let us send a signal to lawmakers that we demand action, not excuses.   12

Check Your Understanding

Review

List three reasons that Cassidy presents for the right to own firearms.

1. _____

2. _____

3. _____

List three reasons Brady gives for controlling sales of handguns.

1. _____

2. _____

3. _____

Fill in the Blanks

Complete the statements by writing the best word in the blank.

1. Cassidy says that owning a gun is a _____

   freedom.

2. Brady says _____ times as many people died

   from handguns in the 1980s as died in the Vietnam War.

3. According to Cassidy, antigun laws _____

   law-abiding citizens.

4. Brady does not question the rights of _____

   gun owners.

5. Brady says police know that _____ periods

   work.

Multiple Choice

Select the letter of the answer that best completes the statement.

_____ 1. Cassidy's main idea is that
    a. laws can't control human actions.
    b. the N.R.A. began a program for hunter safety.
    c. laws for gun control are unacceptable.
    d. criminals can always obtain guns.

_____ 2. Brady's main idea is that
    a. the nation needs strict gun control laws.
    b. the N.R.A. runs ads that say guns are not the problem.
    c. gun violence is an epidemic.
    d. firearms restricitons help control crime.

_____ 3. You can conclude that Cassidy and the N.R.A.
    a. will continue to train young hunters.
    b. will lobby against any laws for gun control.
    c. believe that only police officers should carry guns.
    d. believe that firearms restrictions help control crime.

_____ 4. You can conclude that Brady
    a. does not believe in the Second Amendment to the Constitution.
    b. believes that firearms restrictions will help control crime.
    c. believes that only police officers should carry guns.
    d. does not believe that laws can control gun use.

_____ 5. A detail that both writers accept is that
    a. gun control laws would stop hardened or insane criminals.
    b. waiting periods work.
    c. responsible gun owners have rights.
    d. the Second Amendment guarantees everyone the right to have a gun.

True/False

Label the following statements as true or false.

_____ 1. Brady believes that a waiting period for guns will harass law-abiding citizens.

_____ 2. The use of "evangelism" to describe antigun supporters is name calling.

_____ 3. Military assault weapons can turn our streets into a war zone, according to Brady.

_____ 4. Cassidy believes that human characters can be made more perfect.

_____ 5. Criminals have illegal methods of obtaining guns, according to Cassidy.

_____ 6. Brady says that every day a child loses his or her life to a handgun.

_____ 7. According to Brady, police say that waiting periods are effective.

_____ 8. Cassidy says that police officers know waiting periods and antigun checks are not effective.

_____ 9. Assault weapons are generally used by hunters.

_____ 10. Brady opposes training hunters to use handguns responsibly.

Vocabulary

I. Use these legal terms from the article in the following sentence.

legacy   statutes   legitimate   legislation   testimony

The laws, or _____, are _____ reasons

for giving a statement or _____ asking for

_____ to improve our _____ or inheri-

tance of a great country.

II. Homonyms can be confusing. Fill in the blanks correctly with the correct homonyms suggested by the article. Use your dictionary if necessary.

1. *Principle* should not be confused with *principal.*

   a. A _____ is a rule or standard, while a

      _____ is the chief or first.

   b. A good _____ is to pay your debts.

   c. The _____ of the school called a meeting.

2. *Wave* has several meanings, all different from the meaning of *waive*.

   a. You _____ to say goodbye.

   b. You could _____ or forgo your right to a trial.

   c. Some people _____ or put aside their vacations.

   d. A huge _____ lashed the coastline.

III. Complete these analogies using some of the words listed.

inherent   erosion   carnage   statistics   oracle
inanimate   assassin   flawed   domestic   prone

1. Living is to non-living as animate is to _____.

2. Slaughter is to _____ as murder is to homicide.

3. Sight is to a visionary as speech is to a(n) _____.

4. Unknown is to known as foreign is to _____.

5. Probable is to likely as inclined is to _____.

IV. Use the following words to complete the sentences.

assault   appalling   assassin   heinous   incorrigible
flawed   deterrent   incarcerated   deprived   philosophical

1. The _____ on a police officer was considered a

   _____ crime.

2. The _____ had a(n) _____ character.

3. The judge gave a long jail sentence because he thought

   the criminal was _____.

4. Consequently, the criminal was _____ in a fed-

   eral prison and _____ of the right to visitors.

5. Punishment is supposed to be a(n) _____ to crime.

6. The crime rate in some cities is _____.

7. Sometimes _____ ideas must be supported by practical action.

V. Match the words in column A with the terms in column B by placing the letter before the correct number.

Column A

____ 1. inherent

____ 2. stabilized

____ 3. erosion

____ 4. debunking

____ 5. prohibitionists

____ 6. statistics

____ 7. escalation

____ 8. massacre

____ 9. gratified

____ 10. importation

Column B

a. exposing false claims

b. numerical facts

c. innate

d. slaughter

e. bringing in

f. wearing away

g. established

h. pleased

i. an increase

j. those who forbid

Writing

1. Write a paragraph using specific facts, opinions, or examples supporting your opinion on gun control. You can use material from one or both of the articles, but be sure to identify your source.
2. Evaluate the argument made by one of the two writers. Is it valid? What persuasive techniques are used or misused?

Critical Thinking

1. Both writers use biased words. Mention some of these and discuss their effectiveness.
2. Does either writer use facts, statistics, and authorities more effectively? Explain your choice by giving examples.

3. Regardless of your point of view on gun control, who gives the better argument? Identify strong points to support your decision.
4. Is gun control primarily a moral or ethical issue or an emotional one?

Sometimes people take a position on an issue or controversy like gun control without having listened to or read about both sides of the issue. However, reading two sides of an issue is important in arriving at a valid opinion based on your value system and an analysis of both sides' strategies and evidence. The assignment that follows gives you an opportunity to look at and evaluate both sides of an argument.

Project Assignment: Comparing Views

Your group should choose one of the topics that follow or perhaps one of your own choosing. This assignment works best if some members of your group have one point of view and others hold the opposite point of view.

Step 1

Select a topic agreeable to the group from the list that follows. Once the topic is selected, the group should write about five questions on the topic. For example, for gun control, your group's questions might be:

1. Should we have stronger gun control laws?
2. Should adults be free to purchase handguns?
3. Should police carry guns?
4. Is the waiting period for a gun purchase effective?
5. Is it too easy to buy weapons illegally?

Next, each member of the group should answer these questions before any reading or further discussion. These questions can be used again at the conclusion of the project to see whether reading and discussion changes any group member's original response.

Step 2

Find two articles. One should support one side of the argument, and one should support the opposing view. Keep in mind that it is important to evaluate Internet sources carefully if you decide to use them.

Step 3

Xerox enough copies of the two articles so that each group member has a copy. Be prepared to hand in one copy of each article at the end of the project.

Step 4

All members should read both articles and decide how best to make notes of main ideas. (examples: maps, outlines, paragraph summaries, etc.). Each group member should make a set of notes. After comparison and discussion, the group will select the best representation of both articles.

Step 5

Evaluate the strength of each article. Are the arguments valid, well-supported, true, reasonable? Is one argument stronger than the other? Prepare a group evaluation of each article. (One written paragraph for each article is sufficient.)

Step 6

Redo the self-questioning of Step 1. Has anyone in the group changed his or her opinion on the topic?

Step 7

Hand in the following material, stapled or in a folder, in this order.

   a. Cover sheet
   b. Group evaluation of members' contributions.
   c. Graphic organizers (maps, outlines, summaries) for both articles.
   d. Evaluations of both articles.
   e. Sentence summary of before-and-after self-questioning. For example: *Two members significantly changed their views.* Or: *No one in the group changed his or her view on the issue.*

Possible Issues for Your Project

Discuss these topics in your group and choose one (or another topic of your own choosing) for your project.

   1. Violence on children's television shows is (is not) harmful to children.
   2. The use of animals in research should (should not) be allowed.

3. Drug testing in the workplace should (should not) be allowed.
4. Couples should (should not) live together before marriage.
5. The death penalty should (should not) be allowed.
6. Abortion should (should not) be legal.
7. News media should (should not) be regulated.
8. Genetic engineering of clones is (is not) ethical.
9. Competitive sports should (should not) be allowed in high school.
10. Sex education is (is not) appropriate in school.
11. Evolution should (should not) be taught in public schools.
12. Children's toys encourage (discourage) creativity.
13. The fashion industry does (does not) exploit the consumer.
14. Sexual harassment or racial discrimination in the workplace is (is not) a problem.
15. A President of the United States should (should not) be a moral model.

Credits

Pages 22–26. "Behavior Change Techniques" from *Health: The Basics*, by R.J. Donatelle and L.G. Davis, 2d ed. Copyright © 1997 by Allyn and Bacon. Reprinted by permission.

Pages 28–32. Patricia Skalka, *Six Keys To Quicker Learning*. Used by permission of the author. Originally appeared in *Reader's Digest*.

Pages 70–72. Caryl Rivers and Rosalind C. Barnett, "Just What Family Values Are Normal?" Reprinted by permission of the authors.

Pages 76–82. "Commuter Marriage: Does It Work?" by Elaine C. Ray. Reprinted by permission of the author, from *Essence*, February 1989.

Pages 110–114. "Different Skills to Be Used for Math Courses." Reprint permission by Academic Sciences Press, Inc., from *Winning at Math: Your Guide to Learning Mathematics through Successful Study Skills* by Paul Nolting, Ph.D. For more information about *Winning at Math* call 1 (800) 247–6553.

Pages 119–121. "Public Language Versus Private Language" from *Hunger of Memory* by Richard Rodriguez. Reprinted by permission of David R. Godine, Publisher, Inc. Copyright © 1982 by Richard Rodriquez.

Pages 164–169. "Television's Influence on Attitudes, Behavior, Creativity, and Cognition" from *Human Development*, by R.V. Kail and J.C. Cavanaugh. Copyright © 1996 Brooks/Cole Publishing Company, Pacific Grove, CA 93950, a division of International Thomson Publishing Inc. By permission of the publisher.

Pages 173–178. "Crack and the Box" from *Piecework* by Peter Hamill. Copyright © 1996 by Deidre Enterprises, Inc. By permission of Little, Brown and Company.

Pages 218–221. "Alcohol" from Lester A. Lefton, *Psychology*, 6th ed. Copyright © 1997 by Allyn and Bacon. Reprinted by permission.

Index